As a well-informed church leader who is well versed in Baptist traditions, Dr. Mikhovich gives voice to an unknown, or little known, reality of a church that has suffered under different regimes, and whose suffering, though admittedly softened, is not over yet. In the first part, his review of a wealth of historical archives sheds light on the origins of Baptists in Belarus, providing a historical overview. In the second part, a rich description of contemporary and past worship practices under the Tsar's regime, the Soviet Union, and Perestroika is recorded. Finally, Mikhovich offers thoughts on how to deal with tensions that he perceives between liturgical practices and authoritative voices in the Baptist tradition.

Marcel Barnard, PhD
Professor Emeritus of Practical Theology and Liturgy Studies,
Protestant Theological University, Netherlands

Dr. Mikhovich's work is written to the highest of academic standards in the field. In conversation with respected voices within the current liturgical scholarship it is truly a scientific investigation of the most prevalent form of Baptist worship in Belarus and the Commonwealth of Independent States in general. His argument is coherent, theologically sound, and the results of this study are original and compelling. It is well ordered and described, well-analyzed, and judged on the basis of internal Baptist and external liturgical scientific criteria. Not only is this study an important resource for Baptist worship covering large span of time before, during, and after the Soviet Union, but also, more broadly, for liturgy anywhere in ever-changing times. The results of this work are particularly relevant to the context of Baptist worship in the southeastern and Eastern European context.

Parush R. Parushev, PhD
Associate Professor and Rector,
St. Trivelius Higher Theological Institute, Bulgaria

This book offers a window into the fascinating world of the eastern Slavic evangelical worship tradition, focusing particularly on the Baptist churches in Belarus. Little known outside of Eastern Europe, this unique form of communal worship cannot be understood independent of its historical, religious, and socio-political context, which Leonid Mikhovich traces carefully and convincingly. His description, analysis, and critique of traditional Belarusian Baptist worship will also provide readers with an opportunity to reflect on different expressions of worship and the underlying theological convictions present in their own cultural contexts. This volume will be of value to a wide range of readers who may be interested in the liturgical aspects of church life, Baptist identity, or Eastern European studies.

Lina Toth, PhD
Programme Director, Langham Scholars,
Langham Partnership International
Senior Research Fellow,
International Baptist Theological Study Centre, Netherlands

Traditional Worship in Russian-speaking Churches

Formation, Features, and Internal Conflicts with a Focus on Belarus

Leonid Mikhovich

ACADEMIC

© 2025 Leonid Mikhovich

Published 2025 by Langham Academic
An imprint of Langham Publishing
www.langhampublishing.org

Langham Publishing and its imprints are a ministry of Langham Partnership

Langham Partnership
PO Box 296, Carlisle, Cumbria, CA3 9WZ, UK
www.langham.org

ISBNs:
978-1-83973-661-2 Print
978-1-78641-144-0 ePub
978-1-78641-145-7 PDF
DOI: https://doi.org/10.69811/9781839736612

Leonid Mikhovich has asserted his right under the Copyright, Designs and Patents Act, 1988 to be identified as the Author of this work.

All rights reserved. No part of this publication may be reproduced, stored in a retrieval system or transmitted, in any form or by any means, electronic, mechanical, photocopying, recording or otherwise, without the prior written permission of the publisher or the Copyright Licensing Agency.

Requests to reuse content from Langham Publishing are processed through PLSclear. Please visit www.plsclear.com to complete your request.

Scripture taken from the New American Standard Bible®, Copyright © 1960, 1962, 1963, 1968, 1971, 1972, 1973, 1975, 1977, 1995, 2020 by The Lockman Foundation. Used by permission.

British Library Cataloguing-in-Publication Data
A catalogue record for this book is available from the British Library

ISBN: 978-1-83973-661-2

Cover & Book Design: projectluz.com

Langham Partnership actively supports theological dialogue and an author's right to publish but does not necessarily endorse the views and opinions set forth here or in works referenced within this publication, nor can we guarantee technical and grammatical correctness. Langham Partnership does not accept any responsibility or liability to persons or property as a consequence of the reading, use or interpretation of its published content.

Contents

Abstract xi

Acknowledgments xiii

Abbreviations xv

Transliteration xvii

Chapter 1 1
   Introduction
      1.1. Subject of the Study 1
      1.2. Research Rationale 3
      1.3. The Scope of the Study 6
      1.4. Methodology 9
      1.5. Analysis of Resources 17
          1.5.1. Historical Documents 17
          1.5.2. Ethnographic Data 19
          1.5.3. Content of Questionnaires and Interviews 21
          1.5.4. Theological Materials 24

Chapter 2 29
   The Role of Public Worship in the Belarusian Baptist Context
      2.1. A Source of Spiritual Life in Difficult Times 29
      2.2. Worship as a Refuge 34
      2.3. A Unique Place of Fellowship 40

Chapter 3 45
   Historical Roots
      3.1. The Origins of Evangelical Churches in Belarus 45
          3.1.1. The Second Part of the Nineteenth Century to the
                Early Twentieth Century 45
          3.1.2. Developments After World War I 49
      3.2. Historical and Interethnic Relationships in Identity and
          Worship Formation 54
          3.2.1. Russian Orientation 55
          3.2.2. Western Sources 60
          3.2.3. Local or Foreign, or Both? 65

  3.3. Western Forms in the Eastern Context: Problems of
    Adaptation 69
    3.3.1. Local Context Against "Imported Faith" 69
    3.3.2. Western Christianity on Eastern Soil 71

Chapter 4 79
 Context of Formation
  4.1. Theological Grounds 79
    4.1.1. Back to the Early Church 79
    4.1.2. Unattainable Ideal 86
  4.2. Religious Context 88
    4.2.1. Leaving Orthodoxy 88
    4.2.2. Influence of Orthodoxy on Baptist Worship 98
  4.3. Political Context and the Formation of the Traditional
    Baptist Worship Service 103
    4.3.1. Persecution and Harassment 103
    4.3.2. Motifs of Struggle, Suffering, and Expectation in
      Worship 112
    4.3.3. The Way of Preparation and Presentation 120

Chapter 5 127
 General Structure, Content, Time, and Space of Worship
  Introduction 127
    Service in Church on Fortechnaya 61/1, Brest,
      December 14, 2008 127
    The Service of the Lord's Supper in "Golgotha" Church,
      Minsk, December 2, 2007 131
  5.1. General Structure and Components of Worship 136
  5.2. Content of a Traditional Baptist Worship Service 148
  5.3. Temporal Dimension of Public Worship 153
  5.4. The Use of Space in Public Worship 162
    5.4.1. Houses of Prayer: Status and Place in Worship 162
    5.4.2. The Language of the Interior 171

Chapter 6 183
 Theological Emphases of Traditional Public Worship
  6.1. Centrality of Scripture 185
    6.1.1. The Importance of the Bible in Life, Doctrine, and
      Worship 185
    6.1.2. Back to the Bible 190
  6.2. Edification in Worship 196
    6.2.1. The Role of 'Edification' in Baptist Worship 196

    6.2.2. Towards a Better Theology of Edification 199
  6.3. Evangelism...202
    6.3.1. Evangelism in Life and Worship...202
    6.3.2. Worship as Evangelism 205
  6.4. Simplicity...214
    6.4.1. Pursuit of the "Gospel Simplicity" 214
    6.4.2. From Oversimplification to Creditable Simplicity............217

Chapter 7 225
 Identifying Tensions in Public Worship
  7.1. Freedom and Forms in Tension...226
    7.1.1. Freedom in Worship 226
    7.1.2. Forms in Worship...235
  7.2. The Priesthood of All Believers Versus the Corporate
    Nature of Worship 238
    7.2.1. "Each One . . . Has a Revelation" (1 Cor 14:26)................238
    7.2.2. Individual and Corporate Aspects in Conflict 243
  7.3. Public Worship in the Secular Environment 247
    7.3.1. Traditional Forms and Culture in Conflict........................247
    7.3.2. Cultural Gap..250
    7.3.3. From Culture to Subculture 253

Chapter 8 257
 Overcoming the Tensions
  8.1. Freedom and Forms 261
    8.1.1. Striving for Balance 261
    8.1.2. Freedom and Forms in a Creative Tension 268
  8.2. Individual and Communal Aspects of Worship...........................271
    8.2.1. Priesthood of All Believers in Relation to Worship 271
    8.2.2. Towards a Disciplined Participation 276
  8.3. The Relevance of Worship to the Secular Environment.............280
    8.3.1. Inculturation: Pro and Contra 280
    8.3.2. Inculturation: A Theological Model for Traditional
      Baptist Worship 286
    8.3.3. Inculturation: Building a Bridge in the Practice of
      Traditional Baptist Worship...296

Conclusion 309

Bibliography 317

Photographs of the Houses of Prayer and Sanctuaries...............................353

List of Figures

Fig.1. General schemes of worship for Baptist churches showing the differences between basic and extended forms..........139

Fig.2. Plan of Baptist church hall on Moprovskaya, Pinsk, as a representation of a classical type of the house of prayer building..........176

Fig.3. Photograph of Fortechnaya 61/1 church building, Brest..........353

Fig.4. Photograph of Jackshitsy house of prayer, Minsk region..........354

Fig.5. Photograph of Voropaevo house of prayer, Vitebsk region..........354

Fig.6. Photograph of the "Arc," house of prayer, Volkovysk, Grodno region....355

Fig.7. Photograph of Central Baptist church, Kobrin, Brest region..........355

Fig.8. Photograph of "Light of Gospel" church building, Minsk..........356

Fig.9. Photograph of "Bethany" church building, Kobrin, Brest region..........356

Fig.10. Photograph of "Bethlehem" church building, Minsk..........357

Fig.11. Photograph of textual decoration in Malech house of prayer, Brest region..........357

Fig.12. Photograph of textual decoration in Sadovyi house of prayer, Brest region..........358

Fig.13. Photograph of textual decoration in Pruzhany house of prayer, Brest region..........358

Fig.14. Photograph of textual decoration in Zavelev'e house of prayer, Brest region..........359

Fig.15. Photograph of worship hall Man'kovichi church/house of prayer, Brest region..........360

Fig.16. Photograph of worship hall "Golgotha" church, Minsk..........360

Fig.17. Photograph of worship space Liuban' house of prayer/church, Minsk region..........361

Fig.18. Photograph of worship hall Shatsk house of prayer/church, Minsk region..........361

Fig.19. Photograph of the worship hall Central Baptist church, Gomel (2002) 362

Fig.20. Photograph of the worship hall/space after renovation Central Baptist church, Gomel (2007) 362

Fig.21. Photograph of elevated platform Central Baptist church, Kobrin (2008) 363

Fig.22. Photograph of elevated platform after renovation, Central Baptist church, Kobrin (2017). 363

Abstract

The subject of this study is traditional worship in Baptist churches in Belarus, which is typically composed of a combination of preaching, singing, prayer, and several other components in different forms, quantities, proportions, and order. The focus of this thesis is to explore internal conflicts in worship that result from the process of shaping and adjusting historical contexts of worship to the local and current context.

The first part of this thesis explores primary sources, documents, and texts concerning worship, and covers issues around the origin and development of the evangelical movement in Belarus. It analyzes a variety of influences and connections, and reveals a conflict between local, or Russian-speaking, and foreign traditions that arises within the process of adapting some Western forms for the Eastern situation. It also contains the analysis of the theological, religious, and political contexts that have influenced worship formation and content.

The second part of this study covers the current shape of traditional Belarusian Baptist worship, its structure, content, duration, space of worship, and some of its theological emphases such as simplicity, the centrality of the Bible, the principle of "edification," and evangelistic zeal. Participant observation, historical and contemporary documents, and questionnaires and structured interviews play an important role at this stage of research.

Some inner contradictions are identified between the declared character and the practice of worship. This raises questions regarding the nature of the changes that would be contextually appropriate for this particular expression of Baptist identity. The third part of this study engages in the critique of internal conflicts between freedom and forms, individual and corporate aspects, and the sacral and secular character of worship. Reflections on seemingly conflicting features open the door for possible avenues for holding them in creative tension and enriching the current practice. At the same time, this study demonstrates that tensions are an integral part of worship and that they are in some way inherent in worship itself.

Acknowledgments

It is better to take companions with you on the road to knowledge, especially if you "have not passed this way before" (Josh 3:4). I thank everyone who shared the challenges of my journey, and who was with me while "by day the heat consumed me and the frost by night" (Gen 31:40). First, I thank my promoters – Marcel Barnard, Lina Toth (Andronoviene), and Parush Parushev. They had more faith in the successful completion of my work than I did and have encouraged me along the way. Their sensitivity, patience, and scholarly expertise are wonderful examples for those who seek wisdom. I also appreciate Jim Heizer, who invested so much of his time into compensating for my language imperfections and demonstrating what true academic writing is. The International Baptist Theological Seminary (IBTS) in Prague, and later the International Baptist Theological Study Centre (IBTSC) in Amsterdam, became the oases where a weary pilgrim could restore his strength and be refreshed by their springs of knowledge during colloquium time. I sincerely appreciate school leaders Keith Jones, Stuart Blythe, David McMillan, and Mike Pears, as well as Helen Pears, for their personal interest in my research, and for strengthening "the hands that are weak and the knees that are feeble" (Heb 12:12). The TCM Institute in Austria turned out to be another oasis with "twelve springs of water and seventy date palms" (Exod 15:27), and I am very grateful to the Institute's President, Tony Twist, for allowing me to drink from their springs and to eat the fruit of their trees.

A long journey is impossible without financial support. I am thankful to Langham Partnership and its representatives, Ian Shaw and Riad Kassis, for faithfully covering my expenses, even though the journey was very long. "For even in Thessalonica you sent a gift more than once for my needs" (Phil 4:16).

I thank the staff of Minsk Theological Seminary for doing my work when I was absent during many of my trips. I want to really thank the librarian and translator at the seminary, Valeria Naumenko, for helping me to find my way amid so many books, and for finding "delightful words" (Eccl 12:10) in the translation from the Slavic languages into English.

I thank the Lord for my family who have shared the burden of my journey. My mother Nadezhda has prayed for me. My daughters Natalia and Lilia, and my son Timothy (born during the course of this journey) have suffered my absence resulting from studies at home and abroad. My wonderful wife, Tatiana, has been a faithful companion (1 Cor 9:5), grieving over my failures and rejoicing in my success. She has inspired and encouraged me. I would not have reached the end of this road without her help.

Many other people, whose names will be kept in my memory, have left their good marks on my journey to knowledge, and I trust that they are going to collect good fruit if they do not grow weary (Gal 6:9), and that "good measure, pressed down, shaken together and running over, will be poured" into their laps (Luke 6:38).

Abbreviations

AUCECB	All-Union Council of Evangelical Christians-Baptists
BSSR	Byelorussian Soviet Socialist Republic
CCECB	Council of Churches of Evangelical Christians-Baptists
CIS	The Commonwealth of Independent States
CSHA	Central State Historical Archive
EAAA	Euro-Asian Accrediting Association
EAF	Euro-Asian Federation (of Evangelical Christians-Baptists)
ECB	Evangelical Christians-Baptists
EKhB	Evangel'skie khristiane-baptisty (Evangelical Christians-Baptists)
ICCECB	International Council of Churches of Evangelical Baptist Christians
NARB	National Archive of the Republic of Belarus
NHAB	National Historical Archive of Belarus
Q, 2008	Questionnaire of church ministers (January, 2008)
QM, 2008	Questionnaire of church members (January, 2008)
QM, 2012	Questionnaire of church members (October, 2012)
Q, 2013	Questionnaire of Seminary's students (November, 2013)
RSB	Russian Synodal Bible
RSHA	Russian State Historical Archive
SABR	State Archive of Brest Region
SARF	State Archive of the Russian Federation
SI, 2008	Structured interview of church pastors. Theological Assessment (October, 2008)

SI, 2012	Structured interview of church ministers and members (September, 2012)
USSR	Union of Soviet Socialist Republics
VSEKhB	Vsesoyuznyy sovet evangel'skikh khristian-baptistov (All-Union Council of Evangelical Christians-Baptists)
RSFSR	Russian Soviet Federative Socialist Republic
SSRB	Soviet Socialist Republic of Belarus
UECBB	Union of Evangelical Christians-Baptists in Belarus

Transliteration

In this thesis I am using the established English spellings of common Russian names and terms, as found in common dictionaries. Other Cyrillic words are transliterated by the following system:

А – A;
Б – B;
В – V;
Г – G;
Д – D;
Е – E;
Ж – ZH;
З – Z;
И – I;
Й – I;
К – K;
Л – L;
М – M;
Н – N;
О – O;
П – P;
Р – R;
С – S;
Т – T;
У – U;
Ф – F;
Х – KH;
Ц – TS;

Ч – CH;
Ш – SH;
Щ – SHCH;
Ъ – ";
Ы – Y;
Ь – ';
Э – E;
Ю – IU;
Я – YA.

CHAPTER 1

Introduction

1.1. Subject of the Study

James McClendon states: "The baptists in all their variety and disunity *failed to see in their own heritage, their own way of using Scripture, their own communal practices, their own guiding vision,* a resource for theology unlike the prevailing tendencies round about them."[1] This statement holds true when applied to traditional worship services in Russian-speaking Baptist churches, including Belarus, which is the subject of this study. Traditional worship in this case refers to the average two-hour sermon and hymn-based worship that has prevailed in Belarusian Baptist churches for the last one hundred years or so. Some of its prominent characteristics include two to four sermons, three or four congregational songs using the *Pesn' Vozrozhdeniya* hymnal,[2] the use of the piano and choir, and communal prayer open to all church members. It is easier to describe such worship in contrast to contemporary worship, especially if the latter has a praise/worship band accompanied by electronic instruments leading the praise and worship section. Belarusian Baptists do not use the definition of "traditional" themselves, and such a traditional form is not mandatory for churches. For that reason, the presence, number, and

---

1. McClendon, Jr., *Ethics*, 26. Italics authors. "McClendon identified himself as a "small-*b* Baptist" that includes the radical reformation traditions of the Mennonites, Amish, Brethren and others" (McSwain, ed., *Twentieth-Century Shapers*, 106).

2. *Pesn' Vozrozhdeniya. Sbornik dukhovnykh gimnov i pesen evangel'skikh tserkvey* [Song of Revival, Collection of hymns and songs of evangelical churches]. *Pesn' Vozrozhdeniya* is the most widely used songbook in all churches that follow a traditional style of worship.

sequence of certain components may vary somewhat in different churches at different times. However, Belarusian Baptist churches are united by similar "deep structures" of worship and a stable set of values and characteristics that are the subject of analysis in this thesis.³

In terms of this study, it is necessary to also note the contextual nature of terminology. In most churches, especially those with a well-established form of gathering, getting together is called a *bogosluzhenie* (divine service), which is analogous to the German word, *Gottesdienst*. This term is typically used on the church notice board. This reflects the Russian Synodal translation of the Bible, where the term *divine service* is used four times – Jer 52:18; Rom 9:4; Heb 9:1 and Heb 9:6.⁴ The term *sobranie* (meeting or gathering) prevails in the everyday communications of church members and in worship. *Molitvennoe sobranie* (prayer meeting) is typically used to denote meetings that do not take place on Sundays. The word *poklonenie* (which would be the dynamic equivalent translation of the English word worship) is rarely used in the Belarusian Baptist Union churches that practice traditional worship. It is a common term in new churches and, while it can be used to refer to the whole service, is particularly used to describe the first part of the service which predominantly includes singing. The literal meaning of the Russian word *poklonenie* refers to the position of the body while standing before the Lord and basically means "bowing low." In its broader meaning, this word describes the awe and reverence of God. This dissertation will employ the single term "worship," since it reflects the equivalent of the phenomenon under description in the English-speaking world, but these other terms described above must also be kept in mind.

I explore "Baptist" worship, but the terms "evangelical Christians," "evangelical believers," and "Evangelicals" are also used. These not only refer to

---

3. Ellis, *Gathering*, 68.

4. The Russian Synodal translation of the New Testament was prepared in 1820 and printed in 1825, but the publication was not released due to changes in the political situation in Russia. The four Gospels were later printed in 1860 and the complete edition of the New Testament in 1862. The publication of the Old Testament was completed in 1876. On the history of Synodal translation, see Chistovich, *Istoriya perevoda Biblii na russkiy yazyk* [History of Translating the Bible into the Russian Language]; Rizhskiy, *Istoriya perevodov Biblii v Rossii* [History of Bible translations in Russia], 30–170. Very useful and detailed information can also be found on the official website of the Russian Bible Society, http://www.biblia.ru/reading/new_translations/sinodal.htm, last accessed 12 May 2019.

Baptists but to the various evangelical groups which existed in the Russian Empire and later in the Soviet Union territory until October 1944, when the All-Union Council of Evangelical Christians-Baptists (AUCECB) was established.[5] Thus, after the Second World War, the term "Evangelicals" generally came to mean Baptists, or Baptists and Pentecostals. The latter were forced to join AUCECB in August 1945 on condition of the abandonment of speaking in tongues and foot washing in worship, however they left it once they were able to form their own Union again in 1989. Meanwhile, the term "Evangelical Christians" (with emphasis on the capital "E") refers to a specific group of churches in Russia and the USSR which established their own 'All-Russian Union of Evangelical Christians' in 1909 in St. Petersburg, and then merged with the Baptists in 1944.[6] However, in Belarus the terms "evangelical Christians," "evangelical believers," and "Baptists" are often used interchangeably, and "Evangelical Christians-Baptists" (ECB) and "Baptists" are used as synonyms.[7]

1.2. Research Rationale

Traditional worship in Russian-speaking Baptist churches has not yet been analyzed from historical and theological perspectives. In fact, up to this point

---

5. AUCECB, in Russian VSEKhB (Vsesoyuznyy sovet evangel'skikh khristian-baptistov), was the religious organization of evangelical Christians-Baptists in the territory of the Soviet Union. AUCECB was founded in 1944 in place of the unions of Evangelical Christians (Prokhanovtsy) and Baptists. In the early 1990s, after the breakup of the Soviet Union into independent states, AUCECB was reorganized into national church unions of Evangelical Christian-Baptist churches in these states.

6. On Evangelical Christians see Puzynin, *Tradiciya evangel'skikh khristian. Izuchenie samoidentifikacii i bogosloviya ot momenta ee zarozhdeniya do nashikh dnei* [The tradition of Evangelical Christians. The study of identity and theology from its inception to the present day]; Prokhanov, *V kotle Rossii* [In the Cauldron of Russia].

7. Some authors use the term Protestantism in relation to Baptists and similar groups. In this manner Cherenkov speaks about "Russian Protestantism" in Cherenkov, *Litsom k litsu*, 66–67. Kahle also uses this term along with "Eastern-Slavic Protestantism", in which he includes the Molokans, Mennonites, Shtundists, Evangelical Christians, and Baptists. See Kahle, *Evangel'skie khristiane*, 40, 29. This work was originally published as *Evangelische Christen in Russland und der Sowjetunion*. Lisovskaya uses the term *neoprotestantizm* in order to denote Churches of Christ and Baptists (Lisovskaya, "Neoprotestantizm v Zapadnoi Belarusi v 1921–1939 gg."). It is interesting that Baptists and Pentecostals are often called "believers", as a way of distinguishing them from the Orthodox and Catholics. For further information regarding the term in the Former Soviet Union and Eastern European context, see Parushev and Pilli, "Protestantism in Eastern Europe," 155–160.

there have been no significant studies in the theology and practice of worship in Baptist churches in Russian-speaking countries. Indeed, this may not be unique to the post-Soviet Baptists. Christopher Ellis, a British Baptist theologian, highlights the fact that in the free church tradition, in contrast to the "liturgical" tradition, worship analysis has not been paid much attention.[8] However, in the Russian-speaking context the lack of a theology of worship is perhaps even more acute, since, under the Tzarist and later Soviet persecution, the Baptists had limited opportunities to develop their theological education and theology as a whole. The mere opportunity to be engaged in worship was the primary concern, rather than worship analysis.

At the present time, while there is an opportunity to compare various traditions and make use of theological literature available in other languages, attention should be given to developing theology of worship in the local context and filling the gap in this area of theological knowledge. This is especially important in light of the increasing relevance of the issue: at the beginning of the twenty-first century, in the pursuit of new forms and under the influence of Western churches, some churches are giving up various components of worship or are introducing new forms of worship without much theological reflection. A process of analyzing worship from historical, theological, and cultural perspectives is needed to to help ministers and churches trace its development and map possible directions for the future. This thesis also seeks to demonstrate that it is possible to borrow tools from other traditions to evaluate and analyze local traditional worship. Conversely, this study of worship may hold value for other traditions and researchers who can use its results to enrich their own traditions or to compare different types of worship.

My interest in the topic and my own position as a researcher also need to be clarified here because my upbringing, age, education, and ministry will affect my view.[9] I grew up in a Baptist home and I have been attending Baptist churches since childhood. The first family trips were aimed at attending worship services in remote villages. There, as children and teenagers, we could put our gifts into practice by reciting poems, participating in music ministry, and preaching our first sermons. During the Soviet era, attending the worship of evangelical churches, including illegal gatherings, and participating

---

8. Ellis, *Gathering*, 8.
9. See Barnard, Cilliers, and Wepener, *Worship in the Network Culture*, 8.

in them, determined the identity and way of life of/for a believer to a much greater extent than nowadays. Since various emotions and memories can be considered a type of personal document,[10] these emotional and spiritual ties to the subject of study have certainly implicitly influenced the approach and conclusions of this thesis.

I should also note my personal and professional involvement in the subject. As a participant in worship, I desire that worship be personally fulfilling and meaningful. As a Baptist minister, I am interested in research on worship because I preach on a regular basis and take part in planning and conducting the worship. Furthermore, this subject is important for me as one of the leaders of the Belarusian Baptist Union and as the Rector of the Seminary.

There is an advantage in such a connection to the subject of study. In ethnographic research[11] it takes time to enter another culture and to understand it from the inside, however, in this case these processes have already happened.[12] Being part of the group brings a particular kind of deep understanding.[13] On the other hand, an insider position impacts the selection of information. Familiarity with the topic can have a negative effect since "one may miss out on perceiving its all too familiar characteristics."[14] Furthermore, my personal involvement inevitably influences my analysis and conclusions. "The emic point of view, or inside perspective, on the ritual is confronted with the 'outside' . . . the so-called 'etic' point of view."[15] I work as a researcher and at the same time I am a part of the phenomenon under study. I am involved in worship at different levels which can make it difficult to create an emotional distance from the subject and to interpret it as impartially as possible. Personal interest and the value of the study object to the researcher can indeed make evaluation and analysis more difficult. As Barbara Tedlock notes, "The oxymoron *participant observation* implies simultaneous emotional involvement and

---

10. Tedlock, "Ethnography and Ethnographic Representation," 460.
11. For further discussion on enthography, see section 4 of this chapter.
12. In fact, Denscombe notes, "the most popular development of ethnography in recent times has been its application to lifestyles, understanding and beliefs within 'our own' society" (Denscombe, *The Good Research Guide*, 86).
13. Patton, *Qualitative Research & Evaluation Methods*, 268.
14. Barnard, Cilliers, and Wepener, *Worship in the Network Culture*, 64.
15. Barnard, Cilliers, and Wepener, 53.

objective detachment. Ethnographers attempt to be both engaged participants and coolly dispassionate observers of the lives of others."[16]

I have approached the current project keeping the difficulty of this tension in mind. I also hope that my use of academic tools has helped to minimize the risks since I have been continuously challenged in my understanding and interpretation of worship. "External audit"[17] – that is, the questions and comments of teachers, fellow students, and promoters – has kept this challenge at the fore throughout the study. Visiting public worship both in Protestant, Eastern Orthodox, and Roman Catholic churches has enlarged my vision and stimulated continuous reflection on my subjectivity.[18] In this way, the emic and etic approaches have been continually and intentionally held in tension.

1.3. The Scope of the Study

Before exploring the geographical and temporal framework of this study it is necessary to provide a general overview of the region in the period under discussion – that is, from the second half of the nineteenth to the beginning of the twenty-first century. In the Russian Empire there was no such administrative unit as Belarus: it was part of the Russian Empire (late 1800 – 1917), then of the Soviet Union, and then Poland (the western part of Belarus in 1921–1939).[19] Unified Byelorussia[20] became part of the Union of Soviet Socialist Republics (USSR) and remained so for over fifty years. In 1991, after the collapse of the Soviet Union, it became an independent state and renamed itself the Republic of Belarus.

While this study analyzes traditional worship in Baptist churches in Belarus, due to the close relationships between churches during the formation

---

16. Tedlock, "Ethnography and Ethnographic Representation," 465.
17. Corrine Glesne, *Becoming Qualitative Researchers*, 32.
18. Glesne, 32.
19. *Bol'shaya sovetskaya entsyklopedia* [Big Soviet encyclopedia], vol. 3, 388. *Bol'shaya entsyklopedia v 66 tomah* [Big encyclopedia in 66 vols.], vol. 5, 382. The Law of the Byelorussian SSR from 14.11.1939. https://ru.wikisource.org/wiki/Закон_БССР_от_14.11.1939_Западная_Белоруссия, last accessed 14 May 2019. See also Latyshonak and Miranovich, *Gistoryya Bielarusi ad syaredziny XVIII st. da pachatku XXI st.* [History of Belarus from the middle of the 17th century to the beginning of the 21st century], 154–159.
20. Here I employ "Byelorussia" instead of "Belarus" because it was referenced in this way during the Soviet period.

and development of the evangelical movement, a similar type/form of worship was common across the former Soviet Union from Brest to Vladivostok, and from St. Petersburg to Almaty. Baptist churches in Russia, Ukraine, Latvia, Estonia (Russian-speaking congregations), Kazakhstan, Kyrgyzstan, Moldova, and other republics followed, and a lot of them still follow, the same pattern of worship, with only slight modifications. Therefore, it is possible to use the term *Russian-speaking Baptist worship* as a synonym for traditional worship in all those contexts.[21] Furthermore, many Russian-speaking churches in the United States and elsewhere worship in this "traditional" way.[22]

Indeed, since the Belarusian language and national identity are not more established, one cannot point to a specific "Belarusian" Baptist type of worship.[23] As it now stands, the character of public Baptist worship has been more influenced by regional ties than by national identity. For example, meetings in southwestern Belarus are somewhat closer in spirit to meetings in northwestern Ukraine; these churches have more in common with each other than with the Belarusian churches in the north of Belarus. Geographic proximity and historical ties contribute to their close cooperation, mutual visits, and participation in public worship.

Nevertheless, the main field of this research can be defined as the churches in Belarus, varied in the number of members. The vast majority of them belong to the Union of Evangelical Christians-Baptists in Belarus (UECBB)[24] and, while representing various geographical regions, they are especially

---

21. On worship and preaching in Russian Baptist churches, see Cheprasov, "Formative? Informative?" ch. 5. I have also witnessed this phenomenon personally in my own exposure to Soviet Baptist churches over a number of years. From 1993 to 1997 I was involved in worship nearly every Sunday in Russian churches in Moscow, while studying at Moscow Theological Seminary. Since 1997 I have regularly attended worship in Russian-speaking churches in Ukraine, Estonia, the United States, and Finland. I have also visited Russian-speaking churches in Kazakhstan (Almaty) and Kyrgyzstan (Bishkek, Kant).

22. Since 1988, hundreds of thousands of evangelical Christians have migrated to the United States of America from the former Soviet Union for economic, socio-political, religious, and family reasons. They have established many Russian-speaking immigrant congregations across the country. For a study of how these immigrant churches function in their new cultural, social, and religious contexts, see Vyacheslav Tsvirinko, *Context and Contextuality. Towards an Authentic Mission Perspective for the Churches of the Pacific Coast Slavic Baptist Association* (Carlisle, Cumbria: Langham Monographs, 2018). Unfortunately, no study has so far been conducted on Russian-speaking worship in diaspora.

23. For further background, see Chapter 7.

24. The Union of Evangelical Christians-Baptists in Belarus, official website, http://baptist.by, last accessed 14 May 2019.

concentrated in the southwestern and central parts of the country. In 2020, UECBB had 254 churches. I have visited more than a hundred of them and participated in their worship; on about seventy of those occasions, I took notes, observed the worship, took pictures, and studied the worship space. Several times during my research I also visited two large, influential independent churches in Brest, namely the Church on Fortechnaya 61/1 and the Church "Christmas,"[25] as well as four "unregistered" churches.[26] Visiting the churches was important for gaining a deeper understanding of the character of traditional worship as well as simply getting the facts. Texts of songs or prayers cannot convey the spirit of worship when they are in isolation from worship. The same songs are sung in different ways in different churches and prayers vary in their emotionality.

The majority of this research took place between 2008–2017. During this period the questionnaires were distributed among ministers and church members and results were collected, notes from various worship services were taken, interviews were conducted, and audio- and video-recordings of

---

25. There are around twenty-five Baptist churches in Belarus which are not part of formal church organizations. From 1987 to 1993 I was involved in the ministry of the church on Fortechnaya as a preacher, youth leader, and deacon.

26. There were seventy-three such churches in 2015. "Unregistered," "separated," "initiators," and "Council of churches" are representative of several of the names of this movement among Russian-speaking Baptists which dates back to 1961. It emerged as a reaction to AUCECB's adoption of two documents in 1959, the "Polozhenie o Soyuze evangel'skikh khristian-baptistov v SSSR" [Regulations about ECB Union in USSR] and "Instruktivnoe pis'mo starshim presviteram VSEKhB" [Letter of Instruction to AUCECB Senior Pastors]. See http://baptistru.info/index.php?title=Инструктивное_письмо_и_Положение_ВСЕХБ, last accessed 12 April 2019. The letter was adopted by the December 1959 AUCECB Plenum. The documents recommended restraining missionary and inter-church activity and closely following the Soviet Law about cult practice. Later, on October 15, 1963, an AUCECB Congress abolished the Letter, but the documents evoked widespread dissatisfaction, which later resulted in splitting whole communities, or parts of communities, from the AUCECB. In 1965 a new Union was established: the Council of Churches of Evangelical Christian Baptists (CCECB). Unlike AUCECB churches, CCECB congregations did not register with the authorities. After the breakup of the Soviet Union, CCECB preserved its unity within the territory of the former Soviet Union. Later, it adopted the new name of the International Council of Churches of ECB (ICCECB), uniting Evangelical Christian Baptists in the Commonwealth of Independent States, Baltic countries, Germany, USA, and Canada. One of its distinguishing characteristics has been avoiding any contact with the state. See Tatyana Nikol'skaya, "Kto takiye 'otdelennyye'?" 1–2. *Vestnik Istiny* [Herald of Truth], *Spiritually-edifying Journal of the CCECB*, no 4 (2001), 5. For an English-language study covering the split within the AUCECB see Walter Sawatsky, *Soviet Evangelicals since World War II* (Kitchener, Ontario: Herald Press, 1981); Prokhorov, "The State and the Baptist Churches in the USSR (1960–1980)," 1–62.

worship were compiled.[27] The majority of the photographs of houses of prayer and their architecture belong to this period of time. However, researching the origins and development of the Baptist movement required embracing a period of over a hundred years, beginning from the late nineteenth century. At the same, special attention was given to the initial third of the twentieth century, the time of intensive church growth, and to the last third of the twentieth century, the period characterized by the dominance of Communism and the breakup of the Soviet Union, in which I was also able to incorporate my personal experience of involvement in worship. The beginning of the twenty-first century is especially interesting given the appearance of new styles and forms of worship (chiefly under Western and particularly American influence) driven by the translation of new books on missiology and church structure into Russian, the involvement of Western teachers and preachers in spiritual education and church ministry, and the spread of information on the World Wide Web.

1.4. Methodology

The research question guiding this dissertation has been the following: How is the implicit theology, as it is embodied in traditional Baptist worship in Belarus, related to understandings of established Baptist worship? To be more specific: How have the historical, political, religious, and theological contexts influenced this particular type of worship? How does the relationship between the implicit theology and traditional Baptist worship express itself in structure, content, spatial, and temporal dimensions as well as in values that define the character of worship? What kind of conflicts are of paramount importance for worship, and what are the avenues for a theological interpretation as well as for reconciliation of the existing tensions between form and freedom, the communal and the personal aspects in worship, and between traditional forms of worship and contemporary culture?

In my consideration of the theological patterns of Baptist worship, I largely follow the approach of a British Baptist theologian, Christopher Ellis. Ellis

---

27. The records are limited to a few churches ("Light of Gospel" and "Golgotha" in Minsk, Central Baptist church in Kobrin, and the church in Brest, Fortechnaya 61/1) which model worship for many churches.

engages in a well-documented historical study describing British Baptist worship.[28] In his case, he pays special attention to the spirituality of worship. First, he establishes "the liturgical facts," "the facts of evolving practices," taking into account the development of forms and their place in worship today.[29] Ellis believes that it is important to first learn "what happens, and happened, in worship."[30] Then, following an Orthodox liturgist, Alexander Schmemann, Ellis seeks to provide "the theological analysis of those liturgical facts,"[31] exploring "core worship values which influence worship or are expressed in it."[32] His next step is to draw out the implicit theology underlying a particular expression of worship. This exploration "enables the theology implicit in worship to have a voice."[33] The fourth step for Ellis is to "place the exposition of the faith of the worshipping community under a broader theological scrutiny."[34] Here we engage with "other theological expressions of faith," "such as creeds, confession of faith, analytical theology and, especially, Scripture."[35] In this work I seek to demonstrate how the logic of Ellis's approach can be applied to a different Baptist culture, and thus I do not closely follow the structure of his book. After extended historical study with close attention to the context in Part I, I establish "liturgical facts" in Part II, proceeding with the values which "shape the worship."[36] This enables an exploration of both the visible side of worship as well as what happens behind the scenes. In Part III (which combines steps three and four as suggested by Ellis), several spheres are considered regarding where the theology implicit in worship is in tension with theology expressed in confessions or other theological expressions of faith. This critical analysis of worship allows for a

---

28. Ellis, *Gathering*.
29. Ellis, 23.
30. Ellis.
31. Ellis. See Schmemann, "Liturgical Theology: Remarks on Method," 144.
32. Ellis, *Gathering*, 97.
33. Ellis, 24.
34. Ellis.
35. Ellis. This approach resonates with the theological framework of James McClendon, who suggests that the task of theology is the "discovery, understanding or interpretation, and transformation of the convictions of a convictional community, including the discovery and critical revision of their relation to one another **and to whatever else there is**." (McClendon, *Ethics*, 23. Emphasis in original.)
36. Ellis, *Gathering*, 73.

clarifying theology of worship to emerge against which its practices can be developed and changed.

The method of research is interdisciplinary. It is a combination of the study of history and literature, field research, and theological analysis, all integrated into one framework of research by the main research question and the specific phenomenon under exploration.[37] In the first part, I explore sources related to the origin and development of the evangelical movement and worship service in Belarus. This includes theological, religious, and political contexts and their influence in the process of formation. The primary concern here is to understand the worship of the Baptist community through the process of historical enquiry and theological reflection.[38] A substantive historical examination of the subject raised issues concerning the clashes of different cultures and the influence of context in the process of worship formation. Significant use has been made of primary sources such as archive documents, hymnals, autobiographies and memoirs, newspaper and magazine articles, confessions, reports from conferences and congresses, and government documents. Secondary sources, such as books on history, theses, and reference materials, shed further light on the context and key events that have come to shape Belarusian Baptist worship.

The historical research paves the way for an in-depth understanding of the current shape of worship which is the focus in the second part of this dissertation. Here, ethnographical research has been of particular use, primarily in terms of differing degrees of participant observation.[39] Prolonged time spent in observation has enabled me, as a researcher, to take note of any significant patterns of change.[40] Immersing myself in worship, and forming and maintaining relationships with other participants, has been directed

---

37. Silverman, *Doing Qualitative Research*, 6. According to Ellis, in such a study, "A number of different disciplines may be used in the study of worship – from historical research to ethnographic observation, from liturgical analysis to theological reflection." (Ellis, "Duty and Delight," 330.)

38. Cf. Ellis, *Gathering*, 34.

39. Since levels of participation can vary, Tim May suggests using narrower terms, such as "complete participant," "participant as observer," and "observer as participant." (May, *Social Researcher*, 140). In my practice of visiting churches, these terms could accordingly mean a person who is involved in worship as a leader and preacher, or who joins with church singing and prayer, or who is involved as a listener. On different ways of engaging in worship see section 7.2.1.

40. Fetterman, "Ethnography," 328.

towards the "understanding [of] the meaning of human action"[41] – in this case, understanding the meaning bestowed on the practice of worship.[42] As I engage in the thick description of one of the practices "that shape and are shaped"[43] by people, much attention is paid to context, values, and the definition of the character of worship as the phenomenon under consideration.

Qualitative research can be combined with some elements of quantitative research. In this way, we can "think of quantitative and qualitative approaches as complementary parts of the systematic, empirical search for knowledge."[44] Employing triangulation has allowed for the use of different methods for data collection.[45] This approach enables more precise research of public worship as a social phenomenon, and it strengthens the credibility and validity of the results, taking into account that each method has unique strengths and weaknesses. The validity of conclusions in qualitative methods can be influenced by the researcher's personality and his or her professional training. At the same time, quantitative methods do not pay as much attention to context or the personal characteristics of a particular group. In this way, the use of complementary and independent methods compensates for their faults. In-depth understanding of an individual participant's experience, or of a specific phenomenon, is complemented by the broad coverage of this study in terms of the significant number of churches and public worship services it examines, which suggests a typical experience or phenomenon.

Questionnaires[46] typically belong to quantitative research. In this dissertation, they have shaped the definition and description of the structure and characteristics of, and tendencies in, worship formation. However, the researcher needs to understand the meaning that the participants attribute to certain actions,[47] and the meaning these actions acquire in a particular context.[48] For example, Martin Stringer pays attention to three moments in

---

41. Schwandt, *The SAGE Dictionary*, 248.

42. Creswell, *Qualitative Inquiry*, 71. On ethnography and fieldwork, see the discussion in Schwandt, *The SAGE Dictionary*, 96, and Sandelowski, "Qualitative research," 893–894.

43. Sandelowski, "Qualitative research," 893–894.

44. Silverman, *Doing Qualitative Research*, 9.

45. Glesne, *Becoming Qualitative Researchers*, 32. Patton, *Qualitative Research*, 247.

46. Detailed description of the questionnaires is presented in the following section.

47. Klomp, *The Sound of Worship*, 72.

48. Klomp, 73.

the research: "what a person says they should be doing," "what they say they are doing," and "what they are actually doing."[49] What people say they are doing, and what their understanding is of what they should be doing, can be discovered through questionnaires and interviews. Observation may then confirm or disprove the facts. That is why textual analysis, written questionnaires, interviews and structured interviews, recording, keeping field notes, and conversations should be complemented by observation of the course of worship, the actions of worshippers, and worshippers' reactions to what is going on.[50]

Active involvement in worship may distract from the analytical task. As time goes by, the ethnographer becomes "saturated" with the practice of worship, which can make it more difficult for them to notice details that might grab the attention of a newcomer. Here, notepads, cameras, video cameras, and audio recording equipment, become the researchers' friend due to their "*density* and *permanence*" (emphasis in original).[51] This density allows the researcher to closely examine every element and participant, to pay attention to body language, to follow the words of a prayer or sermon, or to count the number of Scriptures read out loud in worship (as I did for the churches "Golgotha" and "Light of Gospel" in Minsk). They are also very helpful for a thick description. Permanence is expressed in the extension of the time frame of study. Listening to the records of worship, or watching them in the office, while constantly addressing the research framework, and having the opportunity to stop and go back, enables the extraction of new layers of information, which is very important in a thick description, and the checking of conclusions that have already been made. In addition, it helps the researcher to abstract, to look at the worship "from the outside," which is critical for the ethnographer immersed in the subject of study. Given that large churches make their own video or audio recordings of worship, it has been possible to use the fruit of their work (with their permission) to expand the geography of research. However, I recorded most of the visuals on a phone camera. The quality was sufficient for the analysis and conclusions made in section 4.2. The Use of Space in Public Worship.

---

49. Stringer, *On the Perception of Worship*, 50.
50. Klomp, *The Sound of Worship*, 80.
51. Madil, "Ethnography," 291. Also see Gibson, "Videorecording," 916–918.

Gathered data may require clarification or even a change in the collection approach, since "ethnographic research is a reflexive and cyclical process."[52] An ethnographer checks their conclusions both in the light of new information and through the constant evaluation of the influence of their "own culture, social background and personal experiences."[53] In this case, I had to reflect on the multiple ties I had with the subject: convictions and beliefs, personal and academic interests, involvement and experience education and qualifications, and so forth.[54] Self-reflexivity requires responding to such questions as "What do I know? How do I know what I know? What shapes my perceptions and has my background affected the data I have collected and my analysis of those data? How do I perceive those I have studied?"[55] For example, careful consideration needed to be given to the fact that I am a leader of the Baptist Union and Seminary, and I am involved in setting the Union policy concerning worship. This was particularly important when considering the way the information was to be collected by questionnaires and interviews, so that participants did not feel pressure to, respond in a particular way, and understood their right to cease their participation in the project. I also needed to think about my participation in worship not only as an insider, but as an insider who carries a certain degree of power which might influence the worship experience of other participants.

The work of the ethnographer does not stop at the accumulation of information. At the next level the ethnographer "translates this material to make it intelligible to other people by giving a sorted, contextualized description."[56] The study of worship in this dissertation concentrates on the structure, content, and temporal and spatial aspects of worship. Less attention is paid to analyzing the behavior of worship participants, or to the study of individual components such as the music. While an in-depth investigation of these topics would likely shed further light on the theology of traditional Baptist worship, this could not be achieved within the scope of this study. Instead,

---

52. Klomp, *The Sound of Worship*, 75. See also Denscombe, *The Good Research Guide*, 88.
53. Denscombe, *The Good Research Guide*, 90. Also see Russel Ogden, "Bias," 60–61.
54. Denscombe.
55. Patton, *Qualitative Research*, 495.
56. Klomp, *The Sound of Worship*, 74; Stringer, *On the Perception of Worship*, 54.

I have concentrated on what emerged as the key aspects for interpreting the phenomenon under consideration.

The accumulation and processing of information led to further testing and development of the hypotheses regarding the values and beliefs of worshipers as determining the form, structure, content, and design of worship space. Simplicity, the importance of the Bible, edification, and the missiological perspective of worship could be classified as such values or emphases. Alongside the analysis of the information acquired through questionnaires, and the exploration of the documents and texts related to this particular form of worship, participant observation[57] continued to play an important role at this stage.

The third part of this work deals with the problem of discrepancies or tensions between form and freedom, the communal and the personal aspects in worship, and between traditional forms of worship and culture today, conditioned by the context of formation. There is "an *implicit* theology embodied in worship,"[58] which manifests itself in the expectation of believers, their reactions, emotions, and understanding,[59] and in the participants' behavior, the sequence, and the content of the components. There is also an official understanding which is expressed in confessions, articles, manuals, and ministers' statements. Inspired by an approach Ellis sets out in one of his articles,[60] I have explored contradictions between worship in its empirical shape and some of the key tenets of Baptist teaching on worship, or between "primary" and "secondary" theology.[61] This method, aimed at the study of internal contradictions, can be called a dialectical method. It is applied both to individual components, such as prayer, and to the content of the worship

---

57. Cf. Ward, ed., *Perspectives on Ecclesiology and Ethnography*, 8. Barnard, Cilliers, and Wepener think that "Liturgical ritual must be understood in the first place within its cultural and anthropological contexts, that is, within its immediate and wider cultural context, as well as from its anthropological context, that is, from the perspective of its participants or performers." (Barnard et. al., *Worship in the Network Culture*, 39.)

58. Ellis, *Gathering*, 33–34.

59. Stringer, *On the Perception of Worship*, 43; Klomp, *The Sound of Worship*, 74.

60. Ellis, "Gathering Struggles," 4–21.

61. Ellis, *Gathering*, 248. Ellis's ideas of tensions in worship and values, which shape the worship, helped to group and sort out a large amount of material obtained in the process of the research. Other helpful works in systematization and evaluation of the information are Jones and Parushev, eds., *Currents in Baptistic Theology*; Bebbington, "Evangelicals and public worship, 1965–2005," 3–22.

service as a whole, to the participants, and to the relationship between church and society. In Ellis's opinion "to describe Christian worship dialectically . . . can be both creative and illuminating as a theological method."[62] In fact, I began to sense such tensions before becoming acquainted with Ellis's work, and the latter has helped me to clarify and refine my own approach and given me confidence to continue in this direction.

Reflection on discrepancies in worship opens the door for constructive critique and for proposals aimed at reducing the existing tensions. At the same time, the idea of "creative tension"[63] is also developed here. Such dynamic tension is one of the main reasons for the continuous internal development of worship. Therefore, the emphasis is not on completely overcoming the conflict, but rather on using its energy to improve practice and unleash the potential of worship. This approach requires engaging inner resources of local worship, and using resources from other traditions of worship that are able to enrich worship in Baptist churches in Belarus.

Since Ellis devotes little space to culture and its relationship to worship, in the section focused on the relevance of worship to the secular context, I engage with a theological model from the reformed theologian John Witvliet, and particularly with his call to liturgical inculturation.[64] I begin by examining the cultural environment of worship and the relationship between worship and culture. This is followed by a critical assessment of the cultural context and defining extremes, which should be avoided in attempts to adapt or completely reject elements of the local culture. Evaluation of other traditions of worship helps us to understand how "common elements" of Christian worship can be expressed through local worship, avoiding their mechanical repetition. Searching for native equivalents of individual components of worship, possibly by transforming the forms that have been available in a culture, preserves worship uniqueness, and defining basic or common elements characteristic of all Christian tradition preserves worship identity.[65]

---

62. Ellis, *Gathering*. p. 34.

63. This phrase appears in the title of Ellis's article "Gathering Struggles: Creative Tensions in Baptist Worship."

64. Witvliet, *Worship Seeking Understanding*.

65. Witvliet, 109–123.

1.5. Analysis of Resources
1.5.1. Historical Documents

The subject matter and the methodology required the use of a wide range of resources. A considerable contribution to the study of the origins of the evangelical movement and worship formation in Belarus was made by archive research, primarily in the National Archives of the Republic of Belarus, and to a lesser degree in the National Historical Archives of Belarus. The latter holds documents such as the protocols of a police bailiff, reports of district police officers, event reports from the governor, reports of priests and archbishops, information from the governor's office, circulars from the Ministry of Internal Affairs, Mogilev diocesan bulletins, and many others. In the National Archives, the documents of the Council for Religious Affairs are of special value as they contain applications and complaints by Christians, memoranda of authorized representatives, and materials about the activity of religious communities. As with any study of persecuted groups, the shortcoming of such archives is that they mainly deal with evidences provided by the believers' persecutors and adversaries, such as reports from the police and authorized representatives, and materials of official propaganda. Nevertheless, they provide many useful facts and insights.

The repertoire of primary sources is completed by evangelical materials related to the origins and spread of the Baptist faith. CDs with selections of documents (and modern research works) produced by the Euro-Asian Accrediting Association,[66] cannot be overestimated in this regard. For example, the first CD contains two thousand primary sources that cover a wide spectrum of topics linked to the evangelical movement that arose in imperial Russia in the middle of the nineteenth century. The documents include memoirs of key figures of the Evangelical movement, approximately one hundred and fifty interviews, pictures, maps, texts and photocopies of books and journals, state documents, and church and personal archives. However, these documents provide little information on how the evangelical movement spread into the immediate territory of Belarus; their main focus is on the first sites of Baptist origins in the Russian Empire: the Caucasus, Southern Ukraine and St. Petersburg.

---

66. *Istoriya Evangel'skogo dvizheniya v Evrazii* [History of the Evangelical Movement in Eurasia].

Books on the history of the evangelical movement in the Russian Empire and Soviet Union written in Russian and in English (and in some cases in Belarusian and Polish), have been used as auxiliary materials. Among the first of these I should note is *The History of Evangelical Christians-Baptists in the USSR*.[67] This work was prepared and published by AUCECB, summarized a number of sources, and "introduced many new sources and facts into readership circulation, exposing the past of the Baptist movement with scrupulousness as never before."[68] A fundamental work by Wilhelm Kahle[69] also deserves attention, as well as a recently published book by Andrei Puzynin.[70] The works by Heather Coleman and Toivo Pilli[71] are the most valuable among the materials in English. Even though Pilli focuses on a Baptist movement in Estonia, the connection between the churches in the Soviet Union, and the similar political context, make his work a good source for comparison and evaluation. Works by Western historians and theologians have been used for a broader understanding of Baptist heritage and identity, and they include Thomas McKibbens, Ian Randall, Albert Wardin, W.T. Whitley, and Philip Thompson[72] among others.

A significant body of literature contains Orthodox, Russian (until 1917), and Soviet historiography. There are many books of this type in the National Library of the Republic of Belarus. Much of the valuable evidence and a good analysis can be found in the research of the Russian historian A.I. Milovidov,[73] and archpriest A.V. Rozhdestvensky.[74] It is also worth mentioning L.N.

---

67. *Istoriya evangel'skikh khristian-baptistov v SSSR*.

68. Mitrokhin, *Baptizm: istoriya i sovremennost'* [Baptists: History and Modernity], 190. Unless indicated otherwise, all translations from Russian, Belarusian, Ukrainian, and Polish in this dissertation are mine.

69. Kahle, *Evangel'skie khristiane v Rossii i Sovetskom Soyuze*.

70. Puzynin, *Tradiciya evangel'skikh khristian. Izuchenie samoidentifikacii i bogosloviya ot momenta ee zarozhdeniya do nashih dnei*.

71. Coleman, *Russian Baptists & Spiritual Revolution 1905–1929*; Pilli, "Evangelical: The Shaping of Identity," 253.

72. McKibbens, Jr., "Our Baptist Heritage in Worship," 53–70; Randall, Pilli and Cross, *Baptist Identities*; Wardin, Jr, "How Indigenous was the Baptist Movement in the Russian Empire," 29–37; Whitley, ed., *The Works of John Smyth*, vol. 1; Thompson, "Re-envisioning Baptist Identity," 287–303.

73. Milovidov, *Sovremennoe shtundobaptistskoe dvizhenie*).

74. A. Rozhdestvensky, *Yuzhnorussky Shtundism* [Southrussian Shtundism] (Sanct Peterburg: Tipografiya Departamenta Udelov, 1889). Rozhdestvensky wrote about Southrussian Shtundist, which corresponds to the current territory of southern Ukraine. This

Mitrokhin, M.Y. Lensu, and E.S. Prokshina among the Soviet writers, whose works were published in the second half of the twentieth century.[75] However, in Tsarist Russia and in Soviet times, most of the authors were prejudiced against the Baptists and other evangelical groups, considering them to be instruments of Germanisation and agents of Western imperialism, or perceiving them as fanatics and harmful relics of the past. "Extreme bias"[76] is especially typical of the literature published during the late 1920s and 1930s, and then in the 1950s and 1960s. During these times, issues of partisanship decided/affected scientific "objectivity." Thus the objectivity of the thesis by respected modern Belarusian scholar, Tatsiana Lisovskaya, stands out as being of great advantage in this regard.[77]

1.5.2. Ethnographic Data

The second part of my dissertation is devoted to an exposition of the phenomenon of worship. I have been able to explore traditional Baptist worship as an immediate participant and observer. Besides personal observations, impressions, and informal interactions, much information was received concerning church worship. This was primarily a result of the questionnaires and structured interviews conducted over the course of several years which covered churches in different regions of Belarus, but which reflect the fact that most churches are concentrated in the Brest region and in Minsk. Firstly, by random selection and stratification by region, churches of different sizes were singled out to represent the capital, other urban, and rural settings. Questionnaires[78] were offered to one pastor or one preacher from each

---

movement did however contribute to the development of the evangelical movement in the southeast and east of Belarus.

75. Mitrokhin, *Baptizm: istoriya i sovremennost'*; Lensu and Prokshina, eds., *Baptizm i Baptisty. Sotsiologicheskiy ocherk* [Baptism and Baptists. Sociological Digest].

76. Mitrokhin, *Baptizm: istoriya i sovremennost'*, 23.

77. Lisovskaya, *Neoprotestantizm v Zapadnoi Belarusi v 1921–1939 gg.*

78. Q, 2008, *Questionnaire of church ministers* (January, 2008).

church.⁷⁹ I contacted these "gatekeepers" or "key informants"⁸⁰ in person or by telephone about filling out the forms. Instructions on how to fill out the questionnaire and contact information were provided to the participants – mailing address, telephone number and email address – to use when they had any questions or were ready to return their questionnaires. In 2008, information was received from five large churches (four to seven hundred members),⁸¹ including "Golgotha," (the central Baptist church in Minsk which celebrated its one hundred and fifteen anniversary in 2020) five average-sized churches (fifty to one hundred members); and four small churches (up to thirty members). The goal of the initial part of the study was to gather general information about worship services, their structure, content, physical environment, and distinct features. For the most part, the respondents answered open-ended questions, designed to both explain facts and reveal the opinions of the respondents. For example, questions included: "What Bible texts are decorating the walls/pulpit/pictures in your house of prayer (give the reference)? Are the texts replaced for some occasions?" and "What are the main problems of sermons (if there are any)?" Clearly, the questions were not only about the facts and knowledge of the worshippers, but also about their evaluations, feelings, experiences, and perceptions of the subject.⁸² Four out of the eighteen churches did not respond. The information from the questionnaires was digitalized and saved along with the digital questionnaires. The hard copies of the questionnaires are preserved at Minsk Theological Seminary.

While the number of these questionnaires was relatively limited, it was followed by prolonged engagement and extended time in the field, and by another set of questionnaires which engaged lay people of various ages, both men and women. This aspect of the study, which can be identified as

---

79. I should note that, given my personal history and role in ministry, personal acquaintance and good, trustworthy relationships were one of the factors that enabled the extent of this research. As Corrine Glesne observes, "relationship between researchers and people plays an important role" (Glesne, *Becoming Qualitative Researchers. An Introduction*, 43). In the researching and receiving of information, interacting with a researcher who is considered to be a "trusted person" (Glesne, 43) provides a lot of information, including negative aspects of local worship practices that ministers and church members would not share with an outside researcher.

80. Creswell, *Qualitative Inquiry*, 71.

81. There are no such big church congregations in the Vitebsk, Grodno and Mogilev regions, which are three out of six regions in Belarus.

82. Glesne, *Becoming Qualitative Researchers*, 71.

structured interviews administered in writing, was conducted in 2012.[83] The questions were focused on clarifying theological issues related to worship and inviting an analysis of the situation. For example, "How could the participation of many people (everybody volunteering) be reconciled with the importance of the edification of the church?" In addition, there were structured interviews for ministers in 2008, individual church members in 2008 and 2012, and seminary students in 2013,[84] which, although limited in scale,[85] provide a window into "what real people think about their worship and how ordinary churchgoers respond to what happens every Sunday morning in their churches."[86]

1.5.3. Content of Questionnaires and Interviews

The information obtained through surveys and interviews makes it possible to paint a picture of worship as seen by ministers and church members, although this picture is largely determined by the questions posed. It should also be noted that ministers tend to express "official" opinion in their responses, presenting the worship as it should be, while church members express their feelings and impressions, presenting an "outside" perspective. On the other hand, most people are not inclined to write anything bad or negative about worship in their churches, even if they feel a little bit differently.

The vast majority of respondents define church meetings in the house of prayer as traditional worship services or meetings, rather than as worship. They describe the essence of what is happening as glorification, co-worship, and fellowship with God and with each other. The purpose of public worship is to teach, encourage, comfort, inspire, and spend time in fellowship with

---

83. SI, 2012, *Structured interview of church ministers and members* (September, 2012).

84. Respectively SI, 2008, *Structured interview of church pastors. Theological Assessment* (October, 2008); QM, 2008, *Questionnaire of church members* (January, 2008); QM, 2012, *Questionnaire of church members* (October, 2012); Q, 2013, *Questionnaire of Seminary students* (November, 2013).

85. An average 10–12 interviews per set.

86. Stringer, *On the Perception of Worship*, 1. Stringer argued, "the meaning of any act of worship existed primarily withing the minds of the worshippers who attended the rite and had very little to do with the specifics of the text or the actions of the liturgy being used." Later he came to the conclusion, "that the 'answer', so far as there is an answer, must lie somewhere between the text and the minds of the worshippers who use the text." (Stringer, 2.) The ratio between the role of the text and the condition of the worshippers could vary significantly depending on church and individual personality, but the voice of public worship participants should be heard in the process of worship analysis. See Klomp, *The Sound of Worship*, 74.

each other. During worship, such fellowship is of particular value, since the Spirit of God acts in a special way.

It is noted that the form and content of the meeting (especially hymns and the nature of worship) was significantly influenced by the Orthodox context, as well as the context of persecution. The religious context promoted reverence in public worship, emphasis on prayerful meditation, and gave a certain sadness to the meetings. Persecution led to highlighting such themes as suffering, faithfulness, patience, and eschatological motives. Church members believe that in recent years, public worship has become more formal. Western influence can also be traced (which is not always appropriate in an Orthodox context), along with the influence of theological education, primarily on the quality of preaching and the spread of the idea of expositional preaching. People also noted the weakening of the evangelistic aspect (the call to repent of sins is heard less often).

The survey responses allow us to clarify the issues related to planning public worship and to determine its participants, the order of worship, its components, the Christ-focused content of individual elements, the number of public worship meetings and how long they take, as well as physical aspects such as the structure of the sanctuary, interior design, and changes to the space of worship (e.g., some churches strive to give an impetus to public worship by making use of new technological and multimedia tool). The surveys reveal that people consider the most valuable element of worship to be preaching, and then prayer and singing follow. The believers in Jerusalem devoted themselves to the apostles' teaching and the disciples do the same thing nowadays.

Specific guiding questions allow us to assess the instances of tension in public worship between freedom and form (it is a must to have freedom, even spontaneity, and at the same time it is important to prepare for singing, preaching, and systematizing the "ministry of the Word"), between the individual and social nature of worship, (problems associated with large numbers of participants), and between the sacred and secular aspects of the meeting (here more attention is paid to music and singing). The issues related to large numbers of participants and the disadvantages associated with it are of particular interest. A congregation can be dispirited by long and identical prayers, when the same words or phrases are repeated by the same people every meeting regardless of the context or the topic of the worship service.

Too many songs, and too long a sermon or prayer, along with too many topics, is exhausting and frustrating for the congregation. Nevertheless, the Christians believe that it is very important to maintain and encourage individual participation for members' benefit and spiritual growth.

In general, church members are not interested in significant changes to public worship, although, depending on the church, they would be glad to have better quality and better organization, or, conversely, more informality. They believe it is important to preserve traditional church culture in terms of outreach in the Orthodox context. Ministers and church members alike indicate that the most important things they value are humility, openness, kindness, care and love for others, compassion, exemplary lives of believers, and the importance of revealing emotion, warmth, and simplicity in the presentation of the Gospel.

Summarizing the survey results requires cautiousness when drawing conclusions and evaluations. The information should only be perceived as an "attempt to discover an authentic voice."[87] David Silverman asks a fair question: "How far did my respondents' answers to my prepared questions actually reflect their own experiences?"[88] Some respondents may treat the questionnaires and structured interviews casually and may try to respond to them hastily. Others may try to present their church practice in its best light while some others may be critically minded. Thus, the issue of reliability always remains, and the value of observation and the researcher's own involvement is equally important in the process. In order to confirm and clarify some assumptions and details, other sources of information could be consulted, such as private or informal conversations with theology students, musicians, choir members, pastors, and ordinary believers. Indeed, learning to listen well to others' stories and to interpret and retell their accounts is part of the qualitative researcher's trade.[89] Such conversations help us to better understand the influence of worship, the connection between worship and life, and worshippers' individual and collective experiences.[90]

---

87. Ward, *Perspectives on Ecclesiology and Ethnography*, 8.
88. Silverman, *Doing Qualitative Research*, 8.
89. Glesne, *Becoming Qualitative Researchers*, 1.
90. For more about informal conversational interview see Patton, *Qualitative Research*, 342–343. Such informal conversations are characterized by flexibility and spontaneity, and they

1.5.4. Theological Materials

It is hard to imagine a study of worship without an analysis of liturgical texts. Yet, as already noted, there are only a few items directly associated with traditional Baptist worship: namely, the Bible, hymnal(s), and collections of poetry. There are neither prayer books nor written texts or directions for communions, funerals, weddings, ordinations, baptisms, offerings, special days of the Christian year, or regular worship occasions. However, there are still some other useful items that are indirectly related to worship services. *Bratskiy Vestnik* magazine is an indispensable resource for the study and analysis of Russian-speaking Baptist worship, as it was the only legal Baptist magazine published bi-monthly from 1945 to 1993.[91] (In 2005, the publication was relaunched as a press organ of the Euro-Asian Federation of the Unions of Evangelical Christians-Baptists).[92] In the Soviet era, this publication united churches and evangelical groups, and, in the absence of other theological resources and means of communication, it is difficult to overstate its role. The leadership of AUCECB considered "proper formation" of church members "both from spiritual and the civil point of view"[93] as the main objective of the magazine. The magazine covered various issues of church life, and included published sermons, articles for Christian edification, commentaries on biblical texts, and information about how the leadership of the Union and regional units visited churches, and what decisions the Union made. Many communities practiced communal reading of the magazine, such as reading it aloud before the start of a worship service. Nevertheless, it was an official publication, and it was controlled by the Soviet authorities, so a lot of information about the life of churches was avoided, especially regarding

---

can be done if persons are acquainted with each other, work together, visit churches, meet at conferences, and work with pastors.

91. [Fraternal Messenger] (Moskva: VSEKhB). Initially, the magazine's circulation was three thousand copies, from 1957 it increased to five thousand copies, and from 1979 to ten thousand. From late 1949 to 1952 inclusive, the magazine was not published. See *Istoriya evangel'skikh khristjan-baptistov v SSSR*, 278; Kasataya, "Samvydat evangel'skikh khrysstiyan-baptystau u BSSR," 196. Even though the number of magazine copies was small, they were personally handed from one person to another, (judging by the experience of our family) which means that the number of Christian readers was considerably greater and more significant than the number of copies.

92. See all issues of the magazine on the website of the Moscow Central Church of the ECB. http://mbchurch.ru/publications/brotherly_pdf/, last accessed 15 May 2019.

93. *Bratskiy Vestnik*, no. 3 (1969), 65.

forced closing of churches, arrests, and the activity of unregistered churches.[94] Yet, its spiritual influence, in an atmosphere of almost complete absence of other literature and information sources, was felt far beyond Moscow. To provide a personal example, my brothers and I used *Bratskiy Vestnik* in the preparation of our sermons when we were only 14–18 years old, making use of the "Meditations for Preachers" by Karev, one of the most productive authors of the magazine.[95]

A key resource from a theological and analytical point of view is the literature in English on the theology of worship, or Liturgical Theology. First of all, there are the books and articles of Christopher Ellis, John Witvliet, and Alexander Schmemann. Other authors who analyze worship from different perspectives – Methodist, Reformed, Lutheran[96] – have made a great contribution to the understanding of the theology of worship. Their works present tools and methodology for the study of worship, which, due to the lack of research on the topic, are needed in the Russian-speaking evangelical tradition.

Alongside Western scholars we should note contemporary indigenous Russian and Ukrainian scholars, including Seventh Day Adventist, Victor Leahu, and Baptist, Mikhail Cherenkov.[97] The picture is complemented by the recently written dissertations at the International Baptist Theological Seminary, such as the work of Timofey Cheprasov, who explored preaching in the Russian-speaking context, and Constantine Prokhorov, who studied the influence of Orthodoxy on the practice of Baptist churches in Russia. They worked in similar contexts and yielded excellent results on the analysis of the practice

---

94. Kasataya, "Evangel'skiya khrystsiyane-baptysty ý BSSR u 1944 – pachatku 1950-kh gg," 144; Popov, "The Evangelical Christians-Baptists in the Soviet Union."

95. Alexander Vasil'evich Karev (1894–1971) was a pastor, preacher, Christian writer, and theologian, as well as the General Secretary of AUCECB and the chief editor of *Bratskiy Vestnik* magazine (1944–1971).

Cheprasov offers an informative overview of articles on preaching that appeared in the pages of the *Bratskiy Vestnik*. He claims, "The importance and influence of this media is difficult to overestimate, since until 1968 when the Bible Correspondent Courses (BCC) started to work, the only resource available to churches and individual preachers were publications in the *BV* [*Bratskiy Vestnik*]." (Cheprasov, *Like Ripples on Water*, 51.)

96. Wainwright, *Doxology: The Praise of God in Worship*; *Worship Old & New*; Hoon, *The Integrity of Worship*; White, *Protestant Worship*; Barnard, Cilliers, and Wepener, *Worship in the Network Culture*; Lathrop, *Holy People*; von Allmen, *Worship: Its Theology and Practice*.

97. Leahu, "K voprosu o vzaimodeistvii teologii bogosluzheniya i teologii kul'tury v liturgicheskom opyte neoprotestantisma", 46; Cherenkov, *Evropeis'ka rephormaciya ta ukrain'sky evangel'sky Protestantism: Genetiko-tipologichna sporidnenist' i natsional'no-identiphikatsiiny vymiry suchasnosti*, 300; and other books and articles.

of preaching, theological identity and how it was shaped, and the praxis of worship among Russian Baptists.[98]

---

98. Cheprasov, "Formative? Informative?" Subsequently published as Cheprasov, *Like Ripples on Water* and Prokhorov, *Russian Baptists and Orthodoxy, 1960–1990*; Prokhorov, "Russian Baptist and Orthodoxy, 1960–1990: A Comparative Study of Theology, Liturgy, and Traditions".

Part 1

Formation: Exploring the Past and the Context

CHAPTER 2

The Role of Public Worship in the Belarusian Baptist Context

2.1. A Source of Spiritual Life in Difficult Times

Worship has always played a prominent role in the life of Evangelical Christian Baptists, performing a preparatory and hermeneutical function in relation to the everyday experiences of believers. Together with a distinct ethical and outward appearance,[1] public worship has been the principal manifestation of belonging to the church. Describing their attendance of worship, AUCECB senior pastors and leaders would use such lofty descriptions such as "extraordinary meeting of the redeemed,"[2] "blessed prayer meetings,"[3]

---

1. It is possible to read about the behavior and experience of the Baptists from the point of view of secular researchers in the books by Lensu and Prokshina, *Baptizm i Baptisty. Sotsiologicheskiy ocherk* and Mitrokhin, *Baptizm: istoriya i sovremennost'*. The authors of the first book, which was published in 1969, study the history of Baptists in Belarus. On the basis of sociological materials they cover various sides of Baptist psychology and their moral ideals. The book by Mitrokhin was published in 1997, and the author is concerned with the dogmatic and morals of Christians and their "living" religious experience. It is also very interesting to study the practice of creating a family, which, from an ethical point of view, is one of the most fundamental issues in the context of opposing "worldly" morality. Mironova, "Predstavleniya o brake i brachnyye praktiki yevangel'skikh veruyushchikh v Sovetskom Soyuze v 1940–1980-ye gg. Po materialam obshchin yevangel'skikh khristian-baptistov tsentral'no-chernozemnogo regiona" [Marriage Ideas and Practices among Evangelical Believers in the Soviet Union in 1940–1980s. The Case of Central Black Earth Region], 131–162.

2. *Bratskiy Vestnik*, no. 1 (1945), 44.

3. *Bratskiy Vestnik*, no. 3 (1945), 15.

"solemn divine service,"[4] or "blessed hours in joyful communion like on Mount Tabor."[5] It would not be uncommon to note that those who attended "listened to our words with sublime delight,"[6] and though "the meeting lasted for four hours, nobody wanted to leave."[7] A well-known hymn, *Vot nastal molitvy chas* (Time Has Come For Us To Pray), frequently performed before the start of the worship service, illustrates the reverent attitude:

> Time has come for us to pray.
> Faith shall bring us near,
> At the feet of Christ we lay
> Sin and all our fears.
>> This we have to know in faith:
>> He extends His embrace
>> Sending His abundant blessings
>> Unto us all the days.
> Wondrous prayer time!
> Wondrous prayer time!
> Sweetest fellowship, it can be no sweeter!
> Filled with Power Divine.[8]

Baptists consider taking part in worship to be an experience of joy and satisfaction, and also a way of receiving food for one's soul, power to gain victory over sin, wisdom to solve everyday problems, answers to the hard issues of life, encouragement in despondency, and a spiritual supply of energy to live in the secular milieu during the coming week. To inspire each other, Baptists would sing, "We found encouragement in the words of the Lord, so we may go forth with new strength."[9] In the words of one Baptist woman,

> During the prayer service I get charged with power and more faith in God. It may be compared to a light bulb that feeds on

---

4. *Bratskiy Vestnik*, no. 3, 13.
5. *Bratskiy Vestnik*, no. 1 (1946), 43.
6. *Bratskiy Vestnik*, no. 3 (1948), 52.
7. *Bratskiy Vestnik*, no. 6 (1947), 48.
8. *Pesn' Vozrozhdeniya*, no. 2, first stanza and refrain. The songs and poems in the Introduction and Chapter 2 were(put into poetry in English by Viyaleta Saviankova.
9. Hymn "Dorogie minuty nam Bog daroval" [The Lord Has Given Us Precious Moments], *Pesn' Vozrozhdeniya*, no. 679.

a battery. Just as with time going on a battery loses power and it needs to be charged again, so do we. A week goes by and we need to be recharged. For a week we are busy with secular matters, work and care. We seem to be utterly consumed by our surroundings but on a day for public worship we get recharged and our faith grows stronger . . . On Sunday it is impossible to stay home. You are just pulled to the house of prayer. My soul sings and joy flows.[10]

On the other hand, as preachers often warn, disregard for worship services is understood to eventually lead to spiritual coolness and going astray from the church and faith. Admonitions to be zealous in attending public worship are often accompanied by examples and illustrations. A typical analogy compares Christian worship to a burning coal. If a burning coal falls out of a stove it will soon become cold. Likewise, if a Christian is all alone, without fellowship with other Christians, they will grow cold and die spiritually.

Church members who are absent from worship services for several months without a reasonable cause can be disciplined to the extent of admonition, reprimand,[11] or even excommunication.[12] Referring to multiple Scriptural texts (mainly in the Book of Psalms), and practices in the early church (as described in the Book of Acts), official ECB documents, communicate that it is the duty of all church members to attend church services:

---

10. Lensu and Prokshina, *Baptizm i Baptisty*, 209, 202.

11. Measure of church discipline (see 2 Thess 3:14). Church members under admonition are not allowed to take part in any kind of ministry or membership meetings, and cannot participate in the Lord's Supper. A person can be under admonition for a period of up to six months. Then, depending on their behavior, a member of the church may have their rights restored, or be excommunicated.

12. The last stage of church discipline: a member of the church is deprived of all membership rights (see Matt 18:15–17). Questions of admonition or excommunication are the responsibility of the church council or a membership meeting. Yaroslav Pyzh believes that "the practice of New Testament discipline and excommunication vividly proved the high standard applied to church members" ("The Confessional Community as the Ecclesiological Core of the Baptists in the Soviet Union, 1960–1990." Nikolai Levindanto, one of the AUCECB senior pastors, stated that "excommunication could be applied only for cases of revealed and proved sin, apostasy or falling into heresy after all evangelical measures have been taken for the correction of the sinning person while notwithstanding he or she has stayed incorrigible" (Levindanto, "Blagochinie pomestnyh tserkvey ili tserkovnaya distsiplina," 15).

Each church member is called to attend church services and to be worthy to take part in [the] Lord's Supper (Heb 10:25; Ps 16:3; Ps 27:4; Ps 122:1; 1 Cor 11:26–28; Acts 2:42).[13]

In particular each church member is obliged to take part in the Lord's Supper (Matt 26:27; Mark 14:23) and to be diligent in attending all the church services officiated by the congregation both on Sunday as well as on week days (Heb 10:25; Acts 1:14; Acts 2:1; Acts 2:42; Acts 4:24; Ps 27:4; Ps 122:1; Ps 84:1–2). Only in extreme necessity or in sickness may a church member be excused from participating in the Lord's Supper or attending public worship, and especially membership meetings (Ps 116:18–19).[14]

It ought to be noted that admonitions and exhortations to attend public services are hardly needed in the case of the middle-aged and elderly people who attended worship during Soviet times,[15] and who have particular respect and reverence for church services as an inseparable part of their lives. Past experiences cause them to value what they possess today because in the past public worship attendance was tied to overcoming various kinds of difficulties. One of these obstacles was the authorities banning children from involvement in, or from even attending, public worship. It was against the law for a religious organization to "teach minors religion, get them to take part in their choirs, orchestras and crafts groups, as well as hold . . . special prayer meetings for children and teenagers."[16]

---

13. *Verouchenie evangel'skikh khristian-baptistov v Belarusi, prinyatoe na 43-m s'ezde evangel'skikh khristian-baptistov (1985 g.)* [Doctrine of Faith of Evangelical Christian Baptists in Belarus, adopted at the 43rd Congress of Evangelical Christian Baptists (1985)], unpublished material, Section VII, The Church of Christ.

14. *Ispovedanie very khristian-baptistov* [Confession of Faith of Christian Baptists], published by F.P. Pavlov (1906), Section X, On the Church of God. *Vecheria Gospodnia (the Lord's Supper)* or simply *Vecheria* (Supper) (Luke 22:20; 1 Cor 11:25) and *hleboprelomlenie* (breaking bread; Luke 24:35; Acts 2:42), or its short form *prelomlenie* (breaking), are the most used terms in relation to the rite of remembrance of the death and passion of Christ. Another word for Communion, *prichastie* (1 Cor 10:16–17) – which literally means "to become a part of" – is used too, but it is even more popular among the Orthodox Christians. In this work, I will mostly use "the Lord's Supper," but these other terms and their meanings should be kept in mind.

15. Here we focus particularly on the period between 1945 and 1998.

16. Golst, *Religiya i zakon* [Religion and Law], 36–37.

Nevertheless, in spite of the bans, the youth and children of many churches took active part in worship, primarily music ministry. In the 1970s and 1980s, the author, with his brothers

Another difficulty was insufficient seating in the houses of prayer, especially in large cities such as Minsk or Brest.[17] Some church members would arrive at a meeting an hour or two before the start in order to secure a seat. The inconvenient locations of the houses of prayer should also be mentioned. In such cities as Mogilev, Brest, and Vitebsk, the sites were located on the outskirts of the city in remote, hard-to-reach areas. The authorities tried their best to reduce the number of churches which made the situation even harder. To quote the words of the Commissioner for Religious Affairs for the Brest region, "I think it is essential to merge small neighboring church communities (within 10 km) into bigger ones in the nearest future. It will allow us to study them in a deeper way and introduce proper order there."[18] The complaint made to the Commissioner of Religious Affairs in BSSR by members of the Baptist community in Belky, Glubokoe District, Vitebsk Region in 1960 is revealing in this regard: "The majority of our membership of 22 are elderly people, but we want to pray. It is impossible for us to get to any other community since the roads are muddy or covered in clay, and the horses are always busy and on weekends they rest."[19]

Later on, the development of the public transportation system and the personal possession/acquisition of motorcycles and cars relieved the situation for Christians traveling for public worship. Nevertheless, it did not completely solve the problem. As an example, my parents were members of a Baptist church located in a distant area (Svyatopolka, Ivanovo District, Brest Region) because there was no church near our home in Lipniki, Drogichin District. In the 1970s–1980s, our typical trip to a two-hour church meeting involved a walk or ride on bicycles for two kilometers, then a ride of fifteen kilometers

---

and a sister, attended worship services of the churches in Drogichyn and Ivanovo districts, Brest region. There we sang, played the button accordion, domra, and recited poetry, and the older brothers began preaching. In fact, the existence of such bans is proof that these practices were prevalent in some churches at the time.

17. "House of prayer" was and is the common way for Baptist believers to refer to the church building.

18. State Archive of Brest Region (SABR), Stock 1339, File 1, Case 1, 7. Kasataya, "Evangel'skiya khrystsiyane-baptysty ý BSSR u 1944 – pachatku 1950-kh gg.," p. 144.

19. National Archive of the Republic of Belarus (NARB), Stock 952, File 3, Case 21, 280. In the letter to the Commissioner for Religious Affairs under the Council of Ministers of the Byelorussian SSR written on 30 June 1966, the ECB community in Brest noted that "in Voolka Podgorodskaya there is only one bus route. The bus is constantly crowded, so it is not possible to get on it, especially for the senior believers" (National Archive of the Republic of Belarus (NARB), Stock 952, File 3, Case 21, 141–142).

on a bad forest road in a bus, and finally a walk of four more kilometers. Then, returning home, the journey was repeated in reverse order.[20] Such circumstances played a significant role in forming a sense of the special value of worship services and imprinting it onto a Russian-speaking Baptist mind.

2.2. Worship as a Refuge

Besides the politically conditioned limited opportunities associated with attending and participating in worship services, the essential importance of worship services was promoted by an ideological gap between Christians and an antagonistically inclined socialist society. Christians were convinced that "the whole world lies in the power of the evil one"[21] and that corruption at the highest levels indicated the approaching end of this world and the coming of Christ:

> When you look around
> You cannot describe with your pen how many things are
>   doomed for eternal damnation.
> Evil is raging without end, son fights against the father
> And the word of God becomes fulfilled.[22]

Thus, these believers regarded themselves as a "little flock,"[23] travelling on "the narrow way,"[24] rejected by the world and chosen by the Lord.[25] A segment of this separation from the world related to the realm of marriage and

---

20. The situation with public transport still has a negative effect in villages and small towns, and transportation conditions may have a strong influence on the time and attendance of services in churches. In villages such as Lesovnia, Volok, and Starye Terushki in the Minsk region, the church pastor or their assistant goes around several villages before worship starts to gather and bring the elderly worshippers to the church and they then take them home again afterwards.

21. 1 John 5:19. Unless noted otherwise, Bible quotations in English are from the NASB translation.

22. The poem "20-i vek!" [The 20th century!], *Stikhotvoreniya, declamatsii, istorii* [Poems, Recitations, Stories] (Lipniki, 1960s, Unpublished), second verse. Available in Russian through the author.

23. Luke 12:32.
24. Matt 7:13–14.
25. 1 Pet 2:9.

family. Church members who married non-believers[26] (referred to as sinners, "outsiders,"[27] and "Chaldeans"[28]) were excommunicated, for "what fellowship has light with darkness?"[29] Such a perception of the need for separation from the sinful world, and "bad company" which "corrupts good morals,"[30] led to the isolation of Baptist Christians, willingly or imposed, in culture and in everyday life.

Withdrawal from this world also implied a decisive departure from Communist ideology and secular culture. In fact, Marxism–Leninism could be regarded as an opposing religion with its own "trinity" (Marx, Engels, and Lenin), "gatherings" (demonstrations), "Scriptures" (books by Lenin), "saints" (heroes and martyrs of the revolution in 1917 and World War II such as Pavlik Morozov, Nikolai Ostrovskiy, and Zoja Kosmodem'yanskaya), and "rituals" (parades, graduation ceremonies, awarding of honors, and the passing-out parade for the Soviet army). "The cult of worship" of "the ever-living Lenin," as he was typically referred to, and who was entombed in the central "temple" (mausoleum) of the country, was served by the "high priests" of the cult – the Communist Party officials.[31] Indeed, in 1923, the Central Committee of the Russian Communist Party (Bolsheviks) adopted a resolution on anti-religious propaganda in the country which particularly stressed the importance of "replacing religious rites with civil events, that is, religious holidays with civil and industrial holidays (such as harvest festival, sowing festival, etc.), sacraments with solemn civil acts, for example, civil funerals, mourning, weddings, naming and birth registration."[32]

---

26. For marriages among Baptists see Mironova, "*Predstavleniya o brake i brachnyye praktiki yevangel'skikh veruyushchikh v Sovetskom Soyuze v 1940–1980-ye gg. Po materialam obshchin yevangel'skikh khristian-baptistov tsentral'no-chernozemnogo regiona.*"

27. 1 Cor 5:12–13; 1 Tim 3:7.

28. 2 Kings 25:13; Jer 39:8; 51:24. The terms "outsiders" and "Chaldeans" are used by Belarusian Baptists to denote people who do not belong to the evangelical church. The second term is usually used in colloquial speech.

29. 2 Cor 6:14.

30. 1 Cor 15:33.

31. For a consideration of Marxism as a religious outlook and its relation to Christianity, see Parushev, "Marxism and Christianity," 552–554. According to Alexander Schmemann, atheism and secularism have a peculiar longing for a "liturgical" expression (Schmemann, *For the Life of the World*, 119).

32. Yemelyakh, *Proiskhozhdenie Khristianskogo kul'ta*, 187.

It is important to note that Baptists did not officially preach seclusion as a lifestyle. Even in the days of severe persecution, their preaching opposed escapism and references to an ascetic lifestyle. Separation from the world was not required; what was required was to keep oneself from evil while living in the world.[33] However, such avoidance of evil and profanity required estrangement from participation in various forms of "worldly" activities. Thus, Soviet Baptists were unwilling to participate in parades that celebrated Victory Day or the Great October Socialist Revolution. As a rule, they did not attend theaters, concert halls, discos, or mass entertainment events, and held a negative attitude toward television, believing that all these might harm their spiritual life.[34]

Sociological research done in Belarus in the 1960s revealed that 68.7 percent of Baptists read only religious books, primarily the Bible. Only 15.1 percent of them read fiction – mainly books published before the Revolution in Russia or published abroad – and only a few read modern Soviet Belarusian and/or Russian fiction.[35] More than half of Baptists (53.5 percent) were reported to listen to radio broadcasts, although irregularly, and about 19.4 percent to occasionally watch television. At only 9.4 percent, an insignificant portion, of Baptists reported occasionally watching films. In the following years, the number of Evangelical Christians listening to radio broadcasts grew, but their attention was primarily captured by religious broadcasts transmitted using a short-wave range, especially by Trans World Radio and the "Voice of the Andes."[36] Radio broadcast filled the deficiency of public worship par-

---

33. John 17:15–16.

34. Lensu and Prokshina, *Baptizm i Baptisty*, 113, 129.

35. Lensu and Prokshina, 129–130, 164–166. Considering the severe negative bias towards Christians in the Soviet period, during which virtually all the material about believers was written to support Communist Party ideology, one should treat the presented percentages with a certain degree of skepticism, yet the picture presented here does not jar with other known facts of the period.

36. Personal experience of the author's family and other Baptists in Belarus in 1970s-1980s. Trans World Radio was originally called "Voice of Tangier," as it broadcasted from the International zone of Tangier (in Morocco) from 1954 to 1959. Later on, the broadcast station moved to Monte Carlo and it continues broadcasting all over the world to this day (Trans World Radio, official website, https://www.twr.org., last accessed 16 May 2019.).

"The Voice of the Andes" (HCJB) was the first international HF radio in the world and started broadcasting from Quito, Ecuador in 1941. "The Voice of the Andes" broadcast covered an area of eleven time zones in the former Soviet Union. More information on its history can be found on http://www.hcjb.ru/history.htm., last accessed 3 February 2017.

ticipation and compensated for the almost complete lack of Christian books and, frequently, the low level of sermon preparation in churches.

Using these figures, atheist propagandists in the 1960s argued that believers lived in intellectual poverty, lacked public interest and fulfilling hobbies, and showed poor involvement in the lives of teams in the workplace and the country's social and cultural life. Yet for Baptists, worship services defined life's priorities.[37] In their understanding, they had not deprived themselves of pleasure. To the contrary, they believed they had access to the highest joy. Such an outlook is reflected in the following poem which demonstrates the apologetics of the Christian life, and was popular with young people around the time of *perestroika*:[38]

> Christian life is so dull and eventless -
> This is what many people will say.
> They maintain that routine is so endless
> That no dreams will come true anyway . . .
>> We have left evil ways and devotions,
>> Shall we now wipe their dust off our feet?
>> Use your feet for God-honouring motions,
>> Not for dancing or trifling pursuits.
> Our joy is so pure and enduring,
> It is pleasing and good for the soul.
> I must say this with greater assurance –
> Christian life is fulfilling in all![39]

Thus, during the Soviet era the worship service became the main place for self-actualization, the fulfillment of spiritual and emotional needs, the center of Christian fellowship, and a key factor in the transmission of spiritual values. In fact, it played a vital role in the survival and further development of Baptists as a denomination. Participation in worship, as well as Bible studies, choir and orchestra rehearsals, and youth trips to other churches, replaced

---

37. Ignatenko, *Osobennosti psikhologii baptistov,* Avtoreferat dissertatsii na soiskanie uchenoi stepeni kandidata filosofskikh nauk, 15.

38. This is the term for time of radical changes in the economic and political structure in the USSR, which were initiated by Mikhail Gorbachev in 1985–1991.

39. The poem "Khristianskaya zhizn" [The Christian Life], *Stikhotvoreniya, declamatsii, istorii,* first, sixth, and sixteenth verses.

secular cultural and entertainment events.[40] Even atheist researchers noted this characteristic:

> The influence of sectarians among the retrograde part of the population and young people could be explained to a certain degree by the fact that they find various ways of satisfying a person's spiritual interest, presenting them as an alternative to our cultural work among the masses. At the same time an aspiration for full satisfaction of spiritual needs of Christians often goes far beyond the limits of religious interests. In order to attract attention of the youth the sectarians have lately started to arrange their prayer services in a solemn way in an attempt to meet aesthetic and cultural Christian needs. The majority of the sects use theatrical techniques and forms, developing their own amateur theatricals, making performances on the days of religious celebrations intended for attraction of both Christians and non-Christians. With the help of music, skillfully and thoroughly prepared theatrical skits accompanied by prayer, they attempt to bring up the feeling of reverent awe and a "foretaste of heavenly joy," etc.[41]

The development of worship forms, freedom of creativity, depth of fellowship, and preaching of high and pure ideals elevated the spirits of Evangelical Christians. Any lack of worldly entertainment was compensated for by an exciting and plentiful church life. With full assurance, young Christians sang:

> Offering all days to Jesus,
> Vigour and strength, we will give it to Christ,
> We shall approach Him and humbly
> Bring our dear sacrifice!
>> Serving and following Jesus – Nothing compares to this life
>> (this joyful life),

---

40. Some public events related to family life, such as weddings, funerals, births, and birthdays worked in the same way. For example, weddings were turned into worship services lasting for hours or even two days with songs and sermons, that might not have been strictly related to the topic.

41. Garkavenko, *Khristianskoe sektantstvo v SSSR*, 14. Baptists would agree with the author that the aesthetic element had no value in itself, but served as a means to evoke faith and strengthen it.

> All of your heart and your reason,
> Giving Him all of your love (Give him all).[42]

Secular researcher Lev Mitrokhin assessed the situation in the following way:

> As a result sincere Christians (and we can classify most Baptists among them) found themselves to be outcasts in their society, and they were driven to special spiritual "zones." Therefore, they have gone from this world never to return, leaving the cultural achievements, the actual wealth accumulated for centuries by the human thought.[43]

At the same time, many Baptists would have been favorably disposed to the literary richness of Russian culture, especially to literature by Lomonosov, Derzhavin, Lermontov, Tolstoy, Dostoevsky, and other authors who wrote on some biblical themes.[44] However, the attitude toward secular culture as a means of recreation and enjoyment was negative.

In recent years, the understanding that one ought to treat secular culture with reticence has become weaker; the world does not seem as hostile as it was during the times of persecution. Many young Baptists study at secular Universities. Even if unofficially, different kinds of pleasures are enjoyed. Some new believers, along with a significant proportion of young people as a whole, go to theaters and cinemas, philharmonic societies, concert halls, and sports events. The fact that in the twenty-first century some members of "Light of Gospel," "Light of Truth," and "Bethlehem" churches in Minsk work, or have worked, in the Theater of Musical Comedy, the Opera and Ballet, or the Philharmonic, is puzzling to some Christians of the older generation. In this age of computers and other technologies, the issue of having or not having a television at home is no longer important as a "Baptist distinctive." Nevertheless, for the majority of Baptists, public worship still remains the main source of meeting their spiritual needs, especially in small towns and

---

42. "Luchshie dni nashei zhizni" [The Best Days of Our Life], *Pesn' Vozrozhdeniya*, no. 725, first stanza.

43. Mitrokhin, *Baptizm: istoriya i sovremennost'*, 243–244.

44. E.g., Dimitru Sevastian assesses the influence of the literary work of Fyodor Distoevsky on the Moldovan Baptists in his "'Christ's Way:' Biography as Theology in the Literature of F. M. Dostoevsky" (PhD diss., University of Wales, 2012).

villages where people have limited options for their free time and negative attitudes toward secular culture remain dominant.

2.3. A Unique Place of Fellowship

The cultural gap was not the only factor that gave value and prominence to public worship. The isolation of Baptist Christians from the rest of society on a normal everyday level also contributed to that gap. It was typically in the house of worship, which for them represented a time of sacred fellowship, that Christians realized their need of fellowship on vertical and horizontal levels. According to the deepest convictions of the "ones gathered in His name,"[45] worship within a fellowship was the most glorious and comforting moment in a believer's life. Expressing their joy, they sang:

> No greater consolation,
> No fuller joy to gain.
> The Lord of all creation
> Has fellowship with people.
> > It is sweet and wonderful to be in eternal fellowship with
> > Him,
> It is sweet and wonderful to be in fellowship with Him.[46]

Such fellowship with God made it possible for those who shared common faith in the Lord to feel a part of a community of like-minded people. On the one hand, Baptists were unable to have much community experience at school or at work because Communist policies led to animosity against Baptists. On the other hand, practically speaking, the conflict of worldviews did not allow for shared common interests or spending much time with "sinners" outside of an educational establishment or a factory. This was especially true because non-believers might drink alcoholic beverages, smoke, dance, curse, play cards, or engage in other activities that were unacceptable from the Baptist point of view.[47] Children raised in Baptist homes would usually

---

45. Matt 18:20.

46. "Net bol'she uteshen'ya, net radosti polnei" [No Greater Consolation, No Fuller Joy to Gain], *Pesn' Vozrozhdeniya*, no. 171, first stanza and refrain.

47. See autobiographies and memoirs about the life of Evangelicals in the USSR: Bondarenko, *Tri prigovora*; Vladimir Vil'chinskiy, *Nedarom prolityye slezy*; Ryaguzov, *Zhizn'*

not join "the Young Pioneers" or "the Communist Youth League."⁴⁸ Christians were suspicious of different social movements and organizations. In turn, they were discriminated against when applying for a job,⁴⁹ and a student could be expelled from university or technical school if the authorities discovered that they belonged to a "sect."⁵⁰

Family ties were unable to meet the need of fellowship if the relatives did not belong to the church. "Holy fellowship," fellowship "in spirit," was only possible with those who shared a common faith, which primarily happened in public worship, and, to an equal degree, before and after the service. One would often hear this quote from the Psalms at the beginning of, or during, a worship service: "Behold, how good and how pleasant it is for brothers to dwell together in unity!"⁵¹ At the end of an encouraging gathering, the leader might recall the experience of Jesus's disciples on the Mount of Transfiguration, quoting Peter's words, "Lord, it is good for us to be here."⁵²

Considering the substantial role of worship from a cultural, psychological, or social viewpoint, its spiritual value surely cannot be underestimated. Worship was, and still remains, a center for the religious activity of Baptists, a source of spiritual life, a place of repentance and confession of sins, the means

---

vopreki. Ryaguzov was expelled from Kuibyshev Medical Institute in 1973 and blacklisted because of his faith. His letter of protest addressed to Leonid Brezhnev remained unanswered. For many years he was employed as an electrician whilst also serving as a pastor of a Baptist church.

48. On December 21, 1966, Nina Volos, a six-grade student of Pruzhany Secondary School No. 1 came home in tears. She had been expelled from school for not wearing a Pioneer's tie and for supposedly attending the funeral of an elderly Christian neighbor. The school director's reaction towards the parents' complaint was, "She got what she deserved." (National Historical Archive of Belarus (NARB), Stock 136, File 1, Case 4, 118.)

49. To provide a personal example, in 1962 my mother was fired from a school in which she had been teaching dressmaking, on the grounds of her becoming a member of a Baptist church.

50. Alexander Firisiuk, a former President of the Baptist Union in Belarus, shared his story. In 1955 he applied to the Belarusian Forestry Engineering Institute. In 1958 the KGB learnt that Firisiuk was attending ECB worship in Minsk. He was summoned to the KGB office and was invited to provide information about the situation in the church. Firisiuk declined the offer and as a result was expelled from the Institute for his "religious beliefs." With great difficulty he managed to complete his training by correspondence (Personal interview with author, Minsk, 22 April 2011 [Personal notes (2008–2018), 59].). In 1959, the *Chyrvonaya zmena* newspaper no. 206 (CC KCUY of Belarus, October 20), 3 published an article by A. Rydz'koýski entitled "Know Your Comrade in the Lecture Room." The article denounced Firisiuk's beliefs and his belonging to the church. See also Firisiuk, *Radost' seyaniya so slezami*, 25–34.

51. Psalm 133:1.

52. Matt 17:4.

of comfort and strengthening hope for the Second Coming, the main place of meeting with the Lord and keeping the faith to transmit it to future generations, and a special time of prayer and holy fellowship. Moreover, attending church worship was, and remains, an essential component in the formation of Baptist identity and in preserving it in a society in which Baptists saw themselves (and still do) as "sojourners" and "tenants."[53]

Certainly, it is impossible to deny the fact that drastic changes to the political, ideological, and social contexts since the beginning of *perestroika*, and the enlargement of the scope of church activities, has diminished the formerly exclusive role of public worship in Christian life. Moreover, this process is likely to continue. The current structure of Baptist worship life continues to exclude children from participation in public worship. In most churches, Sunday school for children and teenagers is organized during worship, and a children's choir may rehearse at the same time.[54] Sometimes children spend limited time in worship and then go to Sunday school, which is convenient for parents because they do not have to arrive early or wait for their children after the service.[55] It is not surprising that children prefer well-prepared Sunday school classes which are often taught in the form of games, or accompanied by games, to "boring and incomprehensible" preaching. The concern is that they eventually become isolated from the special atmosphere of the church, and the worship service is not their center of attraction.[56]

Diversification of church activities also leads to a shift in focus. Young people experience a wide variety of church activities besides public worship:

---

53. 1 Chron 29:15. A good example might be public worship in the church in Man'kovichi, Stolin district, Brest region. In the 1970s-1980s, meetings on the weekdays began at ten o'clock in the evening and sometimes later. The preaching and singing were well prepared, but after a hard-working day it was difficult to talk about the practical value of the meetings because some of those present could hardly stay awake. Yet, the important fact was presence at, and participation in, the meetings. Believers attended to show which side they were on (The testimony of a church pastor, Vladimir Vandich; Personal interview with author, Man'kovichi, Brest region, 18 May 2008 [Personal notes, 2b].).

54. Sunday Schools in Baptist churches are just for children and teenagers. Adults and youth are usually invited to come to Bible studies on weekday nights.

55. There are some exceptions. Sunday school has classes after morning worship at the "Ark" church in Volkovysk. In this way, children are present with their parents in worship. Only small children (up to 3 years old) can stay in the children's room during worship (Personal visits of the author to the church service, 15 March 2015 [Personal notes, 2b].).

56. Of course, this challenge is not unique to Russian-speaking Baptists, but for many churches and denominations. Some authors explore this challenge, such as Clifton-Soderstrom and Bjorlin, *Incorporating Children in Worship*.

youth conferences and Bible studies in small groups, Christian clubs and hobby groups, and classes in Bible schools and summer camps. Similarly, middle-aged and elderly people now have more opportunities to meet their spiritual needs through internet and satellite television. This access to quality spiritual literature and a wealth of good sermons in electronic, video, and audio formats reduces the importance of traditional preaching in a house of prayer. Of course, this is not at all unique to the Belarusian Baptist context. As noted by the authors of Worship in the Network, "The Sunday service no longer has a monopoly, but stands along 'spectacle worship' at mass events, rituals on the World Wide Web, and private and individual rituals."[57] Nevertheless, worship services remain the most important indicator of spirituality and the means of its expression in Belarusian Baptist life. Demonstrating their belonging to Christ, Baptists in traditional churches get together, bringing along their Bibles and hymnals (which are being gradually replaced by smartphones), to become stronger in their faith and to gain power to live in this difficult world. Fellowship with God and fellow believers in public worship is seen to provide such strength and power.

Summing up the role of worship from an historical perspective, we should note its exceptional value and importance in understanding the identity of believers and their spiritual formation. In difficult times, it sustained the faith of the Baptists and served as a source of encouragement and comfort. An analysis of songs and official documents, as well as personal testimonies and the experience of believers in the Soviet era, show that the value of worship increases in times of persecution and limited opportunities.

Observation, involvement in church life, and external evidence confirm that as a result of isolation, caused by the hostile attitude of the communist regime towards believers, worship has acquired a special status. The political context contributed to the conscious isolation of believers and their separation from the "sinful world", as well as their limited participation in society. Worship, preparation for it, and Bible study were the main occasions for putting skills and gifts into practice, and they became the center of communication, replacing involvement in secular activities.

The isolation and marginalization of believers in society contributed to the growth of ties within the church, which only intensified as result of family

---

57. Barnard, Cilliers, and Wepener, *Worship in the Network Culture*, 14.

bonds and marriages exclusively between church members. Worship became a safe place for like-minded people who were strangers in their own country. At the same time, this study shows that the value of worship decreases with the cessation of persecution, a change in attitude towards believers in society, and the emergence of new opportunities for ministry outside houses of prayer. Nonetheless, worship attendance and participation in it remains the main indicator of spiritual life. Worship continues to play the role of a connecting center and a place of fellowship for evangelical believers. Tthe context of worship formation is examined in the next chapter, and sources of influence that have determined the character of worship are singled out. This is designed to facilitate a better understanding of the indigenous character of worship and its place in the spiritual life of Belarusian Baptists.

CHAPTER 3

Historical Roots

3.1. The Origins of Evangelical Churches in Belarus
3.1.1. The Second Part of the Nineteenth Century to the Early Twentieth Century

Evangelical Christianity reached Belarus from several geographical sources. The authors of a seminal book on the history of ECB churches in the former Soviet Union identify four primary sources of influence: Southern Ukraine, Siberia, Germany and Austria, and the United States.[1] Indeed, the facts reveal that the sphere of geographical influence is even wider. In this chapter I conduct a brief review of the key historical moments in order to trace the sources of influence. This review and analysis of the emergence of the evangelical movement in Belarus demonstrates that while it did come from several

---

1. *Istoriya evangel'skikh khristian-baptistov v SSSR*, 380–391. See also Kanatush, "Istoriya evangel'skogo dvizheniya v Belarusi" 24–32. Even now there is no thorough published research on the history of Baptists in Belarus. There are only a limited number of chapters in books that deal with the history of the Baptist movement in the Russian Empire and Soviet Union, as well as some articles, notes, and memoirs in magazines and encyclopedias. Beside the above-mentioned sources, we should note Lensu and Prokshina, eds., *Baptizm i Baptisty*, and an article by Vladimir Kanatush, "Istoriya evangel'skogo dvizheniya v Belarusi" [The History of the Evangelical Movement in Belarus], 16–20. Recently Minsk Theological Seminary has produced three helpul volumes in Belarusian: Bokun, ed., *Yevanhielskaya tsarkva Bielarusi: gistoryya i suchasnasc'* [Evangelical Church of Belarus: History and the Present; Bokun, ed., *Yevanhielskaya tsarkva Bielarusi: gistoryya i suchasnasc'. Vypusk II* [Evangelical Church of Belarus: History and the Present. Issue II]; and Bokun, ed., *Yevanhielskaya tsarkva Bielarusi: gistoryya i suchasnasc'. Vypusk III* [Evangelical Church of Belarus: History and the Present. Issue III]. In 2019, another helpful book written by a local researcher was published: U. I. Navitski, et. al, *Jevanhiel'skija chryscijanie u Bielarusi: piać stahoddziau historyi (1517-2017 hh.)* [Evangelical Christians in Belarus: Five Centuries of History (1517-2017)].

sources, it was also marked by spontaneity. Although in some areas purposeful missionary activities were carried out, generally speaking the spread of the evangelical movement (or, as some historians term it, the "revival"[2]) was not a planned sequence of events, but was rather conditioned by specific life circumstances as well as political and economic factors.

From the middle of the nineteenth century, poor peasants began to move from Belarus to southern Ukraine in search of employment. After being introduced to the Gospel, some of them were converted and, after returning home, began to preach to their neighbors and relatives, thus establishing the first communities of believers in southeastern Belarus.[3] The Baptist church in the village of Ut', Gomel district, Mogilev province, is believed to have started in the late 1870s, which suggests that it was the first evangelical church on the territory of present-day Belarus.[4] *Mogilevskiye yeparkhial'nyye vedomosti* newspaper reported that there were one hundred and seventeen Baptists in the village Ut' in 1906.[5]

One of a number of peasants who had sought employment in southern Ukraine was Dmitriy Pavlovich Sementsov. There he had encountered Baptists and joined them in Odessa. In 1877 he returned to his village of Usokhi, Gomel district,[6] where he gathered a group of Evangelicals and established a church in 1879.[7] In 1882, this group had twenty-nine members and by 1885 it had grown to ninety-five members.[8] The influence of a southern

---

2. Dyck, "Revival and Baptist Beginning in Russia," 14–22.

3. Yanouskaya, *Hrystsiyanskaya tsarkva u Belarusi 1863–1914 gg.* [Christian Church in Belarus in 1863 -1914], 69. *Istoriya evangel'skikh khristian-baptistov v SSSR*, 381.

4. Kanatush, "Istoriya evangel'skogo dvizheniya v Belarusi," 29. Kanatush notes that Akulina Fyodorovna Kopenkova, a local believer born in 1890, suggested that the Good News was brought to Ut' at the beginning of the second half of the nineteenth century (Kanatush). However, it is not possible to verify this statement.

5. "Polozheniye sektantstva v predelakh Mogilevskoy yeparkhii i mery dlya bor'by s nim" [Position of sectarianism within the Mogilev diocese and measures to fight it], Iz raporta Yeparkhial'nogo missionera na imya Yego Preosvyashchenstva [From the report of the Diocesan missionary to His Eminence], *Mogilevskiye yeparkhial'nyye vedomosti* [Mogilev Diocesan Gazette], no. 8 (1906), 296. According to this report (p. 296) there were one hundred and seventy-two Baptists in the village of Ivaki, seventy in Krasnaya Buda and Nikolayevka, forty-nine in Kozhanovka, and nine in Starye Yurkovichi.

6. Villages Ut' and Usokhi now are in Dobrush district, Gomel region.

7. Central State Historical Archives of the USSR (CSHA), Stock 1284, File 220, Case 12, 40. Report of the Mogilev Governor to the Minister of Internal Affairs, in Lensu and Prokshina, *Baptizm i Baptisty*, 18.

8. CSHA, Stock 1284, File 220, Case 7, 12.

Ukrainian source was also detected in other villages of Gomel district, including Dubovy Log and Stary Krupets as well as the Cherikov and Rogachev districts of Mogilev province, where Shtundists (see footnote below) were reported to be present by 1884–1885.[9] In 1903–1905 there were at least two Baptist churches in this territory.[10] According to the reports submitted by the Orthodox priests of the time, there were about 500 Baptists (including children) in Mogilev province at the beginning of 1906.[11]

Northern Belarus experienced other influences, namely from the Baltic region and the neighboring Russian province of Pskov.[12] Official correspondence gives us some idea of what was happening in Vitebsk province. The Governor's report, in response to the request of the Ministry of Internal Affairs, clearly shows that attempts were made to spread the evangelical faith at the end of the nineteenth century:

> At the end of 1895, in the Lucinski district of the province entrusted to me, a case of emergence of the Shtundist sect was detected, which was brought here from the Ostrovsky district, Pskov province. We were able to deal with the emerging sect in a timely manner by taking appropriate steps . . . So far no new cases of the emergence of Shtundism have been reported in the province entrusted to me.[13]

However, later evidence from reports by district police officers in 1911–1912, show that the authorities were unable to suppress the movement.

---

9. Rozhdestvensky, *Yuzhnorussky Shtundism*, 57. Originally, the Shtundist movement spread in Russia in the nineteenth century among the German colonists. The term "Shtundism" (from the German word Stunde, meaning "an hour" that was devoted to Bible reading and interpretation) is hard to define in relation to Russians, Ukrainians and Belarusians. The same can be said of the essence of Shtundists confessions, "since Shtundism does not represent any definite theological system or as it is revealed in masses of its followers" (S. Mel'gunov, *Tserkov' i gosudarstvo v Rossii* [Church and State in Russia] (Moskva, Zadruga, 1907), 65–66). Sometimes it was simply associated with the Baptist movement (Pavlov, "Pravda o baptistakh. Ocherk istorii, tserkovnogo ustroystva i printsipov baptistskikh obshchin" [The Truth about Baptists. Essay on history, church organization and principles of Baptist communities], 233). The term "Shtunda" was so tied to the Baptists that it was sometimes used even in Belarus, far away from the place of Shtundist origins, even until the second half of the twentieth century.

10. NARB, Stock 952, File 2, Case 5, 254.

11. "Polozheniye sektantstva v predelakh Mogilevskoy yeparkhii i mery dlya bor'by s nim," 295.

12. *Istoriya evangel'skikh khristian-baptistov v SSSR*, p. 382.

13. NHAB, Stock 1430, File 1, Case 43941, 2.

> I report to Your Excellency that in Dvinsk there is a sect of Baptists who broke away from the Evangelical Lutheran confession. It consists of 20 people and they do not have a house of prayer. They invite Jan Kristopov Janson, a Baptist preacher from Jakobstadt [now Jēkabpils, Latvia], to help perform their religious rituals in the place where they get together.[14]

Other officers reported a Baptist family in Drissa district, who originally came from the Baltic countries,[15] and about Baptists in the Dvina uyezd (Letts and Baltic Germans, as a rule). Almost all of them had Lutheran backgrounds.[16] As a result of persecution, the first Evangelicals in northern Belarus had little impact on the development of the evangelical movement in the country as a whole. This is especially true in comparison with their activities in the central and western areas where the Baptist movement started later when the pressure of the authorities was not so strong.

In Minsk, church planting had begun in 1902. According to a report by the chief of the Minsk police, Gerasim Andryukhov and his wife arrived there from Kharkov province that year. Gerasim belonged to a congregation of Russian Christian Baptists in the village of Obody, Kharkov province, and was a street vendor selling Bible Society books. On August 12, 1902, he obtained Permit No. 54 in Minsk to "sell books and pictures."[17] This work yielded so much fruit that it aroused the concern of the authorities, a fact that is reflected in a report by the Head of Minsk Police to the Governor of Minsk province in January, 1914:

> In recent years, a sect called Shtundists is believed to have appeared in Minsk and they have already seduced several Orthodox people and caused them to follow their doctrine . . . Supposedly the sect was organized by German workers, who are also masterminds of their activities. The inspection revealed that there is no such sect as Shtundists . . . but there is another sect, Baptists, which is also currently illegal . . . The people present had

---

14. Report of the Chief of Dvinsk Police, 1911. NHAB, Stock 1430, File 1, Case 48020, 15.

15. Report of the Drissa district Police Officer (January 1912). NHBA, Stock 1430, File 1, Case 48020, 17.

16. Report of the Dvinsk district Police Officer. NHAB, Stock 1430, File 1, Case 48020, 9.

17. NHAB, Stock 295, File 1, Case 8462, 61–64.

the following books: a) a Bible b) Brief index number 105, c) a New Testament, d) *Gusli*, a collection of religious songs edited by I.S. Prokhanov, e) a Christian calendar, f) *Gusli*, Third Edition ... The sect was organized by Georgiy Yakovlevich Slesarenko, Ivan Fyodorovich Byelan and Artem Artemiev Khodasevich ... The Andryuhovs were also actively involved and stayed in touch with the church in Obody, Yastrebinka parish, Sumy district, Kharkiv province. Moreover, Andryukhov, who is a commissioner for the sale of books published by the Evangelical Society, provides local followers of the sectarian doctrine with these books. According to Reverend Kvachevski, Andryukhov is the founder of the sect ... Currently, there are 21 people in this Baptist sect.[18]

There were also influences from northwestern Ukraine. The creation of ECB congregations in Volynia at the end of the nineteenth century, where missionaries from St. Petersburg and southern Ukraine were active, established a foundation for dynamic missionary activity in Polesie, the southern part of Belarus, and in the south-west.[19] It is likely that the first evangelical church in this area was founded in Pruzhany in 1906.[20] According to the same source, in 1910 there were eight Baptist congregations, the largest of which were Shtundo-Baptist congregations in Volynia and the Pinsk districts.[21]

3.1.2. Developments After World War I

Church planting increased considerably during and after World War I (WW1). Returning refugees and military captives, and then returning émigrés from America, contributed to this ministry. In 1916, Nikita Ephimovich Shchelkun served in the army in Kiev where he met Evangelical Christians[22]

---

18. NHAB, Stock 295, File 1, Case 8462., 61–63.

19. T.V. Lisovskaya, "Novye protestantskie denominatsii na zapadnobelorusskih zemliah v kontse XIX – 20 gg. XX veka: Faktory i puti poyavleniya" [New Protestant denominations in West Belarusian territory between the late nineteenth century and the 1920s: Factors and ways of emergence], 42.

20. SABR, Stock 1, File 2, Case 1065, 13. It is likely that the church in Pruzhany was founded earlier and then became legal in 1905–1906 following the liberalization of the law in 1905.

21. SABR, Stock 1, File 2, Case 1065.

22. See footnote 6, on p 3.

from St. Petersburg who told him about Christ and gave him a Bible. When he returned to his home village of Proshchitsy (Slutsk district, Minsk province) he planted a church there. Other people in town were converted, and services started in Slutsk. A house of prayer was opened in Slutsk in 1927 and, by the late 1920s, this congregation was the largest in Belarus. In the late 1920s and early 1930s, more than two hundred people were baptized each year in Slutsk. This church also helped to plant churches in Popovtsy, Tsalevichy, Starobin, Skovshin, and other nearby villages.[23]

During WWI, some citizens in the western regions of Belarus found themselves in Siberia with other refugees fleeing the war zones and became Baptists in local Baptist congregations. Anthon Grigorievich Kirtsun was baptized in 1917 in a church in Omsk, Siberia. When he returned home in 1923, he planted a church in Zelva, Grodno region. Later on, churches were also planted in Volkovysk (where the first baptism took place in 1925) Lida, and other settlements.[24] Kirtsun's followers were called "kirtsuns."[25]

During WWI, some Belarusian soldiers were taken as prisoners to Germany and Austria, where they met Evangelicals, became believers, and later began to spread their faith when they returned home.[26] One of these was Luka Mikhailovich Gladky, who came to faith in 1914 in Austria. When he returned home, he was thought to be deranged because he read the New Testament which he had brought with him, abstained from alcohol and tobacco, and was bold enough to remove all icons from the walls. Eventually his mother and sisters joined his faith, and a house church was founded in Otradnoye, a village near Soligorsk, Minsk province. Then he founded the church in the village of Lesovnia.[27]

Nikita Vandich was converted when ministers from German Baptist churches visited the prisoners of war. He attended classes at the Bible school in Germany, and after returning home he founded over ten churches in the

---

23. Sergei Karchemenko and Sergei Rek, elders of the church in Slutsk. Personal letter to the author, January 5, 2009.

24. Kanatush, "Istoriya evangel'skogo dvizheniya v Belarusi," 28; Leonid Kovalenko, *Oblako svidetelei Khristovykh* [A cloud of witnesses of Christ], 155–156.

25. Grygor'eva, Zavalniuk, Navitski, Filatava, *Kanfesii na Belarusi (kanets XVIII-XX st.)* [Confessions in Belarus (the end of XVIII-XX centuries)], 212.

26. Martsinkovskiy, *Zapiski veruyushchego* [A Believer's Notes], 195.

27. Gladky and Firisiuk, "80 let razluk i vstrech" [80 years of Partings and Meetings], *Krynitsa Zhyttsya*, 18–21.

Stolin area, Brest region. Vandich helped to plant about thirty churches between the 1920s and 1939.²⁸ Clearly, German-speaking Christians were indirectly involved in planting many churches in Belarus.

Another connection can be traced to the United States where some Belarusians went in search of employment. They were converted there and upon their return to the homeland started to share their faith. Anton Kazimirovich Senkevich preached in Nikolaevshchina, Minsk region, Iosif Pukhovsky, who had received theological training in the USA, preached in Pruzhany,²⁹ and Afanasiy Gurin preached in Selishche, Pinsk district, Brest region. When Gurin was asked about his conversion, he replied: "While I was staying in America, I went to a sectarian school, where I learned to read and write and also learned the sectarian doctrine, which was the reason for my joining the sect."³⁰

Tatsiana Lisovskaya, who explored the evangelical movement in Western Belarus in 1920–1930, writes:

> Although there were few Protestants (0.9%) among the émigrés who came back to Western Belarus in 1921–1923, their return was one of the most important factors contributing to the development of Protestantism in 1920–30 because the return of Protestants had the spreading their teaching as its goal . . . Based on the list of elders in the churches of Evangelical Christians and Baptists compiled by the Polesie Voivodship Office, 16 pastors out of 42 were re-émigrés from the United States and Russia who returned from emigration in 1921–1923.³¹

---

28. Information about Nikita Vandich's ministry was received in May 18, 2008, from his namesake Vladimir Vandich, the pastor of the church in Man'kovichi, Stolin district which had been planted by Nikita Vandich, and from other members of that church. (Personal notes, 59b.)

29. Yevtukhovich, *Zhit' – znachit verit'. Iz istorii evangelicheskoi tserkvi v Belarusi* [To Live Means to Believe. From the History of an Evangelical Church in Belarus], 11.

30. The record of missionary trips of a Diocesan missionary to the Pinsk and Mozyr uyezds (NHAB, Stock 136, File 1, Case 38344, 1). The terms "sectarian" and "sect," should likely be attributed to an Orthodox missionary who recorded a conversation with Afanasiy Gurin. Evangelical Christians did not use such terms.

31. Lisovskaya, "Novye protestantskie denominatsii na zapadnobelorusskih zemliah v kontse XIX – 20 gg. XX veka," 45. Based on the materials of the SABR, Stock 1, File 2, Case 2345, 1–11. First of all, the author means Baptists, Evangelical Christians, and Churches of Christ.

Konstantin Yaroshevich, Ivan Bukovich,[32] and Georgiy Satsevich[33] started a Christian missionary center in Kobryn in 1924 aimed at the "concentration of missionary activity on the eastern outlying districts of Poland."[34] In 1926 they registered the Union of Churches of Christ in Poland.[35] Kobryn became the center of activity of the Churches of Christ, uniting about seventy communities.[36]

The evangelical movement continued to spread from the territories of modern Poland. For example, Luka Dzekuts-Maley moved to Brest in 1921[37] after he had been converted in Bialystok, where he met some Evangelicals and was baptized by German Baptists in 1912.[38] He actively ministered in Brest and its neighborhood, and, in 1926, this church had over eight hundred members. Within a few years, nineteen evangelical churches were planted in the Brest region, and services were held in seventy other places.[39] In 1937,

---

32. Konstantin Yaroshevich was born in Belostok province. He went to the United States in 1910 and was converted in New York in 1912. In 1916 Yaroshevich graduated from Johnson's College in Tennesssee. (SABR, Stock 1, File 3, Case 1274, 70.) He worked among Slavic people in America, and returned home in 1921 (Arhivum Akt Novyh v Varshave. Ministerstvo Wyznan' Religiynyh i Osvichenia Publichnego. Referat vyznan' evangielickih. [Archives of Modern Records in Warsaw. Ministry of Religious Affairs and Public Education. Department of evangelical churches.], Sygn. 1455, l. 215). In 1923 the first community of the Churches of Christ was started in the village of Staraya Ves', Belostok province. In 1924 Yaroshevich settled in Kobrin (H. Satsevich and N. Hury, *Word and Life*, no. 4–6 [1995].). Ivan Bukovich was born in Sudzilovichi, Polesie province. In 1908 he went to the United States where in 1911 he was baptized in a Baptist church in Chicago and then studied at Moody Bible Institute (SABR, Stock 1, File 3, Case 1274, 70). He returned home in 1921 and began to work with Yaroshevich in 1923 (H. Satsevich, N. Hury, *Word and Life*, no. 4–6 [1995]).

33. Georgiy Satsevich was born in Zelva. He studied at an Orthodox school and then at the Orthodox Seminary in Kaluga, Russia. In 1920 he was baptized as a believer in Kaluga and returned to Kobrin in 1922. (SABR, Stock 1, File 3, Case 1274, 70.)

34. SABR, Stock 1, File 3, Case 1274., 69.

35. The western part of Belarus, including Kobrin, was part of Poland at the time. See section 1.3.

36. *Istoriya evangel'skikh khristian-baptistov v SSSR*, 390 (SABR, Stock 1, File 3, Case 1274, 62).

37. Brest was also a Polish territory at the time.

38. Kovalenko, *Oblako svidetelei Khristovykh*, 161. Luka Nikolaevich Dzekuts-Maley (1888–1955) is famous as a Belarusian religious and public figure, pastor, preacher, and translator of the New Testament into Belarusian. On his life and ministry see Bokun, ed., *Lukaš Dziekuć-Maliej i Bielaruskija piaraklady Biblii* [Lukash Dzekuts-Maley and Belarusian translations of the Bible], 49.

39. Akinchyts, "120-letie Dzekuts-Maleya" [120th Dzekuts-Maley anniversary], 15.

the Baptist Union, with its center in Brest, had eighty-five churches and two hundred and seventy-five branches with 13,800 believers.[40]

The development of the evangelical movement in western Belarus (part of Poland since 1921) must be treated separately. Here the process of the penetration of evangelical ideas started later than in the eastern part but proved to be especially effective for church planting, despite Poland attempting to quench the movement through local administration and the police. As the majority of Christian books were printed in Russian, the Protestant movement was considered "undesirable for Polish statehood."[41] The authorities adopted a policy of a "neutral unfavorable attitude"[42] and imposed restrictions to avoid the Russification of western Belarus. Believers were forbidden to teach choir singing, to distribute religious literature among church members, and to teach people religion.[43] Nevertheless, Evangelicals there managed to carry out dynamic missionary activity, organizing Bible and choir director courses, and distributing Bibles and New Testaments, because they had more freedom than their fellow believers in the eastern (Soviet) part of Belarus.[44] From 1922 to 1929, the number of followers increased by eight times and reached 7,865.[45] Nowadays, Baptist churches still enjoy the fruit of this activity. For example, Kobryn has the largest Baptist house of prayer in Belarus.

However, opposition and persecution caused considerable hindrance to the development of the movement. P.E. Ermakov in *Baptist* magazine recounts the ministry of Leontiy Demidovich Priymachenko, a former Orthodox deacon who founded the church in Nikolayevka, Gomel district. The account describes the circumstances in which the church was planted:

---

40. Grygor'eva, Zavalniuk, Navitski, Filatava, *Kanfesii na Belarusi (kanets XVIII–XX st.)*, 213. More about the Baptist Union in western Belarus, its organization, and leadership can be found in Lisovskaya, "Struktura yevangel'sko-baptistskogo dvizheniya Zapadnoy Belarusi v 1921–1939 gg." [The Structure of the Evangelical-Baptist Movement of Western Belarus in 1921–1939], 22–23.

41. Lisovskaya, "Deyatel'nost' protestantskikh obshchin i organizatsii v Zapadnoi Belarusi v 1921–1939 gg" [The Activity of Protestant Communities and Organizations in Western Belarus in 1921–1939], 81.

42. Lisovskaya, 82.

43. Lisovskaya.

44. SABR, Stock 1, File 3, Case 1274, 62.

45. Lisovskaya, "Deyatel'nost' protestantskikh obshchin i organizatsii v Zapadnoi Belarusi v 1921–1939 gg," 77.

After his arrest, [Prymachenko's] believers began to have meetings again secretly in the night. At one such meeting, a crowd of about 30 people suddenly broke in. They broke the windows and doors and grabbed three people, including brother Prymachenko. They began to beat them to death and threw brother Prymachenko on the snow, where he spent the whole night until morning. In the morning his father and mother came ... and washed and bandaged his wounds ... Suddenly, the mob appeared again, led by a sergeant, to lynch the family ... Brother Prymachenko begged the Lord to spare his life.[46]

A significant factor in the spread of evangelical doctrine was migration, primarily resulting from wars and economic difficulties in Belarus. In such circumstances, ideas always spread faster. As Belarusians traveled abroad they learned about the new faith and adopted it while in places such as Southern Ukraine and Siberia as well as in North America and Germany. Along with this, the missionary activities of Evangelicals from neighboring territories such as the Russian Empire, and later Poland, led to the planting of new churches. For example, Polish, German, and Baltic missionaries worked in northwestern Belarus which was predominately Catholic.[47] However, as Catholics maintained allegiance to their church, their relationship towards the evangelical Christians was either indifferent or hostile.[48]

3.2. Historical and Interethnic Relationships in Identity and Worship Formation

Various traditions contributed to the shaping of the evangelical movement in Belarus. The evangelical movement in Belarus contained both Ukrainian and Baltic congregations which included Belarusian territory as part of their

---

46. P.E. Ermakov, "Biographiya brata L.D. Prymachenko" [Biography of brother L.D. Prymachenko], 27.

47. Lisovskaya, *Neoprotestantizm v Zapadnoi Belarusi v 1921–1939 gg.*, 30–31.

48. Research of the conversion cases during the Second World War revealed that the Baptist churches mainly grew due to the conversion of Orthodox people (79.1%) and to a lesser extent due to Catholics (4.5%) (Lensu and Prokshina, *Baptizm I Baptisty*, 34). However, the ministry was mainly carried out within Orthodox territory. However, Latvian missionaries established a church in Grodno, where the majority were Catholics (Lisovskaya, "Novye protestantskie denominatsii na zapadnobelorusskih zemliah v kontse XIX – 20gg. XX veka," 42.).

mission field.⁴⁹ Polish and German Baptists, and Evangelicals of the USA and Russia played an important role in this movement through education in theological schools (in Lodz, Warsaw, Hamburg, Chicago, Knoxville, and St. Petersburg) and missionary work. International organizations were particularly involved in western Belarus.⁵⁰ A variety of influences certainly contributed to the evangelical movement in Belarus. On the one hand, this influence was positive in terms of the richness of expression in worship, especially in music ministry, and its broadness and openness. On the other hand, divisions and tensions now occurred between people belonging to different traditions, particularly Evangelical Christians and Baptists. Together all the influences led to "the unique social and theological status of the Baptist movement, its complex, dual and combined European-Russian, universal-local, Protestant-Orthodox cross-cultural and theological identity,"⁵¹ which shaped the tradition of worship services in the churches of the Russian Empire and later the Soviet Union, including Belarus.

3.2.1. Russian Orientation

Studying the history of the origin and spread of the evangelical movement in Belarus highlights two basic sources of influence. In many cases the awakening was conditioned by relations within a Russian-speaking environment, whereas others were more determined by relations with German and English-speaking believers. It is difficult to distinguish clearly between these sources since they often exerted indirect influence in Belarus via Russia and Ukraine, and the types were often mixed. For example, the development of the Baptist movement in the northwest of the Belarusian lands at the beginning of the twentieth century was associated with the activity of "Wilhelm Fetler's Mission." From 1923–1939 the mission supported missionaries in Poland (Western Belarus). Wilhelm (or William) Fetler, who was born on the outskirts of the Russian Empire in Latvia, and received his religious education in London and St. Petersburg,⁵² trained evangelists and missionaries

---

49. Lisovskaya, *Neoprotestantizm v Zapadnoi Belarusi v 1921–1939 gg.*, 31.
50. Lisovskaya.
51. Cherenkov, *Litsom k litsu. Evangel'skaya vera v sovremennoi kul'ture*, 66–67.
52. Bednarczyk, *Historiya Zborow Baptystow w Polsce do 1939 roku* [History of Baptist Churches in Poland until 1939], 119.

for Russia and visited Grodno himself. Fetler was a strong Rusophile, yet his ministry was supported by western resources.[53]

However, it is possible and important to trace the main factors of influence in order to understand the nature of traditional worship. It developed on Slavic soil but was also strongly/significantly influenced by the West. Close connections within the limits of one country (especially in eastern Belarus), culture, language, and the active missionary work of evangelical Christians and Baptists from Russia and Ukraine, all led to the development of new "Russian" communities in Gomel and Rogachev districts, Mogilev region, in Vitebsk region, and later in Minsk and Belarusian Polesie. It is not surprising that early believers in Gomel district called themselves followers of "a newborn Russian brotherhood."[54]

The main factor of influence here was the Russian language. Although in 1920 a Baptist church pastor in Brest, Dzekuts-Maley, under the editorship of Anton Lutskevich, translated the New Testament from Church Slavonic into the Belarusian language,[55] this translation was not adopted as the text for worship and reading in evangelical churches.[56] Instead, the Russian Synodal translation was, and continues to be, used as the main translation. To this day, the Russian language holds a dominant position in the evangelical churches of Belarus as the language of worship.[57]

Belarusian Evangelicals mostly used newspapers, magazines, and books written in Russian, and that remains true at the beginning of the twenty-first century. The insignificant number of publications in Belarusian in western Belarus can be explained by the fact that in the early years of the movement, the majority of religious literature was designated for use by all the

---

53. Fetler was also known by his adopted Russian name, Basil Malof. For a (rather hagiographic) biography of Fetler, see J.A. Stewart, *A Man in a Hurry: The Story of the Life and Work of Pastor Basil A. Malof* (Asheville: The Russian Bible Society, 1968).

54. Yanouskaya, *Khrystsiyanskaya tsarkva u Belarusi 1863–1914 gg.*, 69.

55. Unuchak, "S'vyatar, patryyot, perakladchyk" [Priest, Patriot and Translator], 8–13. New Testament and Psalms were published as one book in 1931 (Unuchak, 8).

56. The full translation of the Bible from Church Slavonic language into Belarusian by Vasiliy Semukha (issued in 2002) is generally not used in worship, with rare exceptions. On Bible translations into Belarusian see Bokun, "Gistoryya pierakladu Biblii na bielaruskuyu movu" [History of translating the Bible into Belarusian], 34. In 2016 there were three translations of the entire Bible into Belarusian, and about ten translations of the New Testament.

57. On the use of Belarusian in worship see footnote 1 on p 258.

communities in Poland,⁵⁸ as well as Russian-speaking believers in Russia, Ukraine, the Baltic States, Moldova, and other territories. Widespread knowledge of the Russian language significantly increased Belarusians' opportunities and their access to Christian literature, and publications printed in Russia and Ukraine enriched their ecclesial life. This is especially true in terms of singing. Hymns (in Russian) published by the leader of the All-Union Council of Evangelical Christians (AUCEC), Ivan Prokhanov,⁵⁹ were especially important in shaping the spirit of worship services. Prokhanov published 1037 lyrics, 624 of which he wrote himself, including the very popular *O, Obraz sovershennyi* (Oh, Perfect Image), *Za evangel'skuyu veru* (For Evangelical Faith), and *Vzoydem na Golgofu, moy brat* (Let Us Go up to Calvary, My Brother).⁶⁰ Prokhanov also translated 413 lyrics from English and German, many of which have become classics for Baptist music ministry, such as *Slushaite povest' liubvi v prostote* (Simple Love Story), *Ne proidi, Iisus, menia Ty* (Pass Me Not, O Gentle Savior), *Lyublyu, Gospod', Tvoy dom* (I Love Thy House, Lord), and others.⁶¹

Evangelical believers in Belarus, and people with similar beliefs in other territories of the Russian Empire and later in the Soviet Union, were brought together by personal relationships as well as by the same Bible texts, songs, and Christian books. As stated earlier, many Belarusians came to faith through the ministry of Christians in Ukraine, Siberia, and St. Petersburg. They also maintained relationships with various figures of influence. For instance, Baptists in Gomel district maintained links with their coreligionists from southern provinces in Russia. Believers in St. Petersburg were sending financial assistance and books to believers in Chechersk, in Rogachev districts,⁶²

---

58. Lisovskaya, "Problema ispol'zovaniya belorusskogo yazyka v deyatel'nosti baptistskikh i pyatidesyatnicheskikh obshchin Zapadnoi Belarusi v 1921–1939 gg" [The Problem of Use of Belarusian Language in the Activities of Baptist and Pentecostal Communities in Western Belarus in 1921–1939], 77.

59. Ivan Stepanovich Prokhanov (1869–1935) – a prominent figure of the evangelical movement, the founder of the All-Russian Union of Evangelical Christians, as well as a writer, poet and translator. See the book by Popov, *I.S. Prokhanov, Stranitsy zhizni* and Prokhanov's autobiography *V kotle Rossii* [In the Cauldron of Russia].

60. *Pesn' Vozrozhdeniya*, nos. 31, 185, 420. Ludvig Shenderovsky, *Ivan Prokhanov* [Ivan Prokhanov] (Toronto: "Evangel'skaya vera," 1986), 117.

61. *Pesn' Vozrozhdeniya*, nos. 1, 30, 248.

62. Lensu and Prokshina, *Baptizm i Baptisty*, 17; *Istoriya evangel'skikh khristian-baptistov v SSSR*, 382.

which demonstrates a relationship with Vasiliy Pashkov's followers.[63] The leader of the Baptists in Brest, Luka Dzekuts-Malei, studied and completed Bible courses for Evangelical Christians in St. Petersburg. The churches of Evangelical Christians, which had an influential center in St. Petersburg, were also actively working with Baptist churches in Brest.[64] Mina Veresov, who founded churches in Bobruisk and the surrounding villages of Bortniki, Dabas, and Vorotyn in Mogilev region,[65] along with Vasiliy Velichko, the presbyter in the town of Slutsk from 1920 to 1928, also completed courses for Evangelical Christians in St. Petersburg. Public worship began in Mogilev in 1917 with some Evangelical Christians involved, including Eumen Prohorov.[66] Evangelicals of Belarusian Polesie established close relations with Baptists and Evangelical Christians in Ukrainian Polesie and Volynia. Later, ties with the center of the Baptist movement in Moscow greatly determined the form of worship for many churches in Belarus: the central and the only Baptist Church in Moscow during the Soviet era became *the* model.

Close ties to other Russian-speaking communities, in addition to ties within Belarus, were leading to the unification of doctrinal beliefs and practices in different regions of the country. Existing differences were further leveled following the integration of all the evangelical churches of the Soviet

---

63. Vasiliy Alexandrovich Pashkov (1831–1902) was a retired Colonel of the Guards, a follower of the English preacher Lord Radstock, and one of the founding fathers of the Evangelical Christian movement in the Russian Empire (common people typically called this movement "pashkovtsy"). On Pashkov's ministry see Corrado, *Philosophiya sluzheniya polkovnika Pashkova* [The Philosophy of Ministry of the Colonel Vasiliy Pashkov] which was originally published as "The Philosophy of Ministry of Colonel Vasiliy Pashkov," (MA Thesis, Wheaton College, 2000); Ellis and Wesley Jones, *Drugaya revolyutsiya. Rossiiskoye evangelicheskoye probuzhdeniye* [The Other Revolution. Russian Evangelical Revival], 87–128. Originally published as *The Other Revolution: Russian Evangelical Awakenings*. Abilene: ACU. Press, 1996.

64. In the Brest area Baptists and Evangelical Christian churches maintained close connections up to the integration into one union. The integration happened in June 1923 in Brest at the Congress of Baptists and Evangelical Christians. The union was called an Association of Evangelical Christians and Baptists of Poland. The Association broke apart at the 4th Congress in Brest on March 17th-19th, 1925, due to conflicts in the leadership of the Association and a different understanding of certain issues, such as military service and the attitude towards the Pentecostal church. (Lisovskaya, "Struktura yevangel'sko-baptistskogo dvizheniya Zapadnoy Belarusi v 1921–1939 gg.," 22–23; Bokun, *Lukaš Dziekuć-Maliej i Bielaruskija piaraklady Biblii*, 162–164.)

65. *Istoriya evangel'skikh khristian-baptistov v SSSR*, 383.

66. Ol'ga Konzevenko, *Istoriya evangel'skikh khristian-baptistov (EKhB) v Mogileve* [Evangelical Christians-Baptists story in Mogilev].

Union into one AUCECB in 1944.[67] For example, doctrinal similarity and the lack of strong national leaders in Belarus transformed the Churches of Christ into Evangelical-Christian Baptists.[68] Today in Kobrin, the former center of the Churches of Christ movement, second and third generation members of the church think of themselves as Baptists, and Kobrin itself is considered one of the centers of the Baptist movement in Belarus.[69]

Thus, the challenging environment, the waves of persecution, political revolutions, two world wars, and the difficult economic conditions under which the churches in Belarus were developing, significantly contributed to uniformity in the expression of faith. The distinguishable characteristics of different evangelical movements were melding and getting lost in the "melting pot" of the imperial and communist regimes. Consequently, we cannot talk of the uniqueness of a "pure Belarusian" style of worship, but rather focus on the uniqueness of the traditional Russian-speaking Baptist service in general with its emphasis on the sermon, its purpose of building up believers and evangelizing non-believers, its restraint in the expression of emotions, and its Christocentrism. These and various other features are explored in the following chapters.

Thus, it is possible to talk about the "Russian orientation"[70] of the evangelical movement in Belarus. Temporary transition under Polish jurisdiction in 1921–1939 and the direct influence of Western Protestantism did not break this dynamic. That is why in order to understand the character, structure, and features of public worship in the evangelical churches of Belarus we can study worship not only in Belarus, but also in neighboring countries which were once integrated by a common language and state. Furthermore, an analysis of

---

67. See footnote 5 on page 3.

68. Lensu and Prokshina, *Baptizm i Baptisty*, 29. With regard to the Churches of Christ, see footnote 5 on page 3.

69. On the relationship of the Churches of Christ with other denominations see Unuchak, "Tserkvy Khrystovyya na Kobrynshchyne u 1920-ya gg.: da pytannya denaminatsyynay toyesnas'tsi i arganizatsyynaga stanaulennya" [The Churches of Christ in Kobrin Area in the 1920s: The Issues of Confessional Identity and Organizational Development]; Unuchak, "Centr Abjadnańnia Cerkvau Chrystovych u Kobrynie (1929–1930 hh.)" [Union Center of the Churches of Christ in Kobryn], 178–185. It should be noted, however, that some Church of Christ ministers and members split from the Baptist Union in 1926. SABR, Stock 1, File 10, Case 2313, 29–30; Case 2279, 38.

70. Lisovskaya, "Novye protestantskie denominatsii na zapadnobelorusskih zemliah v kontse XIX – 20 gg. XX veka," 48.

traditional worship services in the Baptist churches of Belarus can conversely be helpful for understanding worship services in many other churches which share a common historical and religious context.

3.2.2. Western Sources

The connections with other Russian-speaking seats of awakening, and their role in the formation of the evangelical churches in Belarus, are indisputable, especially in the early period leading up to the 1920s. However, Western sources of influence have also been significant. As noted earlier, many of the churches in Belarus were founded by Belarusians who came to faith in Germany or the United States. Therefore, the roots of their practice can be traced back to the Western evangelical churches that have played a key role in forming the "genetic code" of their gatherings. For example, extempore prayer in a Baptist gathering differed (and still differs) so greatly from Orthodox liturgy that it seemed very strange to Orthodox people who were often struck by its novelty and singularity. In his memoirs, Dzekuts-Malei notes that "random visitors, who were neighbors of the house hosts, looked at me, at the congregation, and heard our 'one-of-a-kind' prayers, and they were very surprised with this new faith, asking, 'Where did you borrow it from? What does it mean?'"[71]

Historians and theologians have pointed to the influence of Western Christians over the Russian-speaking Baptists (including Belarusians) and the various ties contributing to that. Alexander Karev, an outstanding figure in AUCECB, states that Baptists in southern Russia were closely connected with German Baptists and adopted the structure of their community system, including the "laying on of hands on each baptized person after baptism."[72] Johannes Dyck also notes that when Vasiliy Pavlov returned from Hamburg,[73]

---

71. Pekun, "Luka Nikolaevich Dzekuts-Maley: zhizn' i sluzhenie" [Luka Nikolaevich Dzekuts-Maley: Life and Ministry], 8. Timofey Cheprasov thinks, that "The absence of rigid liturgy, extemporaneous prayer, and preaching with the anointing of the Holy Spirit were the characteristics that attracted many people to the baptistic churches at the early stages of their development" (*Like Ripples on Water*, 65).

72. Karev, "Russkoe evangel'sko-baptistskoe dvizhenie" [Russian Evangelical Baptist Movement], *Al'manakh po istorii russkogo baptisma* [Almanac on the History of Russian Baptists], 151.

73. Vasiliy Gur'evich Pavlov (1854–1924) was one of the founding fathers and first leaders of the Baptist Union in Russia, a missionary, preacher, and an editor of *Baptist* magazine. He was among the first members of the early Russian Baptist community in Transcaucasia. See

the community in Tiflis (current Tbilisi, Georgia) adopted Johann Oncken's model of pastoral unity of command,[74] and the community order was determined by the Hamburg Confession.[75] This connection with German Baptists contributed to the formation of doctrinal practices, mission organization, the understanding of church discipline, and the order of worship "by its strict organization, highly developed dogma and moral program, and by its missionary emphasis."[76]

German Christians contributed to the content as well as to the spirit of Baptist worship in Belarus. Studying the nature of spirituality in Russian-speaking churches, Gregory Nichols adds German Pietism to the list of sources of evangelical forms of spirituality resulting from the spread of German Pietism in Europe.[77] J.G. Davis notes that in Germany and the Scandinavian countries, where Baptists arose out of the pietistic ferment of previous centuries, worship still contains strong overtones of pietistic devotional life. Bible reading and meditation, spontaneous prayer and introspective hymns characterize such services,[78] and these characteristics are clearly manifested in the worship of the Belarusian Baptists.

---

more about Pavlov in Popov, *Stopy Blagovestnika* [The Feet of an Evangelist]; Kovalenko, *Oblako svidetelei Khristovykh*, 38–42; Viske and Leven ml., *Oni sledovali za Iisusom* [They Followed Jesus], 113–127. In 1885 Pavlov visited the Gomel region and baptized the first Baptist believers there (*Baptist*, no. 3 [1927]: 27–28).

74. Johann Gerhard Oncken (1800–1884) was a German Baptist who was often called the "the 'father' of the continental Baptists." Oncken helped direct and guide the growth of Baptists throughout Germany and across much of Europe for half a century. (Randall, *Communities of Conviction. Baptist Beginning in Europe*, 71–87.)

75. Dyck, "Stanovlenie evangel'skogo baptistskogo bratstva v Rossii (1860–1887)" [Formation of the Evangelical Baptist Brotherhood in Russia (1860–1887), 5.

In 1876 Pavlov translated the Hamburg Baptist Confession into Russian and edited it; the Confession was put together in 1847 by Oncken along with G.W. Lehmann and J.W. Köbner. The document became a model for other confessions of Russian Baptists and Evangelical Christians. (*Istoriya evangel'skikh khristian-baptistov v SSSR*, 438.) For further information on the Hamburg Bapist Confession and its influence on Slavic Baptist churches, see Yaroslav Pyzh, "The Confessional Community as the Ecclesiological Core of the Baptists in the Soviet Union."

76. Mitrokhin, *Baptizm: istoriya i sovremennost'*, 23. An example of the formative influences of German Baptists may be seen in the practice of the Lord's Supper. The Baptists in Belarus accepted a "closed" table, introduced by Oncken, with the prerequisite that communicants must have been baptized as believers, as faith and baptism cannot be separated from each other. Also, children may not partake in Communion. (Kahle, *Evangel'skie khristiane v Rossii i Sovetskom Soyuze*, 57.)

77. Nichols, "Evangelical Spirituality and Russian Baptists," 206–208.

78. Davies, ed., *A Dictionary of Liturgy & Worship*, 66.

Churches in England and North America also influenced Baptists in Belarus. Thus, Wilhelm Kahle argues that Russian-speaking believers build their denominational structure on English and American Baptist models.[79] Connections with English believers tended to be embodied in greater freedom, flexibility, and spontaneity in gatherings, which were viewed as a manifestation of the Spirit in worshipping God, and were valued alongside the requirement of godly order in leading services.[80] Among other notable characteristics, attention to studying and preaching the Bible in mass assemblies were significant.[81] The American revivalist tradition may well have enhanced an evangelistic thrust in traditional worship involving: lively singing, testimonies about the freedom and forgiveness which have come in Christ, spontaneous prayers "in the Spirit," sermons closing with a call to come to Christ, and poems to aid the conversion of sinners.[82]

Numerous songs, especially ones which could be traced to the revival tradition of Dwight Moody and Ira Sankey, were also employed. As a result of his visit to western Belarus in 1926, a correspondent from *The Times* observed that:

> thousands of farmers turn away from traditional services in the Russian Orthodox Church and they have their meetings according to the evangelical pattern as it has been done in Great Britain and America over the last fifty years. Revival hymns are very popular; people listen to a tuning fork and all the congregation unanimously joins in singing. Such worship services of "believers," as these people are called, are so popular that, in one of the villages where I addressed a large congregation, the local parish church was almost empty.[83]

Decades later, the Billy Graham Evangelistic Association's mass evangelistic crusades in Russia, Ukraine, and Belarus continued the same trend. Some of the most popular hymns which represented the English-speaking influence

---

79. Kahle, *Evangel'skie khristiane v Rossii i Sovetskom Soyuze*, 539.
80. Cf. McKibbens, Jr., "Our Baptist Heritage in Worship," p. 63.
81. "British Baptists . . . extend *a legacy of great preaching* in Baptist worship" (McKibbens, Jr.).
82. Cf. McKibbens, "Our Baptist Heritage in Worship," p. 64.
83. Colligan, "White Russia – A Visitor's Impression," 15.

on the formation of the spirit of worship and emotional expressions of faith in Belarusian churches include "Velikiy Bog" (How Great Thou Art), "Vernost' Tvoya velika, o, moy Bozhe" (Great is Thy Faithfulness), "Vsevyshnemu slava" (To God be the Glory), "Chto za Druga my imeyem" (What a Friend We Have in Jesus), "Techet li zhizn' mirno, podobno reke" (It Is Well with My Soul), amongst others.[84]

We can also note the influence of literature, which was mostly characteristic of the Anglo-American relations, particularly given the popularity of such preachers as Dwight Moody and Charles Spurgeon in Russian-speaking areas. Moody's *Pleasure and Profit in Bible Study* and sermons by Spurgeon were very popular until the beginning of twenty-first century and they are still in great demand in Russian-speaking communities.[85]

In addition to the Christian songs and books, the education of several key Belarusian Baptists in the United States contributed to the influence of Anglo-American spirituality in worship. The aforementioned Fetler sent a number of graduates of the Bible Institute in Philadelphia to engage in ministry in Belarus. These included Demid Iosiphovich Polyakov, Korney Petrovich Yurzhits, and Pavel Afanasievich Aksyuchits. Aksyuchits became the founder and pastor of ECB community in Borisov, Minsk region. Polyakov founded an ECB church in the village of Podaresie, Starodorozhski district, Minsk region and was also a director of the community choir.[86] Ivan Vensky, the pastor of Dziarechyn community in Zelva district, Grodno region, had studied at a seminary in the United States for three years before coming to western Belarus as a missionary in 1922.[87]

Furthermore, Western evangelical leaders had an indirect impact on the Baptists in Belarus through such well-known figures of the Russian revival

---

84. *Pesn' Vozrozhdeniya*, nos. 93, 119, 136, 589, 707.

85. Moody, *Pol'za i naslazhdeniye ot izucheniya Biblii* [Pleasure and Profit in Bible study]. In the 1990s many of Spurgeon's works were published, including *Blagodat'yu vy spaseny* [You Are Saved by Grace] (1990), *Sokrovishcha obetovaniy Bozh'ikh* [Treasures of God's Promises] (1991), *Izbrannoye* [Selected Works] (1993), *Sperdzhenskiye konspekty propovedey* [Spurgeon's Sermon Notes] (1996), *Propoved' dlya ishchushchikh Boga* [A Sermon for Those Who Seek God] (1996), *Samyye chitayemyye propovedi* [Most Read Sermons] (1997), *Lektsii moim studentam* [Lectures to My Students] (1998), *12 propovedey o Svyatom Dukhe* [12 Sermons on the Holy Spirit] (1999), and *Evangel'skiye propovedi* [Evangelical Sermons] (1999).

86. *Baptist*, no. 3, 9 (1927); *Baptist Ukrainy* [Baptist of Ukraine], no. 11 (1928 г.); *Istoriya evangel'skikh khristian-baptistov v SSSR*, 384–387.

87. SABR, Stock 1482, File 2, Case 1, 51.

as Lord Radstock and Ivan Kargel. The ministry of Granville Waldegrave Radstock[88] was characterized by several motifs which can be found in many Russian-speaking churches: the yearning for revival and holiness,[89] commitment to restore New Testament Christianity through belief in the absolute authority of the Bible,[90] premillennial theology of holiness, and a precritical method of biblical interpretation, all of which were typical of the Anglo-American evangelical movement in the second half of the nineteenth century.[91]

Ivan Kargel[92] was one of the most popular and respected writers among Belarusian churches. Gregory Nichols argues that Russian-speaking churches have adopted many characteristics from Kargel and other leaders of the Russian Evangelical Christian movement,[93] "such as a distinct revivalist flare in their services and preaching style, a strong yearning for a quietness of the soul before God, a desire for holiness, and a mild disdain for systematic theology which is restrictive."[94]

---

88. Lord Radstock (1833–1913). An English preacher who organized prayer meetings and discussions on Christian topics primarily for the Russian aristocracy in St. Petersburg from 1874 to 1878. Evangelical Christians-Baptists and Pentecostals consider him to be one of the founding fathers of the evangelical movement in Russia. See Ellis and Jones, *Drugaya revolyutsiya*, 63–86; Fountain, *Lord Radstok i dukhovnoye probuzhdeniye v Rossii* [Lord Radstock and a Spiritual Awakening in Russia], originally published as *Lord Radstock and the Russian Awakening* (Revival Literature, 1988); Kovalenko, *Oblako svidetelei Khristovykh*, 69–72. Some interesting information about his ministry in Russia can be found in a story by Russian writer Nikolai Leskov, "Velikosvetsky raskol" [The Great Secular Split], in Leskov, *Zerkalo zhizni* [*The Mirror of Life*], 32–121.

89. Mitskevich, *Istoriya evangel'skih khrisjan-baptistov* [The History of Evangelic Christians-Baptists], 85.

90. Ellis and Jones, *Drugaya revolyutsiya*, 80.

91. Puzynin, *Tradiciya evangel'skikh khristian. Izuchenie samoidentifikatsii i bogosloviya ot momenta ee zarozhdeniya do nashikh dnei*, 56.

92. Ivan Veniaminovich Kargel (1849–1937) was an important figure in the evangelical movement in the Russian Empire, a writer, theologian, and pastor of St. Petersburg church of Evangelical Christians. He is the author of a number of famous books, such as the commentaries on the Epistle to the Romans and the Book of Revelation, *Svet iz teni budushchikh blag* (Light out of the Shadow of Future Blessings), *V kakom otnoshenii ty k Dukhu Sviatomu* (In What Kind of Relationships to the Holy Spirit), and others. For more about Kargel, see Karetnikova, "Ivan Veniaminovich Kargel'" [Ivan Veniaminovich Kargel], 684–688; Nichols, "Ivan Kargel and the Fulfillment of Revival," 23–39; Skopina, "Iz biografii I.V. Kargelya i yego docherey" [From the Biography of I.V. Kargelya and His Daughters], 689–670. See also the detailed research by Nichols, *The Development of Russian Evangelical Spirituality: A Study of Ivan V. Kargel (1849–1937)*.

93. For Evangelical Christians see "Subject of the Study" in Chapter 1.

94. Nichols, "Evangelical Spirituality and Russian Baptists," p. 206.

3.2.3. Local or Foreign, or Both?

Modern Baptist researcher Andrey Puzynin suggests that after the Bolshevik Revolution, along with the memory of its 'aristocratic period', the Western origins of the Baptist tradition, or rather its Evangelical Christian elements, were suppressed in historical memory.[95] The Anglo-American tradition of holiness was then reinterpreted as a native Russian, original, and popular movement.[96] Indeed, some researchers emphasize the local origin of the Russian-speaking brotherhood, primarily referring to the action of the Holy Spirit, spiritual hunger, and the influence of the translation of Scripture into Russian language.[97] Some non-native researchers, including Gregory Nichols and Albert Wardin, also indicate the originality and uniqueness of Russian-speaking Baptists. Nichols notes "that the Russian Baptists have developed independently of the Baptists world-wide. This is due to both the Tsarist and Soviet restrictions concerning communication to the outside world."[98] Wardin agrees that German Baptists "took advantage of the evangelical movement already developing in the Russian Empire. They were not initiators of the movement but facilitators in moving it to what they considered were more consistent biblical principles such as separation from non-evangelical churches and believer's baptism by immersion."[99] The argument is put forward that these groups expressed their faith naturally rather than copying foreign forms.

The first worship services started in small groups of relatives or neighbors. From the beginning they resembled a Bible study or discussions on

---

95. Puzynin uses the term "aristocratic period," to denote a time during which aristocrats came to faith as a result of Radstock's activity, such as guards Colonel V.A. Pashkov, Count A.P. Bobrinsky, Baron M.M. Korf, Princess V.F. Gagarina, E.I. Chertkova, S.P. Liven and others. See also Liven, *Dukhovnoe probuzhdenie v Rossii. Vospominaniya knyazhny S.P. Liven* [Spiritual revival in Russia. Memories of Princess S.P. Lieven].

96. Puzynin, *Tradiciya evangel'skikh khristian*, 333. This statement appears to be true in regard to the twentieth century or older generations of Christians. In contrast, very few young Christians in ECB churches would be familiar with the names of Radstock and Kargel. The voices they hear as a call for sanctification come from contemporary, popular Western writers and preachers such as John MacArthur and John Piper.

97. See *Istoriya evangel'skikh khristian-baptistov v SSSR*, 85–93; P. M., "Istoki evangel'skogo dvizheniya v Rossii" [Backgrounds of Evangelical Movement in Russia], 35; Savinskiy, "Istoriya russko-ukrainskogo baptizma. Uchebnoye posobiye" [History of Russian-Ukrainian Baptists. Study Manual].

98. Nichols, "Evangelical Spirituality and Russian Baptists," p. 205.

99. Wardin, "How Indigenous Was the Baptist Movement in the Russian Empire," p. 36.

spiritual issues, with no final definite form. Their worship was characterized by simplicity of structure and content. Indeed, it would be more appropriate to call them "gatherings": groups of like-minded and sympathetic people getting together. To take an example of the first worship services in Gomel, it is known that "Shtundists" who arrived from Ukraine rented an apartment where "in the evening they gathered in a family circle and were reading the Gospel and singing Psalms."[100] In the same way, opponents of "the sectarians" of Rachkany, Slutsk district accused them of "assembling in a house, reading the Bible and singing their chants. It's their whole worship service."[101] As time passed, worship services developed but the general scheme remained the same. Notes by a Christian who attended a service in Brest in October 1922 describe how a worship service appeared in its more developed form:

> On Saturday night, brother Feodor Trihonyuk harnessed a horse and we went to Brest-Litovsk to the service of God's children. We drove all night and at dawn came into the city. At 10 a.m., brothers and sisters as well as visitors gathered from all the neighborhoods of Brest and the house was filled. The meeting was opened by singing "I Hear Thy Voice" and prayer. Brother Dzekuts-Maley read from the prophecy of Isaiah 12, and instructed brothers and sisters. Two brothers then shared about Christ. The meeting ended at 12 o'clock. After the meeting, four people gave their hearts to the Lord.[102]

However, the thesis of primarily native rather than foreign origins does not answer all the questions posed by the history and practice of worship. Another point of view, already expressed by revival movement participants in the early twentieth century, allows for a greater balance. "The evangelical movement in Russia was not original; it sprouted from the sources that had been provided for us by our Christian brothers from overseas during the great evangelical revival in Germany, England and America."[103] Even earlier

---

100. Kolesnichenko, "Gomel'skoi tserkvi 100 let" [100 anniversary of the Gomel Church], 8.

101. CSHA, Stock 136, File 4, Case 64, 5b; Lensu and Prokshina, *Baptizm i Baptisty*, 19.

102. Pekun, "Luka Nikolaevich Dzekuts-Maley: zhizn' i sluzhenie," p. 9.

103. A.I.K., "Evangel'skaya pesn'" [Evangelic Song], *Utrennyaa Zvezda* [The Morning Star], no. 3–5 (1922): 15.

a Russian evangelist and pastor, Feodor Balikhin, noted that "the light of God's truth began to shine in our country coming from Germany."[104] In his 1911 article, Mikhail Timoshenko declared, "The Baptist movement is not foreign but clearly international. As all people on the earth need bread, water and air, so also all need spiritual nourishment."[105] This kind of thought is also developed by a secular scholar who would have been free from denominational prejudices:

> Although there were valid historical premises for church formation according to the Baptist pattern which was related to the centuries-old legacy of "heresy" and sects, the church received its definitive genetic code from foreign missionaries, and it took a while for the Baptist movement to acquire its own inner impulses, and its own energy to develop itself.[106]

The case of Baptist worship practice in Belarus reveals how Western and local traditions merged and gave birth to an Eastern Slavic form of evangelical Christianity, and demonstrates that this process took place from the very beginning. An outstanding example of this is the aforementioned heritage of music and traditional hymns used in worship services. A collection of songs, *Pesn' Vozrozhdeniya*, which is the definitive resource for traditional singing in the worship of Baptist Churches in Belarus, contains hymns translated from English and German languages, as well as indigenous hymns. However, one of the most beloved hymns of the Mennonites and Ukrainian Shtundists was the Orthodox liturgical chanting "Primi hvalu blagodaren'e, Syn Bozhiy za Tvoyu liubov'" (Accept praise and thanksgiving, Son of God, for Your love).[107] In fact, acceptance of Orthodox music varied. As some people moved away from Orthodoxy they refused to sing such songs, whereas others continued to chant Orthodox texts and music until they developed their own songs.[108]

---

104. Balikhin, "Moya poezdka zagranitsu," p. 15.

105. Timoshenko, "Baptisty i ikh protivniki" [Baptists and Their Adversaries], 69.

106. Mitrokhin, *Baptizm: istoriya i sovremennost'*, 240. The book by Brackney, ed., *Baptist Life and Thought, A Source Book*, is a valuable resource on the development and identity of Baptists.

107. *Pesn' Vozrozhdeniya*, no. 140.

108. Kharlov, "Iz istorii muzikal'no-pevcheskogo sluzheniya nashego bratstva" [From the History of Music and Singing Ministry of Our Brotherhood], 46.

The Molokan tradition[109] exerted strong influence over worship in the Tiflis Baptist community (Transcaucasia) where hymns were borrowed from the German Baptist collection *Glaubenstimme* as another source of the community's singing repertoire. People often composed or selected tunes which were similar to Russian folk songs. Such hymns as "Liubit lish Khristos bezmerno" (Only Christ Loves without Any Measure), "Ya nashel sebe spasen'e" (I Have Found My Salvation)[110] and others were composed in Tiflis.[111] However, Molokan singing, "could not satisfy the evangelicals because it was not in tune with their spirit. The Evangelical Baptist movement did not need plaintive singing, but singing which was cheerful and joyful."[112]

The development of sung worship took another direction in St. Petersburg. Many representatives of the upper class who were fluent in foreign languages began to translate Christian books and hymns into Russian.[113] The favorite songs of the Evangelicals in St. Petersburg were "Radost', radost' neprestanno" (Joyous, Joyous, Without Ceasing), and "V chas kogda truba Gospodnia"

---

109. The term *molokan* was used for the first time in 1785 in relation to a religious group in Tambov governorate, because they were drinking milk (*moloko* in Russian) during lent time. In their turn, the group offered a different explanation for the term referring to the words of the apostle Peter, who called people to "long for the pure milk of the word" (1 Peter 2:2). The movement spread from Tambov province to Saratov, Voronezh, Astrakhan, Kursk, and other provinces. The molokans subscribed to a spiritual interpretation of baptism, the Eucharist, and resurrection, and stood against serfdom and military service. Molokan public worship consisted of Bible reading and singing hymns. In the 19th century the molokan movement was divided into many branches, including "water molokans," who stated that baptism and the Lord's Supper were essential. N.I. Voronin (see footnote 405) was interested in their doctrine. Presently there are a few small groups remaining in Transcaucasia, Ukraine, and the Tambov region in Russia, as well as in the US, Argentina, Canada, and other countries and regions. See *Istoriya evangel'skikh khristian-baptistov v SSSR*, 30–32, 42–43; Mitrokhin, ed., *Khristianstvo. Slovar'* [Christianity. Dictionary], 287–288; Chernov, "Fenomen Rossiyskoy kontrkul'tury na primere natsional'nogo samosoznaniya dukhovnykh khristian-molokan" [Phenomenon of Russian Counter Culture of the Example of National Selfconsciousness of Spiritual Christians-Molokans], 229–233; Chernov, "Inoskazaniye kak kharakternaya osobennost' ucheniya dukhovnykh khristian-molokan" [Circumlocution as Feature of Study of Spiritual Christians-Molokans], 282–288; Lunkin and Prokof'yev, "Molokans and Dukhobors: Living Sources of Russian Protestantism," 85–90.

110. *Pesn' Vozrozhdeniya*, nos. 100, 189. "Only Christ Loves without Any Measure" was originally written as "One There Is, Above All Others."

111. Kharlov, "Iz istorii muzikal'no-pevcheskogo sluzheniya nashego bratstva," 47.

112. Belousov, "Gospod' sila moya i pesn'" [God is My Strength and My Song], *Bratskiy Vestnik*, no. 2 (1966): 74–78, 76. Rudnichenko, "Pesnopeniya v religioznykh ritualakh dukhoborov i molokan Rostovskoy oblasti: sovremennoye sostoyaniye" [Chants in Religious Rituals of the Doukhobors and Molokans in the Rostov Region: Current State], 173–179.

113. Liven, *Dukhovnoe probuzhdenie v Rossii*, 28.

(When the Trumpet of the Lord), as well as "Bog s toboi dokole svidimsia" (God Be With You 'til We Meet Again),[114] translated from English by Alexandra Peyker. Such translated hymns became very popular and were included in one of the most popular collections, *Husly*, along with works by local authors.[115] Thus, these various groups of evangelical believers experienced the influence of different singing traditions: Orthodox, Molokan, and Western-evangelical. The above-mentioned songs are still widely used in traditional worship in ECB Churches in Belarus.

3.3. Western Forms in the Eastern Context: Problems of Adaptation

3.3.1. Local Context Against "Imported Faith"[116]

The inculturation of Western ideas and symbols into an Eastern context was not a simple matter. Moreover, the Tsarist state and Orthodox society strongly opposed "foreign faith" in an attempt to preserve a monodenominational Russian state that had been cherished for many centuries. The mere idea that Russian speakers might convert from Orthodoxy to Baptism was regarded as a threat to the statehood, and the idea of freedom of choice in religion was generally alien to the traditional Russian mind.

One aspect of this conflict of worldviews was described by Alexander Milovidov, an Eastern Orthodox who researched the first Baptist groups and churches in the late nineteenth and early twentieth centuries. He stated his opinion that "a Belarusian is alien to philosophical and rationalistic inclinations of Baptists, which requires more abstract thinking, reasoning and generalizations than modern, common Belarusian people possess."[117] "In

---

114. *Pesn' Vozrozhdeniya*, nos. 176, 665, 686. Goncharenko, "Izdanie sbornikov dukhovnykh pesen v kontekste razvitiya dukhovnoi muzyki evangel'skikh khristian-baptistov Rossii" [The Publication of Collections of Spiritual Songs in the Context of Development of Spiritual Music of Evangelical Christians-Baptists of Russia], "When the Trumpet of the Lord" was originally written as "When The Roll Is Called Up Yonder."

115. Coleman, *Russian Baptists & Spiritual Revolution 1905–1929*, 98.

116. Coleman, "Baptist Beginnings in Russia and Ukraine," 31.

117. Milovidov, *Sovremennoe shtundobaptistskoe dvizhenie v Severo-Zapadnom krae*, 20. It should be noted that even though Milovidov's work was based on wide-ranging research, the author's conclusions indicate his strong interest in defending the Orthodox faith. Linkevich, "Novyye techeniya protestantizma v Belorussii vo II pol. XIX – nach. XX vv." [New Movements of Protestantism in Belarus in the Second Half of the 19th – Beginning of the 20th Centuries], 198.

addition," he continues, "Belarusians are noted for their extreme suspicion of people, especially if these are preachers of some new religious doctrine, which can be explained by painful historical circumstances."[118] Consequently, Milovidov concludes that Baptist beliefs and practices cannot be successful among Belarusians. His view is in unison with Ivan Sokolov's description of the situation in sixteenth and seventeenth century Russia. The latter argued that for the vast majority of Russians "Christianity focused almost exclusively on Byzantine rituals, complicated symbolism and magnificent religious rites. It is not surprising that all Protestant teaching beginning from doctrines to rituals seemed unclear, something strange and even deprived of religious character."[119]

Analysis of the influence of mindset within the historical perspective is complicated by the additional factor of persecution. Results might have been different if there had not been persecution and suppression against evangelical movements throughout the empire. Apostasy from the Orthodox faith was punished as a crime until 1905,[120] although members of other denominations and religions were permitted and encouraged to convert to Orthodoxy without restriction.[121] However, although under harsh conditions resulting from the exile and resettlement of believers, communities began to emerge in Siberia and Central Asia.[122] Therefore, an evaluation of many conversions to evangelical Christianity indicates that they included an expression of protest against the political and religious oppression of the former regime.[123]

Despite active opposition from the state, the State church, fellow-villagers, and even close relatives, conversions to evangelical Christianity were by no means prevented.[124] On the contrary, it contributed to the distinct expression

---

118. Milovidov, *Sovremennoe shtundobaptistskoe dvizhenie v Severo-Zapadnom krae*, 19–20.

119. Sokolov, *Otnoshenie protestantizma k Rossii v XVI i XVII vekakh* [The Relation of Protestantism to Russian in the 16–17th centuries], 42.

120. On 4 March 1905 the edict of toleration of Nicholas II was published as the "Decree on Toleration."

121. *Svod zakonov Rossiiskoi imperii* [Code of Laws of the Russian Empire], vol 14, part 1 (St. Petersburg, 1982), 424, 507.

122. *Istoriya evangel'skikh khristian-baptistov v SSSR*, 125–126.

123. Pavlov, "Doklad na 3-m Vsemirnom kongresse baptistov v Stockgolme, Shvetsiya, 26.07.1923" [Report on the 3rd World Congress of Baptists in Stockholm, Sweden, 26.07.1923," 219.

124. Such a situation is in no way comparable to the deliberate transfer of the Byzantine model of Christianity to the Russian territory many centuries ago. See Prokhorov, *Mezhdu*

of the indigenous culture in areas such as the minor key of many worship tunes. As Pavel Vasil'evich Pavlov, one of the leaders of the Baptist Union (and son of Vasiliy Gur'evich Pavlov[125]), claimed, an exotic plant from overseas would not have survived on Russian soil.[126] Instead, the Russian-Ukrainian-Belarusian evangelical community started with individual communities in the first fifty years of its existence (1867–1917), survived two periods of severe persecution (in the 1890s and in the 1920s and 1930s) both of which aimed at ending the evangelization of the Russian people, and actually grew by more than two hundred thousand members.

3.3.2. Western Christianity on Eastern Soil

Further growth of the evangelical movement in Belarus demonstrates the Baptists' flexibility in adapting forms and content in order to implement Baptist beliefs and practices within their own culture and in order to create distinct Belarusian/Russian churches. As has already been shown, the Evangelical movement grew on traditional Slavic Orthodox cultural soil. In fact, it is difficult to distinguish between culture, national character, and Orthodoxy, since religion determines cultural specifics and culture in turn adapts religion to its traditions. Perhaps the cultural type was a creation of the Orthodox world-view,[127] and the Orthodox faith can be considered a system-forming basis of Russian culture.[128] One cannot be definitive of either the strictly national or the foreign roots of Baptists in Belarus/Russia on the basis of rituals or doctrines. Dostoevsky once described this new phenomenon as "German Protestantism in an environment of Orthodoxy."[129] In 1919, S.V. Mel'gunov made the contestable claim that "Baptists are about

---

Zapadom i Vostokom: Zametki o nachale evangel'skogo dvizheniya v Rossii [Between East and West: Notes on Early Evangelical Movement in Russia], 55, 65.

125. For Vasiliy Gur'evich Pavlov, see footnote 227.

126. Pavlov, "Doklad na 3-m Vsemirnom kongresse baptistov v Stockgolme, Shvetsiya," 219.

127. Matyash, "Pravoslavie kak kul'turny phenomen" [Orthodoxy as a Cultural Phenomenon], 107.

128. Victor Vereshchagin, "O samobytnosti russkoi kul'tury v kontekste globalizatsii" [On the Uniqueness of Russian Culture in the Context of Globalization," 122.

129. Dostoevsky, *Dnevnik Pisatelya, 1873* [Writer's Diary, 1873], 69.

the same as Orthodox but in a slightly distorted form."[130] Along with others, Tatyana Nikol'skaya, a modern Russian scholar, uses the term "Russian Protestantism."[131]

Eastern, or 'Russian', Protestantism was enriched by elements of both Western and Eastern culture. It synthesized the rational and emotional, accepted Orthodox quietism and Protestant activity, and paid attention to worship and the evangelical emphasis on ethics. Thus, Russian-speaking evangelical Christians possess their own specifics. Mitrokhin asserts that this came about

> due to novelty and historical unexpectedness of the combinations, when familiar ideas, subjects, symbols and combinations were interrelated under different historical circumstances, gaining a different meaning . . . As a result of complicated system of ties an 'alien' culture is adopted according to the standards of the domestic one and the emerging hybrids gain viability of [a] self-developing organism.[132]

Evangelical leaders were evidently aware of the problem of adaptation. They wondered how a revival with English characteristics in St. Petersburg could become a Russian revival in the Russian environment. They wondered how a revival with English characteristics could become a Russian revival in the Russian environment, or how a German Baptist movement could become Russia.[133] Such questions addressed doctrinal and social issues in addition to patterns of worship. Prokhanov described the evangelical movement as

---

130. Mel'gunov, *Iz istorii religiozno-obshchestvennykh dvizhenii v Rossii XIX v.* [From the History of Religious and Social Movements in Russia in the XIX Century], 236.

131. Nikol'skaya, "Russian Protestantism at the Stage of Legalization: 1905–1917," 182.

132. Mitrokhin, *Baptizm: istoriya i sovremennost'*, 240, 191. Undoubtedly, not all forms and features of Baptists in Europe and the West could sprout in Belarusian soil. For example, Nikol'skaya notes that "after all, we have unrealized or underdeveloped features of Western Protestantism, such as Protestant business ethics (clearly expressed among Old Believers by the way), the cult of entrepreneurship, personal and professional success, the desire for social integration, and willingness and ability to influence society." ("Uroki istorii dlya EKhB" [History Lessons for ECB], 10.) Nevertheless, Nikol'skaya cites some examples from state archives which show how "sectarians" distinguished themselves from the majority of the Orthodox population in terms of productivity in business, trade, and crafts, because of their diligence in work, reliability, and rejection of smoking and drinking. Nikol'skaya, "Russkiy Protestantism na etape utverzhdeniya legalizacii (1905–1917)" [Russian Protestantism During the Approval of Legalization (1905–1917)], 176.

133. Kahle, *Evangel'skie Khristiane v Rossii i Sovetskom Soyuze*, 425.

a National reformist movement and argued that the evangelical church was equivalent to the restored early Christian church in its teaching.[134]

Just as Prokhanov addressed wider societal and cultural issues alongside the biblical and spiritual, Dzekuts-Maley's work encompassed a variety of aspects including cultural, linguistic, and educational issues. For example, he helped found the cultural society *Belaruskaya hatka*, and he translated the New Testament into the Belarusian language. Educationally, his fellow-workers not only taught about Christianity but also taught general subjects, and, in terms of social aspects, he organized shelters and nursing homes.[135] In this manner he wanted to introduce the gospel into people's everyday lives and promote the Baptist faith and practices which might become a "national" religion in Belarus.

The lower classes appeared to approve of this approach. Kahle notes that it was the masses, not the ruling circles, who defined the strategy. He stressed that "the construction was going and is going in a natural way from the bottom, from among the people, the same way as the church was built in the days of Christ and the Apostles."[136] Heather Coleman argues similarly that:

> as they sought to establish a network of congregations and develop music and liturgies to celebrate their faith, Russian evangelicals repeatedly confronted the problem of establishing a native Russian version of an imported Baptist faith.
>
> ... Russian evangelicals expressed pride in belonging to an international communion and tended to be quite candid about the part that non-Russians had played in the evolution of their church. They insisted, however, that this role was primarily catalytic.[137]

Thus, at the Fourth World Baptist Congress in 1928, a leader of the Baptist movement in Belarus reported that:

> from the outset, the ministry of Baptists in our country is in the hands of the local people of Russia. Baptist missionaries did

---

134. Mitskevich, *Istoriya evangel'skikh khristian-baptistov*, 214.

135. Akinchyts, "... Kab dlya nashaga naroda byla vydadzena Svyataya kniga" [... So that the Holy Book Would be Given to Our People], 14–16.

136. Kahle, *Evangel'skie khristiane v Rossii i Sovetskom Soyuze*, 487.

137. Coleman, "Baptist Beginnings in Russia and Ukraine," 31–32.

not minister in Russia. But throughout our history we have had persistently upheld the purity of Baptist principles in regard to ministry of visiting missionaries of other faiths from overseas.[138]

However, contextualization required time and effort. It took several decades before Eastern Slavic Protestantism learned to write indigenous hymns while, at the same time, the influence of Western singing literature diminished.[139] It is important to note that while evangelicals emphasized independence and originality, they did not reject experience and help from Western believers whose way of thinking about worship could become a model for many churches.[140] Yet, the process of adopting Western ideas was not always smooth, and it was accompanied by both failure and success. In this regard, it is interesting to note how the borrowing of Western hymns by Russian-speaking churches was assessed in different Slavic evangelical contexts. Princess Sophia Liven, an active member of the Evangelical Christian church, addressed the pattern of some educated representatives of the higher class in St. Petersburg translating hymns into Russian. She believed that "the new living church was in need of spiritual hymns . . . but as for the tunes – they were primitive in regard to music, and were somewhat alien to the Russian ear, as they were an exact repetition of the English ones."[141]

On the other hand, the initiator of the Russian Baptist work in Transcaucasia, Martin Kalweit (a German from Memel, East Prussia), explained that because both Russians and Germans were in the congregation, "we use both languages in our service and sing hymns from a Russian collection as well as from the Glaubenstimme. Some of the hymns are the same

---

138. "Doklad P.V. Ivanova-Klyshnikova", 298.

139. Kahle, *Evangel'skie khristiane Soyuze*, 425.

140. Yet, to be fair, there was always a demand for such development. Observations reveal that some new religious churches in Belarus, Russia, and the Ukraine that have been planted by, or in close cooperation with, Western and Korean missionaries in the late 20th – early 21st century are full of people who have grown up in a post-*perestroika* cosmopolitan environment in their formation period. These churches do not hesitate to imitate the order established by the founding missionary or replicate aspects of Western forms and content. Examples of the above would include such congregations as "Light of Christ," "New Earth," and "Light of Hope" in Minsk. The first of these was strongly influenced by Korean missionaries and the others by Western churches and missionaries.

141. Liven, *Dukhovnoe probuzhdenie v Rossii*, 16.

and suit the same tune, but the German are the favorites even with those who understand Russian best, as the words are simpler and the tunes more lively."[142]

In church planting practice such interactions often lead to conflicts. Coleman reports a typical example:

> Foreigners or Russian Germans had provided language and forms that systematized already existing ideas and aspirations. Nevertheless the memoirs and personal correspondence of early leaders reveal the practical and intellectual difficulties of reconciling borrowed structures with popular native aspirations. For example, the influential Baptist missionary and later pastor of Baku, Vasiliy Ivanov, described the tension between Russians and Germans over liturgical practices in his unpublished recollections of the early days of the Tiflis congregation. Although the faith was the same, he explained, "the nation and habits were different." "The Russian Baptists," he elaborated, "wanted to hold to many Molokan ways and performing bows during singing and prayers and so on." The Germans, by contrast, "wanted to toss out everything Russian and Molokan from the service and set up everything in the German manner."[143]

In 1913–1914, shortly before his death, Vasiliy Vasil'evich Ivanov, pastor of the church in Baku,[144] became the chief editor of *Baptist* magazine.[145] In his articles, which were critical of Western Christian culture, he opined that Russian Baptists were carried away by numerous translations of "foreign articles and light stories."[146] He also disapproved of the growing practice of singing by a church choir, while he nostalgically remembered the "common" (probably Molokan) singing by the entire congregation. He critically contrasted one against the other, comparing communal singing to, amongst other things, the first joyful sunbeams against a lifeless electric light.[147]

---

142. Randall, *Communities of Conviction*, 88.
143. Coleman, *Russian Baptists 1905–1929*, 96.
144. Sokolov, "V.V. Ivanov," 47–52.
145. Sokolov, 50.
146. Ivanov, "Obshchiny i presvitery" [Communities and Pastors], 8.
147. Ivanov, 21–22.

Baptist identity and the practice of worship continued to evolve during the Soviet period in mutual interaction with the evangelical faith patterns within the AUCECB.[148] Conflicts were natural consequences of the work of continuing contextualization, and they manifested themselves both in relation to the Western traditions as well as in disputes within the Eastern tradition. This tension remains in ECB churches even today, revealing itself in different perceptions of freedom and order in the service (does one need a preaching/sermon schedule, for example?), in the clash of analytical or rationalistic understandings and intuitive comprehension of the truth (should pastors prepare their sermons or is it sufficient to pray and trust the "provision" of the Spirit to guide their words?), as well as in a combination of sacramental and symbolic approaches to "religious rites" (different conceptions of what is happening at Eucharist).[149]

The issue of contextualization became fresh again after the fall of the Iron Curtain when Western forms and practices were reintroduced to Russian-speaking churches. The links between various Western churches and ECB churches in Belarus encountered similar tensions. Many Baptist believers would express their discomfort with new forms of praying, such as being seated rather than standing or kneeling as had been the custom, or in being asked to pray in small groups of people rather than as a whole congregation. Some believers are offended by humor in a sermon,[150] by laughter and applause in the house of prayer, and by the lack of respect shown to the Bible as a book.[151]

Thus, the analysis of the origin and formation of worship, of international relations, and of observations of its practice today, demonstrate how form,

---

148. Pilli, "Evangelical Christians-Baptists of Estonia: The Shaping of Identity, 1945–1991," p. 253.

149. Concerning tensions in worship see Ellis, "Gathering Struggles: Creative Tensions in Baptist Worship." Detailed discussion of this topic is the subject of Chapters 7 and 8.

150. Almost all popular books in homiletics that are available in Russian are Western translations, with humor and jokes perceived as a natural part of a sermon. Nevertheless, using humor can cause discomfort in a traditional church. To give a personal example, in my sermon in "Light of Gospel" church on 7 November 2012, I used a few funny illustrations. A brother from an unregistered Minsk church approached me afterwards and complained that these illustrations precluded him from grasping the sermon completely.

151. In the early 1990s, when guests from Western Europe and the USA flooded Belarusian churches, the local Christians were appalled by cases of the Bible being treated "improperly." For example, guests putting it on the floor, or casually holding an open Bible with one hand by its corner.

content, and the spirit of worship services in Belarusian ECB churches reveal both Western influence and local roots and how context has contributed to an original form of worship. The Evangelicals who spread in Belarus and throughout the Russian Empire quickly gained particular distinctives in comparison to their western European and North American counterparts. The historical, political, and socio-economic framework of Tsarist Russia and then of the Soviet Union and Poland, alongside ties to religious and Christian movements in Russia in the eighteenth and nineteenth centuries, have had a lasting impact, and thus help explain the uniqueness of the evangelical movement in Belarus and the Russian-speaking context as a whole. Yet, in addition to the historical roots and the clash of Western and Eastern traditions influencing the process of worship formation, other factors have also influenced the content and character of worship. These factors include theological foundations, the dominance of the Orthodox Church, and persecution and seclusion in Tsarist Russia and later in the Soviet period. It is to a careful examination of these particular apects that Chapter Four now turns.

CHAPTER 4

Context of Formation

4.1. Theological Grounds

4.1.1. Back to the Early Church[1]

The culture, spirit, and forms of Belarusian worship have been significantly impacted by the religious environment (namely Orthodox) and the socio-political context. However, other factor such as culture, spirit, and form have also been significant. This thesis contends that the logic of the development of Belarusian evangelical and Baptist worship cannot be properly understood without examination of a distinct theological motivation.[2] The essence of this particular theological-ideological basis can perhaps be encapsulated by the following claim: over time Christians have deviated from the pure teaching of the Gospel; a clear and simple doctrine of salvation gradually became buried under the load of traditions and rituals; the church now needs to get rid of later developments and return to its origins, to New Testament Christianity, and to building life and worship according to the gospel rather than tradition.

An author of one of the articles in *Bratskiy Vestnik* explains it thus:

> The evangelical Baptist movement which demands a return to original Christianity appeared in Western Europe in the sixteenth century. This movement cancelled the division of

---

1. By "the Early church" I mean the church as described in the New Testament, limited to the lifetime of the apostles.

2. On the importance of theological notions see Barnard, Cilliers, and Wepener, *Worship in the Network Culture. Liturgical Ritual Studies. Fields and Methods, Concepts and Metaphors*, 44–45.

Christians into priests and laymen, for all true Christians are priests of the Most High God, and pastoral ministry is only one of many ways to serve God. This movement rejected infant baptism because baptism is a promise of good conscience to God, and only a conscious person is able to give this kind of promise. The Evangelical-Baptist movement declared cancellation of all dubious oral church tradition which contradicts the Scripture, for our doctrine should be based on the Holy Scripture only. The Evangelical-Baptist movement declared that only spiritually regenerated people who gave their hearts to Christ were eligible to be members of a Christian congregation. This movement called for thorough study of Scripture, cancellation of pompous ritual, and worshiping only God, and Christ only.[3]

A particular characteristic of the movement was an emphasis on familiarity with the Bible. Reading Scriptures in plain language, or listening to preaching of the new faith, resulted in the first conversions in the late nineteenth and early twentieth centuries. Some seeker Belarusians began to desire to live and worship "according to the Scriptures." They noticed discrepancies between the teachings of Christ and the apostles, and they started to question various liturgical practices such as worshipping saints, worshipping icons, and baptizing infants, and, most importantly, they recognized their own immoral behavior such as drinking, stealing, fraud, and so on, they

The motif to return to the teachings and practices of the New Testament church is especially clear in songs and poems by Prokhanov, which were extremely popular among evangelicals in Belarus.

> We call the whole world
> To come to the light of early Christianity.
> May centuries-old additions
> Fall off and are destroyed in churches.
> May the Church of the New Days rise
> In the garments of a new revival.[4]

---

3. Belousov, "Gospod' sila moya i pesn'," 76

4. Prokhanov and Zhidkov, eds., *Pesni pervykh khristian* [The Songs of the First Christians], no. 6a, refrain and fourth stanza.

A title of another song by the same author repeats the collection title, "Songs of Early Christians." Prokhanov speaks about the life of the early church as an example for generations to come and asks the Lord to reproduce the church of early Christians.[5] Furthermore, in his poem entitled "Return!" he urges "Back to Christ and the covenant made at Calvary, Back to the earliest age of Christianity" and "Away from the worship of inanimate objects."[6] Other Russian-speaking preachers and theologians also argued that the evangelical brotherhood followed the "apostolic order" and "the path of Christians of the apostolic age."[7] The term "New Testament church" was adopted to describe this movement.[8]

Regarding ecclesiology, such restoration was primarily expressed in the denial of the division of believers into clergy and laity. As elucidated in *Bratskiy Vestnik*, Evangelical-Baptist communities restored the principle of the early Christian church where communities "were not divided into the clergy and parishioners."[9] To emphasize equality, the word "brotherhood"[10] was and still is used in the name of the association of churches. Regarding the clergy, in 1923 Pavel Pavlov, a prominent figure of the evangelical Baptist movement, emphasized that:

---

5. Prokhanov and Zhidkov, no. 3.

6. Prokhanov and Zhidkov, no. 4. Perhaps it is no coincidence that the next song in this collection is called "Forward to the Triumph!" so as not to create a one-sided view of evangelical Christianity. "Go on from the principles of the Doctrine of Christ, from the letters of deadening rituals! Go on to excellence in the knowledge of the Word and in the holiness of actions and views." (*Pesni pervykh khristian*, no. 5, second stanza.)

7. Somov, "Tserkov' Khrista i ee svyashchenstvo" [The Church of Christ and Its Priesthood], 53.

8. Karev, "Svyashchennodeistviya tserkvi" [Sacred Rites of the Church], 36. British Baptist theologian, Paul S. Fiddes, similarly points to the interpretation of Baptist identity by an American Baptist theologian, James Wm. McClendon, commenting that in McClendon's view "the Baptist vision to be nothing other than a shared awareness that the present Christian community *is* the early Christian community and *is* the eschatological community. Baptists understand themselves . . . as living *immediately in* the scriptural story and in the story of the day of judgment, and it is this that shapes their convictions and their ethics." (Fiddes, "Theology and a Baptist Way of Community," 26. McClendon, *Ethics*, 30.

9. Somov, "Tserkov' Khrista i ee svyashchenstvo," 62.

10. The word "brotherhood" is often used as a synonym of the term "union" (e.g. Belarusian brotherhood, or "Brotherhood of independent churches and missions in Ukraine" is the official name of the union) or for a group of churches in a certain territory ("Russian-speaking brotherhood") or that are related by certain characteristics ("evangelical brotherhood," "brotherhood of the Council of Churches"). Nowadays the term is used less and less, especially as the majority, sometimes absolute majority, of the congregation is often composed of women (see footnote 952).

Our movement is growing and expanding because the spirit of the apostolic Church is alive in us, and the lack of financial support is supplemented by enthusiasm. We have almost no professional preachers who receive regular salaries. Our workers, following the example of Apostle Paul, in most cases earn their bread with their own hands, and preach the gospel.[11]

Encouraging large numbers of male believers to get involved in preaching was one aspect of the development of the "brotherhood" idea.[12] A contem-

---

11. Pavlov, "Doklad na 3-m Vsemirnom kongresse baptistov v Stockgolme, Shvetsiya, 26.07.1923," 220. The absence of "professional" pastors and missionaries in Belarusian and other Eastern Slavic churches lasted almost to the end of the twentieth century when, primarily due to the support and influence of Western believers, "professional" missionaries and pastors appeared, being justified "on the basis of the Gospel" prescribing "not to muzzle the ox while he is treading" (1 Tim 5:18). However, the recent economic crisis, coupled with reduced financial support from Western churches at the turn of the twenty-first century, has again forced many servants to earn their bread with their own hands.

12. In the article "About Women's Ministry in Church" the editors of *Bratskiy Vestik* magazine, on the basis of 1 Cor 11:5, Phil 4:2–3, Acts 2:17 and 7:1–6, and Luke 2:38, state that women could minister by preaching the gospel alongside their involvement in charity, singing, and deaconry. (*Bratskiy Vestnik*, no. 3 (1945), 47–49; also no. 1 (1948), 7.) Such a tradition also existed among Pashkov's followers (Margaritov, *Istoriya russkih misticheskih i racionalisticheskih sekt*, 166). However, references to women preaching are very rare. In his section on "*Bratskiy Vestnik* on preaching" Cheprasov notes "that despite the previously noted 'official position' of the Baptist Union and the *BV* [*Bratskiy Vestnik*] on women in preaching, its subsequent publications always referred to preachers using the masculine pronoun 'he.' Similarly, female preachers never appeared on its pages as examples for others (unlike male preachers, such as Prokhanov, Kargel, and many others)." (Cheprasov, "Formative? Informative? Neither? Towards understanding of the practice of proclamation, the core element of Russian Baptist Worship," ch. 4.2.) The involvement of women in preaching activity after the war could be explained by the lack of brothers or their absence altogether. From the early 1990s up to the present, there has not been a single occasion on which I have encountered sisters preaching from the pulpit during regular Sunday worship during my church visits in Belarus, even though witnesses have confirmed that such cases occur. For example, according to Pavel Osenenko, in 1986 two sisters preached in Mogilev church on Saturday, March 8 (International Women's Day). The third, concluding, sermon was preached by a church pastor. (The testimony of Pavel Osenenko, Personal interview with author, 7 March 2017, Minsk [Personal notes, 53].)

Women are not ordained for pastoral ministry in Baptist churches in Belarus either (let us note that preaching and ordination are not directly linked. Both ordained and non-ordained brothers can preach in churches). The other denominations in Belarus stick to the same practice regarding women preaching and being ordained. This includes the Russian Orthodox Church, Roman Catholic, and Christians of Evangelical Faith (Pentecostal). Russian-speaking Baptist Unions of Russia, Ukraine, Moldova, and Central Asia do not ordain women either. Currently, only men have the right to preach with some rare exceptions. So far, the status quo has not raised significant issues or discussions in the church or society. Regarding the religious and social context of church ministry, no important changes can be foreseen in the near future.

porary historian of the evangelical Baptist movement in Russia puts it in the following way:

> [A] democratic approach to the ministry of the word, that could be traced back to the New Testament and inherited by evangelical Christian Baptists in Russia from their forefathers, brings an essential component of creative diversity into public worship, thus creating good atmosphere for the development of the ministry of the word and allowing the missionary spirit to take hold of all the congregation.[13]

On the grounds of overthrowing "ancient accretions," Baptists rejected anointing,[14] compulsory confession, making the sign of the cross, prescribed fasting, and infant baptism, following instead the model of Christ and also of the Ethopian eunuch by being baptised as believers.[15] Believers' baptism and adult membership were given particular attention. Martsinkovskiy, a Christian publisher, preacher, and the leader of the Russian movement of Christian students who was deported from the Soviet Union in 1923, insisted that new birth should precede baptism. "At that time the Orthodox Historic Church puts baptism first, and then revival, preaching baptism as the source of revival. The Free Church puts revival before baptism, seeing that this is required by the Word of God and that this is justified by real life."[16] Baptist minister Konstantin Somov in *Bratskiy Vestnik* later confirmed the commitment to this practice: "The communities adopted people who consciously believed in Christ and gave Him their hearts."[17]

The perception was that it was necessary for public worship to be primarily founded on New Testament principles which included components of early church worship. For example, Acts 2:42 indicates that the worship services

---

13. Popov, "Otechestvennaya shkola propovedi v tserkvakh evangel'skikh khristian-baptistov" [National School of preaching in Evangelical Christians-Baptists churches], 44.

14. In the Orthodox tradition, a priest anoints and crosses the human body with scented oil, the chrism, through which divine grace is transmitted and the Holy Ghost descends.

15. Matt 3:13–17; Acts 8:36–39. The theology of returning to apostolic origins plays an even more important role in the radical rejection of any practice which "does not follow Scripture." In fact, this negative aspect of the elimination of accumulated "layers" was at the forefront of the return to "the basics."

16. Martsinkovskiy, *Zapisky veruyuschego*, 191.

17. Somov, "Tserkov' Khrista i ee svyashchenstvo," p. 62.

of Christian communities in the apostolic age were composed of reading the word of God, instruction, and teaching; therefore, these should be a central part of our worship services.[18] Great attention is given to preaching, teaching, singing, and prayer with reference to Matthew 21:13, Acts 1:14, 2:42, 4:24–31, and 12:12, to 1 Corinthians 14:26, Ephesians 5:19, and Colossians 3:16. Former AUCECB Chairman Jacov Zhidkov described an ideal worship time:

> Under guidance of their beloved brother pastor some able brothers and sisters took part in sharing the Good News. They read the Holy Scripture, explained the passage and applied it to Christian life. Some others glorified the Lord with singing. And some offered up their petitions and praise to the Lord in brief and clear words. So it happened as the Apostle Paul teaches in his Epistle to Colossians 3:16: "Let the word of Christ richly dwell within you, with all wisdom teaching and admonishing one another with psalms and hymns and spiritual songs, singing with thankfulness in your hearts to God."[19]

Some scenes from the life of Christ have also become models to be imitated. An example of this would be the current practice in some, especially smaller churches, of greeting at the entrance to the hall where those entering after silent prayer welcome others with the words "Peace be with you." The response is: "With peace." This practice is based on the text: "On the evening of that first day of the week, when the disciples were together, with the doors locked for fear of the Jewish leaders, Jesus came and stood among them and said, "Peace be with you!"[20]

It should be noted that the perceived close spiritual connection to the "New Testament church" is not to the exclusion of the Old Testament, and this is also reflected in the worship. For example, choir members in Belarus are often called Levites, referring to temple worship in Israel. The orchestras and musical groups "solemnly and reverently praise the Savior, worthy

---

18. Motorin, "O bogosluzhenii v dni apostolov i v nashi dni" [On Worship in the Days of the Apostles and Today], 8. Q, 2008. This perception was confirmed via the questionnaires and was specifically addressed in questions A3 and A4.

19. "Vzglyad nazad" [A Look Back], *Bratskiy Vestnik*, no. 1 (1948): 5–11, 7.

20. John 20:19. In this regard, it is interesting to note that the use of the Lord's Prayer caused a split of opinion at the early stage of the evangelical movement in Russian-speaking communities. See Shipkov, "Molitva Gospodnya" [The Lord's Prayer], 4–5.

of continuing the traditions of their predecessors, the Levites of the Old Testament."[21]

Early Russian-speaking Baptists also used the Old Testament, specifically the Psalms, to justify the introduction of musical instruments into worship services (in contrast to the Orthodox practice):

> You know that I was raised in a Molokan family and all my ancestors strictly adhered to Molokan practices, said Vasily Gurievich [Pavlov]. "We always sang psalms without musical accompaniment. I do not, however, find any ban on music in the Bible. Let us recall the psalmist David, who praised the Lord not only with his lips but with musical instruments. 'Praise Him with the sound of the trumpet, praise Him with the psaltery and harp, praise Him with strings and organ,' the singer of Israel called to the faithful. Why should we forbid worshipping our Creator and Savior on musical instruments?"[22]

Other features of a traditional service indicate further references to Old Testament practice. Among these would be the significance of the celebration of harvest.[23] Furthermore, men and women sit separately from each other in many churches imitating the model of the temple and synagogues. A house of prayer is sometimes called a "temple," and consecration of the houses of prayer follow the example of Solomon's dedication of the temple (see 5.4.1. below). The Old Testament idea of holiness in the place where God dwells is applied to the house of prayer: a reverend attitude, and appropriate behavior in the house and in its territory are required, as well as special solemnity and reverence in worship.[24]

---

21. Volchanskiy, "O sluzhenii orkestrov" [On the Orchestra Ministry], 55. A minister may pray "for the blessing of the Levitical ministry," and a choir director may ask, "Lord, bless us, the Levites" (12 October 2008). It is interesting that a regular youth music festival of the Baptist Union in Russia is called the Levites (Union of Evangelical Christians-Baptists of Russia, official website, http://baptist.org.ru/read/article/96272, last accessed 2nd March 2017).

22. Popov, *Stopy Blagovestnika*, 250.

23. See footnote 118 on page 159.

24. QM, 2012.

4.1.2. Unattainable Ideal

These examples illustrate the role of the theology of returning to the origins. However, the New Testament, and even more so the Bible as a whole, does not offer a single example of the worship service. In fact, the New Testament demonstrates that the worship service is subject to a specific logic of development, as can be seen by comparing the description of the service in Acts with those in the Epistles of Paul.[25] Indeed, the sheer variety of approaches to worship in the evangelical environment indicates that automatic transfer is not possible: it will inevitably be context-dependent. That is why Karl Barth defined such attempts as "ecclesiastical romanticism."[26] Or as well-known liturgist, Robert Taft, puts it:

> For Christians, the only "ideal period of liturgy" is the one they are living in. A nostalgic vision of Christian tradition was a basic error of the Protestant Reformation, the notion that there was some ideal evangelical past to which one could return. Some lovers of Eastern liturgy make the same mistake, playing the same "pick a century" game. The only difference is that they pick the classic patristic age of late antiquity, whereas the Protestant Reformers opted for apostolic times. But Paul tells us in Second Corinthians 6:2, "Behold, now is the acceptable time . . . now is the day of salvation."[27]

The lack of detailed information about early church worship, coupled with the understanding that there have been a variety of forms, and paying heed to the danger of legalism in conducting worship services, ought to make one exercise restraint in claiming to adopt New Testament church practice and in identifying present forms as apostolic ones. This note of caution is indeed echoed by a number of authoritative ministers in the Russian-speaking fellowship, including some of the shapers of the tradition, who have warned against simplistic arrangements and legalism in the practice of worship. Ivan Gnida, a prominent minister of AUCECB, states: "We do not find an unambiguous description of worship service order or church statutes in the New

---

25. Mikhovich, "Pokloneniye i bogosluzheniye" [Worship and Public Worship], 177–178.
26. Barth, *Church Dogmatics*, *IV/1*, trans. G.W. Bromiley, "The Doctrine of Reconciliation," 704.
27. Robert Taft, S.J., "'Eastern Presuppositions' and Western Liturgical Renewal."

Testament."[28] Consequently, as long as a worship service contains sermons, singing, and prayer,[29] any kind of order could be adopted by the church if everything is "done properly and in an orderly manner,"[30] and if it generally corresponds to the New Testament spirit.

As for the Old Testament, the references are contradictory. On the one hand, the Old Testament is used as the basis for the employment of musical instruments since it encourages worshipping the Lord "with stringed instruments and pipe."[31] Yet, on the other hand, traditional worshippers are usually apprehensive about "loud cymbals", as found in the next verse, and even more so about "timbrel and dancing."[32] David's psalms are used in congregational singing on very rare occasions. No importance is attached to the fact that in Old Testament times only the Levite men ministered as musicians. In this respect, Russian-speaking Baptist churches provide an example of the significant hermeneutical problem of the Old Testament's relevance in the life of the "New Testament church."

In seeking to go back to Christian origins, churches operate within a simple standard for worship evaluation. On the one hand, they cling to an anchor, which remains firm and stable regardless of the present frightening diversity. They hold a compass in their hands that guides their way. So, in each particular context, a new "New Testament church" is born. On the other hand, paying exclusive attention to "the biblical basis" leads to neglect of the history of public worship (assuming that nothing good occurred between the early Christians and today's church), and often precludes evangelical believers from examining and learning from almost two thousand years of church history and valuable church traditions. Traditional churches limit themselves, especially in music, to a period of about the last one hundred fifty years (which is nevertheless considerably larger than the churches promoting modern worship styles). Thus, they deprive themselves of the treasures of centuries

---

28. Gnida, "Poryadok provedeniya bogosluzhenii v tserkvakh evangel'skikh khristian-baptistov" [The Order of Worship in the Churches of Evangelical Christians-Baptists], 71.

29. Karev designates these components "sacred rites" ("Svyashchennodeistviya tserkvi," 36).

30. 1 Cor 14:40.

31. Psalm 150:4b.

32. Psalm 150:4a.

of church worship, and it is another reason to be reluctant about concentrating on either the Old or the New Testament as the basis for public worship.

4.2. Religious Context

4.2.1. Leaving Orthodoxy

The religious – and particularly Orthodox = context has played an important role in the formation of worship.[33] This section examines early relations between the evangelical movement and the Russian Orthodox Church and Orthodox services. It demonstrates that negative attitudes toward Orthodox services influenced the formation of evangelical worship in large measure, but at the same time some features of Orthodox worship were retained.

Liturgy has a dominant role in Orthodox worship. Fundamentally, Orthodoxy is a church performing liturgy.[34] When an Anglican minister asked Patriarch Aleksiy of Moscow to describe the Orthodox Church in a sentence, he was famously told, "It is the church which celebrates the Divine Liturgy."[35] Considering the fact that almost all pioneers of the evangelical movement in Belarus came out of an Orthodox environment, it is noteworthy that the Baptists rejected that familiar, rich form, and preferred to adopt a simple fellowship, consisting of unsophisticated Bible interpretation, simple-hearted prayers, and common non-professional singing.[36] How could

---

33. The Roman Catholic church is the second largest denomination in Belarus. According to the official website of the Roman Catholic Church in Belarus there are 1, 402. 605 Catholics in Belarus (around 15% of the population) (http://www.catholic.by/2/belarus/dioceses.html., last accessed 16 May 2019.) However, it has not had such an important role in shaping Baptist identity as the Orthodox Church. First of all, this relates to the fact that the Orthodox Church was dominant during the early stages of the evangelical movement. At the same time, in western Belarus, which happened to be under the dominion of Poland from 1921 to 1939, the Roman Catholic church enjoyed a privileged position, which led to the percentage of Catholics growing from 42.7% in 1921 to 48% in 1931. (Vabishchevich, "Zachodniaja Bielarus pad uladaj Pol'shchy. Dukhounaje zhytsia va umovakh palanizatsyi" [Belarus Under the Rule of Poland. Spiritual Life in Polanization], 438–441.)

34. Stamulis, ed., *Pravoslavnoye bogolovie missii segodnya* [Orthodox Mission Theology Today], 253.

35. Hilborn, "[An] Evangelical Perspective on Orthodox Liturgy. The Place of Liturgy in Orthodoxy and Evangelism," 64.

36. Archive records allow us to come to the conclusion that a number of Baptist communities appeared due exclusively to conversions of the Orthodox population, e.g., in western Belarus in the 1920s and 1930s (Vdovichenko, *Kritika ideologii sovremennogo baptizma (po materialam Belorusskoy SSR). Avtoreferat dissertatsii na soiskanie uchenoi stepeni kandidata philosophskikh nauk* [The Critique of Modern Baptist Ideology (according to the records

a Belarusian with high regard for ritual and liturgy go along a path of such a reduction of religious tradition? How could they turn to an "alien faith" if, in Dostoevsky's words, "everything he is looking for [is] in Orthodoxy?"[37]

To answer this question, an Orthodox scholar has suggested that:

> the Belarusian nature includes a trait which is instrumental in being attracted to Baptist doctrine . . . For him (the Belarusian), as a practical man, it seems very attractive and tempting to get that easy salvation which Baptists preach because it requires neither to keep a priest, nor to build temples, nor to buy candles and communion bread. It is necessary only to believe, and good people, the leaders of the community will teach you for nothing how to believe.[38]

If a peasant could not pay for baptisms, weddings, funerals, sprinkling cattle and crops, and other services in the church, or if he had to arrange a feast for christenings, weddings, and church festivals, then financial interest might be one of the reasons for rejecting Orthodoxy, but it seems unlikely that this was a significant consideration; one might just as easily save money by rejecting alcohol.[39] Moreover, by becoming Baptist, they accepted strict ethical standards which were backed by church discipline, and were at risk of persecution which often included serious material losses.[40]

---

of the Belarussian SSR), 5). The situation would be similar in other parts of Belarus in the early period, although there were variations over time. For example, the archive of a church in Lesovnia, Minsk region indicates that nine people were accepted into the community in 1979 and that they all came from Orthodox homes. In 1983 there were ten more and they all had Orthodox backgrounds (Archive, Church ECB in Lesovnia, Minsk region). A report by a Representative of the Council for Religious Affairs under the Council of Ministers of BSSR, dated 15 January 1986, states that 62% of the people who joined Baptists, Pentecostals, and Seventh day Adventists by water baptism came from believers' homes, 31.4% from Orthodox homes, 6.0% from non-Christian homes and other religions, and only 0.6% came from Roman Catholic homes between 1965 and 1985.

37. Dostoevsky, *Dnevnik Pisatelya*, vol. 12, 70.

38. Milovidov, *Sovremennoe shtundo-baptistskoe dvizhenie v Severo-Zapadnom krae*, 20.

39. Shtundists and Baptists took a strong stance against drunkenness. In 1912 an Orthodox priest in Tver' A. Vvedenskiy wrote in his article, "Village people are hungry in the Orthodox church and they get rich if they belong to Shtundists. Why is that? It is because they used to drink and when they join the sect, they stop drinking." ("P'yanstvo i sektantstvo (k nashey polemike s sektantami)" [Drunkenness and Sectarianism (about our polemic with sectarians)], 697.)

40. There were, however, some benefits that promoted Baptist faith across the land. For example, the priests of Mogilev Orthodox eparchy believed that a considerable growth in

In fact, an argument could be made that many God-seekers among the Orthodox were hungry and thirsty for righteousness,[41] and that "the Orthodox Church was failing to meet many of the religious needs of the population."[42] Historians who have assessed the situation also point to the declining numbers of Orthodox churches and clergy in proportion to the increasing population. "For every Orthodox inhabitant of the empire at the end of the nineteenth century, there were half as many churches, two and a half times fewer monks, and almost a sixth as many monasteries than half a century before."[43] Some researchers believe that by 1918, only one person out of a hundred was an active and conscious believer in Russian society.[44]

However, from an evangelical point of view, the primary problem was the Orthodox liturgy itself. The nature of the celebration of the liturgy was one question but, more importantly, the liturgy was not associated with ethical teaching. A large number of complex, prescribed rituals expressed in an ancient language were essential to formal participation in the liturgy. As noted by the Romanian Orthodox theologian Ion Bria, "if the language and vocabulary make the text impossible to understand, the people are bound to ignore it. This inevitably breaks any connection between the liturgy and the

---

the number of "sectarians" was due to the high level of charity or mutual assistance in Baptist churches. The priests proved the point by citing the common beliefs of Orthodox village people, "Whatever you may say, . . . that guy got a horse, . . . a house was built for that man . . . and new clothes were made for those children . . . they helped to sow a field for that man . . . They do it for each other . . . And here we are: nobody will stretch a hand for you to pull you out of water if you drown . . . You could starve to death and nobody cares . . . as if I am not a Christian . . . well, it seems that they have the truth." ("Polozheniye sektantstva v predelakh Mogilevskoy yeparkhii i mery dlya bor'by s nim," 298.)

41. It is interesting to read about spiritual movements in the Russian Empire which did not conform to the State, including the Strigolniks, the Khlysty, the Baptists, and others. See Serge Bolshakoff, *Russian Nonconformity*.

42. Wardin, "How Indigenous was the Baptist Movement in the Russian Empire," 32.

43. Kantor, "Impersky kontekst russkogo pravoslaviya" [The Imperial Context of Russian Orthodoxy], 54. Data from P.N. Milyukov, *Ocherki po istorii russkoi kul'tury* [Essays on the History of Russian Culture], Collection in 3 vols., vol. 2, 198.

44. A.B. Zubov, "Sorok dney ili sorok let?" [Forty days or forty years?] *New World*, no. 5 (1999); Kantor, "Impersky kontekst russkogo pravoslaviya," 55.

liturgy after the liturgy."⁴⁵ "The necessary balance between the content of the faith and its external religious demonstration" is not preserved.⁴⁶

Another argument was the claim that pagan ideas were present in Orthodox life and ceremonies. Georgiy Florovskiy, an Orthodox thinker, theologian, and historian, wrote about a "second culture," a kind of syncretism, "in which local pagan 'experiences' were fused with stray motifs of ancient mythology and Christian imagination."⁴⁷ In everyday life, "koliady," an ancient pagan festival related to the winter solstice was mixed up with the celebration of Christmas. Simple Orthodox people who diligently attended the church could believe "in a bogeyman, and also wood and water goblins."⁴⁸ Such superstitious everyday phenomena, albeit at the level of folklore and not at the level of official Orthodox theology, provided many reasons for the criticism of Orthodoxy by evangelical Christians. Large-scale conversions into Shtundism and Baptist expressions of faith in the early years of the movement attracted the attention of the authorities who considered the relationship to Orthodoxy as an expression of loyalty to the State itself.⁴⁹ It must be taken into account that the Orthodox Church in the Russian Empire was identified with nationality, and that the majority of Belarusians, as well as Russians and Ukrainians, were considered to be Orthodox by birth. At the end of the nineteenth century, "unauthorized conversion from Orthodoxy to any other denomination" had been declared "a forbidden and even criminal act."⁵⁰

---

45. Bria, *The Liturgy after the Liturgy*, 23. The author uses the expression "The liturgy after the liturgy" in order to demonstrate the relationship between worship and engagement in the life of the society.

46. Borisov, *Pobelevshie nivy. Razmyshleniya o Russkoi Pravoslavnoi Tserkvi* [Whitened Fields. Reflections on the Russian Orthodox Church], 100. This problem characterizes not only the past but also modern times. Thus, a contemporary scholar of religion in the south of Belarus believes that the current situation is deteriorating and that Orthodoxy is increasingly evolving towards belief in the rites. (Predko, *Dinamika sinkreticheskoi religioznosti zhitelei byelorusskogo Poles'ya*. Avtoreferat dissertatsii na soiskanie uchenoi stepeni kandidata philosophskikh nauk [Dynamics of Syncretic Religiosity of Belarusian Polesie residents. Abstract of Dissertation for the Degree of Candidate of Philosophical Sciences], 3.)

47. Florovskiy, *Puti russkogo bogosloviya* [Ways of Russian Theology], 3. Also, Fairbairn, *Eastern Orthodoxy through Western Eyes*, 132.

48. See Nikol'skaya, *Russkiy Protestantism i gosudarstvennaya vlast' v 1905–1991 godakh* [Russian Protestantism and the Government in 1905–1991], 37.

49. Milovidov, *Sovremennoe shtundo-baptistskoe dvizhenie v Severo-Zapadnom krae*, 28.

50. Decision of the Government no. 10, Sept. 1891. In Milovidov, *Sovremennoe shtundo-baptistskoe dvizhenie v Severo-Zapadnom krae*, 29–30.

Laws gave local administrative and police authorities opportunities to appoint "a competent official for attending ['sectarian'] worship and prayer services," who should oversee that

> a) another meeting would not take place as an excuse of being a worship or prayer service, and b) there would not be any desecration or defamation of dogmas, rituals and traditions of the Orthodox Church, nor any profanities in regard to it or its faith objects; and there must not be any invitation toward apostasy from the Orthodoxy.[51]

A Circular of the Department of Religious Affairs, Ministry of Internal Affairs, directed to the Office of the Minsk governor, explained that meetings of sectarians "allowed not only for public vilification of the teachings of the Orthodox Church and its institutions, and an open call for the rejection of Orthodoxy, but also blasphemy."[52] According to the Circular,

> signs of Baptist crimes . . . presented the following elements of their worship: a) general singing of specially selected Bible verses and hymns from the liturgical books of the sect, such as "Voices of Faith," "Spiritual Poems," "Offerings of Christians," and others, and b) reading selected portions of Scripture by any member of the congregation, or preaching and interpreting false doctrine in the spirit of the sect, and c) kneeling prayers or the utterance of improvised, inspirational prayers, without the use of the sign of the cross.[53]

It is important to note that the opposition to evangelical groupings was a gradual development. Many Shtundists were initially slow to officially withdraw from the Orthodox Church and to organize their own communities. They often continued to attend Orthodox services while, at the same time,

---

51. *Baptist*, no. 6 (March, 1909), 21. See also Cirkulyar MVD, Departament dukhovnyh del – Gubernatoram, Nachal'nikam oblastei, Gradonachal'nikam ot 4 oktyabrya 1910 g. [MIF Circular letter, Department of Spiritual Affairs to the Governors, Oblast leaders and City leaders, written on October 4, 1910], NHAB, Stock 295. – File 1, Case 8462, 9. These decisions were seldom carried out in practice (Milovidov, *Sovremennoe shtundo-baptistskoe dvizhenie v Severo-Zapadnom krae*, 29).

52. NHAB, Stock 295, File 1, Case 8462, 6. It is possible to interpret what is meant by "blasphemy" in the light of this circular of the Minister of Justice, April 3, 1900 no. 10677.

53. Bonch-Bruevich, *Iz mira sektantov* [From the World of Sectarians], 175.

gathering separately to study the Bible.⁵⁴ Even though some peasants in Belarus had embraced evangelical faith, "yet [they] did not dare to openly declare the final break with Orthodoxy."⁵⁵ On 24 August 1878 government officials took the following report from the Dubovy Log Baptists in Gomel district: "Although we never avoided the holy sacraments and rites of the Orthodox Church, and as peasants at first considered such ceremonies as external and not essential, in the future we will remain her faithful sons forever, sacredly and steadily preserving all of its decisions to the end of our life." However, a year later they announced a decisive break from the Orthodox Church, declaring: "We are of the evangelical faith and we belong to the new Russian Christian fellowship." These peasants, it was reported, "publicly [expressed] contempt for icons, [called] the church a whore, and [criticized] fasting."⁵⁶

Several reasons contributed to a formal separation from Orthodoxy. First, frequent attacks from government officials, Church authorities, and the "Orthodox folk" pressed Evangelicals, often against their own will, to the other side. Even those who did not actively oppose the dominant religion were accused of being "enemies of the people" through hostile actions on the part of the Orthodox Church hierarchy and secular authorities because the "evangelical form of life represented a theological and political threat to Orthodoxy."⁵⁷ Thus, they had to choose whether to remain within Orthodoxy or to claim allegiance to the Gospel as they understood it.⁵⁸ Second, the hoped-for changes in Orthodox churches had not occurred, and, realizing the futility of their efforts to revitalize Orthodoxy, a number of evangelicals decided to concentrate on developing their own churches.⁵⁹ Third, awareness

---

54. Hebly, *Protestants in Russia*, 50.

55. See Coleman, *Russian Baptists & Spiritual Revolution 1905–1929*, 16; *Istoriya Evangel'skikh khristian-baptistov v SSSR*, 59; Rozhdestvensky, *Yuzhnorussky Shtundism*, 98.

56. CSHA, Stock 1284, File 220, Case 12, 14, 21b. Report of Mogilev Governor to Minister of Interior Affairs, in Lensu and Prokshina, *Baptizm i Baptisty*, 16.

57. Puzynin, *Tradiciya evangel'skikh khristian*, 84.

58. Cherenkov, *Evropeis'ka rephormaciya ta ukrain'sky evangel'sky Protestantism*, 16.

59. Some attempts were made by Evangelical Christians and Baptists who hoped for the reformation of Orthodoxy in the evangelical spirit and were attempting to join efforts for the spiritual and moral renewal of the Church and people. For example, Prokhanov in 1922 addressed the Orthodox with a plea to start a reformation in the spirit of the Gospel of Jesus Christ, publishing 100,000 copies of "Evangelsky klitch." (Mitskevich, *Istoriya Evangel'skikh khristian-baptistov*, 214.) Prokhanov sought contact with such "dissenters" ("renovators") as

of their particular identity eventually led to separation. The Pashkovtsy, for example, did not plan to leave the church, but, as Geoffry Ellis and Wesley Jones say, "the trappings of Orthodoxy such as the worship of the Virgin Mary, prayers to saints and prayers for the dead, devotion to icons and relics, and the doctrine of salvation by good works were becoming less and less acceptable with increasing knowledge of the Bible."[60] Such separation in any case became inevitable because the history, theology, and liturgical practice of these new communities and the Orthodox church differed too much for it to be possible to work together in the spiritual revival of the people.[61]

4.2.2. The Shaping of Worship in Opposition to the Orthodoxy
Radical simplification of liturgy, and the rejection of rituals, was indeed a reaction against Orthodoxy rather than a simple import from the West. One can speak of "resistant"[62] or "negative identity,"[63] of evangelical believers, or "anti-Orthodox doctrinal orientation of doctrinal and religious principles of those structures" in early and modern forms of Belarusian Protestantism.[64]

"Living Church," "Ancient Apostolic Church," and "Church renewal" (Shenderovsky, *Ivan Prokhanov*, 128–129). There were also several cases of Baptist and Evangelical Christians being invited to preach in Orthodox churches (Martsinkovskiy, *Zapisky veruyuschego*, 195).

60. Ellis and Jones, *Drugaya revolyutsiya*, 125.

61. An observation of the present situation shows that the romantic idea of the possible cooperation of Evangelicals and the Orthodox is as in the past, alive only within a few members who keep contact with Orthodoxy at the level of a conference or educational programs. Ordinary believers, familiar with local Orthodoxy, do not generally see opportunities for collaboration. On differences in the doctrine and practice of the Evangelical Christians-Baptists and the Orthodox from a Baptist viewpoint, see for example, Trubchik, *Vera i traditsiya* [Faith and Tradition]. Trubchik, a Belarussian author, editor of *Krynitsa Zhyttsya* magazine and Baptist church minister, contrasts Orthodox and evangelical teachings against each other as "outward and lifeless forms" and "the essence of Christ's teaching" (290).

62. Barnard, Cilliers, and Wepener, *Worship in the Network Culture. Liturgical Ritual Studies. Fields and Methods, Concepts and Metaphors*, 90.

63. Cf. Pilli, "Evangelical Christians-Baptists of Estonia: The Shaping of Identity, 1945–1991," 139.

64. Rekuts, *Protestantism i khudozhestvennaya kul'tura Belarusi* [Protestantism and Artistic Culture of Belarus], 3.

In this regard, the comprehensive doctrinal statement of the Pentecostal church in Belarus seems instructive. They carry out their ministry in the same Orthodox and partly Catholic context. While they defined their doctrinal stand, generally matching the Nicene Creed, they also included a chapter into their doctrinal statement on Confessional features of the Pentecostal Church. Except for the first point, the entire chapter is based on negations, such as "we do not believe . . ." or "we do not practice . . ." Among the aspects negated are relics, special priestly robes, the sign of the cross, icons and statues, infant baptism, and prayers to the saints and the Virgin (capitalized in the original) Mary. See *Verouchenie Ob'edinionnoi tserkvi khristian very evangel'skoi v Respublice Belarus'*, izd. 2 [Doctrine of Faith of the United Church of Christian of Evangelical Faith in Republic of Belarus, sec. ed.], 19–21. It is interesting to note, that in new

From the evangelical point of view, the magnificence of liturgy, enigmatic beauty of Church Slavonic language, gorgeous decorations, and luxurious priestly garments became obstacles to knowing God; aesthetic or mystical experience replaced a truly spiritual relationship with the Heavenly Father. Thus one of the first evangelical Christians in St. Petersburg, describing the situation in the Orthodox Church at the end of the nineteenth century, noted the pomp and luxury of the worship and complained that "instead of making [the Gospel] easier for a person to understand great truths of God, [the rites and priestly garments] made it even harder."[65] Prokhanov, analyzing the situation in Russia at the turn of nineteenth and twentieth centuries, made similar criticisms:

> The [Orthodox] church appeared to be flourishing. There were luxurious temples with golden domes. Worship service was held in the midst of splendorous golden glitter, silver, precious stones and decorations, and expensive priestly garments. Externally it all looked admirable, but what was the internal condition of the hearts? The service consisted mostly of ritual liturgy and there was almost no room for edification and sermon. The people did not know the Word of God.[66]

As a reaction, evangelical Christians firmly rejected the liturgical practices of the Orthodox Church, as well as other liturgical and doctrinal expressions of the Orthodox faith. An accusation against evangelical peasants in Dubovy Log village in Gomel district are a typical example: "Ivan Ivanov, Alexander Andreev, Zakhar Grigoriev, Semion Fedorov and their families stopped performing Orthodox rites, do not come to church, do not keep the fast, and do not honor saints . . . these peasants try to spread the above-mentioned doctrine in their village."[67]

Special attention should be given to the rejection of icons and their use as objects of worship, along with the removal of the breast cross, which became

---

churches professing modern styles of worship, worship is formed in opposition to traditional Baptist worship, rather than to Orthodox liturgy. For a residents of large cities, Orthodoxy no longer plays such a significant role as before.

65. Liven, *Dukhovnoe probuzhdenie v Rossii*, 21.

66. Prokhanov, *V kotle Rossii*, 20.

67. CSHA, Stock 1284, File 220, Case 12, 1, 1b. Report of Mogilev Governor to Minister of Interior Affairs, in Lensu and Prokshina, *Baptism i Baptisty*, 17

a distinctive characteristic of new converts, and which remains one of the key issues dividing the Eastern Slavic Baptists and the Orthodox. Thus, in the 1920s, Orthodox priests were known to order people not to associate with "apostates who reject the Lord's cross and holy icons."[68] According to some accusations, "sectarians" dared to take down icons and to be disrespectful to them. Sometimes icons were thrown out or even destroyed.[69] An example of an iconoclastic conflict took place at the beginning of the twentieth century in the Slutsk district, Minsk province where peasant Karl Korshunov declared: "'We do not have to worship the cross, or icons, because these are only the portraits.' [Korshunov's] brothers who saw that he was not even at confession, did not like such apostasy . . . and beat him the other day."[70]

A mid-twentieth century anti-Orthodox poem expresses the perspective of Baptists in Belarus towards icons:

> My God is no icon with smouldering incense,
> Old women in churches can worship such gods.
> For God is no image, so still, unconvincing,
> Unable to wake people's hearts.
>   This image can hear no cries of the hopeless
> Because it was painted by hand
>   I see someone leaning on it, weak and forceless,
> In hope that their struggles will end.
> But this is an image, so still and unmoving,
> It hears no entreaties or prayers of men
> You leave unallayed and with no consolation
> And plunge into worries again.[71]

---

68. Akinchyts, "120-letie Dzekuts-Maleya," 14.

69. On examples of extreme disregard of icons, especially among Shtundists, see S. Margaritov, *Istoriya russkih misticheskih i racionalisticheskih sekt* [History of Russian Mystic and Rationalistic Sects], 4th ed., corrected and supplemented (Simpheropol': Tavrich. gub. tip., 1914), 183; Kahle, *Evangel'skie khristiane v Rossii i Sovetskom Soyuze*, 526; Rozhdestvensky, *Yuzhnorussky Shtundism*, 186.

70. The Case of Conversions of Karl Korshunov's Recalcitrant Peasants from the Orthodox Church into Shtundism (Rachkan village, Slutsk uyezd). The protocol was composed by a police officer in Slutsk. (National Historical Archive of Belarus (NHAB), Stock 136, File 1, Case 37077, l-2.

71. The poem "Moi Bog" (My God), *Stikhotvoreniya, declamatsii, istorii*, first – third verses. Songs and poems in chapters 3–5 are put into poetry in English by Oksana Ostapovich.

The negative attitude of Baptists towards icons became a kind of trademark. It radically transformed both the worship space and its meaning. At the same time, the denial of priesthood was of no less importance. A clear-cut division between the priesthood and the laity in the Orthodox tradition yielded to the priesthood of all Christians in the evangelical communities, which meant that all Christians were expected to take part in the worship service. This requirement was met in the attention to common singing, the usage of musical instruments, and such elements as testimonies, recitations, and participation in prayer of all those who would volunteer.

Assuming that the Orthodox liturgy left no room for instruction, evangelicals put forward the preaching of the Gospel rather than liturgy ("plenty of instruction by the Word of God") which meant a radical shift to a verbal mode of communication. Regarding this, the meetings of the first Christians were again taken as an example: "Christians gathered in the true sense of the word around the Word of God."[72] Special attention was paid to instruction which helped apply truth in life and associate worship with behavior. Interestingly, however, at the same time Baptists continued to use the Synodal translation, itself richly endowed with Orthodox vocabulary.[73]

Rituals, which were seen as obstacles to the knowledge of God, gave way to "personal" communication with God – an opportunity afforded by extempore prayer as opposed to the prescribed Orthodox prayers. Baptists emphasized prayer as a simple, sincere conversation with God from the heart. This practice remains a distinctive feature of evangelical churches.

The changes conditioned by negative attitudes to Orthodox forms were truly dramatic. It was not a reformation or modification of a cult, but a radically different kind of worship. If initially there had been some attempts to achieve compromise, the evangelical Christians later came to the conviction that "returning to the New Testament church" required a complete break; correction and modernization seemed inappropriate.

---

72. Somov, "O propovedi I propovednikakh" [About Preaching and Preachers], 33.

73. There are a lot of words adapted from the Orthodox lexicon in the Synodal translation, for example, "iyerey" (high priest, Hag 2:4), "ipostas'" (exact representation, Heb 1:3), "kadilo" (censer, Ezek 8:11), "kivot" (ark, 1 Kings 14:18), "ladan" (frankincense, Matt 2:11), "lampada" (lamp, Exod 25:37), "milot'" (mantle, 1 Kings 19:13), "podir" (robe extending down to one's feet, Rev 1:13), "poprazdnestvo" (solemn assembly, Neh 8:18), "prepodobnyy" (godly ones, 2 Chron. 6:41), "riza" (robe, Isa 6:1), "tainstvo" (mystery, 1 Tim 2:9), "felon'" (cloak, 2 Tim 4:13).

"But no one puts a patch of unshrunk cloth on an old garment; for the patch pulls away from the garment, and a worse tear results. Nor do *people* put new wine into old wineskins; otherwise the wineskins burst, and the wine pours out and the wineskins are ruined; but they put new wine into fresh wineskins, and both are preserved" (Matt 9:16–17).

"New" garments and "new" bottles were needed for new movements; "old bottles" which interfered with spiritual life and freedom of fellowship with God had to be forsaken.

4.2.2. Influence of Orthodoxy on Baptist Worship

Life and ministry in the Orthodox environment left its mark on Baptist worship.[74] This is expressed both in the spirit or atmosphere of the worship and in its content and form. One could immediately mention services dedicated to events in the life of Christ such as the Lord's Baptism, The Meeting of the Lord,[75] or the Transfiguration. Annunciation Day draws attention to Mary, but she is presented not as an intercessor, patron, or the Mother of God, but as a good example of humility and obedience to God's will, and as one who also needs salvation. The name of the holiday, The Annunciation,[76] indicates that the most important thing is the good news of the birth of the Savior of the world.[77]

Major holidays of the year, Easter and Christmas, also have the imprint of an Orthodox milieu. The All-Night Vigil at Easter[78] and singing the Easter

---

74. See Prokhorov, "Baptists and the Orthodox Church," 98–112.

75. A Christian festival held on February 15 to commemorate the presentation of Christ in the Temple (Luke 2:22–35). The Slavonic name of the festival – *Sretenie* – is literally "The Meeting."

76. In Russian, *Blagoveshchenie* literally means "the proclamation of the good news."

77. Luke 1:47.

78. By the beginning of twenty first century the practice of holding all-night services has virtually become a thing of the past. Yet churches, especially in villages, used to hold these, and the author himself took part as a child in Easter services which started at 10 p.m. and ended at 4 or 5 a.m. Preachers usually spoke about the sufferings of Christ until midnight; after midnight, the same preachers announced His resurrection. An all-night celebration took place in Voolka, Brest region in 2014. In Schatsk, Minsk region, Easter is celebrated from 11 p.m. to 1 a.m. On this practice in the Russian Orthodox Church see Krasovitskaya, *Liturgica* [Liturgics] chs. 2, 8, 15; Orthodox encyclopedia under the editorship of Cyrill, Patriarch of Moscow and all Russia, on-line version, vol. 9, http://www.pravenc.ru/text/155522.html., last accessed 16 May 2019.

troparion from then until Ascension Day clearly illustrate this.⁷⁹ The dates of the celebrations also reflect the context. The twenty-first century has seen the transition of most Belarusian Baptist churches to celebrating Christmas in line with the Western Church, that is, on December 25th. However, taking context into account, many churches continue to celebrate Christmas for a second time on January 7th, using the "second Christmas" primarily for evangelism in the Orthodox context.⁸⁰ "First Christmas" is for "internal church use" and an awareness of unity with evangelicals in other countries. The content of both the worship services is generally no different. The preachers use the same texts, and there are the same Christmas hymns. Yet in January, to take "Golgotha" church in Minsk as an example, the worship service has an evangelistic focus and there is a call to repentance. In other churches, such as "Light of Gospel" and "Bethlehem" in Minsk, there may be evening theater performances for non-Christian audiences.⁸¹

Orthodox origins and surroundings, perhaps in combination with national specifics, also explain restraint and reverence, especially in prayer, and demonstrate respect for the worship location.⁸² In particular, kneeling during prayer is practiced in traditional Baptist worship services, though in recent

---

79. "Troparion" is the main festival hymn which highlights the most important points of the Church's teaching about the holiday. The Paschal *troparion*, sung three times at the beginning and three times at the conclusion of the meeting goes as follows: "Christ is risen from the dead, trampled death by death, and to those in the tombs He gave life." (Krasovitskaya, *Liturgica*, ch. 5. Voskoboynikov *Illyustrirovannaya pravoslavnaya entsiklopediya. Tolkovaniye simvolov i obryadov. Opisaniye glavneyshikh pravoslavnykh svyatyn'* [Illustrated Orthodox Encyclopedia. Interpretation of Symbols and Rituals. Description of the Main Orthodox Holy Places], 250.) For Christmas time "Silent Night," which came from the West, is the main festival hymn.

80. The difference in the dates results from using either the Julian or Gregorian calendar. The Gregorian calendar was introduced in Russia (across the territory controlled by the Soviet Union) on January 26, 1918. There was an unsuccessful attempt to switch to this calendar in the Russian Orthodox Church in 1923 but it still uses Julian calendar (usually referred to as "an old style"). According to the old style, Christmas is celebrated on January 7. Other celebrations have also shifted two weeks ahead in comparison to Gregorian calendar (new style). For example, the Presentation of the Lord is celebrated on February 15 according to the old style and on February 2 according to the new style. Easter and related feasts sometimes coincide but more often they are celebrated later. On Julian and Gregorian calendars see Voskoboynikov, *Illyustrirovannaya pravoslavnaya entsiklopediya. Tolkovaniye simvolov i obryadov. Opisaniye glavneyshikh pravoslavnykh svyatyn'*, 282; Orthodox encyclopedia under the editorship of Cyrill, Patriarch of Moscow and all Russia, vol. 29, http://www.pravenc.ru/text/1319949.html., last accessed 16 May 2019.

81. Personal notes, 20b.

82. Wardin, "How Indigenous Was the Baptist Movement in the Russian Empire," 36.

times people may stand during the service. Prayer in the sitting position during a traditional meeting would not be considered appropriate.

Restraint and austerity are also expressed in relation to clothing. Cosmetics and jewelry are not encouraged, because immodest clothing might hurt the pious feelings of Christians in a house of prayer.[83] At the service there would be no room for entertainment, jokes, laughter, or any other sort of informality, which would be perceived as a loss of reverence.[84] (Likewise it is impossible to imagine laughter and jokes during Orthodox liturgy.) "Reverence" is accompanied by a special humility,[85] contrition, and awe before the God of gods.

The content of a traditional Baptist worship service often contains discernible aspects of Orthodox theology. These include an emphasis on good works and their importance in salvation, grief, weeping over sin, humble appeals to His mercy, and awareness of one's own sinfulness and unworthiness in the sight of God. These are reminders of a well-known Orthodox motif, expressed in a prayer song "Lord, Have Mercy" (*Kyrie eleison*).[86] This feature is illustrated by one of the most famous Baptist hymns, beginning with the following words:

> Oh, I'm a poor sinner! Honestly, I'm such a person;
> If eternal God was not full of gifts,
> If He was not full of love and He didn't save me,
> I'd have perished in this world many years ago.[87]

Singing is one of the bridges by which Orthodox theology and worship character permeate ECB communities. As far back as the 1860s, some evangelical Christians who had split from Orthodoxy continued to sing Orthodox songs before their own songs were written.[88] One favorite hymn

---

83. Shchavelin, "O blagogovenii v dome molitvy" [On Reverence in the House of Prayer], 41–43, 42.

84. Q, 2008.

85. Gnida, "Poryadok provedeniya bogosluzhenii v tserkvakh evangel'skih khristian-baptistov," 72.

86. It is interesting that this motif finds no place in contemporary worship in Baptist churches in Belarus. Perhaps this is explained by different life circumstances (such as the lack of persecution) and close ties to Christians in the West, who rather stress the assurance of salvation and joy in the Lord.

87. "O, ya greshnik bednyi" [Oh, I'm a Poor Sinner], *Pesn' Vozrozhdeniya*, no. 68, first stanza.

88. Kharlov, "Iz istorii muzikal'no-pevcheskogo sluzheniya nashego bratstva," 46.

of evangelical believers is "Strashno bushuet zhiteiskoye more" (The Sea of Life Is Terribly Raging), written in the nineteenth century by Ivan Kulzhinsky, an Orthodox school teacher in Chernigov.[89] As an example of the spread of Orthodox hymns, the author's ad hoc examination of the repertoire of the first choir of ECB "Light of Gospel" church in Minsk in 2008 revealed that a third of the hymns that were regularly sung in worship were the work of Orthodox authors.[90] Yet, the Baptist style of performance tends to be more classical and vivacious compared to the singing style of the same hymns in an Orthodox church.

One may also note a contrast between the themes of joy and sadness in singing. In 1933, Prokhanov, whose songs are widely used in traditional worship, contrasted evangelical music with Orthodox and folk music in the following way:

> The Orthodox Church music was beautiful, but sad, and this is quite natural, because their religion was pessimistic. The Orthodox Church said nothing about the new birth and renewal; it did not meet the needs of the people. On the other hand folk music also was full of grief and couldn't be useful. Having for centuries remained in serfdom and under the pressure of autocratic power, people were constantly living in fear and anxiety. All Russian music was mainly pessimistic and in a minor key. The music of the Evangelical Christian movement could not be sad, like popular folk music. It was not supposed to be similar to the minor [key] music of the Orthodox churches. Every evangelical Christian passed from darkness into light through his [sic.] conversion, feeling indescribable joy and happiness. His whole life was illuminated by bright rays of salvation in Christ, so I decided to do my best to make Gospel music express the supreme joy that exists on the earth, the joy, proceeding from heaven (Luke 15:7–23). Music should be of the same nature as the Gospel that contains joy. The rays of sunlight filled with optimism should penetrate through the rainy clouds of pessimism.[91]

---

89. *Pesn' Vozrozhdeniya*, no. 87.
90. Personal notes, 60.
91. Prokhanov, *V kotle Rossii*, 142–143.

Indeed, Prokhanov was a real optimist, and he was inspired by church growth and the triumphant development of the evangelical movement in Russia and the Soviet Union in the first third of the twentieth century. However, many years of persecution, including prisons and deportations, along with "sad" national and religious environments, made a strong impact on the character and practice of church ministry, and many of the hymns sung by today's Baptists are in the minor key.

Another key point is the way in which Baptists use general terms for the Lord's supper, baptism, marriage, dedication, ordination, consecration prayer, and prayer over the sick. They are referred to as "church acts,"[92] but the terms "sacred rites," "commandments," and even "sacraments" are also in use,[93] and this must be considered an influence of the Orthodox environment. Thus it is not uncommon for a preacher, when praying for the bread before communion, to ask "Oh, Lord, bless this sacrament," or for a believer to pray for the "holy sacrament of Eucharist."[94] However, in paragraph 8.1 of the Doctrine of the Evangelical Christian Baptists Faith in Belarus, (adopted at the ECB Congress of Belarus on March 15, 2003) baptism and the breaking of the bread are named as the Lord's commandments, and other "rites" (marriage, dedicating the children, ordination, consecration of the house of prayer, and prayer over the sick) are considered to be "church acts."[95] It is noteworthy that the document lists seven of them suggesting that they parallel the seven sacraments of the Orthodox Church.

One more point of influence concerns special prayers for the needs of believers. As in the Orthodox Church, these play an important role in the

---

92. "Tserkovnyie ustanovlenia."

93. "Svyaashchennodeistvia," "zapovedi," "tainstva."

94. Baptist church in Borovliany, Minsk region, 7 October 2012 and 5 March 2017 (Personal notes, 28). This does not mean the preacher or the female believer believe in transubstantiation. The term simply reflects their awe and respect for the elements.

95. Different views on "sacred rites" are reflected in Russian-language Baptist literature. For example, Karev considered "sacred rites" to be church preaching, church singing, church prayer, baptism, Communion, ministry of Christian love, keeping peace in church, and especially highlighting the word preached. ("Svyashchennodeistviya tserkvi.") Kolesnikov presents a more sacramental position, bringing water baptism, Communion (Lord's Super), ordination, marriage, prayer for the sick and children, dedication of houses of prayer, and funerals into the category of "sacred rites." (Kolesnikov, *Khristianin! Znaesh li ty kak dolzhno postupat' v dome Bozhiem*? [Christian! Do You Know How to Act in the House of God?], 6.) Here are his words about water baptism, "God works out the sacrament of ordaining and transference of grace of the priesthood" (Kolesnikov, 48).

Baptist worship service. In small churches, believers name their prayer requests aloud, while in larger churches, worshippers send notes listing their requests to the pastor before or during the service. This practice resembles prayer in Orthodox churches, but, unlike Baptist churches, Orthodox churches have established a set of rules for writing and submitting prayer notes; for example, these notes should not contain a person's last name or middle name (patronymic), their ranks, titles, or degrees of relation.[96]

Even a general comparison of worship services in Orthodox and Baptist churches demonstrates that Baptists in Belarus continue some aspects of the pre-Baptist context and reflect the spirit and character of the Orthodox tradition. On the other hand, the comparison also indicates a conscious and decisive rejection of much liturgical practice, ceremonies, and external attributes of worship such as icons, candles, special garments, and so forth. Here we again see the desire to go back to the origins, to follow the Bible commandments in a more literal way (for example, the second commandment of the Decalogue in relation to icons) and to pour "new wine into new wineskins." It is paradoxically through both the imitation of the Orthodox tradition (whether consciously or unconsciously) and its total denial that new communities have been formed and evangelical Christian Baptist public worship shaped.

4.3. Political Context and the Formation of the Traditional Baptist Worship Service

4.3.1. Persecution and Harassment

The origin and spread of the evangelical movement in the Russian Empire took place within a context of hostility, animosity and opposition from the state and the Russian Orthodox Church. This led to severe persecution and the

---

96. For example, some of the rules are listed on the website of the Cathedral of Intercession of the Most Holy Theotokos in Minsk. http://pokrovhram.by/index.php?id=7, last accessed 7 March 2017. For examples of notes in a Baptist church see section 5.2. Content of a traditional Baptist worship service.

oppression of evangelical Christians.⁹⁷ Under Konstantin Pobedonostsev's⁹⁸ leadership, the 1891 resolution of the Second All-Russian [Orthodox] Missionary Congress stated:

> The rapid growth of sectarianism is a serious danger for the state. All sectarians should be prohibited from leaving their place of residence. All trespasses against the Orthodox Church should be brought to a religious court and not to a secular one. Passports of sectarians should be marked in a special way so that nobody would employ them or let them live until life becomes unbearable for them in Russia. Their children should be removed from them and be trained in an Eastern Orthodox faith.⁹⁹

The years from 1882 to 1905, and especially from 1894 to 1896 which were known as the period of "Pobedonostsev's persecution," were extremely hard on evangelical Christians. Articles added to the criminal code enabled punishment for leaving the Orthodox Church and especially for the spread of "heretical" or sectarian doctrines. As a result, several prominent pioneers of the evangelical movement were arrested and banished, notably Nikita Voronin,¹⁰⁰ Vasiliy Pavlov, Ivan Riaboshapka,¹⁰¹ and Vasiliy Ivanov. Moreover, evangelicals often experienced violence and mocking from the local

---

97. See State Acts Governing the Life of Evangelical Believers in the Russian Empire, http://anabaptist.ru/obmen/hystory/ist1/files/books/book_002/0060_t.html., last accessed 16 May 2019; *Polnoe sobranie zakonov rossiiskoy imperii* [Complete Collection of Laws of the Russian Empire] Collection 3. V. III, http://nauka-i-religia.narod.ru/religioved/garadga/docum.html., last accessed 10 November 2012; V.I. Yasevich-Borodayevskaya, *Bor'ba za veru* [Fighting for the Faith].

For more details on the Mission Congresses of the Russian Orthodox Church and the mission witness of Baptists in the Orthodox Context, see Parushev, "Mission as established presence and prophetic witness in culturally Orthodox Contexts," 57–111. For a general study of the church-state relationship in the USSR see Bourdeaux, *Religious Ferment in Russia*.

98. Konstantin Pobedonostsev (1827–1907) was a Russian statesman, writer, translator, and church historian. In 1880–1905 he held the position of Attorney-General of the Holy Synod, which was the highest authority of the church-state administration of the Russian church during the period from 1721 to 1917.

99. Mitrokhin, *Baptizm: istoriya i sovremennost'*, 243–244.

100. Nikita Isaevich Voronin (1840–1905) became famous as the first Russian Baptist person in the territory of the Russian Empire. The date of his baptism on the river Kura in Tiflis, August 20, 1867, became the birthday of the Russian Baptist movement. (Mitrokhin, *Khristianstvo. Slovar'*, 90.)

101. Ivan Grigor'evich Riaboshapka (1831–1900) was one of the pioneers of the evangelical revival in the Ukraine.

population, and the authorities did not usually attempt to protect them.[102] The savage waves of violence abated after Nicholas II published a "Decree On Toleration" on 17 (30) April 1905.[103] Yet, after war began with Germany in 1914, the situation deteriorated. Evangelical believers in unoccupied Russian territories were accused of communicating with the Germans.[104] Religious freedom only came after the February revolution of 1917, which evangelicals greeted with great enthusiasm.[105] Then, after the Bolsheviks came to power, the first Constitution of July 1918 stated that "the right to religious and anti-religious propaganda is recognized for all citizens."[106] Early Bolshevik policy was supportive of the Evangelicals' struggle for religious freedom,[107] but the communist policy toward them soon changed. "Sectarians" began to be accused of counter-revolutionary activity, of opposition to the cultural revolution, and of ties with Western imperialists.[108] The Antireligious Commission, established by the Politburo of the Russian Communist Party (Bolsheviks) on October 19, 1922, began to make provisions in order to limit Baptist and Evangelical Christian activity, and stressed the necessity for a "rapid increase in the decomposition of sectarianism."[109] Persecution mechanisms slowly

---

102. Lensu and Prokshina, *Baptism i Baptisty*, 20. In fact, the authorities were trying to make the life of sectarians in Russia unbearable (Mitrokhin, *Baptizm: istoriya i sovremennost'*, 243–244).

103. Ukaz Ob Ukreplenii Nachal Veroterpimosti 1905. [Decree on Making Toleration Foundation Stronger 1905]. This decree recognized that falling away from the Orthodox faith and espousing other Christian faiths or doctrine should not lead to prosecution. Parents were allowed to raise their children under fourteen years of age in their faith. Some opportunities emerged for the construction of houses of prayer and for the legal ministry of the leadership of the communities. Dr. James L. Heizer, who gained a PhD at the University of Kentucky for his work on the cult of Stalin in 1929–1939, also studied the reign of Nicholas II, and he believed that his Decree on Toleration was intended to favor Old Believers rather than evangelical Christians. Evangelicals and Baptists may have only been the indirect beneficiaries of the decree. (Personal letter to author, 31 August 2012.)

104. See Linkevich, *Mezhkonfessional'nye Otnoshenia v Belarusi (1861–1914gg.)* [Interdenominational Relationships in Belarus *(1861–1914)*], 56.

105. "Tserkov' dolzhna ostavat'sya tserkov'yu. Neobratimye desyatiletiya: 1917–1937 gody v istorii evangel'skogo I baptistskogo dvizhenii" [The Church Must Remain the Church. Irreversible Decades: 1917–1937 Years in the History of Evangelical and Baptist Movements]. Documentary material about the history of the Baptist Church in Russia (Mezhdunarodnyy sovet tserkvei evangel'skikh khristian-baptistov: Istoriko-analiticheskiy otdel, 2007), 5–6.

106. The Soviet Constitution of 1918, Part 2, Chapter 5, Clause 13.

107. Lensu and Prokshina, *Baptizm i Baptisty*, 22.

108. Lensu and Prokshina, 25.

109. Mitrokhin, *Baptizm: istoriya i sovremennost'*, 362.

began to accelerate. Anti-religious literature was produced on a large scale.[110] In 1925 an all-union anti-religious society "Sojuz bezbozhnikov" (Union of Atheists) was established, which in 1929 was renamed "Soyuz voinstvuyushchikh bezbozhnikov" (the Union of Militant Atheists),[111] and the children's anti-religious movement became "the Young Militant Atheists Organization."[112] Evangelical Christians soon felt the heavy hand of the Communist Party on their shoulders. Houses of prayer were closed and remodeled into schools, clubs, kindergartens, cinemas, anti-religion museums, collective farm canteens, barns, and archives, amongst other things.[113] Christians of all denominations experienced severe repression, especially from 1929 to 1937, when many ministers, including Orthodox priests, and church members were arrested, killed, or banished as "enemies of the nation."[114] Evangelical churches remember the execution of Christians, especially in the purge of 1937, in the following song:

> You will not find their names in statistic data,
> Nor are their relics found in museums.
> What is left after them is the bright light

---

110. See Glan, *Antireligioznaya literatura za 12 let (1917–1929)* [Anti-religious Literature for 12 years (1917–1929)]. The list of children's books alone had sixty-seven titles. The whole list (occasionally with brief notes in one to three sentences about the contents of a certain book) had as many as two hundred and thirty-four pages. As Russian philosopher Nickolai Berdyaev noted, its quality did not match the quantity: "Soviet literature on the anti-religious propaganda is at a very low intellectual level and is aesthetically intolerable according to its style -- this is the lowest kind of literature in Soviet Russia" (N.A. Berdyaev, *Sochineniya* [Essays] (Moskva: Raritet, 1994), 389).

111. The word "bezbozhnik" ("atheist" or, literally, "godless") became a popular term and was used in various spheres. A "Bezbozhnik" aircraft, "Bezbozhnik" tank and "Voinstvujushchiy [militant] bezbozhnik) submarines were built. High-powered atheist work teams were opened in kolkhozes and factories. See Krapivin, *Nepridumannaya tserkovnaya Istoriya: vlast' i tserkov' v Sovetskoy Rossii (oktyabr' 1917-go – konets 1930-kh godov)* [True Church History: Power and the Church in Soviet Russia (October 1917–late 1930s)], 196.

112. The Union of Militant Atheists ceased its activity in 1947 to be replaced by the All-Union Society on Dissemination of Political and Scientific Knowledge (the "Knowledge" Society). In 2008 a Union of Militant Atheists of the Russian Federation was established as an heir of the Union of Militant Atheists of the USSR in order to fight religion in the Russian Federation. It states its task as uniting people for the active, systematic, and consistent fight against religion in all its forms and kinds, since religion is considered to be a brake on the socialist and cultural revolution. See the Union web-page: http://svb.net.ru/., last accessed 24 June 2014.

113. "Tserkov' dolzhna ostavat'sya tserkov'yu," 30.

114. *Istoriya evangel'skikh khristjan-baptistov v SSSR*, 221–228.

Of their great deeds as an example to follow.
You will not find a path to their graves
In the midst of taiga and the Ural Mountains.
At these graves, you will see no flowers
Laid by their friends' caring hands.[115]

Church historian, Dmitry Pospelovsky, believes that Belarus holds a special place in Soviet political history as it was officially the first completely atheistic Soviet republic.[116] The attempts to fight religion were obvious. There were no functioning evangelical churches in the Soviet (Eastern) part of Belarus by the end of 1937, and not a single church had been opened throughout the entire Minsk region by the time of the Nazi occupation in 1941.[117]

During the Second World War, persecution in the Soviet Union weakened because the country needed support from every possible group, including religious groupings.[118] In July 1941, the publication of the magazine *Bezbozhnik* (Atheist) was cancelled.[119] In Minsk, at the beginning of the occupation, Pavel Ivanovich Laguta began to bring together the scattered Baptists and Evangelical Christians to hold Bible studies, and he subsequently started meetings in the area of the present Bicycle Plant. Laguta was assisted by Anton Mitrofanovich Ketsko and other brothers in the faith.[120]

On 26–29 October, 1944, Evangelical Christians and Baptists established one Union, and in 1945 began publishing the Union's official magazine *Bratskiy Vestnik*.[121] During and after the war many Christians who had fallen

---

115. "Protiv tserkvi vozdvignut val" [They Build an Rampart to Fight against the Church], *Pesn' Vozrozhdeniya*, no. 999, second stanza and refrain.

116. Pospelovsky, "Stalin i tserkov': "konkordat" 1943 i zhizn' tserkvi" [Stalin and the Church: The "Concordat" of 1943, and the Life of the Church], 223.

117. Pospelovsky, 103. The persecutions included the Orthodox among other groups. According to D.V. Pospelovsky. at the end of 1936 only 11% of the Orthodox "cult buildings" were functioning in contrast to the days before the Revolution in Belarus, and 28.5% in the USSR. (Pospelovsky, *Russkaya pravoslavnaya tserkov' v XX veke* [Russian Orthodox Church in the 20th century], 167.)

118. Pospelovsky, 185–189.

119. Orthodox encyclopedia under the editorship of Cyrill, Patriarch of Moscow and all Russia. On-line version, vol. 4. http://www.pravenc.ru/text/77798.html., last accessed 16 May 2019.

120. Reminiscence by V.Y. Kanatush, preacher and writer from Minsk, 23 April 2005.

121. "Vsesoyuznoye soveshchaniye evangel'skikh khristian i baptistov v Moskve s 26 po 29 oktyabrya 1944 g. (Zapisi zasedaniy)" [All-Union Conference of Evangelical Christians and Baptists in Moscow from October 26 to October 29, 1944 (Recordings of Meetings)], 11–38.

away as a result of persecution returned to church. The Soviet authorities allowed the registration of a third, (1,696) of five thousand Baptist congregations.[122] However, the Council for Religious Affairs, which was established in May 1944, sought to control the church, and destroy it from within.[123] Antireligious policy became tougher and Christians in local churches were persecuted. For example, in the village of Rogozno, Brest region in 1949, Kirichun Feodosiy was forcefully relieved of pastoral responsibilities and convicted of anti-Soviet activities. The community of one hundred and nineteen members had their house of prayer closed.[124]

Later the Soviet government brought down its suppression on all denominations in an attempt to destroy church ministry from both outside and from within. The Council for the Affairs of Religious Cults was ordered to "prevent orchestras, choirs and preachers from coming to other houses of prayer," "take measures in order to put an end to 'outreach' among youth and women," and put a stop to such activities as art and music events.[125] As recently as 1959, senior pastors in the Soviet Union complied with the requirements to restrict "unhealthy missionary efforts" and to limit the evangelistic potential of worship services.[126]

In 1957, "scientific" atheism replaced "militant" atheism.[127] Nikita Khrushchev became famous for de-Stalinization and ending the notorious political purges, but he soon renewed the severe persecution of churches.[128] A

---

122. Alexeeva, *Istoriya inakomysliya v SSSR. Noveishy Period* [History of Heterodoxy in the USSR. The Newest Period], ch. 11.

123. *Gistoryia Bielarusi* [History of Belarus], vol. 6 (Minsk: Sovremennaya shkola, Ekoperspektiva, 2011), 356.

124. NARB, Stock 952, File 1, Case 21, 2, 2a.

125. "Instruktivnoe pis'mo Soveta po delam religioznyh kul'tov" [Letter of instruction of the Council for the Affairs of Religious Cults] (April 1957), SARF (State Archive of the Russian Federation) Stock R-6991, File 148, Case 3, 3–4. (The website of the Russian Association of researchers of religion. http://www.rusoir.ru/president/works/214/, last accessed 31 March 2011.

126. "Instruktivnoe pis'mo starshim presviteram VSEKhB," §§ 3–4.

127. Savinskiy, *Istoriya evangel'skikh khristian-baptistov Ukrainy, Rossii, Belorussii. Chast' II (1917–1967)* [History of Evangelical Christians-Baptists in Ukraine, Russia and Belarus. Part II (1917–1967)], 196. In 1959 they began publication of the "Nauka i religia" (Science and Religion) magazine. Its goal was equipping the readers to spread a materialistic worldview.

128. In April 1960 a house of prayer was torn down in the village of Rechky, Logishin district, Brest region. NARB, Stock 952, File 3, Case 21, 155. In August an extension was demolished in Podoressie community, Starodorozhsky district, Minsk region. (NARB, Stock 952, File 3, Case 21, 250–251.) In November the Christians of Krasovshchina ECB community, Molodechno district, Minsk region complained that the local authorities "wrenched out the

poem in an unpublished, hand-written collection of the 1960s describes the atmosphere that prevailed during the Khrushchev years. The author recounts how persecution directly affected his family. He presents suffering as a natural consequence of faith and preaching the Gospel but, at the same time, he also expresses complete assurance that it is true happiness:

> We were little kids back then,
> But it is still so vivid in my memory:
> That day our father was taken away from the family
> For telling the truth to people,
> > For having a burning heart for God,
> > For calling sinners to repentance,
> > For fighting a good fight for God's cause
> > And proclaiming Christ's death on the cross …
> A thorny path has now become my portion,
> But I have only found happiness walking this path.
> Just like my dad, courageously and devoutly,
> I want to walk my path in life.

Many Soviet authors published books that accused Christians of "antisocial, sectarian activities," manifestations of "fanaticism," and "clandestine activities."[129] Another notable event was the release of the anti-religious motion picture, *Tuchi nad Borskom* (Clouds over Borsk), which portrayed the tragic involvement of a Komsomol girl in a Pentecostal sect until she was nearly killed by ritual sacrifice.[130] Another film, *Greshnitsa* (Sinner), displayed the fate of a young girl who was forced to get married against her will by "sectarians", but who ran away from home, and escaped from religion.[131]

---

locks, broke down the door, burst in, crushed the furniture in the house of prayer as well as all the worship utensils, threw the curtains from the windows into the mud and smashed the pulpit." (NARB, Stock 952, File 3, Case 21, 307–309.)

129. Belov, *Sekty, sektantstvo, sektanty* [Sects, Sectarianism, Sectarians]; Fedorenko, *Secty, ikh vera i dela* [Sects, Their Faith and Acts]; Kalinicheva, *Social'naya sushchnost' baptisma* [Social Essence of Baptists]; Sulackov, *Na iskhode nochi* [At the End of Night]; Ryabushkin, *Kto takie sektaty* [Who Are Sectarians].

130. Directied by V. Ordynsky (Mosfilm, 1961). See Kasataya, "Sud nad baptystami': savetskiya kinastuzhki yak metad barats'by suprats' evangel'skikh khrystsiyan baptystau u BSSR" [The Baptists' Trial: Soviet Movies as a Method of Fighting against Evangelical Christian Baptists in BSSR], 240–251.

131. Directied by F. Philippov (Mosfilm, 1962).

Motion pictures typically represented evangelical believers as old women whose lives seemed bleak and devoid of all joy, or as "sectarians" who were fanatical zealots. At work and in school, Evangelicals experienced official and personal insults, oppression, and harassment. Protestant Christians suffered from show trials. For example, Vladimir Kanatush, a preacher of "Golgotha" church in Minsk, was arrested in 1950 and sentenced to twenty-five years of prison camps, but was released in 1955, after Stalin's death.[132] In March 1963, church leaders in Brest were sentenced to three to five years in prison.[133] In Zelva, Grodno region, on January 14, 1970, Nikolai Shugalo and Nikolai Lazuta were sentenced to five years in prison as the leaders of the local Baptist community.[134] The story of the Vilchynski family is famous in Brest. In 1968, the pastor of an unregistered Baptist community,[135] Vladimir Vilchynski, was sentenced to five years in prison. In 1979, his daughter Galina, aged 21, was sentenced to three years in prison because she had been teaching Bible lessons. In 1986, Zinaida Yakovlevna, Vladimir's wife, was also arrested for

---

132. Kanatush, "Svidetelstvo o pape" [Testimony about My Dad], 24.

133. Their names are Grigoriy Shepetun'ko, Stepan Matveyuk, Ivan Kotovich and Yevgeniy Fedorchuk (Gardzienka, *Religiynaya apazitsyya na Belaruskim Palesśi u 1960–1980-ya gady. Zagaroddze-3. Materyyaly navukova-krayaznauchay kanferentsyi "Palesse u XX stagoddzi"* [Religious opposition in Belarusian Polesie in 1960–80-ies. Zagaroddze-3. Proceedings of regional research conference "Polesie in the twentieth century"], 222). They were accused of holding illegal prayer meetings at private apartments and of calls to summon an ECB Congress. There were five court cases in Brest. (*Gistoryya Bielarusi*, 354.)

134. *Gistoryya Bielarusi*, 356. Dzmitry Lazuta, Nikolai Lazuta's grandson, is a pastor of "Light of Truth" Baptist church in Minsk. The Baptist church members' trial in the village of Borodichy, Zelva region, became a basis for the documentary "The Baptists' Trial," which was shot in 1970. For the analysis of the events and the film, see Kasataya, "The Baptists' Trial: Soviet Movies as a Method of Fighting against Evangelical Christian Baptists in BSSR," 240–251.

135. See footnote 26 on page 8.

her activity in the Council for Relatives of Prisoners[136] and was sentenced to two years in prison.[137]

Fortunately, the severity of persecution relaxed somewhat in the first half of Brezhnev's governance (1964–1982).[138] Toivo Pilli refers to these years as the "transition period from 'administrative methods' to more 'educational methods,' including sociological arguments against religion."[139] However, persecution did not cease until the celebration of the Millenium anniversary of the baptism of Kievan Rus'[140] in 1988. The last prisoner of conscience, Vitaly Boiko, a pastor from Odessa, was only set free in 1989.[141]

When the Soviet system broke up in 1991, evangelical Christians were afforded opportunities which would have been unimaginable earlier. They started holding evangelistic meetings and worship in clubs, houses of culture,

---

136. The Council for Relatives of Prisoners (1964–1987) was established by the Council of Churches of Evangelical Christians-Baptists in order to provide help for imprisoned Christians and their families. See *Vestnik Istiny*, no. 4–5 (2009) dedicated to the 45th anniversary of the Council's ministry. On September 25, 1987, by the decision of the Council of Churches of Evangelical Christians-Baptists a new department was formed under the Council of Churches, named the "Department of Intercession of CC ECB." (*Vestnik Istiny*, no. 3 (2001), 32–33.) See also Walter Sawatsky, a researcher of the Russian-speaking Baptist movement: *Evangelicheskoye dvizheniye v SSSR posle Vtoroy mirovoy voyny* [Evangelical Movement after World War II], 396. This work was originally published as *Soviet Evangelicals Since World War II* (Kitchener, Ontario: Herald Press, 1981). For a helpful source on the role of women in "unregistered" evangelical communities see Belyakova and Dobson, *Zhenshchiny v evangel'skikh obshchinakh poslevoyennogo SSSR. 1940–1980-ye gg. Issledovaniye i istochniki* [Women in the Evangelical Communities of the Post-War USSR (1940s–1980s). Documents and Analysis].

137. Vil'chinskiy, *Nedarom Prolitye Sliozy*, 3.

Other prisoners' names could be mentioned in regard to the 1960s and 1970s. In Dobrush, Gomel region on April 24, 1968, there was a legal trial against the chief "schismatics," who were active in the village of Ut'. These were Tretinnikov Kuz'ma Nikitovich and Abushenko Nina Korneevna. They were prosecuted and condemned. Tretinnikov was sentenced to 3 years and Abushenko to 2 years of work camps. (NARB, Stock 136, File 1, Case 13, 123–132.) On August 15, 1968, there was a court trial against the leaders of Gomel church, Kolesnichenko Mikhail Andreevich, Kozin Nil Petrovich and Frolov Andrey Fedorovich. They were condemned according to article 139 of the Criminal Code of BSSR and sentenced to three years in prison. (NARB, Stock 136, File 1, Case 13, 125.) The list is not exhaustive.

138. On this historical period see Natallya Baltrushevich, "Uzajemadačynienni dziaržavy i pratestanckich cerkvau u BSSR u 1965–1985 hh." [Mutual Relations of Protestant Churches in the Byelorussian SSR in 1965–1985], 220–237.

139. Pilli, "Evangelical Christians-Baptists of Estonia: The Shaping of Identity, 1945–1991," p. 49.

140. Kievan Rus' is an ancient state in eastern Slavic lands which shaped the Old Russian language, culture, and people.

141. "Obnovliat'sia i byt' samobytnym" [Be Replendished and Be Original] *Logos: The Bible, Education, Music*, no. 1(13) (2005), 8.

stadiums, and movie theaters. From September 14, 1992 to December 28, 1994 the religious programs "Golos druga" (Friends' voice) and "Sutnasts'" (Essence), prepared by TWR studio in Brest, were broadcast by the first channel of Belarusian radio in prime-time.[142] Legal opportunities arose for publishing Bibles, song collections, Christian newspapers and magazines, and other Christian literature. Dozens of churches and missions were registered. In 1989 Bible courses were begun by Belarussian Baptists, and the Bible Institute, Bible School, and the Seminary were established in 1991, 1993, and in 1997 respectively.[143] The authorities provided Christians with plots for the construction of houses of prayer, and the "Light of Gospel" and "Bethlehem" houses of prayer were built.[144] A door was opened for missionaries, teachers and preachers from other countries. However, when the President Alexander Lukashenko consolidated his power, some limitations were put in place. In the opinion of some experts, the law "On Freedom of Conscience and Religious Organizations" (passed on October 31, 2002, no.137-3) impairs Christian freedom of conscience and belief.[145] Nevertheless, in comparison to the Soviet era, the evangelical Christians continue to possess ample opportunities for evangelism and worship.

4.3.2. Motifs of Struggle, Suffering, and Expectation in Worship

Constant hostile pressure from outside forces, and interference in the life of Christian communities and their ministries during the Tzarist and Soviet eras, resulted in a particular type of worship that was based on the opposition to and separation from "the world". The emphasis on the idea of struggle, on a willingness to suffer for the faith, and on eschatology, illustrate the nature of the conflict between these churches and the world. Sermons, songs, and

---

142. Since 1991 I have been involved in broadcast ministry in Brest as an author of some broadcasts and the Chairman of the Board of Trans World Radio in Belarus (official website. http://twr.fm., last accessed 16 May 2019.

143. Since 1997 I have been involved in the Seminary's work as an Academic Dean and (since 2010) as the Rector. Minsk Theological Seminary, official website, http://www.mbseminary.org., last accessed 16 May 2019.

144. "Light of Gospel" church in Minsk, official website, http://www.glchurch.by, last accessed 9 March 2017. "Bethlehem" church in Minsk, official website, http://iisus.by/o-tserkvi/история, last accessed 16 May 2019.

145. See discussion in the minutes of the Council of the ECB Union in Belarus, no. 59 (30 October 2002) and no. 60 (18–19 December 2002), Minsk, Belarus.

poems often stressed fighting against the world and against the flesh while striving for salvation. One popular song captured a similar sense of the fierce struggle and suffering that was present in the early church, and also challenged Christians to continue spreading the Good News:

> All along the thorny way of suffering,
> We see bloody traces and stains -
> It is the first Christians walking here,
> Who showed a great act of love.
> The storm of evil could not put out
> Their holy heavenly flame,
> And the old grey-haired men
> Brought it to us through many trials.
>> They preserved it but lost many brethren
>> During the years of relentless fighting.
>> Now they call on us, the young and strong,
>> To join them and fill in these losses.
>> If we are ready to give up our lives
>> For the great cause of our ministry,
>> God calls us to join without delay
>> His army of salvation volunteers.
> We will take the flags of Christ's teaching
> From their weakening hands
> And carry this light of truth in the darkness
> Through ages and generations.
> Our path may be full of hardships,
> But soon the Sun of eternity will rise for us -
> Our happiness will be revealed, outside this troubled life,
> In the reign of truth and much-desired freedom.[146]

Baptists in particular responded to idealism with songs that summoned them to "holy war." These texts often included such military terminology as feat, trial, struggle, sacrificing life, army, banners, victory, and battle. Two popular hymns of the Evangelical Christians-Baptists perhaps illustrate how

---

146. "Nyne Bozh'ya lyubov' obnimayet" [Now God's Love Embraces], *Pesn' Vozrozhdeniya*, no. 716, second– fourth stanzas.

ideas of struggle influenced worship. A hymn written by Prokhanov served as a *sui generis* hymn of the evangelical brotherhood during the first third of the twentieth century and it is still used to the present day. Unfortunately, the written text is not able to convey all the expressive dynamics such as the explicit march beat.

> For evangelical faith
> And for Christ we will stand up;
> Following His example,
> Forward all, forward after Him.
>> It is a fierce battle and a devastating fire,
>> Which make the earth shudder;
>> Hold up your flag,
>> The banner of the victorious Christ.
> A closely knit and joyous family,
> His united people,
> Having one heart and one soul
> Onward, you who follow Christ![147]

Another "militaristic" text was written by Nikolai Khrapov, who was arrested five times and spent more than twenty-eight years in prisons and camps, where he eventually died. This poem, which became a song, was primarily addressed to young people. Singing these and similar hymns spiritually united twentieth-century Christians with those early believers who also worshiped in secret. All had to be ready to enter the arena in face of the fear of bloodthirsty lions or martyrdom:

> We greet you, Christ's blossoming people,
> Born in storms by the great destiny,
> The end times come to you with a threatening face,
> They call you for the last decisive battle!
>> The steel wall of troops is set against us –
>> It is unbelief fighting against us fiercely.
>> Let us close up our file,
>> Young soldiers, keep up in this decisive battle!

---

147. "Za evangel'skuyu veru" [For Evangelical Faith], *Pesn' Vozrozhdeniya*, no.185, first and second stanzas and refrain.

Sound the victory! May the holy flame burn more brightly over
   the ruins of evil!
Bring forth the Christian banner
Of unselfish love and Christ's goodness![148]

A somewhat unusual example may be added to the songs cited above. This was an alteration of the text of "The International," the international proletarian anthem which became the anthem of the Soviet state from 1918 until 1944. This revised text was not widely spread, but it is known that it was sung in the Slavgorod district, Mogilev region,[149] and Kobrin district, Brest region.[150] Evangelical Christians replaced the fight against "the international bourgeoisie" with the struggle against sin and evil, which can be defeated by the blood of Christ.

Arise, oh world steeped in sin,
The world of the hungry and slaves
Arise and fight for your life,
You will fight for life or death.
   The whole world of violence will pass away,
   It will be destroyed to the ground and then
   Love and truth will reign
   And there will be no evil at all.[151]

Such struggles required complete determination, selfless devotion, and firmness to the end. There could be no easy way to victory, and song lyrics warned about the possibility of martyrdom. Life with Christ, even risking martyrdom, appeared to be the best option because even dying for Christ was better than living without Him.

---

148. "Privet vam, Khristovo tsvetushcheye plemya" (We Greet You, Christ's Blossoming People), *Pesn' Vozrozhdeniya*, no. 718, first-third stanzas.

149. Khaytun and Kapayevich, *Suchasnaye sektantstva na Belarusi* [Modern Sectarianism in Belarus], 48. This details the situation of Christians in the village of Urech'e, Propoysk (nowadays Slavgorodsky) district, Mogilev region.

150. Alexander Firisiuk, Personal interview with author, Minsk, 22 April 2011 (Personal notes, 59).

151. *The International*, first stanza (Khaytun and Kapayevich, *Suchasnaye sektantstva na Belarusi*, 48).

> May young hearts sound in unison
> At Christ's bosom today!
> Tomorrow a furious crowd may as well lift someone
> And nail them to the cross![152]

Other popular songs also called for self-sacrifice, self-denial, and dedication.

> Living for Jesus,
> Dying with Him,
> Can there be a better life than this?
> It is worth humbling oneself for,
> It is worth fighting for,
> It is worth giving up your life for.[153]
> We have few concerns of our own,
> But let us not be preoccupied by them.
> We should sacrifice our forces
> Not for ourselves, but for others.
>> Oh fresh youth, the spring of life!
>> Do not spare forces and health (for people),
>> Keep your spirit burning for the Lord (more and more).[154]

The frequent use of military language in hymnody demonstrates how Baptists expressed a dualistic perception of the world. There existed only darkness or light, black or white. The world, with its culture and political order, was considered hostile towards citizens of the kingdom of heaven, and it appeared ready to use any opportunity to destroy believers. Believers were not to become involved with the world because it could not be changed, transformed, improved, or corrected; they could only fight against it. They believed that a person's culture and way of life must oppose the world, and that then the victory, although it might cost your life, would be won.

Opposition to the world, the struggle with sin, and separation from the world, naturally led to suffering. Although evangelicals believed that the

---

152. *Pesn' Vozrozhdeniya*, no. 718, fourth stanza.

153. "Zhit' dlya Iisusa, s Nim umirat'" (Living for Jesus, Dying with Him), *Pesn' Vozrozhdeniya*, no. 287, first stanza.

154. "Poka ogon' lyubvi chudesnoy" (While the Fire of a Wonderful Love), *Pesn' Vozrozhdeniya*, no. 720, fourth stanza and refrain.

Lord sometimes sent peaceful and quiet times,[155] they often quoted another text from the Second Epistle to Timothy, "all who desire to live godly in Christ Jesus will be persecuted."[156] As a member of an "unregistered" church preached, "the way the true church chooses contains suffering, the catacombs, amphitheaters, fires, torture, and prison. It remains the same until now and for those who love the Lord it is pleasing, beautiful, because it leads to eternal life."[157]

To a certain degree, one could even speak of a "psychology of martyrdom"[158] or a "cult of the Way of the Cross,"[159] which remains evident at the present time in reading magazines or attending worship services of the ICCECB churches. The appeal to suffering constantly feeds the spirit of worship and the faith of believers who continue to speak about persecution taking place in their churches, who continue to send information about persecution, fines, and bans from the authorities, and who read these aloud at public meetings. A typical example occurred during a meeting of an ICCECB church, where information of a fine imposed on one of the churches of the Brest region was presented, along with news of the persecution of believers in Turkmenistan.[160]

A positive attitude toward suffering can be attributed to several factors. First, there is a strong belief in retribution, and that a special glory awaits those suffering for their faith. Second, suffering and persecution serve as the confirmation of being chosen to follow the narrow path because evil forces always oppose truth. This theme resembles Shtundist preaching from as early as the 1880s which argued that "if Shtundism was not the true, holy faith, it would not have been subjected to harassment, and the early days of Christianity would not have resumed."[161] Third, suffering for righteousness is seen to increase one's faith and bring the faithful closer to God. "Every difficulty," Karev proclaimed, "is a breeze which drives us towards the harbor of

---

155. 2 Tim 2:2.

156. 2 Tim 3:12.

157. Misiruk, "Tserkov' Khrista – eto maloe stado . . ." [The Church of Christ is a Little Folk . . .], 2–3.

158. Nikol'skaya, "Uroki istorii dlya EKhB," p. 10.

159. Mitrokhin, *Baptizm: istoriya i sovremennost'*, 446.

160. Personal visit of the author to the church service, Church of ICCECB in Minsk, 9 September 2007 (Personal notes, 59b).

161. Rozhdestvensky, *Yuzhnorussky Shtundism*, 83.

Christ." A good example of desire and pleasure in suffering was narrated by a preacher in the "Light of Gospel" Church in Minsk on November, 13, 2008.

> A brother was in jail in the 1930s. He was often called in for questioning, and at the end of the questioning he always thanked the investigator. "Thank you for allowing me to suffer for Christ." He was transferred to another cell with the worst conditions of life, and he again thanked the authorities: "Thanks, now I can testify about Christ to new people." His term in prison was extended by four years, and he commented on this: "Thank you, I have several more years to suffer for my Lord."[162]

However, suffering is not presented as hopeless. Although "life is always good, even in suffering,"[163] other songs and poems reflect that the Lord alleviates suffering and that all suffering is a foretaste of the coming joy. One section of the hymnal is entitled "Consolation for the Sick, Suffering, and Prisoners," while another section is devoted to "Christian Joy." When announcing a hymn for singing, a worship leader often begins with the words: "For our encouragement let us sing hymn no. . . .," or "let us be encouraged by singing the hymn . . ." Direct encouragement during worship is in mind, but it is assumed that the encouragement will also accompany the believers after the meeting closes. Particularly popular in terms of comfort are hymns such as "Kogda odoleyut tebya ispytan'ya" (When Trials Prevail Against You), "Techet li zhizn' mirno, podobno reke," (If Life Goes Smoothly Like a River), and "Ty moy Bog Svyatoy" (You are My Holy God),[164] which express confidence in God's consolation and protection in the different circumstances of life.

The key moment of comfort is to become like Christ during the suffering, which is expressed in a Russian saying: "Christ has suffered and told us to do so." This idea is voiced by the following poem:

> I am the Teacher and God,
> I have travelled all this way,

---

162. "Light of Gospel," Minsk, 13 November 2008 (Personal notes, 59). See also the title of the hymn "Yest' radost' v tom, chtob lyudi nenavideli" [There Could Be Joy When People Hate You], *Pesn' Vozrozhdeniya*, no. 815, first stanza.

163. "Kogda odoleyut tebya ispytan'ya" [When Trials Prevail Against You], *Pesn' Vozrozhdeniya*, no. 553.

164. *Pesn' Vozrozhdeniya*, nos. 553, 707, 789.

> Are my disciples greater than Me?
> If I walked this thorny path to Calvary,
> It means that you will have to walk it, too.[165]

Attention to struggles, suffering, and social protests against the ungodly system naturally result in a strong eschatological emphasis. This is reflected by significant interest in the book of Revelation, prophesies, the millennium, and questions around subjects such as "the end of the world," the Second Coming, the end of suffering, and the victory of Christ and those on His side. It is interesting to note that the first books by native Baptist authors published in Belarus after the beginning of *perestroika* were *The Mystery of the Apocalypse* by Vladimir Kanatush and *Prophecy of the Bible* by Pavel Makarevich.[166] Eschatological themes were expressed in the work of evangelical believers, as demonstrated in a poem by Galina Vezikova which was popular in the 1980s and 1990s:

> Do you want to be taken to heaven? –
> I want so much to shake the earthly dust off my feet
> And step into eternity with the hope that all troubles end.[167]

It was during times of persecution that eschatological aspects were expressed most powerfully, envisioning Christians as aliens in the world who longed for life in heaven:

> I am an alien here; this is a strange country to me,
> And everything is strange to my soul.
> I long, with all my soul, for the vast sweep of heaven,
> A better, brighter and lighter place.[168]

Convinced that many signs indicated that Christ would soon return, suddenly and without further warning, preachers would appeal to each person

---

165. The poem "Khristianinu" [To a Christian], *Stikhotvoreniya, declamatsii, istorii*, first and second verses.

166. *Taina Apokalipsisa* (Minsk: "Probuzhdenie," 1993) and *Prorochestva Biblii* (Minsk: 1993).

167. http://www.blagovestnik.org/books/00430/db/v838593.html., last accessed 16 May 2019.

168. "Ya zdes' ne svoy" [I Am an Alien Here], *Pesn' Vozrozhdeniya. Sbornik dukhovnyh gimnov i pesen evangel'skih tserkvey s notami, tom 1* [Song of Revival. Collection of spiritual hymns and songs of the Evangelical Churches with music] (Samohvalovichi: ODO "Dubki," 2006), no. 1146.

with exhortations. However, waiting and longing for Christ's return introduced a certain kind of optimism and hope into the worship services of the persecuted. It was joyful for worshippers to realize in the midst of persecution and oppression that there is a place without evil, where injustice and animosity will be replaced with eternal love.

> We face our future with hope and joy,
> Your soul will find rest only there.
> You will forget things of the past and come to your heavenly home,
> You will come to your heavenly home, this wonderful place.[169]

4.3.3. The Way of Preparation and Presentation

The influence of persecution in worship can be seen in other aspects of the worship service, including the quality of content and the ways of presentation. For example, because of the difficulties in acquiring higher education[170] (not to mention theological education), the isolation of the theological community from the West, the lack of Bible dictionaries, reference books, and commentaries, interpretation of the Bible by allegoric methods or spiritualization flourished. Preachers did not have resources for historical-grammatical text analysis, and so searching for allegory and hidden meaning within the text was the preferred method. Preachers omitted historical context and would instead immediately apply the truth to the lives of their congregations. Below is an interesting example of how the text from Luke 2:43–44 would be applied; all details are directly related to everyday life.

> Mary and Joseph lost Jesus. What does this fact tell us about? Undoubtedly, we can easily do the same in our fuss, concerns, tedious thoughts, misunderstandings in life, indignation filling us when we do not understand God's will, when everything in us is against God, because His direction does not correspond to our desires, or as we think, our needs. Young people lose Jesus even easier! Running after joys of this life, its satisfactions they aim only at one thing – the satisfaction of their desires. In this

---

169. "Zachem stradat', moy drug, zachem grustit' poroy?" [Why Should You Suffer, My Friend, Why Should You Be Sad At Times?], *Pesn' Vozrozhdeniya*, no. 780, fifth stanza.

170. See footnote 47 on page 40 and footnote 50 on page 41.

situation Jesus disappears and leaves their life. Jesus is not lost immediately, but gradually. Most of human fallings are also done gradually, not at once.

Mary and Joseph started looking for Jesus not where he could have been found. . . . But there is only one place in the world where you can and should look for him, and you will certainly find him there. It is the church! This place is his saved church! And how can you find him there? The only way is through holy repentance.[171]

As a result of bans against theological education and the publication of theological literature, the idea of intuitive knowledge emerged superior to analytical thinking because a person could receive this without the help of dictionaries, encyclopedias, or commentaries. Since "the Holy Spirit directly reveals the knowledge of truth," then the historical, cultural, and contextual analyses do not seem to play an important role in comparison to spiritual preparation, especially prayer and meditation.[172] This understanding continues to flourish, despite modern preachers having many reference books at their disposal. This fact indicates that the approach is only partially explained by the context; indeed, it could be argued that it is inherent in the Baptist method of reading the Bible – as McClendon notes in what he describes as the 'baptist vision'.[173]

Since most preachers had only a Bible and a concordance, they often preached topical sermons. Before studying at Moscow Theological Seminary, I myself followed this pattern with mostly thematic or textual preaching on topics such as "Love," "Fear," "Hope," "Freedom," "Forgiveness," or sermons on Jesus' parables or miracles but not in a series.

Spatial limitations also often influenced the form of public worship. The small space in private houses did not allow for a stage, or pulpit, and preachers often preached from where they sat holding the Bible in their hands. The lack

---

171. Adamovich, "Poteryanny Khristos" [Lost Christ], 43–46.

172. Inevitable subjectivity in such cases is compensated by the authority of the brotherhood, older brothers, or traditions. For a negative evaluation of this phenomenon, see Cherenkov, *Evropeis'ka reformatsiya ta ukrains'kiy evangel's'kiy protestantizm*, 318; Alexander Negrov, "Hermeneutics in Transition: Three Hermeneutical Horizons of Slavic Evangelicals in the Post-Soviet Period," 40.

173. McClendon, *Ethics*, 26–34.

of space in small houses of prayer limited opportunities for having a large choir. Less importance was given to external aspects of public worship. For example, beautiful robes for choirs were an unknown phenomenon.

However, persecution could not stop the development of the worship service. For example, an unregistered church in Brest developed its activities with even more energy than many registered communities.[174] There were Sunday school classes for children which, of course, were illegal; there were rehearsals for a brass band for playing and singing; and special youth services.[175] Interestingly, public worship during the pre-*perestroika* period allowed for greater diversity because the shortage of printed songbooks indirectly encouraged creativity among church members and led to the creation and use of hand-written songbooks, even if the quality was not always high. By the beginning of the twenty-first century, churches had fully provided themselves with the *Collection of Christian Hymns* and *Songs of Revival*. The collection is now considered to be the musical canon in traditional churches.[176] Many collections of poems have been published, and these publications contributed to the unification of worship in churches, at the expense of decreased local creativity.

The end of persecution has led to less of an emphasis on the idea of the struggle against the world, and a decrease in the tension of chiliastic expectations or motifs of suffering. Although older preachers attempt to call attention to the struggle with the world and the flesh, there is a general shift in preaching toward spiritual growth, purity, ethics and Christian character, appeals

---

174. In May 1960, the house of prayer in Shirokaya street was torn down and on November 5, 1960 the Council on the Religious Groups Affairs in BSSR canceled church registration. They suggested the Christians in Brest join a Baptist community in the village of Voolka Podgorodskaya, which is three kilometers away from the city. (*Gistoryya Bielarusi*, 354.) In fact, the house of prayer in Voolka was not big and it could not meet the needs of Christians. See footnote @@.

175. See interview with a pastor Vladimir Klopot, "Bozh'e voditelstvo" [God's guidance], *Gost'* [Guest], no 5–6 (2014): 16. I was a member of this church from 1987–1991 and personally met many eyewitnesses of the events described. For further information on the history of Brest ECB church in Fortechnaya, see the material provided by the church deacon, Stepan Pekun: "Krestnyy put' Brestskoy tserkvi YEKHB" [The Way of the Cross of Brest ECB Church], 23–26; "Krestnyy put' Brestskoy tserkvi YEKHB" [The Way of the Cross of Brest ECB Church], 14–19.

176. Some churches provide almost all their participants and guests with songbooks. These contain only lyrics. Songbooks with sheet music are used by musicians and choir singers. Since the same songs have been sung in churches for many years, everybody knows the tunes by heart.

to good works, Bible reading, attending services, and, especially, praying and participating in the ministry of the church.[177] However, the leadership of traditional churches is mostly composed of people who experienced persecution, who continue to emphasise the idea of the struggle against the world, and it is they who determine the direction of worship services in large and influential churches such as "Golgotha" and "Light of Gospel" churches in Minsk, the central Baptist church in Kobrin, churches on Fortechnaya 61/1, Voolka, and "Christmas" in Brest, the church in Man'kovichi, Brest region along with Slutsk and Soligorsk, Minsk region, and others.

As a result of evangelism after *perestroika*, a considerable number of new people have joined the congregations, especially in the large churches in the cities. However, they are not yet likely to hold leadership roles. First, they would not be regarded as having met the requirement of maturity and stability in their spiritual life. Second, they do not have sufficient support in the already existing structure. Third, some are barred due to past family problems: in Baptist churches, at least until 2017, divorced and/or remarried people could not be ordained. Therefore, it is not surprising that the spirit of the worship service, along with the theological-ideological basis and influence of the Orthodox environment, reflects the difficult history of survival and struggle for evangelical Christians, nor that this attitude is passed on to their children and the new generations of converts. Historical connections and context have also shaped worship practice, worship structure, content, and temporal and spatial characteristics, factors that are addressed in the fifth chapter.

---

177. QM, 2012. My personal experiences and visits to churches would corroborate this statement.

Part II

An Analysis of the Practice of Traditional Worship

CHAPTER 5

General Structure, Content, Time, and Space of Worship

Introduction

The following two sections seek to provide a thick description[1] of a regular worship service and a service which includes the celebration of the Lord's Supper.[2]

Service in Church on Fortechnaya 61/1, Brest, December 14, 2008[3]

Sunday morning worship starts at 10.00. Many show up twenty to thirty minutes earlier and park their car in a church parking lot. Some of the people are picked up by a church bus and some walk from the nearest bus station.

---

1. On thick description see Clifford Geertz, "Thick descriptions toward an interpretive theory of culture," 3–30. Such an ethnographic description has three characteristics: "it is interpretive; what it is interpretive of is the flow of social discourse; and the interpreting involved consists in trying to rescue the "said" of such discourse from its perishing occasions and fix it in perusable terms." (Geertz., 13.)

2. I know these churches very well, as I was a member of the first church from 1987–1993 and have continued to visit it regularly. I have also attended worship services in "Golgotha" church several times, so in general I am familiar with the context. When describing these worship services, I am relying on my personal participation and observation. I have reviewed the videos of worship (which people made at my request to make the most of visual and auditory functions several times), and I also talked with some participants to clarify the details, especially regarding the preparation and holding of the Lord's Supper.

3. See worship in the church's website https://www.youtube.com/channel/UCvEaSKjb9PUvyDI6oUFn_2g. Last accessed 14 December 2020.

People come in small groups or families to the house of prayer and take their seats in the sanctuary. Most people flood into the sanctuary in the last ten minutes before worship starts. In general, sisters take their seats to the left of the central aisle and brothers go to the right. Nevertheless, some couples sit together in the "male" section. The families with small children are in the balcony; there are many young people there and there is no gender segregation. The ordinary members do not take their coats off. There is a small check-room at the basement; choir members and preachers make use of it. Married women and elderly ladies wear headscarves, although the headwear of some is inconspicuous. Some walk towards their seat and keep standing, praying silently. It is not until later that they take their seats in order to talk to a neighbor or just wait for the worship to start. Three minutes before the worship is due to begin, the sanctuary is filled with three to four hundred Christians. There are slightly more women than men. The people sit tightly together but there are some spare seats on the first two rows in front of the pulpit. There are two people in wheelchairs in the central aisle.

Ministers and preachers gather in the basement in the "brothers' room" ten to twenty minutes before worship starts. Here they clarify who is going to preach (if there are no guests, according to the previously approved schedule); then they get on their knees and some of them pray. Following that, the brothers go to another room in the basement, where the choir is already waiting for them. The pastor clarifies anything related to the choir participation, the choir director asks one of the choir singers to pray, and then the choir members leave the basement on both sides and enter the sanctuary. They are followed by the preachers, and the senior pastor closes the procession. Choir members come to the stage facing the audience. The ministers, dressed in suits and ties, take their seats on the left. There is a pulpit in the left corner of the sanctuary. The piano is located in front of the choir, to the right, and microphones are placed in the center. There is a table on the stage in front of the ministers for Communion.

The senior pastor immediately proceeds to the pulpit and the entire congregation stands up. He opens with a greeting "Peace to you, dear brothers and sisters." He notes that the Lord has shown His grace and he calls the congregation to prayer. The pastor prays for about one minute, asking for the Holy Spirit's blessing through singing and the word. He closes with "Amen," which is unanimously repeated by church members. The pastor announces the hymn number for the congregation to sing. The choir members pass hymnals with just lyrics, and people in the congregation open their own hymnals. The pianist plays two lines of the hymn, and the choir director gives a sign to start the singing. Many Christians know the hymn by heart, and they do not need any text. The singing is harmonious, but it is not too emotional: the faces stay solemn and focused. While the congregation sings, latecomers enter the sanctuary and are guided to seats by the male ushers.

The pastor leaves the pulpit after the hymn and the first preacher comes to the pulpit to begin his sermon with the words: "Peace to you, dear brothers and sisters." He reads Psalm 96 and encourages the church to praise the Lord. Some people open their Bibles and follow the passage. The sermon lasts for about six minutes and the preacher asks everyone to bow down in prayer. The people kneel and most of them bend their heads, clasp their hands and close their eyes. A sister from the congregation is the first one to pray. She praises the Lord for providing all the necessary things, asks a blessing for the church, for "those who share the Word with the people," for individuals praying, and for non-Christians so that "the Lord may be revealed to them." The sister prays for about a minute, and then a brother from the congregation takes a little bit longer to pray and thanks the Lord for the opportunity to serve and worship the Lord. When his prayer is over, another brother continues to pray but another sister raises her voice at the same moment. Her voice sounds agitated and stirred, so the brother stops and the sister prays out loud for the pastors, choir, and young people ("this young vineyard"), and asks a blessing for the worship service. Her prayer lasts a little bit over a minute and the second pastor continues. He thanks God for the worship, for good days, for daily bread, for the house of prayer, and he makes requests for the sick and non-Christians, so that "many people would receive You, the Lord and Savior." Each person praying concludes with "Amen" and the rest of the people echo "Amen." The preacher is the last one to pray. He thanks the Lord for His majesty and mercy, for Jesus Christ, and for the essentials in life. He also expresses his desire to glorify the Lord and to witness about Him. Finally, he prays for the rulers to "rule with wisdom", for the sick, and for the congregation.

After the prayer people get to their feet. Some of them brush their knees. Then everybody takes their seats and listens to the hymn "Do not Despair, the Lord Is Always with You," which is performed by a solo singer and accompanied by the choir. Immediately after the song, sixteen smartly dressed children, ages 3 to 5, with their Sunday school teacher and musician come up to the stage. Seven boys and girls recite short poems (one or two verses). One of the boys is too shy to speak and they pass a microphone to the next one in line. Sometimes it is hard to make out what the children say, but it seems that their participation is the most important thing. The adults listen with tenderness and smile even when they cannot understand what is being said. The teacher prompts the words if the children forget them. The children sing a song accompanied by the piano. The song has a verse repeated, "I am a small sheep, I follow Him through a narrow trail up to Jerusalem." Eight more children recite poems and one boy sings.

After eight minutes on the stage, the children leave holding hands. A sister from the choir recites an old Chinese story with the theme "Forget about Yourself for the Sake of Others." She encourages people to imitate Christ, who walked from house to house comforting and supporting people. She concludes with, "Do not merely look out for your own personal interests, but also for the interests of others" (Phil 2:4). The choir continues in worship by singing about great and marvelous acts of God.

The final preach is by one of the deacons. He begins with the words, "I greet everybody who has gathered at the house of prayer, in the name and love of our Lord Jesus Christ." The audience stands up and responds, "It is mutual." Then the brother reads Proverbs 2:1–8 and advises the congregation to seek wisdom from God, as Solomon did. The sermon is preached for twenty-four minutes. The preacher calls on listeners to cultivate a virtuous life and to be constant in good deeds. He reminds the people that they will not be able to enter the heavenly pure and holy gates by their own righteousness. He lists sins which are an abomination to the Lord (Prov 6:16–19), and calls people to avoid them.

People kneel to pray again after his sermon. Two brothers and a sister pray (her words are hard to discern). They express their desire to live according to what they have just heard. The preacher concludes in prayer, thanking God for His Word and His love, and for giving purpose in life, as well as for his brothers and sisters in faith. The brother asks the Lord to let His word be proclaimed to all people, to let Christians live to the glory of God. He also prays for people experiencing difficulties. Sighs, coughs, crying children are heard in the sanctuary. It is likely that people have grown tired.

The prayer is over, and the congregation sings a well-known hymn "Let Jesus Take over My Heart". The senior pastor comes up to the pulpit and calls the congregation to pray for a sister who has broken her leg, and for another sister who is in hospital in a grave condition, that the Lord would give her comfort and support. In his prayer immediately after the announcements, the pastor gives thanks for the Word and its power, and he asks for a blessed ability to hear the word. He prays for the requests expressed and concludes with the words of 2 Corinthians 13:14, "The grace of the Lord Jesus Christ, and the love of God, and the fellowship of the Holy Spirit, be with you all. Amen."

Then the pastor announces, "Our worship is over, I ask our church members to stay for the members' meeting. (You may leave) with God's peace." The noise of people moving drowns out his words, as the people begin to pack their things, leave, or take their places again. Since the members' meeting was scheduled to take place right after worship, the service lasted for an hour and twenty minutes instead of the usual two hours. Nevertheless, all public worship elements were present. Had it been the usual two-hour service, one more brother would have preached (there would have been three sermons in total), the entire congregation would have sung two more hymns, and there would have been additional choir, solo, and music group singing.

The Service of the Lord's Supper in "Golgotha" Church, Minsk, December 2, 2007[4]

The central Baptist church in Minsk holds Communion on the first Sunday of the month, as do other Baptist churches in Belarus. The decoration of the sanctuary reminds all attendees of the nature of the event: there is a table in front of the pulpit, covered with a white tablecloth embroidered with a short version of 1 Corinthians 11:25: "This cup is the new covenant in my blood; do this, whenever you drink it, in remembrance of me."[5] The sanctuary is lit up. There are about four hundred and fifty people there. There are many elderly sisters in the sanctuary, especially in the front rows. They have their heads covered by scarves, kerchiefs, warm hats, and berets. On the balcony there are young and middle-aged people. There is a choir in the balcony in

---

4. See fig. 16.
5. The table is prepared on Saturday evening, and on Sunday morning, about an hour before the meeting, the sister in charge pours wine into chalices and puts the bread out.

front of the organ and opposite the pulpit. The choir consists of about fifty people and two-thirds of them are women.

The Lord's Supper is celebrated during the second half of the two-hour meeting. Until then the worship proceeds through the regular order: there is prayer, church singing, choir singing accompanied by the organ or piano, an eight-minute sermon about the passions of Christ (Luke 22:63–71), people kneel down to pray (two people from the audience and the preacher pray one after another), choir sings (Lord's prayer – the audience listens standing), then comes the second sixteen-minute sermon about God's grace on 1 Timothy 1:15–17, a solo, and a poem. All worship components are united by the general theme of the passion and death of Christ. Finally, there is a third sixteen-minute sermon on 1 Corinthians 11:25–33 (the third sermon usually lasts around twenty-five to thirty minutes, but today it is shorter because of Lord's Supper) and people kneel down to pray again. When they get to their feet, they look focused and solemn. It seems that the theme of passion is reflected in their faces. They take their seats, and the choir members begin to sing with the same solemn or even grim countenance about the struggle of Christ in Gethsemane.

During the singing the pastor leaves his place on the platform by the pulpit. He approaches the table and lifts half of the tablecloth for everybody to see seven wooden plates.[6] There are big round loaves of bread baked by a sister on two of the plates.[7] The pastor nods to the deacons to join him. Three brothers in their forties, and another one about 65 years old, come to the pastor and take their places – two on the right and two on the left.[8] They all have dark suits and light-colored shirts and ties. Then they all wipe their hands against a big white wet towel which the pastor folds and puts aside on the table. The deacons fold their hands in front waiting for the singing

---

6. The church used to have five glass plates and two metal ones.

7. Besides two big loaves of bread, which are about thirty centimeters in diameter, they bake a smaller loaf for the ones taking Communion at the evening worship. It is prepared for Sunday school teachers who are busy teaching the children in the morning, for some of the parents who stayed at home with their little ones in the morning, and for church members and guests who cannot partake in the morning Communion for a variety of reasons. They also bake 50–60 small buns for the Communion taken to people's homes after the morning meeting. There are many elderly members in Golgotha church and some of them are sick. The deacons and preachers visit them at home with Communion.

8. Fifteen minutes before the worship starts the pastor announces the names of the brothers who are going to join him for breaking the bread. Then they leave and wash their hands.

to stop. Meanwhile, the pastor opens his Bible, looks in it and then casts a glance to the choir.

The singing is over, people get to their feet, and the pastor addresses the congregation (there is a microphone stand on the Communion table, so everybody can hear his voice). "Dear brothers and sisters, as we begin the Lord's Supper, Vasily Moiseevich [one of the deacons by the table] is going to pray." Brother Vasily gives thanks for the opportunity to remember the death of Christ, asks Christ to forgive his sins, and prays that partaking of the Communion will be to God's glory. Then the pastor reads 1 Corinthians 11:23–29, reminding people of how great our Lord is, Creator of heaven and earth, who became a Lamb and made us His own in Christ. He also mentions that we follow the precept in remembrance of His redemptive death. He reads 1 Corinthians 11:23b-24 again and takes a plate with the bread in his hands. The second plate is taken by the deacon on the Pastor's left. The Pastor pronounces the words of his prayer distinctly, solemnly, stressing the words, and it takes him about a minute. In his prayer he thanks Christ for enduring curses, whipping, suffering, and death. He asks for a blessing on the bread, for the people present to have clean hearts, and that they would take communion to the glory of God. The deacons standing nearby keep their heads down and their eyes closed. After the prayer the choir begins to sing about the crucifixion passions and God's love. People keep standing.

The presbyter breaks the two loaves into four parts each (the loaves are prudently incised at the bottom); he puts a piece into each of the seven deep plates and puts two smaller pieces into the last plate. Then he gives a sign to the deacons standing near him and they begin to split the bread into small pieces. The whole procedure takes three minutes. The choir keeps singing and church members are waiting, some with heads bowed in reverent silence. The choir's singing and the preparation of the bread cease at almost the same time. A few seconds before this happens, the pastor nods his head to invite three more brothers to the table. So, there are eight people by the table before the pulpit.

In the ensuing silence some people are coughing, and the pastor announces, "All God's children can take part in the Lord's Supper, those who have received holy water baptism [meaning only those who have become church members through baptism at the age of reason from 17–18 and above], and who have peace with the Lord and each other. [In some churches they add, "those who are neither admonished not excommunicated"]. The visitors to our church may take part in the communion following the same principle. May the Lord bless the whole church as we partake in this commandment."

The Pastor passes the plates to his assistants and the congregation starts the hymn "Gospod', kogda uchenikam Ty smert' Svoyu yavil," (Lord! When You Revealed about Your Death to the Disciples),[9] which is, in essence, a paraphrase of 1 Corinthians 11:23–28. The deacons go into the sanctuary, to the balcony, and two brothers turn back to serve the preaching brothers and other ministers sitting on the platform (there is a 79-year-old retired senior pastor of the church and a former Chairman of the Baptist Union in Belarus in this group of people). The people stay in their places and take Communion while standing. The deacons pass the plates with the bread across the rows of people. The people take small pieces of bread. Some of them eat it immediately and some have some moments of silent prayer and then put the bread into their mouths. Some people have put aside their hymnals to free their hands (the majority are familiar with the hymns sung during communion). In some of the rows people take the plate from the deacon's hands and pass it on to others who cannot reach it. During this time, the Pastor takes care of the tablecloth, folds it, and takes away the napkins from the tops of chalices filled with wine.

Having sung two stanzas of the hymn, there is a short period of silence before the choir director announces another hymn about the sufferings of Christ, which begins with the following words, "V bagryanitse stoish' Ty v ternovom ventse," (You're Standing in the Purple Robe with a Crown of Thorns).[10] The deacons have gone around the sanctuary passing bread. It has taken them about five to six minutes. They return and put the plates back on the table arranging them in two rows. The last deacon passes his plate to the pastor and the pastor offers the bread to the deacons. After that, he takes the bread while the organ is playing. Two deacons raise the tablecloth on both sides and cover the plates with the leftover bread.[11]

---

9. *Pesn' Vozrozhdeniya*, no. 416.

10. *Pesn' Vozrozhdeniya*, no. 419.

11. After worship, the bread is collected onto one plate and it is taken to church office, where the brothers finish it. The wine is poured into small bottles that are used for taking Communion to people's homes. The leftover wine is poured into a jar and kept in the refrigerator until the next month when it is used again.

The singing and the music ceases. The Pastor opens up his Bible and reads from 1 Corinthians 11:25 and then continues, "Anatoly Semenovich [one of the deacons] is going to pray over the chalice". The pastor takes one of seven chalices filled with wine and passes it to brother Anatoly. He gives a short prayer, giving thanks for the blood of Christ, and asks for a blessing on the chalice and to be worthy of partaking of it. The congregation gives a unanimous response to his prayer, "Amen". Immediately after the prayer the church continues to sing a hymn from *Pesn' Vozrozhdeniya*, 416, starting from the third stanza, "Then You took a cup with wine". Meanwhile, the pastor is passing chalices and fabric napkins to the deacons. Following the same order, the deacons go to the congregation. People sip from the chalice and the deacon wipes the rim of the chalice with a napkin and passes it to the next person. Sometimes the congregants pass the chalice to each other, and the deacons wipe the rim of the chalice after two or three people. Some church members close their eyes after they drink from the chalice to have a moment of silent prayer, and then continue to sing.

After a minute and a half, two brothers come up to the table, taking the jars of wine and go to the hall to pour more wine into the chalices, a process that happens twice. During this time of communion the church finishes singing the hymn, and then sings another song about the suffering and the death of Christ, and then another one.[12] The singing is rather slow and drawn out. The deacons return, give the chalices to the pastor, which he puts on the table to the sounds of the organ; the deacons put napkins on the table. The pastor gives the last chalice to the deacons, who take a sip. Then the pastor wipes the rim of the chalice, sips the wine and puts the chalice back on the table. In the ensuing silence someone coughs again. Two deacons raise the tablecloth from both sides and cover the plates and chalices.

The pastor congratulates the church on their participation in the Lord's Supper, and the audience responds amicably "The same to you". He reads Hebrews 9:28 and asks one of the deacons who remains on the platform to pray. The latter thanks the Lord for participation and asks Him to fill the church with faith and love. In essence, the Lord's Supper is concluded with this prayer. However, it is followed by singing, the collection of donations,

---

12. "U kresta khochu stoyat'" (I Want to Stand by the Cross) and "Grekh pobedit', o, zhelayesh' li ty?" (Do You Want to Have Victory over Sin?), *Pesn' Vozrozhdeniya*, nos. 427, 443.

prayer, and choir singing. This time the people who have been standing all this time sit down. It is obvious that some are tired, given that many church members, especially the elderly, keep with tradition and do not eat in the morning until they take part in communion. The pastor makes announcements, receives greetings from other churches, prays at the conclusion of worship, and dismisses the meeting with the words, "Let us greet each other. With the peace of God." The brothers greet each other with handshakes, and the sisters, especially the elderly, greet each other with a Holy Kiss. Some people stay to talk with each other and gradually leave.

5.1. General Structure and Components of Worship

The study of a worship service begins with an analysis of its actual structure and components. So the primary concern of this chapter, as Christopher Ellis states, is not 'What *ought* Baptist worship to be?' but 'what *is* Baptist worship and what has it been?'"[13] The testimonies and observations of public worship participants become an important resource, especially in light of the claim of Martin Stringer that "understanding of the texts rather than that of practice" does not allow observing the whole picture of worship.[14] This is particularly true of traditional Baptist worship which has no set text except that of the Bible and the hymnal. The attention to current changes in worship is also helpful in defining its parameters.

> A typical traditional Baptist service is composed of a combination of preaching, singing, and prayer, in various forms, proportions, and sequences. Its duration generally varies from an hour and a half to two hours, with a two-hour service as the most common model used in both larger and smaller churches.[15] A certain scheme or "skeleton" remains unchanged from Sunday to Sunday and characterizes the traditional public worship of Baptist churches, not only in Belarus, but in former Soviet Union

---

13. Ellis, *Gathering*, 40.
14. Stringer, *A Sociological History*, 5.
15. Q, 2008. It is recommended that services last no longer than two hours because two hours is quite sufficient for two or three sermons, several songs, and for listening to special music by the choir (Motorin, "O bogosluzhenii v dni apostolov i v nashi dni," p. 9).

countries, and also emigrant Russian-speaking churches. The latter seek to preserve their identity and avoid assimilation, thereby following the traditional way of worship even more consistently than some churches in Belarus or Russia. Paradoxically, freedom of religion has led to the same closing in and conservation of the subculture that characterized the churches during the period of persecution in the Soviet Union.[16]

The above-mentioned form has been typical for Baptists since the emergence of these churches in the Russian Empire. According to Directive number 10677, issued by the Ministry of Justice on April 3, 1900, criminal behavior of Baptists included the following elements of a prayer meeting:

> a) congregational singing of specially selected Bible verses and service songbooks of the sect such as "The Voice of Faith," "Spiritual Poetry," "Christian Offerings," etc.; b) reading of selected scriptural passages by a member of the meeting, with their sermon-like interpretation in the spirit of the "sect's" teaching, and, finally, c) prayer on bended knees, with improvised inspirational calls, without making a sign of the cross.[17]

Considering that worship is usually two hours, the sequence of singing, preaching, and praying is convenient from a physiological point of view because worshippers can relax their entire bodies by doing "religious" physical exercises – members of the congregation sit during the sermon, stand to sing, and kneel or stand when they pray. Changing positions helps to increase the body's ability to concentrate on the "abundant instruction" provided by brothers from the pulpit. The alternation of the components also helps to maintain the intensity, although too-long sermons or prolonged prayers may sometimes quench the spirit of participants.

The general scheme reflects both the basic forms (in small churches or on the weekdays) (1) and the extended forms (in large churches or on holidays)

---

16. A few examples are Brookhaven Slavic Evangelical Baptist Church, PA, http://bsebc.com; First Russian Baptist Church in Gorham, ME, http://frbcme.org/language/ru/; First Russian Baptist Church in Harrisonburg/Mt. Crawford, VA, http://frbcva.org; ECB Church "Bethany" in Tallinn, Estonia, http://vifania.ee. All websites were last accessed 16 May 2019.

17. Bonch-Bruevich, *Iz mira sektantov*, 175.

(2) of a regular service.[18] The leader (usually the pastor of the church) prays at the beginning, leads worship, announces the upcoming participants and hymn numbers, and makes announcements. The scheme of worship generally fits the picture of Baptists worldwide, taking into the account the importance of the Bible, prayer, preaching, and singing in worship. The differences relate mostly to the form, and, in particular, to the shorter worship service common in Baptist churches in the West, where there is typically only one sermon and Bible reading is a separate component, which is very rarely practiced in churches in Belarus.[19]

---

18. The first form is typical of small churches that do not have a choir. Due to the lack of preachers in small churches there may be no sermon in the middle. Both schemes could describe the same church: Sunday evening worship or evening worship on a weekday (column 1) and Sunday morning worship, which is the main church public service (column 2).

19. See, e.g., examples of descriptions and different orders of service in Ellis, *Gathering*; Rodney Wallace Kennedy and Derek C. Hatch, *Gathering Together: Baptists at Work in Worship* (Eugene: Wipf & Stock, 2013). As a researcher, I also compared the structure of worship by visiting and participating in the worship of Baptist churches in the USA, England, Sweden, Norway, the Netherlands, and other countries. A similar picture would emerge from a web search of terms such as "order of service in Baptist churches," "Baptist worship/structure" and viewing the first 10–12 links to the churches of the United States, Canada, or the UK.

1.	2.
Pastoral greeting	Pastoral greeting
Pastoral prayer	Pastoral prayer
Congregational singing	Congregational singing
First sermon	Singing of the choir
Congregational prayer	First sermon
Congregational singing	Congregational prayer
[Second sermon]	Congregational singing
[Congregational singing]	Singing of the choir
Ministry of the congregation	Second sermon
Poetry	Singing of the choir
Solo or group singing	Ministry of the congregation
Testimonies	Poetry/Solo or group singing
Congregational singing	Children's participation (poems, songs)
Third sermon	Congregational singing
Congregational prayer	Third sermon
Congregational singing and offering	Congregational prayer
Prayer of thanks for the collection	Call to repentance
Announcements	Congregational singing and offering
Pastoral prayer	Prayer of thanks for the collection
	Announcements
	Greetings from guests and other churches
	Pastoral prayer (prayer for requests handed as written notes)
	Blessing

Fig. 1. General schemes of worship for Baptist churches showing the differences between basic and extended forms.

The schemes outlined in Figure 1 do not take into consideration all the nuances, since each individual church adapts the structure and the number of elements in worship as required; typically, little consideration is given to the structure, because attention is placed on the content.[20] Some churches, for example, concentrate on individual participation (singing, poetry, and testimonies) in the middle of public worship, calling it "congregational ministry."

---

20. Cf. Ellis, *Gathering*, 74.

To give a few illustrations of this, during "congregational ministry" time an elderly sister may sing two songs, another sister may give her testimony, the third one sing a solo, and the fourth one recite a poem.[21] Or a sister may recite a poem, then there may be presentations of two books from the church library, Psalm 112 could be recited by heart, and a duet could follow.[22] Some new elements could be added to public worship, such as a sermon for children. Probably adopting the practice of some Western churches, special sermons for children are now included in the "Beam of Hope" church in Minsk; "Salvation," Kolodishchi, Minsk region; "Light of Truth," Minsk.[23] Nevertheless, such instances do not invalidate either the general scheme or the approach to public worship organization.

In most churches, worship services currently have three sermons[24] while simultaneously increasing the duration and improving the quality of preaching. This stems from the development of the system of education and the professionalization of ministry.[25] Tradition is maintained in a variety of ways. An experienced minister explained to me that in the absence of other preachers he would deliver two or three sermons, but only out of practical considerations because it is difficult for people to listen to one long sermon; it is better to break it into smaller parts of fifteen to twenty minutes each.[26] This was the case during the Transfiguration celebration and the worship service extended into two hours.[27]

---

21. Church in Borovliany, Minsk region, 24 February 2013 (Personal notes, 40).

22. Church in Machulishchi, Minsk region, 12 May 2014 (Personal notes, 40).

23. Personal visits of the author to the church services, 31 May 2009, 27 June 2010, and 26 August 2012 respectively (Personal notes, 9b). In December 2013, the church in Borovliany Minsk region, introduced a five-to-seven minute talk for children in the middle of public worship. This was something that I, as a pastor of the church since 2012, personally introduced. A few other churches practice something similar.

24. In the last decade of the twentieth century churches usually had four sermons.

25. Ivanov, *Dukhovnost' evangel'skikh khristian-baptistov* [Spirituality of Evangelical Christians-Baptists], 20–21.

26. Pavel Obrovets, personal interview with author, Minsk, 18 November 2012 (Personal notes, 4b).

27. Morning worship, 19 August 2014 (Personal notes, 4b). In 2002, when visiting a church in Stebrovo, Brest region, southwest Belarus, I was asked to deliver three messages at the same meeting: at the beginning, in the middle, and at the end of the two-hour meeting. However, in such a situation the pastor typically preaches two times – at the beginning and at the end of worship.

It should be noted that it is the Sunday morning worship that principally fulfills the task of teaching the congregation. There are Sunday school classes only for children; for adults,

In the basic type of worship service, the first sermon is the shortest, while the last is the longest.[28] The goal of the first sermon is to guide the congregants into the right mindset for communication with God, and to prepare their hearts for meeting with Him. The sermon in the middle of the service, in conjunction with the last one, is meant for instruction, encouragement, and evangelism, and both can end with a call to a holy life, the life of following God's commandments, and a call to repentance. The sequence is often determined by the talent and reputation of the preachers: the last ministers of the word are the more prominent and titled preachers, the pastor himself, or guest speakers, and thus the intensity increases.

Prayer and singing complement the sermons. During the congregational prayer, two to five brothers and sisters take turns praying aloud for several minutes and the preacher then prays in conclusion. As one of the hymns puts it, in a "living Church" "the prayer as a mountain stream flowing into heaven."[29] In the house of *prayer*, less time is devoted to prayer than to sermons and singing, but prayer is regarded with special reverence, piety, and awe.[30] In a traditional meeting, in contrast to the churches practicing contemporary worship, many people still kneel down to pray during the congregational prayer (after the first and last sermons). However, kneeling prayers gradually give way to prayers while standing. Members of churches explain this fact by the lack of space (narrow aisles), by floor covering (tiles) being uncomfortable for kneeling prayers,[31] and by non-Christians attending, who could be put

---

both tradition and the lack of space do not allow cutting worship in order to give time to Bible study in groups. Bible studies for young and older adults are held in the evenings on working days – usually separately for youth and older believers.

28. This is one of the unwritten rules of Baptist worship. The total time of preaching is from forty-five minutes to an hour; sometimes longer. At Communion services, participation in the Lord's Supper takes fifteen to thirty minutes and public worship can take a little bit longer than usual. The Lord's Supper could replace a sermon or the number of songs and poems could be reduced.

29. "Izvestna mne tserkov' zhivaya" [I Know a Living Church], *Pesn' Vozrozhdeniya*, no. 247.

30. On average, the opening and closing pastoral prayer, the congregational prayer after the first and the last sermon (which involves two to five "praying believers"), and the special prayers of thanks and prayer requests take an average of fifteen minutes, which is about one fifth or sixth of the service.

31. Cf. The instruction on doing church worship in the model of the Central Moscow ECB Church. "If the room is full then congregational prayer is done while everybody is standing. If there is an opportunity, then the people kneel to pray." (Motorin, "O bogosluzhenii v dni apostolov i v nashi dni," p. 9.)

in an awkward position by this tradition.³² Such explanations make sense, yet the changes would not have been possible without knowing the traditions and forms of other churches, especially evangelical ones in the United States, nor without the influence of theological education, all these factors have contributed to an awareness of the diversity of forms in worship.

The third essential worship component is singing.³³ Article 26 of the Charter adopted by AUCECB in 1963 states: "The churches of Evangelical Christians-Baptists have preaching and prayer as well as congregational and choir singing accompanied by music as a part of their worship service."³⁴ Baptists sing for encouragement and edification, they also use songs as praise and prayer, and as an evangelistic tool.³⁵ Singing is often called "another pulpit"³⁶ and singing in the choir is often referred to as "a sacred calling."³⁷ In fact, the worship services of the evangelical Christians in the territory of modern-day Belarus (as in general in the Russian Empire) began with Bible reading *and* singing, as is typically illustrated in the following: "[In 1907 in Gomel] brothers [Prikhodko] . . . rented an apartment in Fedoseevsky str., 21 (now Tsiolkovsky), where the people got together in a family circle in the evening read the Gospel and sang psalms."³⁸

Today, the traditional worship service features a rich musical tradition, representing a variety of styles and forms: congregational singing, choir singing,³⁹ the singing of men's and women's groups, solos, duets, pop-groups, brass

---

32. The pastor in Ushachi, Vitebsk region, reported that they had replaced kneeling prayers by standing prayers for the sake of non-Christian visitors, who were not used to kneeling down to pray. (Petr Lukashevich, personal interview with author, Ushachi, 1 June 2014 (Personal notes, 18). According to Lukashevich, now the church wants to return to the earlier practice, since fewer non-Christians attend worship anyway (Personal notes).

33. The number of congregational songs varies from three to five. Taking into consideration the additional singing of three/four songs by the choir, music groups and individual church members, singing can take more than thirty minutes.

34. Belousov, "Gospod' sila moya i pesn'," p. 74.

35. See more about the purpose of the Christian hymnody in Remmel, "'Wake up, my Heart, and Glorify the Creator in Singing!' Sense of Virtue in the Primary Theology of Anabaptist and Estonian Baptistic Hymnody," 58–59.

36. Karev, "Svyashchennodeistviya tserkvi," 39.

37. Kholm, "Poite Gospodu" [Sing to the Lord], 30.

38. Kolesnichenko, "Gomel'skoi tserkvi 100 let," 8.

39. There could be several choirs in a large church, such as "the first," "youth," "teenage" and "children's" choir. Toivo believes that particular attention to choir singing could be explained by the fact that in the Soviet era it was virtually the only legitimate form of church group activity. (Pilli, "Evangelical Christians-Baptists of Estonia: The Shaping of Identity, 1945–1991," 86–88.)

bands, orchestras of folk instruments, symphony and string orchestras,[40] and so on. There are a variety of song lyrics and themes that reflect the diversity of religious feelings, as well as the history of the growth of the churches across the Russian Empire and their relationships with believers in other countries. In some churches, the choir may occasionally sing the Creed.[41] The main instrument is typically the piano, but the organ,[42] electric organ,[43] guitar, tape recorder,[44] button accordion,[45] synthesizers, small music groups, and, recently, even recorded music streamed from a computer[46] to accompany the singing. Besides these, in the traditional Baptist service there can be various types of wind instruments, violins and cellos, electric guitars, cymbals, or bells. Having more instruments, and a variety of them, is encouraged and can be traced in the example of the Baptist church in Orsha. Initially the church did not have any musical accompaniment. In the middle of the twentieth century they got a harmonium, and during the opening of the new house of prayer in 1995 there was a piano. Now the church uses electronic and string instruments, as well as musical audio records.[47]

Poetry starts our list of "minor" components. The tradition of using poetry goes back to the beginning of the twentieth century. A 1928 issue of the *Khristianskiy Soyuz* magazine includes a report of a meeting in which the "boys recited Christian poems and sang to the glory of God."[48] Another magazine describing the situation in Western Belarus gives a similar example: "There were children involved in the second day of the celebration. They sang and recited poems to the glory of the Lord and for the encouragement of the people present." "Our young people presented a program of songs, poetry,

---

40. This reflects the fact that the Baptists now have opportunities for getting graduate degrees in music and it facilitates professionalism in music ministry, especially in large churches.
41. Church on Fortechnaya 61/1, Brest; "Golgotha," Minsk (Personal notes, 15b).
42. "Golgotha," Minsk (Personal notes, 16b).
43. "Light of Gospel," Minsk (Personal notes, 16b).
44. "Revival," Mogilev, 2005; Church in Borovliany, Minsk region, 2012 (Personal notes, 16b).
45. Churches in Gorodets, Brest region; Bol'shaya Ganuta, Minsk region (Personal notes, 16b).
46. Music is in harmony with the lyrics projected on the screen. Naroch and Rudensk, Minsk region, 2012 (Personal notes, 16b).
47. Orsha, 7 June 2009 (Personal notes, 16b). In 2018 the church in Orsha celebrated its centenary.
48. Savik, "Radost' vsyakoy dushe" [The Joy of Every Soul], 164.

good wishes, and instructions."[49] In fact, reciting poetry became one of the ways to involve young people in ministry.

The beginning of the twenty-first century was marked by fewer people (especially the young) getting involved in reciting poetry in traditional churches, perhaps because of the passivity of the participants or the loss of interest in poetry in general. This tendency prompted the authors of Vestnik Istiny to write an article entitled "Recitation Is Also an Important Ministry." The authors emphasize that recitation (of different kinds of poems) is a special and challenging type of ministry. The general idea of the article is that one must employ a serious approach to all aspects of this ministry: selecting the text, praying, learning the text (preferably by heart), loving the audience, being expressive, and using appropriate intonation. The authors write, "With the assistance of the Holy Spirit poems can affect the hearts of the audience in the same way as through a good sermon."[50]

Testimonies of church members may also feature in the service, even though this is not done regularly. In the "House of the Gospel" church in Vitebsk, the pastor typically asks someone in the congregation to share "how the Lord has led him or her during this week." A similar practice exists in the church in Luninets, Brest region, but here church members themselves volunteer to share.[51] A testimony may focus on the person's walk with the Lord, God's protection, care, or miracles in their life, including healing. Women tend to be more active in this.[52] New converts share about discovering their way to the Lord. Such testimonies about conversion and God's providence

---

49. *Slowo Pojednania* [Word of Reconsiliation], no. 1(4) (January-February, 1939), 62.

50. "Deklamatsiya – trud tozhe otvetstvennyy" [Recitation Is Also an Important Ministry], 50.

51. Q, 2013, Questionnaire of Seminary students (November, 2013).

52. In an evening worship service at the "Light of Gospel" church, a sister in Christ gave a ten-minute testimony about the blessings she encountered as a result of her lung cancer diagnosis and subsequent surgery. Before and after the surgery she felt the constant support of her husband, daughter, and other relatives. She expressed her happiness for having faith in the Lord, for belonging to a church, and having Christian relatives, implying that Christians have a better chance of enduring sickness. She remarked that non-Christians who had been in the hospital with her were not doing so well. (Personal visit of the author to the church service, 14 April 2013 [Personal notes, 42].) Another testimony in the church in Borovliany, Minsk region went as follows: "The Lord taught me to be humble . . . I lost my monthly ticket and I wondered why the Lord let it happen. In a while I lost another monthly ticket . . . I thought again, 'What does the Lord want to tell me?' I remembered Job who lost everything and said, "blessed be the name of the LORD." I also blessed the Lord and later on I found one of the monthly tickets." (Personal visit of the author to the church service, 24 February 2013 [Personal notes, 42].)

in personal life were more common in the 1990s, when there was an influx of new people. As the membership of the congregations has stabilized, new converts' testimonies are less frequent.

In addition to the components listed above, the ministry of the congregation may also involve quoting the Bible from memory, reading articles from *Our Daily Bread* or a Christian newspaper or book,[53] and the participation of children (singing and reciting poetry) which can take up to a third of the worship time in small or medium-sized churches. For example, during Christmas worship in Berezino, Minsk region, more than an hour between the two sermons was filled with children and youth participating, with poems and singing, a solo, singing by small groups, and receiving greetings from other churches.[54]

In the majority of churches, the collection of offerings is usually done at the closing of the service every Sunday morning, or in some cases only once or twice per month. Before the collection, the pastor makes an announcement along the lines of, "Brothers and sisters, at the time of congregational singing the [serving] brothers will collect your donations for the needs of the church and God's work."[55] The term "plate collection," which was used in the twentieth century, along with the practice of collection by using plates or baskets, now generally belongs to the past. Today, in most churches, the servers use specially made bags, which suggest discretion and respect for the mystery of the giving.[56] However, some small churches practice another method: while

---

53. Starye Terushky and Zhdanovichi, Minsk region. Personal visits of the author to the church services on 29 May 2011 and 31 August 2011, respectively (Personal notes, 53b).

54. Personal visit of the author to the church service, 7 January 2009 (Personal notes, 53b). This church has sixty-seven members (2011), as well as many children and teenagers.

55. The hymn "Vsio Iisusu otdayu ya" [All to Jesus I surrender] is commonly sung during the collection, emphasizing the idea of dedication, sacrifice, and commitment. The first stanza and chorus are as follows:
All to Jesus I surrender, I belong to my Saviour,
In the hope and humble spirit, in His light I long to walk.
I give it all to You, that is what I pursue,
All to You, my precious Saviour, I give it all to You. (*Pesn' Vozrozhdeniya*, no. 397.)

56. This reflects the Soviet society's value of the collective over against the private. Private information was typically made publicly available, such as one's salary or grades at school and University. The collapse of collectivist ideology was followed by an increased respect for privacy. In the context of traditional Baptist worship, it was also reflected in leaving "the plates" behind, so that donations are no longer open for the public to see when they are being passed around. Nevertheless, some churches, for example the church in Redigirovo, Brest region, continue to use open baskets.

the congregation sings, people come forward and place banknotes on the table by the pulpit.[57] The offering is not explicitly related to the rest of the worship. "Material ministry," as the collection of offerings is typically termed, is seen to relate to one's spiritual well-being in general, and "to a certain extent it could be used as an indicator of the spiritual life of the whole church, and of the passion of its members for God's ministry."[58]

The end of the worship service may include greetings from guests and other churches, as modeled by greetings recorded in Paul's epistles,[59] announcements,[60] a call to repentance (depending on the church and the presence of non-believers this could take place at almost every meeting, or very rarely), the final prayer (sometimes with the recitation of "grace"),[61] dismissal

---

57. Church in Liuban', Minsk region, 2010. Some churches do not have any collection in public worship. Their church members can put their gifts in a box for donations by the entrance of the house of prayer. E.g. Rudensk, Minsk region, 2013; Mal'kovichi, Brest region, 2008. There are also times when church members bring their donations once a month to a minister or cashier who keeps a careful record of gifts from each church member, encouraging them to be sacrificial and give a tithe. E.g. Churches in Volok, Liubacha, Minsk region, 2013. (Personal notes, 39). Belarusian Baptists generally do not hold to the doctrine of tithing, but some pastors insist on this practice in their churches.

58. Gnida, "Poryadok provedeniya bogosluzhenii v tserkvakh evangel'skikh khristian-baptistov," 72–73.

59. Such greetings may be received as someone passes a note or immediately addresses the congregation. In most cases, the pastor asks people present if anyone brings greetings to our church, to which individuals may rise and say something such as "Church 'Golgotha' in Minsk sends its greetings," "Please accept greetings from the church in Kobrin," "Sister Anna Pavlovna is in hospital; she sends her cordial greetings to the whole church and asks us to pray for her," or "Brother Klopot Ivan Karpovich called from America and sent his greetings to the church." At the end of these greetings, the pastor leads a traditional response on behalf of the whole church:
"For the greetings you have sent we say . . ."
"Thank you," – the congregation continues,
"And we ask you to send our greetings to the churches you are going to visit."
"We ask!" – the congregation confirms. (Personal notes, 46b.)

60. Announcements can be divided into two broad categories – church announcements (related to the schedule of church services, various kinds of church ministries for the next week such as Bible studies, choir practices, visiting guests, special meetings for the youth and Sunday school teachers, weddings of church members, a reminder about fasting on Fridays, preparing oneself for the Lord's Supper, information on church discipline, funerals, events in the brotherhood, conferences, and subscriptions to Christian newspapers and magazines) and social announcements (related to the everyday life of church members and their relationships; this may include announcements about people in the church looking for a jobs or offering jobs, apartment-to-let offers, or rental-apartment announcements, etc.). (Q, 2008.)

61. The last pastoral prayer could have final words such as: "The grace of the Lord Jesus Christ, and the love of God, and the communion of the Holy Ghost, be with you all. Amen" (2 Cor 13:13).

("With God's peace"), and an exhortation "Let us greet each other," which is perceived as a call for exchanging handshakes. Some female members (and, much less frequently, the males) still keep the tradition of the "holy kiss",[62] but on the whole it is getting rarer in traditional worship due to societal changes, an influx of members who do not come from an evangelical background, and foreign guests visiting and introducing other greeting habits such as handshakes and hugs. Nevertheless, the pursuit for the "New Testament church" and fulfilling the Scriptures in a literal way[63] contributes to keeping the tradition in some ECB churches, especially in southern Belarus and in some rural churches.[64]

The Lord's Supper is the last element to be mentioned here, since it is practiced only once a month and is not a part of traditional weekly worship.[65] It is celebrated on the first Sunday of each month during the morning service.[66] It is usually served at the end of the worship service, while the preceding part of the service prepares the congregation for taking part in the sufferings and death of the Lord, as each member should to "be worthy to take part in Lord's Supper."[67] One is expected to prepare for the Lord's Supper in advance, "so that each church member could test himself or herself in the light of the Word of God, as well as personal relationships with the Lord, brothers and

---

62. For further on this practice amongst Eastern Slavic churches see Keith G. Jones, "Kiss of Peace," in *A Dictionary of the European Baptist Life and Thought* ed. John H.Y. Briggs (Bletchley: Paternoster, 2009), 290.

63. 1 Pet 5:14; Rom 16:16; 1 Cor 16:20; 2 Cor 13:12.

64. Q, 2008. At the same time, developments in theological education, and in the availability of books on hermeneutics, resulted in a rejection of literal interpretations. Practices such as greeting each other with a holy kiss as well as the controversial issue of head coverings for women (1 Cor 11:1–16) is explained by some as a cultural context.

65. Jean-Jacques von Allmen calls it "a solemn exception," *Worship: Its Theology and Practice*, 289. Some identify the Lord's Supper as the "Great Omission," as "protestant worship shifted from the centrality of sacrifice to the centrality of scripture." See Moody, *The Word of Truth: A Summary of Christian Doctrine Based on Biblical Revelation*, 480.

66. As most Baptists present it, the Lord's Supper is not celebrated too frequently in order to avoid familiarity, and it is not celebrated too rarely lest we forget about the death and passion of Christ. On the differences in the frequency of celebrating the Lord's Supper throughout church history, see Moody, *The Word of Truth*, 473. Christopher J. Ellis believes, the Eucharist becomes "central to a worshipping community without it needing to be weekly" (*Gathering*, 252).

67. *Verouchenie evangel'skikh khristian-baptistov v Belarusi, prinyatoe na 43-m s'ezde evangel'skikh khristian-baptistov (1985 g.)*. Unpublished material. Section VII, The Church of Christ.

sisters and the neighbors".[68] A prominent minister of ICCECB recommends abiding in "fasting and prayer, staying away from intimate relationships in marriage, and the whole body should be pure and properly clothed (1 Cor 7:6; Heb 10:22)" in preparing to take part in the Supper.[69] The very act of participating "asks for special attitude, such as special focus, special state of prayer, silence and awe."[70] Even though the bread and the cup are often called "symbols" they are understood to be endowed with special qualities, since it is a symbol of the body and the blood of *Christ*. Hence there are no hesitations about drinking from the same cup from a hygienic point of view, as the Lord is seen to be acting in a special way through this rite (the same degree of confidence is expressed when people state that one cannot catch a cold while being baptized in an ice hole in winter). Traditional churches would have a negative attitude towards replacing the common cup with a set of individual cups. Such careful preparation towards taking part, and such reverence in attitude, stresses the special significance and value of the person of Christ, His passion, and death.

5.2. Content of a Traditional Baptist Worship Service

The topic or the theme(s) of a traditional meeting is not usually planned beforehand. The only predictable element is the general structure of the meeting, while the content of its specific parts depends on the inspiration of its participants. A meeting may appear to be (in an observation from a different context which nevertheless aptly describes the issue in Belarusian churches) "an unassembled potpourri with no frame or motif unifying them."[71] Preachers usually speak on different topics, based on what "God puts in their hearts." An example from one church illustrates this situation. In the

---

68. Gnida, "Poryadok provedeniya bogosluzhenii v tserkvakh evangel'skikh khristian-baptistov," 73.

69. Khrapov, *Dom Bozhii i sluzhenie v nem. Prakticheskoe posobie dlya sluzhiteley tserkvi. Pererabotannoe izdanie* [The House of God and the Ministry There. Practical guide for ministers. Revised Edition], ch. 10, http://www.blagovestnik.org/books/00280.htm#40, last accessed 16 May 2019.

70. Vysotskiy, "Znacheniye i sila dukhovnoy muzyki" [The Importance and Power of Spiritual Music], 61.

71. Hoon, *The Integrity of Worship*, 279.

morning service, the first preacher talked about walking in the light, the second taught about obedience to God, and the third dwelled on God's greatness and glory. In the evening service, the first preacher spoke about the importance of attending meetings, the second spoke about a Christian's heart and peace in the heart, while the third contrasted the role and the work of Satan with that of God.[72] Such sermon topics, deductive in structure, are largely designed for believers, and the sermons aim at strengthening the relationships of Christians with the Lord. Speakers assume that attendees are familiar with the Bible, its historical and cultural background, Christian terminology, and sometimes church history.

The subject of any prayer is determined by the direct inspiration of the prayer. Baptists take a stand against any formal prayer written beforehand out of fear that the prayer may become a ritual. Even opponents of evangelicals stressed this point, commenting that many "instructions for members of sectarian churches state that prayer should not be automatic and that a person should put all their feelings into it and feel connected to the deity at the time of prayer."[73] Yet prayers do share some common motifs. At the very beginning of the meeting, the pastor, and then after the first sermon, members (as everyone has opportunity to pray), give thanks for the wonderful opportunity to come to the house of prayer and worship the Lord, to see each other's faces, to listen to preaching, to sing, and to ask for a blessing over the worship, preachers, choir members, and other participants in the meeting. They also ask the Lord to prepare them for listening and praise. At the end, after the last sermon, they give thanks for the instruction they have received, and for the wonderful (regardless of their quality) sermons and singing, and they ask for the strength needed to "dissolve by faith"[74] what they have heard.[75] Quite often the prayer is completed with these words "In the name of the Father, the Son, and the Holy Ghost, amen" or by a phrase such as "in the

---

72. "Light of Gospel," Minsk, 14 December 2008. In "Golgotha," Minsk, 20 November 2011 the first preacher read James 3:17 and Prov 8:11 and spoke about wisdom coming from above; the second talked about God's grace in Eph 2:4–9; the third meditated about the future and the comfort which Christians have in the Lord, referring to Rev 1:8; 21:1–7. (Personal notes, 9.)

73. Belov, *Sekty, sektantstvo, sektanty*, 89.

74. Heb 4:2, literal translation from the Russian Synodal Bible (RSB).

75. Cf. Lensu and Prokshina, *Baptizm i Baptisty*, 208.

name of Jesus we ask, amen," as the literal interpretation of Christ's teaching about the efficacy of prayer.[76]

Baptists in Belarus do not separate the prayer at the meeting into different types, such as invocation, adoration, thanksgiving, supplication, intercession, or confession; they consider prayer as communion with God in general. Regular prayer includes thanksgiving (for spiritual blessings, opportunity to be at the meeting, preachers, singers, and youth), petition (asking for forgiveness for "voluntary and involuntary" sins, for the strengthening of the faith), and intercession (primarily prayers for the repentance of unbelieving children, grandchildren, husbands,[77] relatives, and neighbors, especially those who are enslaved by alcoholism).[78] The content of prayer is usually limited to the personal requests of the members and to church ministry. Only in rare cases is it possible to witness specific prayers about Christians in other countries or prayers about racial, social, or economic justice. However, many churches did begin to pray regularly for Ukraine in connection with the outbreak of hostilities in April 2014 as Ukraine borders Belarus. It is assumed that temporal, earthly, issues are not worth paying much attention to. The main task is to save human souls. Past political isolation and a negative attitude towards mass media and the news in general also play a certain role.

Nevertheless, some congregants ask for prayer about their individual "earthly" needs, presenting them to the congregation in their notes. They most often ask the church to pray about their health and the health of their family (while pastors often try to emphasize the primary importance of spiritual health), and about their unbelieving relatives, or some other urgent daily-life requests.[79] These requests often concern issues like moving to a new place, entering a university or looking for a job, or sometimes to thank God for various blessings such as the birth of a child or healing, and answered prayers. There is an assumption that pastoral prayer is particularly powerful and effective. Pastoral prayer is considered the prayer of the whole church

---

76. John 14:13.

77. Prayer topics reflect gender dynamics in churches. It is unusual for the husband to be a member and not his wife, but there are a number of female members whose spouses do not belong to the congregation. For example, a church in Borovliany, Minsk region, has seven female church members who have non-Christian husbands, while only one male member in the congregation has a non-Christian wife.

78. Q, 2008.

79. See Motorin, "O bogosluzhenii v dni apostolov i v nashi dni," p. 9.

to which the congregation expresses its assent by a loud "amen". The prayer requests that may be sent over to the pastor are typically characterized by the following: 1) "Dear brothers and sisters, I would kindly ask you to pray to our Lord Jesus Christ about my brother Vasily Stepanovich who is now going through a medical examination in Minsk City Hospital no. 3. His stomach will not take any food. For over two weeks his life has been supported through an intravenous line. Brother Dmitry." 2) "My dear church, I thank you for your prayers. My son Victor has had no fever for two days over a month since he felt sick. Praise the Lord. I would also ask to pray that the Lord may touch his heart and call him onto the way of salvation. Sister Praskovia." 3) "I ask the church to pray that the Lord may bless me on my trip and keep me safe on the way. I am going to Sevastopol. Thank you all. Sister Tatyana." 4) "The Melyanets Family, Alexander and Tatyana, thank the Lord for the safe birth of a daughter. We ask that the Lord may bless this baby as it grows up and restore the mother's health. Thank you. Alexander Melyanets."[80]

Songs, and pieces of poetry specially selected for the subject of the sermon, make the diversity of topics less noticeable and smooth out the structure of the service. Besides, the very diversity and disconnectedness of themes is not regarded as a failure of the service. The Holy Spirit is understood to address each person according to their spiritual needs. If it becomes evident that two of the preachers have selected the same Scripture text on which to speak, the second one may decide that his sermon approaches the text from a different perspective, or he may have an extra message based on a different passage, just in case.[81] In practice, a variety of topics, but within certain limits, is seen to be better than repetition of the same thoughts. Listeners do not complain about the diversity but about the quality of the material, or the extent of one component of the meeting at the expense of another.

---

80. "Light of Gospel" church in Minsk, 16 and 23 March, 2008 (Personal notes, 18b).

81. Personal interview with the pastor of the Baptist church in Man'kovichi, Brest region, 18 May 2008. I had this experience when preaching in the evening in "Light of Gospel," Minsk (15 September 2013). For the conclusion (the third sermon) I decided to preach about the ten virgins (Matt 25:1–13). However, the second guest preacher came to the pulpit and read the same text as the basis of his sermon. My dilemma was resolved in a rather surprising way. First of all, the guest preacher "embarked" on the Old Testament in the third minute of his sermon and never came back to the parable. Secondly, his sermon took such a long time that there was no time left for the third sermon. So, when I came into the pulpit, I could only read the parable in another translation and invite people to pray. I preached the sermon I had prepared the following Sunday.

In addition, traditional worship is held together by an evident common motif, or the "main focaliser," namely the motif of "the cross, or more precisely, the broken and glorified body of Jesus Christ who descended to the earth and ascended into heaven."[82] The centrality of the motif of the cross can be recognized both in the official statements made by church leaders[83] and the content of songs, prayers, and sermons themselves. Among the most popular hymns are songs about Christ:[84] "Vest' ob Iisuse skazhi mne" (Tell Me the News About Jesus), "Ne proidi, Iisus, menia Ty" (Pass Me Not, the Gentle Savior), "Iisus, dushi Spasitel'" (Jesus, Savior of My Soul), "Ty dlya menia Spasitel'" (For Me You Are the Savior), " Ot greha ya spasion" (I Am Saved from Sin), "Iisusa imia sladko mne" (Jesus' Name Is Sweet to Me).[85] During the Lord's Supper, songs which focus on Christ are sung, describing His sufferings and filled with feelings of pain and Jesus' death. Every first Sunday of the month, Baptists sing "Gospod', kogda uchenikam Ty smert' Svoyu yavil," (Lord! When You Revealed Your Death to the Disciples), "Kto podnimet svoy vzor na Khrista na kreste," (Who Will Raise His Eyes to Christ on the Cross), "V bagryanitse stoish' Ty v ternovom ventse," (You're Standing in the Purple Robe With a Crown of Thorns), "Vzoydem na Golgofu, moy brat" (Let Us Go Up to Calvary, My Brother), "Znayesh' li ruchey, chto bezhit," (Do You Know the Stream That Flows from the Cross)[86] and similarly themed hymns.

The interior of church buildings also typically indicates the centrality of the motif of Christ and his cross. One of the most popular texts which can be seen on the front wall of the house of prayer says: "We preach Christ who was crucified, was resurrected, and is coming again."[87] A Christocentric approach is applied to interpreting the Old Testament, generally in the form of seeing it as allegorical for/to the life of Jesus. Alexander Negrov states that in a similar way to the Orthodox tradition:

> evangelical readers of the Bible tend to interpret the rituals of the Old Testament as typological references to the life and deeds

---

82. Barnard, Cilliers, and Wepener, *Worship in the Network Culture. Liturgical Ritual Studies. Fields and Methods, Concepts and Metaphors*, 6.

83. Ivanov, *Dukhovnost' evangel'skikh khristian baptistov*, 15.

84. Q, 2008.

85. *Pesn' Vozrozhdeniya*, nos. 9, 30, 50, 138, 230, 745.

86. *Pesn' Vozrozhdeniya.*, nos. 416, 417, 419, 420, 421.

87. See footnote 647.

of Jesus Christ. Of course, in this regard we may say that the Christocentric reading of the Bible by evangelicals parallels not only Orthodox tendencies, but also reflects the indirect theological influence of the Protestant Reformation in Europe.[88]

5.3. Temporal Dimension of Public Worship

The aspect of time in church worship or the correlation of worship services to different time cycles is not given much coverage in articles, notes, or practical guidelines on the structure of church worship. However, there is a subsection called the "liturgical calendar of Evangelical Christians-Baptists"[89] in a manual published in 2010. Attention is given to the content of a particular worship service and its influence on those attending the house of prayer, but not to the relation of the service to the preceding or the following services. Nevertheless, there is some allowance for distinguishing between the weekly, monthly, and yearly cycles of worship in Baptist churches.[90] "Resident aliens"[91] live according to a different calendar from Sunday to Sunday, from the first Sunday of the month when they have the communion to the first Sunday of the next month, and from Christmas to Easter, making brief stops at other feasts, then proceeding through Pentecost and Harvest before going back to Christmas.

The foundation of the weekly cycle is Sunday. In Slavic languages other than Russian, the word for Sunday (Belarusian "nyadzelya," Bulgarian and Ukrainian "nedilya," Czech "nedele," etc.) denotes abstaining from "doing," and means "not working". It is often used in casual speech in many rural communities in Belarus. However, the main theological meaning of Sunday is not

---

88. Negrov, "Hermeneutics in Transition: Three Hermeneutical Horizons of Slavic Evangelicals in the Post-Soviet Period," 41–42.

89. Ivanov, *Dukhovnost' evangel'skikh khristian-baptistov*, 13.

90. For the history of the origins of the Christian Calendar and the meaning of the Seasons see the following: Metford, *The Christian Year. An Indispensable Companion to the Holy Days, Festivals and Seasons of the Ecclesiastical Year*; McGowan, *Ancient Christian Worship. Early Church Practices in Social, Historical, and Theological Perspective*, 217–260. The book by Robert E. Webber is very useful for preachers: *Ancient-Future Time: Forming Spirituality Through the Christian Year*.

91. From the title of the book by Stanley Hauerwas and William H. Willimon, *Resident Aliens: Life in the Christian Colony*.

related to leisure but rather to worship,[92] and this is reflected in the use of the language itself. The word for Sunday in Russian (the language of worship in Baptist churches)[93] is "voskresenie," which literally means "resurrection." It is the Lord's Day, and each Sunday is a little Easter. In the Orthodox tradition it is also a day of worship and joy, "the queen of days."[94] The authors of the Orthodox dictionary note that "having and attending Sunday services was considered so important in ancient times that it was not canceled even during the period of persecution."[95] Usually one (morning) or two (morning and evening) worship services are held on Sunday, and they begin at 10.00 a.m. and 6.00 p.m., although some congregations may slightly vary these times. Numbers 28:9–10 is used as a biblical foundation for the tradition of holding two meetings on Sunday (a double offering on the day of Sabbath), and most Baptists interpret this as a good tradition.[96] In practice, around fifteen out of sixty-four churches of the Association of Baptist Churches in Minsk and Minsk area had evening worship services on Sundays in 2013. The others limited themselves to only one service. There are various reasons for this: some church members cannot attend evening worship because of the great distance they must travel, public transport schedule limitations, or poor health; some congregations do not have their own buildings but rather rent a room for a limited number of hours on Sundays; in some distant rural areas there are no ministers able to take an evening worship service.[97]

---

92. Due to the specifics of their work some Christians can neither have rest on Sundays nor come for church worship, and others may not experience much rest since they are busy with involvement in two services and other Sunday events. The concept of the Lord's Day as the day of liberation and rest as expressed in Exod 20:8–11 and Deut 5:12–15 remains a challenge. (Searle, "The Church Gives Thanks and Remembers," 15–16.)

93. See footnote 1 on page 258.

94. *Polnyy pravoslavnyy bogoslovskiy entsiklopedicheskiy slovar', t. 1* [Unabridged Orthodox Theological Encyclopedic Dictionary, v. 1], 564.

95. *Polnyy pravoslavnyy bogoslovskiy entsiklopedicheskiy slovar'*, 564–565.

96. Q, 2008.

97. Some churches are exploring alternative forms of fellowship. For example, by 2010, because of low attendance, churches in Machulishchi, Slutsk, Stolbtsy, Minsk region had replaced the Sunday evening service with Bible study in groups. (Q, 2013.) The new practice was not accepted in Slutsk because of some internal conflicts, and at the beginning of 2013 the church went back to holding Sunday evening services. (Gennadiy Ralko, personal interview with author, Minsk, 11 February 2014 [Personal notes, 20].) Ralko is a Deputy senior presbyter in the Minsk area and pastor of ECB church in Slutsk. Another church in the Minsk region, "Bible Church" in Borisov, reinstated evening services in the summer of 2012 having stopped them in the mid-1990s. They believed this would encourage church discipline and Christian maturity.

The weekly cycle also consists of one or two services on weekdays in addition to Sunday services.[98] A service held during weekdays has the status of a prayer service with the distinguishing feature of prayers by church members (mostly on their knees) not only at the beginning and end of the service, but also after each sermon. These services are not usually intended for unbelievers, although they are welcome, but rather are designed for the needs of the church and its members. On average, the attendance at these meetings is lower, sometimes significantly so, compared with attendance at services on a Sunday morning.[99] Some church members regard these services as meetings for the most committed and spiritual church members.[100]

The monthly cycle of services is centered on the Lord's Supper. The meeting with the breaking of bread serves both as the beginning of the cycle in the current month, while also marking the end of the cycle because preparation for the Lord's Supper, including the traditional fast on Friday, begins during the previous week.[101] The monthly cycle is particularly significant for those church members who are not able to attend church worship as a result of their poor health or advanced age. On the first Sunday of the month, the brothers (primarily pastors and deacons) visit such people at home and in hospitals

---

(Interview with pastor Sergei Zhukovskiy, Minsk, 11 February 2014 [Personal notes, 20].) My personal experience of visiting churches shows that evening services are still well-supported in Brest, Kobryn, and other places in the Brest region. There are many Christians of the third and fourth generation there, and attending all church services is considered natural.

98. On weekdays, services may start a little later so that church members and guests may come to worship after work; these services may start as early as 6:30 p.m. or as late as 8 p.m. In Kobrin, Brest region, services take place on Wednesday and Friday evenings. Services at "Emmanuel" Church in Mogilev on Thursdays and Saturdays start at 10:00 a.m. because their building is located on the outskirts of the city and because most of those who regularly attend services on weekdays and Saturday are the elderly, and it is difficult for them to return home late in the day. (Personal visit of the author to the church service, 26 February 2019 [Personal notes, 20].)

99. "Golgotha," the oldest Baptist church in Minsk, has worship services on Thursday and Saturday evenings (prayer meetings) as well as on Sundays. In 2013, less than ten percent of members attended the service on Saturdays, because for most people it was a very inconvenient time. In the church council and members' meetings they often raise the issue of canceling the service but there is no consensus so far. (Pavel Osenenko, Minsk, personal interview with author, 7 March 2017 [Personal notes, 20].)

100. Q, 2008.

101. The preachers frequently stress the importance of preparation for the Lord's Supper. CCECB minister Khrapov made the recommendation, "It would be better to abide in fasting and prayer, abstaining from the intimacy in marriage and the body should be pure and properly clothed" (1 Cor 7:6; Heb 10:22). (*Dom Bozhii i sluzhenie v nem*, ch. 10.)

holding small worship services with communion there. In this way, people can be involved in church life at least once a month.[102] The monthly cycle is also important in terms of preaching in the church. Many churches arrange their preaching schedule for a month, and this determines the preparation for, and involvement of, preachers in the worship services.[103]

The yearly circle encompasses the key festivals related to the events of Christ's life and the life of the church. Observance of such special days is conditioned by both the Orthodox environment and references to the Old Testament,[104] such as the use of the text "Observe the Feast of the Harvest"[105] by a number of preachers during the celebration of the Day of Harvest. The Baptist church calendar used to be identical to the secular calendar and began with a New Year's celebration which was followed by Christmas on January 6–8. However, in the early 2000s most Baptist Union churches in Belarus changed the former tradition and now celebrate Christmas in late December. This has produced a positive result in terms of transition from the secular to the ecclesiastical calendar. New Year receives less prominence than Christmas, and Christmas, in fact, becomes the first holiday of the coming year. So far, Advent (as the special four weeks before Christmas) has not found expression in the traditional worship of the churches in Belarus.[106]

The holidays continue with New Year,[107] celebrating the "Orthodox" Christmas on January 6–8 (often with a stronger emphasis on evangelism),

---

102. An authoritative AUCECB minister has proposed that there is no need to have Communion in houses every month. "The practice of life shows that the Lord's Supper is served at home for the sick and handicapped, who are not able to attend worship for a long time . . . only on the request of the sick person who has been ill for a long time. There is no reason to practice it every month and on the same day." (Kolesnikov, *Khristianin! Znaesh lit y kak dolzhno postupat' v dome Bozhiem*? 53.)

103. Q, 2008. A preaching/sermon schedule usually comprises of a list of the preachers' names, dates of their sermons, and their order (the first, second, or the third).

104. Ivanov, *Dukhovnost' evangel'skikh khristian-baptistov*, 14.

105. Exod 23:16.

106. *Nastol'naya kniga presvitera* [The Pastor's Handbook], vol. 1, 286–291. This new Handbook does not even list the New Year as a celebration. Cf. "Tserkovnye prazdniki EKhB na 1976 God" [Church Feasts of the ECB for 1976], *Bratskiy Vestnik*, no. 6 (1975), 75. This list begins with the New Year (January 1) and finishes with New Year's Eve (December 31), following the secular calendar.

107. Most of the churches have worship services before the New Year (December 31 in the evening) and on New Year's Day (January 1 at midday or in the evening). As an example, in the Baptist church on Fortechnaya 61/1 in Brest, on New Year's Eve the worship service lasts about three hours. It starts at 10 p.m., then congregational prayer starts at about 11:55

followed by the Lord's Baptism (January 19), The Meeting of the Lord (February 15), Annunciation Day (April 7), and the feasts related to Easter. Palm Sunday (in Russian literally Willow Sunday) is celebrated a week before Easter, then Holy Thursday (The Lord's Passion in Gethsemane with the Lord's Supper during an evening gathering), rarely Good Friday, then Easter,[108] the Ascension, and the Day of Pentecost (Trinity Day).[109]

During holiday seasons, especially around Christmas and Easter, the number of services substantially increases. Christmas, Easter, and Pentecost celebrations in many churches last two or three days (if the third day at Christmas time is a Sunday). A 1976 edition of *Bratskiy Vestnik* magazine mentions as holidays the third day of Christmas (January 9), and the third day of both Easter and Whit Monday (the second day of Pentecost).[110] At the beginning of the second decade of the twenty-first century, these feasts are hardly celebrated. Nevertheless, the number of public worship services can be significant, particularly if we consider the "week of prayer" which takes place at the junction of the old and new years.[111] Churches that follow this tradition

---

p.m. and lasts 10–15 minutes. Thus, believers begin the New Year on their knees (Personal notes, 21.). As people come to church reflecting on the past, they thank the Lord for all the blessings of the year, and ask for more blessings for the coming year. The New Year songs (*Pesn' Vozrozhdeniya*, nos. 612–620) are about the Second Coming of Christ, the transience of life, and close encounter with Christ.

108. On this day churches gather from 10:00 – 11:00 a.m., as usual, but some churches change the time of worship. In the Baptist church on Fortechnaya 61/1 in Brest, on Easter Sunday morning the worship service starts at 6 a.m. (Personal notes, 21.)

109. In the Western liturgical calendar, Trinity Sunday is the one after Pentecost, but for Belarusian Baptists it is the same Sunday and they use both names for the Holiday.

110. "Tserkovnye Prazdniki EKhB na 1976 God," p. 75.

111. The schedule of the church on Fortechnaya 61/1, Brest represents a typical example of the 2012–2013 holiday season in large churches:
December 23 (Sunday) – a morning and an evening service.
December 24 (Monday) – an evening service on "Western" Christmas Eve.
December 25 (Tuesday) – a morning and an evening service on Christmas Day.
December 26 (Wednesday) – a morning and an evening service on the second day of Christmas.
December 27 (Thursday/Friday) – regular weekly prayer service.
December 30 (Sunday) – a morning and an evening service.
December 31 (Monday) – a New Year Eve evening service.
January 1 (Tuesday) – a New Year daytime service.
January 2, 3, 4 (Wednesday to Friday) – prayer services every evening.
January 6 (Sunday) – morning and evening services on "Orthodox" Christmas.
January 7 (Monday) – morning and evening services which continue Christmas celebrations.

hold prayer meetings every night for a week during the first days of the new year. Before the new year, the Union of Churches sends the churches a prayer calendar, suggesting a prayer request for each day.[112] For example, the Union of Evangelical Christian Baptists declared 2013 to be the year of the family, so many of the prayer requests dealt with family life issues. The crossover where one year ends and another begins is a special period dedicated to being alert, even though numerous Christmas events and concerns do not always allow concentration on prayer. Yet, committed church members try to attend all worship services resulting in up to twenty services in a period of sixteen days. However, this is the only time of the year when there are such a large number of meetings, and it also results from "two" Christmases as well as New Year between them. Whatever day of the week Christmas or New Year fall on, Sunday services are never canceled.

Easter season is marked by less frequency, although there may still be eight services in nine days (Palm Sunday to Easter Monday).[113] However, the importance of Easter is especially reflected by the length of the season. Christmas motifs are gone within a week or two after Christmas. In contrast, Easter is remembered for forty days in many churches. On Easter day itself, besides the singing of the *troparion* by the congregation, the ministers greet participants with the words "Christ is risen!" This is usually repeated three

---

112. A reduced version of the "Week of Prayer Program for 2013 in Baptist Churches in the Republic of Belarus" is as follows: December 30 (Sunday) – Prayer of praise, confession, and forgiveness. Thank God for the Christian family, which He has established and continues to bless.

> December 31 (Monday) – The prayer of gratitude for evangelism. Prayer for Christian families to be aware of evangelism, maturity of each member of the church, being faithful to the Great Commission and spreading the gospel to all people in Belarus . . .
> . . . January 5 (Saturday) – Prayer and thanksgiving for the death and resurrection of Jesus Christ. Prayer for the unity of the people of God, the unity of our brotherhood, and the unity of the churches.

113. An example of Easter services in "Light of Gospel," Minsk in 2014:
> April 13 (Palm Sunday) – a morning and an evening service.
> April 17 (Thursday) – service with Lord's Supper in the evening.
> April 19 (Saturday) – service in the evening (reading from the Gospels about Christ's suffering and death along with singing and praying).
> April 20 (Easter Sunday) – services in the morning and in the evening.
> April 21 (Easter Monday) – services in the morning and in the evening.

times and the church responds each time by saying: "He is risen indeed!" Worship services continue to begin in this manner until Ascension.[114]

The Transfiguration is celebrated on August 19 in memory of the transfiguration of Christ on Mount Tabor, and it is the last holiday of the yearly Baptist church calendar associated with the life of Christ here on earth. The celebration is not so important in comparison with Christmas and Easter. In the main collections of Christian hymns used in traditional worship there is only one hymn for this occasion "Tam na vershine ozarionnoi" (There, on the Illuminated Mountaintop).[115]

The importance of the celebrations for worship life can be measured by the number of songs in the collection that correspond to the event. In Pesn' Vozrozhdeniya there is only one hymn for Ascension Day,[116] and there are no hymns directly addressing the Lord's Baptism, The Meeting of the Lord,[117] Annunciation Day, or Palm Sunday. Other hymns about Christ and life with Jesus are sung in church worship on these days. On the other hand, in the collection there are twenty-two songs for Christmas, twenty-two for Easter, twelve for the Day of Pentecost, nine for New Year, and ten for the Day of Harvest.

The Day of Harvest, or Harvest Festival (the name Thanksgiving Day is used occasionally), is celebrated in the fall.[118] Harvest Festival summarizes the fruit of a spiritual harvest and thus closes the yearly holiday cycle very appropriately. This celebration provides an abundance of topics on various aspects of Christian life: gratitude for the harvest and spiritual blessings,

---

114. The forty-day period could be explained by Christ appearing to His disciples for forty days (Acts 1:3).

115. *Pesn' Vozrozhdeniya*, no. 676. The song is a kind of Bible lesson about the transfiguration and subsequent events. The author explains that in life, after the triumph of transfiguration, the Christian should expect sorrow, temptations, and hard work, but if Christ is in front of us we should have no doubt about the victory.

116. "O, kakoy nam put' otkrylsya" [Oh, what a way was opened for us], *Pesn' Vozrozhdeniya*, no. 675. This song reveals the way of the Cross, the promise of the Holy Spirit, and the main topic of the celebration is a return of Christ in glory.

117. See footnote 380.

118. Prokhorov notes that this feast did not come from the Orthodox tradition, and "the Russian celebration was drawn from the tradition of German Baptists and Mennonites" (Prokhorov, "Russian Baptist and Orthodoxy, 1960–1990: A Comparative Study of Theology, Liturgy, and Traditions," 202). Prokhorov refers to P.M. Friesen, *Die Alt-Evangelische Mennonitische Bruderschaft in Russland (1789–1910) im Rahmen der Mennonitischen Gesamtgeschichte* (Halbstadt, Taurien: Raduga, 1910), 422, 561.

encouragement to engage in activity (primarily to save the lost), spiritual sowing and harvest in the Christian life, and the Second Coming and God's judgment. On this day there is a tradition, especially in rural areas, of offering an abundant meal to every attendee. Guests may be invited from other communities. Harvest Festival is usually celebrated on the last Sunday of September, but may be moved to another Sunday in October or even to the beginning of November in order to visit other churches or invite guests.

In Soviet times, churches celebrated another holiday in the fall: the so-called "Day of Unity." It was originally established in 1945 in memory of the historic merger of the two brotherly movements, the Evangelical Christians and the Baptists, into a single Union in the fall of 1944.[119] In 1953 the editorial of Bratskiy Vestnik wrote, "We announce that two dear celebrations, such as the Feast of Harvest and the Day of Unity, are established this year: the first one on Sunday, September 27, and the second one on Sunday, October 25."[120] With the collapse of the AUCECB in 1992,[121] and the formation of separate unions in the newly independent states, the Day of Unity began to lose its place in the church calendar, and is hardly mentioned in Belarusian churches in the early twenty-first century.[122]

Currently, apart from Christmas and Easter, the focus on Christian holidays is weakening, especially in large cities. When the celebration of the Meeting of the Lord (the commemoration of the presentation of Christ in the Temple) falls on a working day, only two churches, "Light of Gospel" and "Golgotha", of the seventeen Baptist churches in Minsk celebrate that holiday. The churches outside of Minsk, and churches in the country, are more zealous in holding to Christian celebrations, since they have a strong sense

---

119. *Bratskiy Vestnik*, no. 3 (1948).

120. *Bratskiy Vestnik*, no. 2–3 (1953).

121. In fact, AUCECB was reorganized into the Euro-Asian Federation of ECB unions, but the main leadership functions of AUCECB were delegated to the national Baptist Unions. EAF only has a role in coordination and serves to connect the unions in the Commonwealth of Independent States.

122. Nevertheless, the Day of Unity is mentioned in a new Pastor's Handbook, published by the Russian Baptist Union. On this day the churches are called to talk about the "spiritual unity of all Christians, local churches, and regional unions that make together ECB Russian Union" (*Nastol'naya kniga presvitera*, vol. 1, 291).

of tradition and a large stratum of older believers who have free time, value traditions, and cannot justify any work on holidays.[123]

High regard for the celebrations enables them to play an important role in enriching the practice of worship. First, they become a kind of compass, pointing to Christ, and the redemptive acts of God in Christ; they take us on a year-long walk with Christ from his birth to his ascension. They also present a whole picture of his ministry and himself, as the observance of the Christian year is "a celebration not of what Christ did or said, but of Christ himself,"[124] (and indeed of the Trinity as evident in the Lord's Baptism or Pentecost). Second, preparation for the celebrations and relating them to each other may provide a framework for organizing Bible reading and preaching. However, in traditional Baptist churches the yearly cycle of festivals is not associated with lectionaries or any other scheme for systematic reading of the Bible. Thus, much of the potential of the festival seasons is lost, as are opportunities for systematic training and spiritual preparation for the celebrations.[125] In that sense, Baptists in Belarus have yet to rediscover the importance of time and seasons, and to move to a richer Christian calendar that can serve as a catalyst to worship renewal.[126]

---

123. From my personal experience (I grew up in a village and regularly visit churches in villages), commitment to resting from work particularly applies to people in rural areas. Even if it is a working day, on Christian holidays they try not to do work publicly in their fields and gardens. They perform only the most necessary steps to care for the cattle and the house, lest they should offend the Orthodox people.

124. Benjamin Gordon-Taylor, "Time," 113.

125. Before Christmas and Easter churches spend much time advertising meetings, the preparation of music programs, and evangelistic and social projects. On the other hand, Evangelicals have rejected Lent since it is not considered to be prescribed by the New Testament. Moreover, Lent was understood as a part of Orthodox rites which contradict the doctrine on salvation by faith. For example, Pashkovtsy's evangelical confession states that "only the righteousness of Christ justifies us by faith in the eyes of God, and not Lent, charity, bows to the ground or any other kinds of acts. Even though good works are inseparable from the true and living faith they can neither meet the requirements of the Law of God about sins nor they can save us." (http://slavicbaptists.com/2012/06/01/pashkavconfession/, last accessed 16 May 2019.

126. See White, "A Protestant Worship Manifesto," 84.

5.4. The Use of Space in Public Worship
5.4.1. Houses of Prayer: Status and Place in Worship[127]

It would be reasonable to assume that Baptist houses of prayer reflect the spirit of Baptist approaches to public worship, and that an examination of their design and composition can provide insight into the role, meaning, and components of worship.[128] However, the space in which traditional Baptist worship takes place has not yet been analyzed or critiqued, neither on the church level nor or as an element of theological education in Belarus, and, for this reason, the rest of this chapter pays significantly more attention to examining this particular issue. In the Russian-speaking environment, only two major articles on this topic have been published within the last three decades – both of them in the *Bogomyslie* journal.[129] Perhaps this is due to the fact that during the Soviet period churches had extremely limited opportunities to build any houses of prayer.[130] It was not until 1980 that permission was

---

127. See photos of houses of prayer, worship halls, and decorations in the worship halls in Appendix.

128. Nigel Yates provides a good overview of the interrelationships between theology and the structure of church buildings, as well as their history in the various denominations. Yates, *Liturgical Space. Christian Worship and Church Buildings in Western Europe 1500-2000*.

129. Ryaguzov, "O tserkovnoi arkhitekture" [On Ecclesiastical Architecture] and Golodetsky, "Kakim byt' domu molitvy" [What Should the House of Prayer Be Like], 250–261 and 262–266. The first author is himself a professional architect. In 2016 and 2017, *Bogomyslie* published articles by Ivan Gutsul. In the first article Gutsul discusses Christian symbolism in protestant architecture in Ukraine, and the second article contains a brief overview of the approaches to building houses of prayer in church history. See Gutsul, "Khristianskaya simvolika v sakral'noi arkhitekture protestantov Ukrainy – visual'noe vyrazheniye dukhovnosti veruyushchikh" [Christian Symolism in Protestant Sacred Architecture in Ukraine – The Visual Expression of the Spirituality of Believers], 27–345; "Molitvennyy dom – sakral'nyy khram ili mnogofunktsional'nyy kompleks?" [Is the House of Prayer a Sacral Temple or a Multifunctional Complex?], 73–95. In the last section of the second article the author describes "modern protestant temples in Ukraine."

130. For example, since October 1948, and until the end of Stalin's rule, 100% of the appeals by Christians to let them open a house of prayer were declined. (Sinichkin, *Vlast' i sluzhiteli tserkvi na etape formirovaniya VSEKHB (s 1944-go po 1949 g.). Traditsiya podgotovki sluzhiteley v bratstve evangel'skikh khristian-baptistov. Istoriya i perspektivy: Sbornik statey* [Authorities and church officials at the stage of AUCECB formation (from 1944 to 1949). The tradition of the training of ministers in the brotherhood of Evangelical Christians-Baptists. History and prospects: Collected papers] (Moskva: Rossiiskiy soyuz evangel'skikh khristian-baptistov, 2013): 162.) In the first third of the 20th century, the situation was more favorable (see 4.3.1.), even though the number of houses of prayer was very limited. In 1912 there was a house of prayer in the center of Minsk. (*Istoriya evangel'skikh khristian-baptistov v SSSR*, 83.) The first worship service in Slutsk was held in a Calvinist church, and in 1924 a house of prayer was built there. One poor brother donated a cow to build the house, and this inspired other Christians. (*Istoriya evangel'skikh khristian-baptistov v SSSR*, 385.) In Brest the Christians gathered in a

granted to rebuild a modified private home that had been the only Baptist prayer house existing in the capital of the country, Minsk, prior to the 1990s (Appendix 2.1.16).[131] The house of prayer in Brest, Fortechnaya 61/1, was built in 1986 (Appendix 2.1.2; Figure 2).[132] It became the first specialized cult building after the Second World War owned by Baptists in Belarus. In 1987, the church in Gomel received permission to build a new house of prayer. Its construction was completed in 1990.[133]

> New opportunities suddenly caught believers by surprise, and in a massive push for construction and the acquisition of houses of prayer, enthusiasm preceded theological considerations.[134] Each congregation made their own decisions about construction based on pragmatic, legal and financial opportunities, or

---

basement, then they rented a theater hall, and in 1926 they built a house of prayer. Around the same time, small houses of prayer were built in Pinsk and Grodno. (*Istoriya evangel'skikh khristian-baptistov v SSSR.*, 389, 391.)

131. Kanatush, "Istoriya evangel'skogo dvizheniya v Belarusi," 18. From March 1942 the church held its worship services in a former fish warehouse in Nyamiha str., 2 in downtown Minsk. In 1965 the government decided to use the area for the construction of Dom Mod (Fashion House) and the church acquired an unfinished house on the outskirts of Minsk. The Baptists finished the building at their own expense, but according to the decision of the City Council no. 46 on 18 February 1965, the building was legally taken away from the church, and then the church was allowed to rent it from the local authorities. When the church became a legal entity in 1990, much effort was required to acquire the documents for the building. It only became church property officially in 1999, after many appeals and negotiations.

132. Klopot, "Bozh'e voditelstvo," p. 15.

133. Navitski, *Jevanhiel'skija chryscijanie u Bielarusi: piat' stahoddziau historyi (1517–2017 hh.*, 357. When the church in Gomel received permission, it had three hundred and fifty-five members. For thirty-six years, the worship services had taken place in an expanded private home. From the Second World War to the early 1990s almost all the churches gathered in private homes or private homes converted for worship. There was a lack of space, especially in urban areas. In a letter to the Commissioner on Religious Affairs under the Council of Ministers of the Byelorussian SSR written on 30 June 1966, the believers of another community in Voolka Podgorodskaya, Brest complained about their lack of space. The area of the house of prayer was 60 sq.m., with an extra 20 sq.m. in an extension without any heating. That church had four hundred members, excluding *priblizhionnye*. (NARB, Stock 952, File 3, Case 21, 141–142.) The term *priblizhionnye* denotes adult believers, attending church for a long time (several years), but who have not yet been baptized, and so are not church members.

134. By 2012, seven buildings were built in Minsk and the Minsk district by churches in the Union of Baptist Churches in Belarus ("Bethlehem," "Light of Gospel," "Light of Truth," "Revival," Minsk; churches in Churilovichi, Machulishchi, and Zaslavl', Minsk district), six buildings bought and renovated ("Beam of Hope," "Good News," "Nativity," Minsk; churches in Gatovo, Sokol, and Zhdanovichi, Minsk district), and six other houses of prayer were in the construction process ("Resurrection" and "Sun of Righteousness" in Minsk; churches in Borovliany, Kolodishchi, Ratomka, Yuhnovka, Minsk district).

guarantees by donors, on professional training, and on individual preferences. Pastors were often personally involved in the construction, endeavoring to compensate the lack of experience with enthusiasm. Many new churches bought private residences for remodeling, adding additional space, removing or altering some walls to create a worship hall, and so forth. Such new buildings generally preserved the architecture of the residences they replaced.[135] In other instances, the buildings reflected the creative work of non-Christian architects whose primary concern may have been the outward appeal of the building without considering its functional role for worship as well as the theological significance of particular architectural arrangements.[136] However, as an exception to the rule, the "Ark" church building in Volkovysk, Grodno region, is worthy of attention, since the architect tried to present it in the form of an ark (Appendix 2.1.34; Figure 5).[137] Later, the extension of the church ministry, along with a greater familiarity with the architecture of Western churches, contributed to the construction of several multifunctional complexes which contain a hall, Sunday school classrooms, a canteen, a hall for church celebrations, and offices.[138] Thus, as noted in relation to other evangelical churches, "the gathering places can range from simple meetinghouses to elaborate buildings."[139]

---

135. Churches in Jackshitsy (Figure 4), Molodechno, Zhodino, Minsk region; churches in Voropaevo, Vitebsk region (Figure 5); Stebrovo, Brest region; Kalinkovichi, Gomel region, and others.

136. "Light of Gospel," Minsk (Figure 8); "Salvation" in Kolodishchi, Minsk region. In fact, ministers were involved in the decision-making. In 2012, "faith"-based decisions of former pastors in "Resurrection" church, Minsk and "Salvation" in Kolodishchi, Minsk region resulted in the sale of an unfinished building of "Resurrection" church after eleven years of construction, since there were no finances or prospects for continuing the construction. "Salvation" church is still in the process of construction after fifteen years.

137. See Houses of Prayer by the same architect in Appendix 2.1.7; Figure 8; Appendix 2.1.9a, 2.1.9b.

138. Churches "Bethlehem" and "Light of Truth" in Minsk (Figure 10); "Hope" in Grodno; "Salvation" in Brest. In the latter, the worship hall is transformed into a gym. It is a unique case among the churches in Belarus.

139. Stamoolis, ed., *Three Views on Eastern Orthodoxy and Evangelism*, 23.

Theological uncertainty about church architecture is further evidence of the minor role of church buildings in Baptist belief and worship in comparison to the Russian Orthodox church. Tatyana Nikol'skaya draws attention to the fact that during the Soviet era Orthodox communities often ceased to exist after authorities closed their church building, while Protestants adjusted more easily to the new conditions. Their services did not require specially equipped facilities or special liturgical objects, other than the Bible.[140] Such an approach to worship is reflected in the Baptist reference to "the gathered church."[141] The primary interest of Baptists was in opportunities to assemble and worship rather than in a building or its status, for the church is "where two or three are gathered together in my name,"[142] as expressed in the following hymn:

> Not a temple covered with gold
> Not a circle of chosen men
> The Church of Christ is a congregation of
> People redeemed by the cross.[143]

Evangelical Christians also argued against the splendor of church buildings. Magnificent decoration and ornamentation of cathedrals was interpreted

---

140. Nikol'skaya, *Russkiy Protestantism i gosudarstvennaya vlast' v 1905–1991 godakh*, 37.

141. Haymes, "Theology and Baptist Identity," 2. Keith Jones posed legitimate theological objections to the use of this term in favor of 'gathering community', see his "Towards a Model of Mission for Gathering, Intentional, Convictional Koinonia," 5–13. Also, Parushev "Gathered, Gathering, Porous: Reflections on the nature of baptistic community," 35–52.

142. Matt 18:20.

143. "Ne hram, ne zolotoye zdanie" [Not a Temple Covered with Gold], *Pesn' Vozrozhdeniya*, no. 252. Text by I.S. Prokhanov.
Negative attitudes towards Orthodoxy are clearly stated here. The lyrics and words of the song below hint at the fact that Evangelicals thought Orthodox practices unscriptural:
> My God doesn't live in churches with crosses
> Where incense and candles emit fumes.
> My God searches for acceptance and simplicity
> As well as passionate love to lighten the gloom.
> God is watching over everything,
> Fields and forests are His dome,
> To all He gives deliverance from sin,
> Humans' hearts He makes His home . . .
> My God dwells not in temples, I know,
> He's inside me; before the King I bow.
> His love embraces me and further flows
> To warm and lighten weary souls . . .

(Poem "Moi Bog" [My God], *Stikhotvoreniya, declamatsii, istorii*, fourth, fifth, and sixteenth stanzas.)

as an obvious deviation from the simplicity of Gospel teaching and the nature of God who does not need such buildings:

> Israel, you're trying to earn my endorsement
> With shining temples full of icons
> Full of glittering and tinsel, incense burnt,
> Where day and night, the lights are on.
> What should I do with pompous works?
> Soulless stone is dust of the earth.
> I created the waters and the sun,
> I by hand draw the skyline.[144]

To justify this position, it was not only the Bible that was employed,[145] but also historic interpretations:

> From the time of Emperor Constantine, the Christian church began to rapidly fall astray from the teaching of Christ.... For some people the glitter of gold became more precious than the light of teaching of Christ.... In order to please wealthy and famous parishioners, who were in essence pagans, the Christian temples were being decorated with much splendor and glitter in the same manner as pagan ones.... But following pagan examples Christians started to worship their temples, considering them to be holy. They began to decorate them with gold, silver and stone and worship this manufacture of human hands.[146]

Thus, the evangelical houses of prayer are valued above all from a practical point of view. And if worship services continue to be held in converted houses, or in the homes of the pastor's family,[147] the situation prompts a purely utilitarian approach to the building and its function. The house of prayer must encourage the edification of believers, provide space for

---

144. Hymn "Israil', moi narod, vnimai!" [Israel, My People, Hearken!], *Pesn' Vozrozhdeniya*, no. 125, Second and third stanzas. Originally published in *Vestnik dukhovnykh khristian-molokan* [The Journal of Spiritual Christians Molokans], no. 1–2 (1925), 19. The author of the poem is the Russian poet–theologian A.S. Khomyakov (1804–1860). When he refers to "the new Israel", he is speaking of the church of his own day.

145. John 4:24; Acts 7:48–50.

146. Somov, "Tserkov' Khrista i ejo Svyashchenstvo," 60.

147. Rudensk, Sokol, Zhdanovichy (Appendix 2.1.39), Minsk region and others.

fellowship, and meet evangelistic purposes. Orderly from the outside and modestly decorated inside, buildings are seen to develop positive attitudes among and toward Baptists, and to encourage visitors to return.[148] The place of worship should promote "the spiritual mood to think about biblical truths and create an atmosphere of prayer."[149] It is therefore preferable to have a specialized building, but if such does not exist, a congregation can meet in different premises. In fact, starting in the 1990s, over a period of about fifteen years, a number of Baptist churches rented lecture halls, cultural centers, clubs, cinemas, educational establishments, and back rooms.[150] Room composition, furniture, acoustics, time, and the cost of renting the premises could be seen as a disadvantage. Yet no theological arguments were raised against using secular rooms.

However, the utilitarian attitude is in tension with the idea of the sacredness of a building where appearance may sometimes be more important than functionality. Ideas around buildings holding elements of sacredness are likely derived from the Orthodox environment and are perhaps accepted more readily in situations where any historical or ongoing conflict with Orthodoxy is perceived less sharply. As opportunities arose, some churches were able to build magnificent purpose-built structures, preferring respectful appearance to the notion of "inexpensive church."[151] This alternative theological vision is reflected in new Baptist terminology: following the Orthodox pattern, large houses of prayer are sometimes called "temples."[152] This suggests evidence of

---

148. Compare this with an understanding of beauty in Orthodox theology as a reflection of the glory of God. See Bulgakov, *Pravoslavie* [Orthodoxy], 243; and Schmemann, *For the Life of the World*, 29–30.

149. Ivanov, *Dukhovnost' evangel'skkih khristian-baptistov*, p.17.

150. After the new edition of the Law "On Freedom of Religion and Religious Organizations" came into force on November 16, 2002, it has become more difficult to rent public buildings.

151. Cherenkov, *Litsom k litsu*, 75.

152. "Light of Gospel" and "Bethlehem," Minsk (Appendix 2.1.15; Figure 7 and 2.1.17; Figure 9); "Salvation" church in Kolodishchi, Minsk region (Appendix 2.1.9a and 2.1.9b); central Baptist church in Kobrin, Brest region (Appendix 2.1.8; Figure 6); church on Fortechnaya 61/1, Brest (Appendix 2.1.2; Figure 2).

Indeed, even a small house of prayer could be referred to in the same manner because it is also a place where God dwells among the believers. A pastor in his opening prayer of public worship might pray "I thank you, Lord, for being able to come into Your temple," as was the case in a church in Berezino, Minsk region.(Personal visit of the author to the church service, 7 January 2009 [Personal notes, 88b].). Such prayers are not uncommon from the mouths of traditional Evangelicals. A text in the worship hall of a rather small house of prayer in Shatsk,

the influence of Orthodox theology and cultural expressions, coupled with Old Testament worship imagery. Practically, this lofty terminology also reflects an awareness and awe of the Lord's presence. During worship even the least appealing building becomes "a temple:"[153]

> When you walk into the house of God
> Throw away your anxiety and watch your heart and feet,
> So as to hear, to hear the Word of God.
>> This place is holy, sacred is this place here,
>> This is the house of God, the house of God.
>> This is the house of God, sacred is this place here.
>> This is the house of God, sacred is this place here,
>> This is the house of God, here are the gates of heaven . . .
>> Throw away your anxiety, heed the words of Christ.[154]

Minsk region reads: "That Your eyes may be open toward this temple night and day," taken from 1 Kings 8:29, translation from the Russian Synodal Bible (Appendix 2.3.10.2).

153. Schmemann analyzes the "transposition" of the idea of the temple at the beginning of Christianity. In his opinion the role of the building was instrumental (as the place of gathering) in the pre-Constantine Church. He claims that "The church building was gradually freed from subordination to its ecclesiological meaning, acquired its own independent significance, and the center of attention was shifted from the Church assembled and realized within it to the church building itself, as in fact a sanctified building or sanctuary." (Schmemann, *Introduction to Liturgical Theology*, 113–114.)

154. *Notny sbornik dukhovnykh pesen* [Music collection of spiritual songs], vol. 3, part 1 (Moskva: Vsesoyuznyy sovet evangel'skikh khristian-baptistov, 1988), no. 11.

The notion of the sacredness of a house of prayer is expressed in a special service after the completion of the construction, or a reconstruction of a newly acquired building, a service of "consecration" or "dedication" of the house of prayer. The text in I Kings 8 relating the story of the dedication of the first temple is often recited during such a service as the congregation prays that the glory of the Lord may fill "this temple" and that the name of the Lord may be glorified in this place through church ministry and the conversion of unbelievers. The pastors and senior pastors raise their hands as they say a special prayer of blessing and dedication. During the consecration of a rather small church building in Volozhin, Minsk region, sermons and prayers contained such words and phrases as "temple," "holy place," and "Your home" (Personal visit of the author to the ministers' meeting, 14 October 2012.). Indeed, the Baptist doctrine of faith in Belarus considers the consecration of the house of prayer to be a sacred rite (*Verouchenie evangel'skikh khristian baptistov v Belarusi, prinyatoye na s'ezde EKhB v Belarusi 15.03.2003 goda.* [Doctrine of Faith of Evangelical Christian Baptists in Belarus, adopted at the Congress of ECB in Belarus 15.03.2003], Unpublished material, 8.1). Consecration of the house of prayer is a regular worship with solemn congratulations and one special feature – the ministers say a prayer with their hands lifted up.

The concept of a house of prayer as a place where God is especially present can sometimes lead to unexpected problems and discussions. For example, is it permissible to have lavatories or a table-tennis table in the house of prayer? Can non-Christian neighbors borrow benches from a house of prayer for use in a wedding? In the latter case, a congregation may refuse the request, believing that benches of the house of prayer should not be used in situations where people would drink alcohol and so bring dishonor to the Lord.[155] A House of prayer belongs to God as it is called "My House," and it needs more care than a private house. It is also understood to be different from other types of buildings. Ivan Gutsul, a modern Ukrainian art critic, believes that "the house of prayer, where the community of believers gets together, should . . . dominate over other buildings by its architectural spiritual symbolism . . . [it should not lose its] 'sacral spirit.'"[156]

The status of "the Lord's house" demands a corresponding statement in design and decoration. Large, wealthy congregations, especially in south-western Belarus, along with the central Baptist church "Golgotha" in Minsk (Appendix 2.2.4.1, 2.2.4.2, and 2.2.4.3), creatively decorate their church space with refined ornaments, paintings, carved balustrades, original light fixtures, engravings, mosaic floors, stained glass, and so on.[157] These buildings also display calligraphically written or sculptured Scripture texts; modeled, carved or embroidered pictures of an open Bible, cups and loaves of bread, grapes,

---

155. Related by a guest preacher from the Ukraine with regard to the service in church on Fortechnaya 61/1, Brest, 12 October 2008. It is interesting to make a comparison with the rules of the Orthodox church, such as, "the temples should not be robbed and turned into regular dwelling and a transformed one should be restored . . ." or "one should not eat and sleep inside the temple." (*Kniga Pravil svyatykh apostolov, svyatykh Soborov Vselenskikh i pomestnykh i svyatykh ottsov* [The Book of the Rules of the Holy Apostles, the Saints of the Ecumenical and Local and Holy Fathers], Moskva, 2004). Cited in Verhovih, "Kanon v Arkhitekture pravoslavnoy tserkvi" [Canon in Architecture of the Orthodox Church], 27.

156. Gutsul, "Molitvennyy dom – sakral'nyy khram ili mnogofunktsional'nyy kompleks?" 94. Gutsul refers to Matt 5:14 among other references, groundlessly applying the image of the city on a hill to a church building.

157. The standard of life of evangelical Christians in the south-west of Belarus is higher than in Belarus in general, as reflected in the number and quality of private cars in the church parking lots. Being so close to the border with Poland contributes to the development of cross-border trade and other kinds of business. Those living in the capital of Minsk enjoy better financial life than those in the other regions, since the main sources of income are from within the city and the labor market is developed.

or the cross; paintings of nature that occupy almost the entire front wall;[158] or paintings on the ceiling.[159] Onlookers may observe that while the ornate beauty of Orthodoxy is avoided in favor of simplicity in Baptist houses of prayer,[160] some churches nevertheless no longer perceive stark simplicity as their guiding principle, and only financial limitations restrain their zeal.

Thus, two visions of church buildings seem to exist among Baptists of Belarus: a utilitarian structure on the one hand, and the church building as a temple on the other. The historical development of Baptist identity in the region requires simplicity in relation to the house of prayer, and focusses on the people, not the building.[161] At the same time, the influence of the Orthodox environment, the personal convictions of some pastors and believers, and the newfound ability of the church to acquire plots and build has led to the construction of "temples" that the church may later struggle to maintain.[162] In turn, the presence of grand buildings brings temple-terminology back to life. Thus, the two theological approaches coexist, and it seems that only the political and economic situation currently provide any correctives either in constraining meetings within the house church model, or in restraining the practical implementation of a larger, church building vision.

---

158. Church in Man'kovichi and church on Moprovskaya, Pinsk, Brest region (Appendix 2.2.24a; Figure 15 and 2.2.30).

159. Church in Man'kovichi, Brest region (Appendix 2.2.24a and 2.2.24b; Figure 15); church in Shatsk, Minsk region (Appendix 2.2.35a and 2.2.35b; Figure 18); central Baptist church in Gomel (Appendix 2.2.1.1; Figure 19).

160. Harris, *Toward an Understanding of Russian Baptist Worship*, 6.

161. At the consecration of houses of prayer, preachers often repeat texts such as the following: "The God who made the world and all things in it, since He is Lord of heaven and earth, does not dwell in temples made with hands." (Acts 17:24); "Or do you not know that your body is a temple of the Holy Spirit who is in you, whom you have from God, and that you are not your own?" (1 Cor 6:19).

162. Houses of prayer in Divin (Appendix 2.1.3) and Kamenets, Brest region; Volok (Appendix 2.1.35) and Chalevichi, Minsk region. In the last two there were no worship services during the winter of 2012–2013 since the churches consisted of small groups of retired people who were not able to pay the heating bills when the prices dramatically increased. The members gathered for worship in a small house of prayer belonging to another church in the neighborhood or they worshipped in the houses of the church members.

It is important to mention that financial opportunities and low energy prices were not the only reasons for building houses of prayer that proved to be too big. It was also due to the enthusiasm associated with a significant influx of people into the church in 1990. At present, the inflow has lessened, and many villages are dying out as young people leave for the cities.

5.4.2. The Language of the Interior

Turning to the worship hall specifically, we will begin with a particularly notable feature: the "sacramentalisation" of walls decorated with biblical texts. Such designs are especially customary in villages and small towns.[163] In contrast to the emphasis on Christ the Almighty, the Pantocrator in Orthodox church design, a particularly common Scripture is a fragment of 1 John 4:8 or 4:16: "God is love." This text is often displayed in large letters on the front wall of the worship hall. The intent is to shape the context of worship,[164] while another text, "We preach Christ crucified,"[165] explains the aim and purpose of the worship service. In contrast to the cult of the saints and Mary in the Orthodox tradition, the message being conveyed here is that the focus of worship and preaching is to be Christ. The same focus is also reflected in the inscription "And behold, I come quickly,"[166] indicating an expectation of Christ's Second Coming. Closely connected to this eschatological emphasis is the call to repentance: "The time is fulfilled, and the kingdom of God is at hand; repent and believe in the gospel."[167] Other Scriptures bring the elements of praise and enthusiasm to the notion of worship by inviting everyone to

---

163. Liuban', Minsk region (Appendix 2.3.5; Figure 17); Svyatopolka, Golovchitsy, Drogichin (2.3.3), Zaveleve (Appendix 2.3.12; Figure 13) Brest region. There are six texts in the house of prayer in Liuban' – Matt 11:28; 2 Cor 1:23; John 3:16; Rev 22:7; John 8:11 and "God is love" on the front wall. On 13 May 2012, the church in Drogichin consecrated a new house of prayer. Hereinafter, the data relating to the church in this thesis describes their former building, which had been functioning up until that time.

164. "Golgotha" in Minsk (Appendix 2.2.4.1; Figure 16); central Baptist church in Gomel (Appendix 2.2.1.1); church in Man'kovichi (on the signboard of the house of prayer) and Pruzhany, Brest region (Appendix 2.1.14 and 2.2.31; Figure 12); Machulishchi, Mar'ina Gorka, Molodechno, Soligorsk, Minsk region (Appendix 2.2.22, 2.2.3.2, 2.2.26, and 2.2.36).

165. I Cor 1:23-24. Church in Voolka, Brest (Appendix 2.3.13); churches in Pruzhany, Voolka, Luninets district, and Zaveleve, Brest region (Appendix 2.2.31, 2.2.39, and 2.3.12.1); churches in Machulishchi and Slutsk (on the pulpit), Minsk region (Appendix 2.2.22 and 2.2.6.5). Its broader version is "We preach Christ [who was] crucified, resurrected and [is] coming again," As in the Central Baptist church in Kobrin, churches in Drogichin, Malech, Brest region (Appendix 2.2.1, 2.3.3.1, and 2.2.23a); church "House of Gospel" in Vitebsk (Appendix 2.3.24); central Baptist church in Gomel (Appendix 2.2.1); church "Hope" in Grodno (Appendix 2.2.15a); church in Liuban', Vileika district, Minsk region (Appendix 2.2.21). In Drogichin and Molodechno the text is carved in the pulpit.

166. Rev 22:7. Central Baptist church in Kobrin and church in Malech, Brest region (Appendix 2.3.4.2 and 2.3.16; Picture 9); church in Ilich, Gomel region (on the pulpit) (Appendix 2.2.16).

167. Mark 1:15. Also Hosea 10:12, Matt 11:28. Church in Malech, Brest region (Appendix 2.2.23a); church on Fortechnaya 61/1, Brest (Appendix 2.3.2.1); church in Mar'ina Gorka, Minsk region (Appendix 2.3.7.4).

praise and give all glory to the Lord (such as Psalm 19:1, Psalm 29:1b, Psalm 146:1, or Rev 14:7).[168]

An assumption can be discerned here that God's Word has the ability to change people without further explanation, preaching, or commentary: a soundless sermon can touch people's hearts even before the worship service starts.[169] Each person present at worship can learn about God's love, repent of their sins, receive salvation through our crucified and resurrected Christ, and glorify the Lord for salvation. The transforming character of the worship service is revealed through the fact that a person may return home as a new being. "Go your way. From now on, sin no more"[170] is often written above the exit. This serves as a warning, reminding the worshippers of the inseparable connection between worship services and daily life.

In addition to the Scriptures that are permanently in view, temporary, seasonal texts may also be displayed. "For today in the city of David there has been born for you a Savior, who is Christ the Lord;" "For to us a child will be born, a son will be given; And the government will rest on His shoulders; And His name will be called Wonderful Counselor, Mighty God, Eternal Father, Prince of Peace,"[171] and other similar texts mark Christmas. On the Day of Harvest, "Observe the Feast of the Harvest" may be exhibited.[172] For the New Year, a church anniversary, or the sanctification of the house of prayer,

---

168. "The heavens are telling of the glory of God; And their expanse is declaring the work of His hands;" "Ascribe to the LORD glory and strength;" "Praise the Lord, O my soul!" "Fear God, and give Him glory." (Appendix 2.3.6.1, 2.3.21, 2.3.3.4, and 2.3.8.4).

Some of the texts are found in singular variants. The church in Molodechno displays the text, "To guide [sic] our feet into the way of peace." (Luke 1:79 [Appendix 2.2.8.5]). This particular Scripture text survived in the house of a church member during the many years when the Soviet authorities abolished all the texts that referred to anything "religious," such as a call to repentance, or in which the name of God was mentioned. This particular text was written in such a way that it did not formally represent a threat to the authorities; on the contrary, it spoke about peace, a theme which was very popular with the Soviet regime. (Victor Butrovich, Pastor of Molodechno Baptist church, personal interview with the author, Molodechno, 20 April 2012 [Personal notes, 88b].)

169. Decorations and painting in the Orthodox church also preach to those who can understand this sermon. In the words of Archpriest Alexei Vasin, "When I enter church, I enter the Bible." ("Round table," organized by Minsk Theological Seminary on 13 October 2016.)

170. John 8:11. Churches in Drogichin, Malech, Brest region; churches in Liuban', Mar'ina Gorka, Minsk region (Appendix 2.3.3.2, 2.2.23b, 2.3.5.5, and 2.3.7.2).

171. Luke 2:11; Isa 9:6. Church "Light of Gospel," Minsk (Appendix 2.3.17a and 2.3.17b). See also Matt 1:23b in "Quiet Haven" church in Bobruisk, Mogilev region (Appendix 2.2.10b).

172. Exod 23:16. (Personal notes, 88b.)

"Thus far the LORD has helped us" would be another popular decoration.[173] These Scriptures are *sui generis* justification for the centrality of the Bible in traditional Baptist worship.

The tradition of decorating houses of prayer with biblical texts goes back to the beginning of the evangelical movement in Belarus,[174] starting with the believers' houses where worship services were held. Even today, in the "red corner" (the corner of the sitting room opposite the entrance and between the windows, where there would be a cross and/or an icon in an Orthodox household) elderly Christians often display the text, "God is spirit, and those who worship Him must worship in spirit and truth"[175] – a clear indication of the disapproval of the Orthodox practice. It would be much easier to place framed Scripture on a wall but, located in the corner where it replaces an icon, the reference to worshipping in spirit and in truth explains the absence of an icon. However, such artefacts could also gain an "iconic" value themselves.[176] The zeal in filling a house or apartment with Scriptures could possibly explain a recommendation in *Bratskiy Vestnik* (taking into account the political and religious circumstances of that time), that "in a home of a Christian everything should contribute to spiritual joy and glory to the Lord. There should be no more than two or three Scriptures in austere frames, bookshelves with good books, and some reproductions of paintings on religious topic or landscapes, etc."[177]

However, the post-Soviet period has witnessed changes in terms of the use of biblical texts. Firstly, aesthetic considerations and relevancy play an increasingly significant role. Scripture texts in the worship hall are expected to represent a certain artistic value, to be in harmony with the surroundings, and to be perceived as "beautiful." Similar changes can be noticed in the houses of young Christians where one finds fewer Scripture texts, and those that do exist are exhibited mainly because of their artistic value and design. Secondly, the number of texts has decreased in the houses of prayer, or in some cases

---

173. 1 Sam 7:12. Church "Hope" in Grodno; church "Ark" in Volovysk, Grodno region (Appendix 2.2.15a and 2.2.38a).

174. Milovidov, *Sovremennoe shtundobaptistskoe dvizhenie v Severo-Zapadnom krae*, 9.

175. John 4:24. (Personal experience of author's family and other Baptists in Belarus.)

176. Cf. *Evangel'skie khristiane v Rossii i Sovetskom Soyuze*, 423.

177. A.R., "Khristianin v bytu" [A Christian in Everyday Life], 65–67, 65.

there are no decorative texts left at all.[178] They are beginning to be replaced by symbols, such as beautifully illuminated crosses,[179] banners and tablets,[180] menorahs,[181] or open Bibles. Among young people, symbols are generally gaining importance . Modern tendencies could probably be viewed as part of a shift towards a new paradigm, where symbols are regaining importance.[182]

Turning to the interior architecture, we can talk about five liturgical spaces: *a gathering space* in a vestibule, the rear part of the hall itself, or even a courtyard; *a congregational or seating space* which may include a balcony; *a space for movement* (this serves for collecting offerings, distributing the elements of the Lord's Supper, and for special acts such as wedding ceremonies); *a space for the choir and musicians*; and a *space for ministers and preachers*.[183]

---

178. "Bethlehem" and "Light of Truth" churches, Minsk.

179. Churches in Slutsk, Stolbtsy, and Zhodino, Minsk region (Appendix 2.2.6.1, 2.2.34, and 2.2.40); churches in Novopolotsk and Ushachi, Vitebsk region (Appendix 2.2.27 and 2.2.37).

180. Churches "Hope" in Grodno and "Emmanuel" in Mogilev (Appendix 2.2.15a and 2.2.25).

181. "Grace of God," Bobruisk, Mogilev region. (Personal notes, 88b.)

182. Webber, *Ancient-Future Faith: Rethinking Evangelicalism for a Postmodern World*, 34. Walter Ong, in his analysis of the main stages in the history of the word and in evaluating the decreased role of the text, speaks about "secondary orality," replacing the oral-aural period. See his *Orality and Literacy: The Technologizing of the Word*, 85.

183. Cf. terminology in White and White, *Church Architecture. Building and Renovating for Christian Worship*, 18, and Jones, "We Are *How* We Worship: Corporate Worship as a Matrix for Christian Identity Formation," 359.

Remarkably, baptisteries are extremely rare in traditional Baptist houses of prayer. The exceptions in this regard are churches in Voolka, Brest, central Baptist church in Kobrin, Brest region; Machulishchi, Minsk region; "Bethlehem," "Light of Truth," and "Light of Gospel," Minsk (Appendix 2.2.5.3), and a few more. (Personal notes, 2.) There is a clear preference of baptizing in rivers or lakes (Appendix 2.4.1), the roots of which are historical. In the days of persecution, it was necessary to conceal the time and place of baptism, especially the baptism of young people, so such services often took place in hard-to-find open water locations. For example, see Sawatsky, *Evangelicheskoye dvizheniye v SSSR posle Vtoroy mirovoy voyny*, 375–376. After the collapse of the Soviet Union, the churches could baptize openly, and they did it with evangelistic purposes in mind. It is interesting that up until 2017, "Light of Gospel" church in Minsk, which has a baptistery, conducted baptisms not in the house of prayer but in a river flowing a hundred meters away from the building. Baptisms in the house of prayer were an exception, happening in circumstances such as someone's poor health or disability which made it impossible to perform the baptism in open water. Since 2017, because of the difficulties in obtaining permissions for open-air baptisms, the church has moved its baptismal acts to the baptistery. The lack of finances and pragmatic concerns has also influenced the churches' decisions to forego the installation of baptisteries; in small churches, for example, the baptism of one or two believers once a year does not justify the expense of having a baptistery. However, "Bethlehem" and "Light of Truth" churches in Minsk (Appendix 2.4.2) actively use their baptisteries which allows them to incorporate baptism in regular worship. Baptism in baptisteries is becoming popular among young churches in Minsk, and they occasionally rent baptisteries from other churches.

The main activities during the meeting take place around the aforementioned liturgical spaces for the choir, musicians, ministers, and preachers on an elevated "stage." Many churches avoid this term because they are apprehensive of the connotations of secular culture, and prefer more neutral words, such as the "elevation" or "elevated platform." The lack of terminology for describing architectural features of the church building from a liturgical point of view is suggestive of a lack of attention to the theology of space. The choir occupies the largest area on the elevated platform, and its prominent location emphasizes the importance of the "rite of singing."[184] The pulpit provides the liturgical focus and is usually located in the center[185] or to the left (as the congregation looks at the preacher) of the elevated area.[186] Its prime function has been to provide the necessities for preaching: the platform elevates the preacher so that they may be seen and heard, it provides a ledge to hold their Bible and manuscript, and perhaps a sounding board or microphone to increase their audibility.[187] The central position, dominance, size, and decoration of the pulpit stress the importance of preaching.

Furthermore, since the baptism in the house of prayer is more convenient and does not require permission from the local authorities, the need for a baptistery is likely to become increasingly important. It is notable that in 2014 "Golgotha" church in Minsk rented the baptistery in "Light of Gospel" for the first time in twenty years because of lack of time to obtain permission to hold open water baptism as a result of the new governmental regulations. In 2015 and 2016 "Golgotha" rented the baptistery in "Bethlehem" church in Minsk. (Pavel Osenenko, personal interview with the author, Minsk, 7 March 2017 [Personal notes, 32].)

Like the baptistery, a table for the breaking of bread does not play a particularly important role, and may even be completely absent during regular worship meetings. At the same time, the rise in the notion of the sacrality of the house of prayer as a building and aesthetic pursuit have resulted in specially decorated communion tables which are architecturally harmonious with the pulpit. This can be seen in "Light of Gospel," Minsk; Pershai and Zhodino, Minsk region (Appendix 2.2.5.1, 2.2.29a, and 2.2.40).

184. Karev, "Svyashchennodeistviya tserkvi," 38. (See Appendix 2.2.1.2; 2.2.2.2; 2.2.5.1; 2.2.24a; and 2.2.30).

185. "Golgotha," Minsk (Appendix 2.2.4.2; Figure 16), Lesovnia and Mar'ina Gorka, Minsk region (2.2.19 and 2.2.3.1 and 2), church on Moprovskaya in Pinsk and church in Sadoviy, Brest region (2.2.30 and 2.2.33; Figure 11).

186. Churches in Malech, Man'kovichi, Brest region (Appendix 2.2.23a, 2.2.24a; Figures 10 and 15); churches in Slutsk and Machulishchi, Minsk region (2.2.26.1 and 2.2.22).

187. The pulpit is sometimes also used as a storage space or a small locker that holds the baskets or plates for the offering, plates and chalices for the Lord's Supper, songbooks, and other Christian literature.

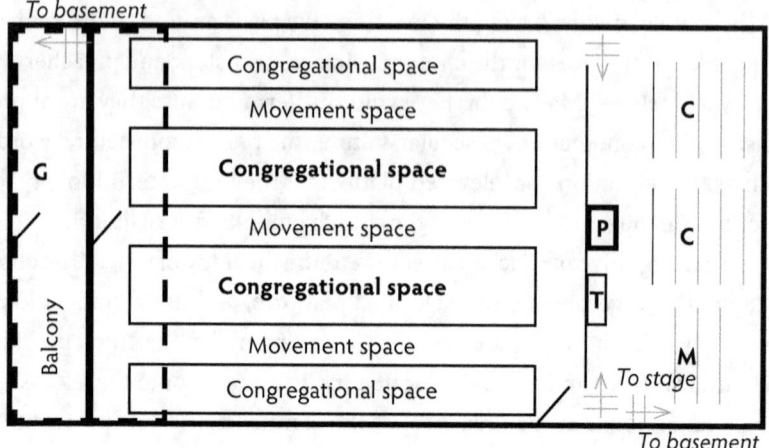

Fig.2. Plan of Baptist church hall on Moprovskaya, Pinsk, as a representation of a classical type of the house of prayer building.[188]

In the twenty-first century, new designs or alterations reflect a shift from the pulpit to the stage as a whole.[189] Altering the size and position of the pulpit frees the central part of the stage for other components of the worship service, or alternatively it becomes just one of the details on the stage. Very large pulpits between the listeners and the choir on the centroidal axis may hide part of the choir who in turn view the back of the preacher without any visual interaction. In some churches, pulpits have become smaller and more elegant,[190] while other churches have moved the pulpit from the elevation

---

188. The chart presents a classical type of the house of prayer building. Key: G – gathering space, P – pulpit, T – table, M – ministers space, C – choir space. On sanctuary structure see Overbeck, "The Worship Environment," 578. A new trend is to have a creche in one of the corners of the hall, at a distance from the pulpit. The creche is isolated from the hall, but its big windows and audio system allow parents with little children to hear and see what is going on in worship. This is the case in Central Baptist church in Kobrin, Brest region; "Christmas" and church on Fortechnaya 61/1, Brest.

189. Compare the new and old structures in Central Baptist church in Gomel (Figures 19 and 20) and in Central Baptist church in Kobrin (Figures 21 and 22).

190. "Light of Gospel," Minsk; Voolka, Brest; Central Baptist church in Gomel and church in Slutsk, Minsk region. The last three churches used glass to build a new pulpit.

down to the main floor, and/or replaced it with a movable pulpit[191] or music stand.[192]

Another significant aspect is the fact that churches are paying more attention to music ministry. Here the model of edification may be giving way to a more entertainment-based model, with the design of worship halls resembling that of concert halls. The stage, therefore, becomes more spacious and beautiful. Some churches are also switching to a more participatory style, and an easily accessible stage can be used for the participation of children and all members of the church.[193] A hierarchical interpretation of liturgical space is being replaced by what Tomas Schattauer, Lutheran Professor of Liturgics, calls "non-hierarchical arrangements of space,"[194] in response to challenges by ministers who want to convey that they are part of the worshipping community and that the Holy Spirit, not them, is in control of the meeting. As a result, the barrier between the hall and the stage is diminishing, as ministers and other worship leaders move from an elevated area to the first row of seats in the hall; the distinction of "ministers' space" thereby merges with "congregational space."[195]

However, at the same time, traditional conceptions about the structure of the worship hall continue to be preserved and remain strong. Those who oppose the types of changes outlined above consider shifts to "theatrical presentation" to be a censurable imitation of the world with its performance-culture, as a "deviation from the true Christian spirit", and as an unacceptable confusion of "the spiritual and the mundane."[196] From their perspective, "the barrier" which divides the worship hall between pastors and congregations is not really a barrier, because any worship participant may come forward

---

191. Central Baptist church and "Bethany" in Kobrin, church in Pruzhany, Brest region; church in Novopolotsk, Vitebsk region.

192. "House of the Gospel," Vitebsk. (Personal visit of the author to the ministers' meeting, 1 July 2015 [Personal notes, 2].) In the church in Mar'ina Gorka some preachers do not come up to the pulpit, but simply stand in front of the stage, and turn to the congregation with the Bible in their hand (Personal visit of the author to the church service, 2 October 2011 [Personal notes, 9].)

193. See, e.g. the newly rebuilt "friendly" arrangement in Slutsk and Berezino, Minsk region.

194. Schattauer, "Liturgical Studies: Discipline, Perspectives, Teaching," 129.

195. Churches "Light of Gospel" and "Bethlehem" in Minsk; church in Slutsk, Minsk region; church "Hope" in Grodno and church "Ark" in Volkovysk, Grodno region. (Personal notes, 2.)

196. Golodetsky, "Kakim byt' domu molitvy?" 263.

and offer a poem, song, testimony, or (in some cases) sermon; the physical division of the space is only a reminder that participation in worship services requires special dedication, solemnity, and responsibility. The fact that the ministers are elevated does not contrast them with the congregation, but only provides them with more authority as God's servants. In addition, the elevated position allows the ministers to observe the congregation, and an experienced pastor is thereby able to notice those who are constantly late, those who spend time in the hallway, and those whose seats are vacant. Therefore, the desire to preserve the status quo remains strong enough to preclude widespread, rapid changes in the configuration of the liturgical space.

Following the collapse of the Soviet Union, circumstances changed dramatically, confronting evangelical believers with new questions. If Christians before the 1990s were concerned with the opportunity to have a house of prayer, now their concern is to establish what 'the house of prayer' or 'the temple' look like? If earlier they were concerned with the mere fact of the worship service as an opportunity to get together for singing, prayer, and Bible study, greater importance is now applied to the environment of that meeting, to the architecture, design, and ornamentation of the house of prayer. If Christians were previously interested in the opportunity to take a seat at a house of prayer, the focus now is also on the quality and comfort of the benches or the look of the stage.

Some churches strive to give an impetus to public worship by making use of new technological and multimedia tools.[197] Congregations including the Central Baptist church in Kobrin, Brest region, the church in Voolka, Brest, and "Light of Gospel" in Minsk have installed projectors or LCD monitors to project lyrics and Scriptures.[198] It is the argument of this thesis that the lack of a theology of worship more generally impacts all other areas of the worship service, including the criteria by which changes and alterations in form and in the worship space itself are assessed. Suggestions for change, and decisions relating to the actual alterations undertaken, do not usually involve serious theological discussion and tend to be primarily guided by questions of aesthetics, comfort, and financial resources.

---

197. SI, 2012.

198. Personal visits of the author to the services of the church 25 October 2015, 9 October 2016, and 2 July 2017, respectively (Personal notes, 2b.)

At this juncture, the work of Baptist theologian James McClendon in his book *Doctrine*, offers a helpful framework for use in making a more theological appraisal of what the current situation with regard to worship spaces might tell us about worship thinking. McClendon undertakes a study to discover what the biblical requirements might be for defining a worshipping community, particularly a baptistic community, and how these can be reflected within the gathering of believers for worship. He summarizes his understanding in a number of principles that could be applied to any place in which Christians gather to worship – whether a dining room or crumbling basilica, a "temple" or small meeting house. McClendon stresses the principle of accessibility for all who may wish to come, to make it comfortable for the strangers and the lame; there are no unwelcome visitors. Then, in order to maintain fellowship with one another and with God, he notes the importance of visibility and audibility, we must be able to both see and hear one another and hear prophetic preaching. Next is the notion of modesty, as "church space is servant's quarters, not a princely palace." Balance is important here; we welcome quality but not luxury. Finally, it should be a place where Christians experience God's presence – what McClendon calls "numinous space."[199] That is something that could happen even in the open field, not just in a building.

Evaluating the present state of houses of prayer in Belarus against McClendon's criteria highlights several areas in need of more careful consideration and interrogation. Theological uncertainty around the status of the house of prayer, and practical factors such as the lack of experience and resources, may play a key part in any lack, but the issues revealed by such an assessment are useful lessons and focus attention on the nature of the challenges faced. Regarding the principle of accessibility, quite often steps, a complicated system of stairs, or a steep ascent interfere with access to the house of prayer for the elderly and especially for the disabled who are not able to overcome those obstacles without some external aid. This is true for old, reconstructed, and new buildings. No Baptist house of prayer in Belarus has an elevator, and the cost of equipment tends to preclude any installation. In addition, the negative attitude of the authorities to the Evangelicals has

---

199. McClendon, Jr., *Doctrine, Systematic Theology*, vol. 2, 414–415. Cf. Irvine, "Space," 111–112. "In considering the design, reordering and assessment of liturgical space" Irvine pays attention to "(a) visibility, (b) audibility and (c) the acoustic of the building."

resulted in many houses of prayer being built on the periphery, thus making it more difficult to reach them without personal transport.

Despite the commonly repeated verse that "faith *comes* from hearing,"[200] acoustics in worship halls often suggest a different order of priorities, with audibility not necessarily high on the list. The lack of special training in the field of acoustics for architects and building-engineers, coupled with the lack of resources, can lead to a worship hall being shaped and decorated in ways that do not allow for the natural flow of sound. Even small sanctuaries may need microphones, amplifiers, and speakers to facilitate communication. Nevertheless, technical solutions cannot always compensate for the faults of construction; any inefficient microphone use by musicians or reciters makes the problem even worse.[201]

Regarding the principle of visibility, the issue of the field of vision is usually successfully resolved because halls are open; they have good lighting and high ceilings, though in some cases people in the balcony may experience discomfort if the height and size of the balcony are disproportionate to the size of the worship hall or if the view is obstructed by columns.[202] Although the verbal nature of a service does not set high requirements for visibility, limited visibility can easily hinder the comprehension of speech and does not create the feeling of belonging and community among the people present in the worship hall. The oblong shape of the sanctuary (in most houses of prayer) limits opportunities for the whole congregation to be able to see and interact with each other. The focus of attention is shifted to the "front" and communication between members becomes subservient to edification.[203]

Reflecting McClendon's principle of modesty, here the simplicity of decorations is indeed the result of theology, but also of financial limitations. Yet in this area there is a need to guard against another extreme, as McClendon reminds us: "Lavish use of costly materials strikes the wrong note, but so does pinchpenny construction . . . tightfisted builders waste more than those who plan (and spend) well."[204] In the 1990s, when many houses of prayer were

---

200. Rom 10:17.

201. The lack of good audibility stands at odds with an emphasis on spiritual formation and edification.

202. Church "Light of Gospel" in Minsk.

203. See section 6.3.

204. McClendon, *Doctrine*, 415.

quickly constructed, very limited finances and a deficit of good building materials in Belarus, had a negative effect on quality and soon the buildings were in need of repairs.

However, well-crafted services can compensate for shortcomings and lead to encountering God's presence. As McClendon points out, Jacob experienced God's presence "at a lonely wayside shrine, where in his sleep he had dreamed a dream (Gen 28:11–17)," and that presence can be experienced in exactly the same manner in the 'simplest chapel in the wood', or even in a place with no building at all, as in the grandest artistic monument.[205] Christ is in the midst of His faithful ones when they are gathered together in His name.[206]

At the beginning of the second decade of the twenty-first century, Baptists in Belarus have accumulated significant experience in the construction and reconstruction of houses of prayer, but much of that experience remains unclaimed. The period of intensive construction has ended, church growth and the process of planting new churches has slowed, and new buildings are not being filled. It is harder to find the funds from donors in the West, and it is almost impossible to get land and permission for the construction of a house of prayer in Belarusian cities. Churches are now reaping what has been sown over the period of about twenty years, from 1990 to 2010. Some of the faults have been gradually corrected: churches alter the elevated platforms, improve the acoustics, and replace heating systems and windows, but many churches live under the consequences of their earlier choices. If a comprehensive theology of worship is to be developed, then more attention needs to be given to the role of the physical place of worship itself. Further study is needed to explore how our theology is reflected in architecture and internal organization, and what the choices we make about our buildings says about the nature of the community that gathers there for worship.

---

205. McClendon.
206. Matt 18:20.

CHAPTER 6

Theological Emphases of Traditional Public Worship

The first part of the thesis sought to explore the historical, political and theological contexts in which traditional forms of Baptist worship developed in Belarus. This part of the thesis has sought to analyze in detail the form, content, and physical space of worship in order to understand the actual practices of the worship itself. Having laid this groundwork, Chapter 6 turns to a more detailed and specific examination of what theological emphases those practices express, and the theological understandings they reveal. The final chapter will then bring all the elements together to discuss the tensions inherent in their interaction and how these tensions may in fact hold the key to contextually appropriate, theologically grounded ways forward in developing this expression of Baptist worship in Belarus.

There are some common values that are frequently emphasized regarding traditional Baptist worship. As will be argued below, these values include simplicity, the central role of the Bible, an emphasis on edification, and evangelism. This list is a product of engagement with other studies on Baptist worship, and the analysis of the formation, content and form of Russian-speaking worship itself. It is largely these emphases that determine the characteristics of traditional worship in Belarusian Baptist churches.

Christopher Ellis, exploring "The Soul of Baptist Worship," lists simplicity, attention to Scripture, devotion and openness to the Spirit, fellowship, and kingdom focus as the key elements or characteristics of Baptist worship.¹ Thomas McKibbens defines those elements as including "simplicity, dependence on the Holy Spirit, the centrality of preaching, the prevalent anthropocentrism."² In fact, all these characteristics describe traditional Baptist worship in Belarus to various degrees. However, observation, experience of participating in worship, interaction with participants, and review of the materials by indigenous writers direct the research to these specific areas: the centrality of the Bible, simplicity, edification, and evangelism. "Openness to the Spirit" or "dependence on the Holy Spirit" will be studied in the final part of the thesis from the point of view of tension between freedom and form in worship.

The central role of the Bible is the main focus of the worship. The authors of the official history of ECB churches in the USSR stress that it was the Bible which defined the form and content of the worship of evangelical Christians. They argued that matching the "practice of Christian life against the teaching of the Gospel" brought people "to reject rites and rituals of Orthodoxy."³ Karev states that "the Word of God has the most important role in evangelical worship."⁴ This idea is supported by the references to creeds and hymnals in section 6.1.

Edification, the importance of "instruction by the Word of God"⁵ is related to the Bible. Konstantin Somov highlights this in his article and contrasts it to the Orthodox understanding of worship.⁶ First, edification is achieved in worship.⁷ This term was often used by ministers and church members in the research questionnaires, when they were seeking to explain the purpose of worship.⁸

Inclusion of evangelism in the list is justified, as we will see later, by the content of worship, the nature of the worship space (see section 5.4.2. The Language of the Interior), the texts of hymns, and the results of observations

---

1. Ellis, *Gathering*, 71–99. See also Ellis, "Duty and Delight: Baptist Worship and Identity," 337.
2. McKibbens, "Our Baptist Heritage in Worship," 66.
3. *Istoriya evangel'skikh khristjan-baptistov v SSSR*, 154.
4. Karev, "Slovo Bozhie" [The Word of God], 14.
5. Somov, "O propovedi I propovednikakh," 33.
6. Somov.
7. Karev, "Svyashchennodeistviya tserkvi," 38.
8. QM, 2008; Q, 2008.

by secular and Orthodox researchers. Personal experience and the experience of worship participants also indicate the importance of evangelism.

The last theological focus could be defined as simplicity. From the very beginning of the gospel movement in the Russian Empire its apologists called for the simplicity of worship, and they were critical of the outward magnificence, luxury, and splendor of the Orthodox liturgy.[9] Later, in 1966, on the pages of *Bratskiy Vestnik,* Baptist worship was contrasted to a "pompous ritual" of the Orthodox Church.[10] The official website of the Russian Baptist Union states that "our worship services are distinguished by external simplicity, in such a way that the pomp of the rite and external attributes could not obscure somebody's fellowship with the Living God."[11] The evolution of worship in the future may require changes or additions but the proposed list sufficiently covers the current situation.

6.1. Centrality of Scripture

6.1.1. The Importance of the Bible in Life, Doctrine, and Worship

The first theological emphasis of traditional Baptist worship is the centrality of the Bible. Scripture, the Bible, or God's Word – terms which are used interchangeably – is proclaimed to be the foundation of worship. The authors of the official history of the Baptist churches in the Soviet Union stress that the Bible determined the shape and content of Baptist worship from the very beginning, pointing out that the movement itself "began as a result of comparing Christian practice with the teaching of the Gospel, and it led to abandonment of Orthodox rituals and statutes."[12] Thus "Bible-believing" Christians read the Bible, listened to the sermons, and expressed sentimental and tender love for this Book in their songs. A few lines from a popular hymn illustrate this sentiment, combining devotion and a reverent attitude towards the Bible as a book:

---

9. Prokhanov, *V kotle Rossii,* 20. Liven, *Dukhovnoe probuzhdenie v Rossii,* 21.
10. Belousov, "Gospod' sila moya i pesn'," p. 76.
11. https://baptist.org.ru/read/article/94201, last accessed 4 November 2019.
12. *Istoriya evangel'skikh khristian-baptistov v SSSR,* 66.

> Living Word divinely spoken, wonderful and true!
> My heart delights in you!
> What a gift for every day! You direct me on my way
> To my homeland where the Lord will take me soon.[13]

Another well-known song speaks of the exceptional value of the Bible in the believer's spiritual life:

> I will never forsake the holy Bible,
> For in it I found salvation and eternal joy.
>> I trust only the Holy Bible, it gives me truth and light,
>> It is the spring of life and there is nothing like it.
> Never will I abandon the Holy Bible,
> Never will I abandon this Holy Book.[14]

The shortage of Bibles suffered by evangelical Christians up to the time of *perestroika* enhanced the value attached to the Bible as a book for those who sang these hymns. As illustrated by a letter from the leadership of AUCECB to Baptist churches in 1957, churches were able to obtain a small number of Bibles, primarily for the preachers. Supplying every church member was out of the question,[15] although Christian families may have had a copy of the Bible at home. The situation improved by the mid-1980s, but even then, many Baptist believers would have obtained their personal copy illegally (that is, a copy that would have been smuggled into the country), and it may well have cost a whole month's salary.[16]

In the wider context, the extraordinary importance of the Bible in public worship has been associated with the crucial role attributed to Scripture in terms of daily Christian life, doctrinal statements, and the personal devotion of Christians. The description of Baptist worship in Estonia by Toivo Pilli, who speaks of a Word-orientated understanding of faith,[17] can also

---

13. "Kniga Bogom mne dana" [God-Given Book], *Pesn' Vozrozhdeniya*, no. 754, refrain.

14. "Naveki ne ostavliu Svyatuyu Bibliyu" (I Will Never Forsake the Holy Bible), *Pesn' Vozrozhdeniya*, no. 701, first, forth stanzas, and refrain.

15. *The History of the Evangelical Movement in Eurasia* 4.0, Primary sources, EAAA, 2005.

16. This was also my personal experience; my first Bible was obtained illegally, and it cost the equivalent of my mother's monthly salary. Usually small-size Bibles were smuggled into the country. For a background story of 'Bible smugglers', see Brother Andrew, *God's Smuggler*.

17. Pilli, "Evangelical Christians-Baptists of Estonia: The Shaping of Identity, 1945–1991," 164. Also see Pilli, "Baptists in Estonia 1884–1940," 27–28.

be applied to the Belarusian context. According to the Statement of Faith of Belarusian Baptists, "Holy Scripture is the source of Christian faith and spiritual guide for believers."[18] However, this statement is not as categorical as the 1928 Confession which proclaimed that the Bible was "the only source of knowledge about God as well as the only rule and measure of our faith and conduct."[19]

The Bible functions as the key tool for personal worship, which is basically defined as Scripture reading and prayer. As one Western researcher observed in the 1960s, "it was the specific contribution of the 'sectarians' to the religious life of Russia that they helped to fill the gap of [the knowledge of the Holy Scriptures]."[20] A Soviet author noted, "Many Orthodox Christians have no Bibles and have a vague idea of what it is about. In contrast, the sectarians view the Bible as their handbook. It is recommended that they spend much of their free time reading 'Holy Scripture.'"[21]

The contrast drawn between the Baptists and the Orthodox believers is helpful for understanding the essential role of the Bible. The first evangelical believers in the Russian Empire pointed to a disastrously poor knowledge of the Bible and indifference to God's Word among the Orthodox parishioners, stressing that "all worship was reduced to mere rituals and ceremonies and it rested upon people's ignorance, their age-long desire to worship tangible objects, saints and relics."[22] In 1876–1877, such a lack of biblical literacy was acknowledged by the famous Russian writer and Orthodox apologist Nickolai Leskov, although in a much more sympathetic tone: "Russian people have a good and warm faith, although most of them are not versed in Scripture."[23]

Vladimir Martsinkovskiy, Christian thinker, lecturer, and one of the leaders of the Russian movement of Christian students, describes a typical episode. After the 1917 Revolution, he was on a train with Red Guard soldiers.

---

18. *Zayavleniye very evangel'skikh khristian-baptistov v Belarusi, Mart 2002* [Statement of Faith of Evangelical-Christians-Baptists, March 2002], Unpublished, 1.5.

19. Odintsov, ed. *Ispovedanie very khristian-baptistov, 1928* [Christian Baptist Confession, 1928], https://slavicbaptists.com/2012/02/10/verouchenie1928/, last accessed 16 May 2019.

20. Kolarz, *Religion in the Soviet Union*, 298.

21. Ryabushkin, *Kto takie sektanty*, 13.

22. Kruedener and Lion, *Evangelist. Zhizn' i sluzhenie Ivana Onishchenko* [An Evangelist: The Life and Ministry of Ivan Onishchenko], part 1, ch. 25, http://www.blagovestnik.org/books/00092.htm., last accessed 16 May 2019.

23. Leskov, "Velikosvetsky raskol," 81.

One of the soldiers was boasting of his "exploits," robberies and murders that he was involved in during the revolution. The author writes: "I couldn't stand it anymore, so I rose from my place and asked the man, "Did Jesus teach you to do this in the Gospels?" to which he replied, "Do you think we read it? We only kissed the cover of the Book . . . But we have no idea what's written in it.""[24] Similarly, Ivan Prokhanov complained that "people's religious ignorance takes grotesque forms. If you ask somebody, 'Who is more important, Saint Nicholas or Jesus Christ?' most frequently you'll hear the answer, 'Of course, Saint Nicholas.'"[25]

However, defining themselves as against the Orthodox was not the only factor which contributed to the centrality of Scripture in the public worship of the Baptist churches. Baptists also saw themselves as a part of the Reformation tradition with its emphasis on the Word,[26] and more specifically, the heirs to the radical Reformation, in which there were no "fathers," no "tradition," and no authorities or sources of faith other than the Bible. As Steven Sheeley put it, "Baptists, that unmanageable subset of Protestant Christians, have styled themselves as 'people of the Book.'"[27] The Orthodox priests also noted that Baptist preachers paid special attention to the knowledge of the Bible. A. Vvedensky reflected that Baptist preaching was so successful because of the efforts and care invested in literacy, reading the Gospel, and religious conversations.[28] From the Baptist point of view, their desire to follow "the first Christian Church of the Apostolic period"[29] encouraged them to gather "around the Word of God passed on by the Apostles and later their successors."[30]

The value of the Bible in public worship is expressed in the significance attached to the Ministry of the Word in an assembly of believers. In fact, the major elements of this type of worship are not the Word and the sacraments, as in classical Protestantism, but the Word (understood to be both Scripture as well as the sermon(s) on that Scripture), prayer, and singing.

---

24. Martsinkovskiy, *Zapiski veruyushchego*, 48.
25. Prokhanov, *V kotle Rossii*, 21.
26. Engle, series ed. and Basden, gen. ed., *Exploring the Worship Spectrum*, 176.
27. Sheeley, "Baptists and the Bible Translation: Toward a Deeper Understanding," 8.
28. Vvedenskiy, "P'yanstvo i sektantstvo," 698.
29. Somov, "O propovedi i propovednikakh," 33.
30. Somov.

These are the staple elements of weekly worship,[31] with the Word considered to be of primary importance.[32] Thus, preaching takes most of the time in public worship; the latter is in fact "a service of the Word set in the context of prayer and praise."[33] Nikolai Alexandrenko, an author of a book on homiletics for Russian-speaking readers, states, "preaching is basically worship."[34] Alexander Karev likewise writes that "preaching is the central sacred rite of the New Testament Church."[35] The structure of the hall, or more specifically the place of the pulpit, also reflects the idea of the centrality of the Word.[36]

The written Word is to direct listeners towards the Word Incarnate, Jesus Christ, and it is through faith in Him that people can be saved. God's Word is therefore called the first instrument of grace God uses to draw sinners to Himself because it enables men and women to awaken from their deep sinful

---

31. Cf. Jones, *A Historical Approach to Evangelical Worship*, 83.
32. Q, 2008; QM, 2008.
33. McKibbens, "Our Baptist Heritage in Worship," p. 61.
34. Alexandrenko, *Homiletica* [Homiletics], 26.
35. Karev, "Svyashchennodeistviya tserkvi," 36. In a few churches, a text on the pulpit surface facing the preacher says, "The place where you are standing is holy" (Josh 5:15) in order to fill the preacher with awe and a feeling of responsibility (Church on Fortechnaya 61/1, Brest; Church in Svyatopolka, Brest region, Personal visits of the author to the church services 11 December 2011 and 12 February 2012, respectively [Personal notes, 11]).

36. A number of churches would traditionally keep a big Bible on the pulpit, which created an inconvenience for preachers who usually preferred to use their own Bible. Examples of such churches would be the following: in Pinsk (on Moprovskaya) and Yatskovichi, Brest region; church "Ark" in Volkovysk, Grodno region; church in Mozyr', Gomel region; churches in Soligorsk (Appendix 2.2.36) and Slutsk, Minsk region; "Grace of God," Bobruisk, Mogilev region. In Volozhin, Minsk region, a new house of prayer was built in 2010 and a large-size Bible was placed on the pulpit. In some churches, like in Mikashevichi, Brest region, the Bible was removed or moved to the shelf inside the pulpit, or moved to Communion tables, such as in Ushachi church, Vitebsk region and Liuban', Minsk region. In the Central Baptist church in Kobrin, Brest region, until 2010 there was an old pre-revolutionary copy of the Bible for people to see on the pulpit. Later on, it was only displayed once a year during the Day of Harvest, when it was elevated next to the fruit of the earth with gratitude to the Lord for the physical and spiritual bread. Some churches keep the Bibles on the pastor's table, as in Central Baptist church in Gomel' and the church in Novopolotsk, Vitebsk region. This information was gathered from Q, 2013. Regarding this, Barnard, Cilliers, and Wepener make an insightful remark: "An always open Bible on the pulpit is a fallacious symbol, especially if it is an antique exemplar that is not in use – as is the case in many churches. The center of worship is not an exhibition space, the Bible is not a museum piece." (*Worship in the Network Culture. Liturgical Ritual Studies. Fields and Methods, Concepts and Metaphors*, 96.)

sleep, acknowledge their sins and guilt, and show true repentance for these sins.[37] Or, following the lines of a song,

> Oh Holy Bible! It alone
> Has the power to correct people' life.
> There we see
> How our Savior suffered for us.
>> Oh Holy Bible! It alone
>> Brings a message of life
>> In the Father's love and Jesus' blood
>> That He shed on the cross.[38]

6.1.2. Back to the Bible

The analysis of worship in traditional Baptist churches provides sufficient ground for the centrality of Scripture, but it also reveals a tension between the proclaimed role and the actual role of the Bible. The claim to Bible-centeredness is not always supported by the actual content of worship. Indeed, this is not unique to Russian-speaking Baptists, but may signal a wider problem amongst those claiming Baptist heritage. As preachers do not follow any kind of lectionary and have freedom in choosing the topic and passage for the sermon, this results in "a sad lack of Scripture reading in many Baptist churches."[39] Contemporary North American Baptist theologian Steven Harmon comments, "Although Baptists have sometimes called themselves "people of the Book," many Baptist congregations hear very little Scripture in the context of worship."[40] A similar picture emerges in traditional Baptist services in Belarus.[41] As text choice is conditioned by

---

37. Cf. Odintsov, *Ispovedanie very khristian-baptistov*, chs. 6 and 7.
38. "Svyataya Bibliya" [Oh Holy Bible], *Pesn' Vozrozhdeniya*, no. 824, first and second stanzas.
39. McKibbens, "Our Baptist Heritage in Worship," 67.
40. Harmon, *Towards Baptist Catholicity: Essays on Tradition and the Baptist Vision*, 161.
41. To take the example of three worship services in "Light of Gospel" church in Minsk, their nine sermons (the duration of each being fifteen to twenty minutes) included the following texts: (1) Acts 2:42–47; Matt 12:15–21; Eph 2:11–12; (2) Phil 4:4–7; John 1:40–42; Jer 24; 29:7; (3) Eph 3:14–21; Rom 8:2–6; 2:13; Eph 2:11–12. Although the preachers read other short texts to support some of their ideas – usually one or two verses – given that the total duration of the sermons would be over six hours, this does not stand out as a great amount of Scripture. (Personal visits of the author to the church services, 1 July 2007, 8 July 2007, and 13 January 2008 [Personal notes, 10b].)

preacher preferences, some biblical books or texts could be forgotten entirely, with preachers preaching a significantly reduced Scriptural canon instead of "the whole purpose of God."[42]

The above is an indication of a shift from reading Scripture to explaining Scripture, or from Bible-centrism to sermon-centrism.[43] Anatoly Rudenko, director of the Russian Bible Society, speaks of "the cult of the sermon," where "the preacher is the only one who addresses the audience, and the Word of God, the Bible, is only a source of quotations which the preacher uses to support his ideas and exhortations."[44] This may not be universally true; some preachers may engage with long Bible passages and stay with the text, but the tendency is obvious.

In the past, faced with an almost complete lack of reference literature and no access to theological education, many preachers simply retold Bible passages, and even today one can still hear this from elderly preachers in small churches. This approach could also be supported by an understanding of the sufficiency of Scripture. An outline of this type of sermon, recorded during worship in a Baptist church in Molodechno, Minsk region, is presented below. The text for this sermon was Psalm 67.

> "May God . . . make His face shine upon us . . ." We also ask about it. What happens when the Lord makes His face shine upon us? What will we see in our heart?
>
> "May the peoples praise You." Who do people praise today? They praise many people, rulers, celebrities. But we should praise God . . . Brothers and sisters, let us praise God.
>
> "And all the ends of the earth will fear Him." Right now people fear no one. More than that, they are proud of their achievements and exalt themselves. But a time will come when they will fear the Lord Most High. In contrast, believers fear the Lord,

---

42. Acts 20:27.

43. It may be pointed out that while the law of God was read out loud clearly and then "interpretation was added" (Neh 8:8, literal translation from Russian Synodal Bible) during that period of worship in Jerusalem, nowadays many preachers first interpret and then add the text to their interpretation.

44. Rudenko, *Kul't propovedi i sluzheniye slova* [The cult of the sermon and the ministry of the word]. http://gazeta.mirt.ru/stat-i/vzglyad/post-1657/, last accessed 14 August 2014.

praise Him and serve Him. May the Lord help us praise Him and do His will today, too.[45]

Cheprasov believes that this form of recounting the text with "unsophisticated interpretation played a formative role in the establishing and spreading of the Russian Baptist movement."[46] This method at least allowed the Bible to speak for itself, to some extent replacing reading the text in worship, and it also increased overall biblical literacy in the days when the Bible was rare. Worship in general had a formative role, since preaching was not as important as the possibility of gathering and spending time together.

The method of recounting the text with attendant unsophisticated interpretation appears, with the advent and use of theological literature, to be too naive and simplistic for reinvigorating the centrality of the Bible. The goal might be better achieved by reviving the ancient practices of Scripture reading, Bible-focused preaching, and of bringing the Bible into other components of worship. Indeed, some churches do read the Bible before or during their regular worship as a separate element that is not directly related to the sermon.[47] In "Golgotha" Church Minsk, passages of the passion of Christ are read before the first Sunday of the month, as worship participants prepare for Communion. Of special note is the practice of the "Light of Gospel" Church in Minsk; here the story of Christ's sufferings and death is usually read once a year on Easter Saturday. The reading involves twelve to fifteen readers, each of whom reads between five and twelve verses, while the choir sings the same theme between the readings.[48]

---

45. Personal visits of the author to the church service 9 November 2008 (Personal notes, 10b).

46. Cheprasov, "Formative? Informative? Neither? Towards understanding of the practice of proclamation, the core element of Russian Baptist Worship," 14.

47. "Hope" church in Grodno reads a chapter from Scripture during each service. In 2013, the Baptist church in Slutsk, Minsk region began to read one chapter from the Bible at the beginning of the service. "Gospel of Light" church in Minsk began to read one chapter from the Bible at the beginning of the worship in 2016. (Personal visits of the author to the church services 26 November 2017, 26 March 2017, and 7 August 2016 respectively [Personal notes, 11].)

In some churches the Bible is read before the start of the service, as in Ushachi, Vitebsk region and Zaslavl', Minsk region till 2010. (Personal visit of the author to the church services 4 November 2014, 26 April 2009 and 1 January 2012 [Personal notes, 10].)

48. Bible reading can take various forms in public worship. It may consist of one chapter from the Gospels (in the morning) and the Epistles (in the evening) followed by a brief explanation if necessary. Von Allmen, following modern Reformed lectionaries, suggests the three major types of witness in the Bible – the prophet, the apostle, and the Lord – should be

Responsive reading could also prove helpful for encouraging interaction with Biblical texts. It allows people present in worship to listen and read the Bible, thus enabling their better memorization of the texts. A recently revised hymnal for Baptist churches based on the *Song of Revival* includes texts from Scripture which participants may read responsively in their worship.[49] However, such practice is not currently a general part of worship apart from some rare exceptions.[50] There are other options for reading (some of them tested by the author in the same church in Borovliany), which might include role-play reading of a book or part of a book of the Bible.[51]

Churches also need to revive Bible-focused preaching. Partially, this can be realized in expository preaching practice. In fact, systematic study of the Bible in preaching and, accordingly, consistent reading of the Bible in the church, has just now begun to gain momentum in the first decade of the twenty-first century. Some churches study specific books of the Bible, such as Romans, 2 Corinthians, Galatians, and James; in other churches preachers preach on popular Bible passages like the Sermon on the Mount, the Decalogue,[52] and so on.[53] However, established habits and ministry experience in the Soviet era discourage or prevent some pastors from using the benefits of in-depth

---

read every Sunday (*Worship: Its Theology and Practice*, 135). In addition, before prayer (call to worship) or singing, passages from Scripture on the topic of worship can be read, mostly from the Book of Psalms. In conclusion, the meeting could close with biblical benedictions from the Book of Psalms or the Epistles. In fact, 2 Cor 13:14 ("The grace of the Lord Jesus Christ, and the love of God, and the fellowship of the Holy Spirit, be with you all") is regularly heard in concluding prayers in traditional worship.

49. *Pesn' Voskhozhdeniya. Sbornik tserkovnykh gimnov i pesnopenii* [Song of Ascension. Collection of Spiritual Hymns and Songs of Evangelical Churches] (Bryansk: Muzikal'no-khorovoi otdel Bezhitskoi tserkvi EKhB, 2009).

50. "House of the Gospel," Vitebsk (Timofei Egorenkov, Personal interview with author, Minsk, 26 November 2015 [Personal notes, 10b].) As another example, a church in Borovliany, Minsk region, read Psalm 103 in this manner at the Harvest feast at the beginning of the service on 8 October 2017 (Personal notes, 11). Sheets of paper with passages highlighted for reading were distributed before public worship. The church has 27 members, uses temporary premises for worship, and does not use a multimedia projector.

51. *The Dramatized Bible* can provide good ideas for reading the Scriptures (Michael Perry, ed., *The Dramatized Bible* [London: Marshall Pickering/Bible Society, 1989]). There is another way of structuring Bible reading that reveals the unity of the Scriptures. Texts read at Christmas or Easter could be arranged according to the pattern of "prophesy-fulfillment." Initially people read Old Testament passages and then the corresponding ones from the New Testament.

52. Q, 2008.

53. Preaching "verse by verse" is practiced in "Hope" church, Gomel (Gospel of Mark); "Bethlehem," Minsk (Acts); "House of the Gospel," Vitebsk (Galatians); and Krasnosel'sky,

Bible study in the context of a sermon. For some preachers, the emphasis on the Scriptures does not mean serious exegesis, and, according to Cheprasov, preparation for preaching is only regarded as a "spiritual exercise for preachers' hearts and minds, which involves prayer and a good knowledge of the Bible."[54] It is true that a preacher's experience and personality may seem more important than his education and Bible knowledge, and in practice the latter may mean only a general acquaintance with the text of the Bible, the ability to find and quote the necessary verse, rather than understanding the context, the historical and cultural background, the genre diversity of the Scripture, or the meaning of words. Thus, the revival of Bible-focused preaching is impossible without transforming the preachers and their attitude towards education, along with returning to the understanding that the sermon is a work of the Spirit, the exercise of the preacher's mind, inspiration from above, and careful meditation over the text of the Bible. "Ministry of the Word," that is defined only as "the ministry of the Spirit,"[55] cannot encompass its full potential.

The centrality of the Bible in worship can be fostered through bringing the Bible into other components of worship so that "Scripture permeates worship."[56] Yet the biblical content of songs, prayers, poetry, and preaching is often determined by the worship leader and may vary significantly. Many hymns used in traditional worship express a subjective perception of Christ's sacrifice and suffering with an emphasis on personal experiences,[57] while the biblical-theological component is not given enough attention, although

---

Grodno region (Psalms). Q, 2013. The negative side of this approach is the overload of sermons with historical and cultural analysis data.

54. Cheprasov, "Formative? Informative? Neither? Towards understanding of the practice of proclamation, the core element of Russian Baptist Worship," 128. In her article, Olga Bokova discusses tensions between traditional and new principles and methods of Biblical exegetics and hermeneutics in Russian Evangelical Christian-Baptist theology, and this analysis is relevant in the Belarusian context.(Bokova, "Bibleiskaia Ekzegetika i Germenevtika Sovremennikh Evangelskikh Khristian – Baptistov: Traditsii i Novatsii" [Biblical Exegetics and Hermeneutics of Contemporary Evangelical Christian-Baptists: Traditions and New Trends], 216–226.)

55. Cheprasov, "Formative? Informative? Neither? Towards understanding of the practice of proclamation, the core element of Russian Baptist Worship," 129.

56. Forrester, McDonald, and Tellini, *Encounter with God: An Introduction to Christian Worship and Practice*, 64–67.

57. On this subject, see McKibbens, "Our Baptist Heritage in Worship," where he discusses a shift from theocentricsm to anthropocentrism in worship.

it is assumed that hymns are based on the Bible and that "each of them uses a particular passage from Scripture."[58]

Worship time can be filled with the Bible, yet this should be accompanied by an understanding that reading alone is not enough. The Bible is not a collection of quotes, and the number of texts read and listened to is not a decisive factor. From the very beginning of the evangelical movement, Christians were interested in practical applications and their aspiration shaped Baptist churches.[59] Biblical narrative, especially the gospel accounts of Christ, became part of their life and helped them to survive persecution even when Christians were not able to get together to read the Bible.

Listening to the Bible and reading it is not only limited to worship. The Scripture is a part of "congregational life."[60] According to McClendon, the Bible works "as a congregational textbook, source of sermons, classroom handbook, devotional guide, practical norm."[61] Such a holistic use of the Bible can transform the believer's life.

And lastly, Christians worship the incarnate word, not the written word or the Bible.[62] All eyes in the church are fixed on him.[63] Such truly Bible-centered worship, focused on God and revealing His will by the Holy Spirit through the Bible, and revealing Himself through Christ who died and rose again, will lead worshippers into fellowship with the Father, the Son, and Holy Spirit, and with each other.

---

58. Somov, "Pesnya v zhizni khristianina" [A Song in the Life of a Christian], 29.

59. Cheprasov, "Formative? Informative? Neither? Towards understanding of the practice of proclamation, the core element of Russian Baptist Worship," p. 149.

60. Cheprasov.

61. McClendon, *Doctrines*, p 35.

62. Cheprasov, "Formative? Informative? Neither? Towards understanding of the practice of proclamation, the core element of Russian Baptist Worship," 149–150.

63. Luke 4:20. Cf. Barnard, Cilliers, and Wepener, *Worship in the Network Culture. Liturgical Ritual Studies. Fields and Methods, Concepts and Metaphors*, 96.

6.2. Edification in Worship
6.2.1. The Role of 'Edification' in Baptist Worship

The next characteristic which follows the emphasis on the Bible and the Word-oriented nature of public worship is edification (*nazidaniye*).[64] Edification is the guidance, teaching, and nurturing of the Christian in their faith, wisdom, holiness, or moral instruction received when participants enrich each other with the knowledge and application of Scripture.[65] Although encouragement, comfort, evangelism, fellowship, inspiration, and praise are acknowledged goals in worship, ministers and members of congregations practicing traditional Baptist worship consider edification to be the most important, and "edification" is often explicitly referred to in discussing the quality of worship.[66] Singing from the section in the hymnal titled "Before the Beginning of Worship,"[67] believers ask that through the Holy Spirit the Lord would help them understand and apply His Word:

> O Savior! Pour out Your grace on the good news;
> Let us understand all the words of Your love.
>> Open up the hearts of all, and plant Your Word in this good soil,
> Let the dew of mercy and Your love fall on our hearts![68]

Then, at the conclusion of the worship service, the congregation promises in song to keep instruction in their hearts and expresses a desire to continue the process at the next worship service:

> We have had a time of learning, now we leave this place –
> As we go, we treasure dearly all the words of grace.
>> We will wait for Sunday morning to come back again,
> For another time of learning on this happy day.

---

64. The Russian equivalent means "to instruct, teach, train, and improve, especially in moral and religious knowledge; to be edified; edification; edifier" (Dal', *Tolkovyy slovar' zhivogo velikorusskogo yazyka v chetyrekh tomakh* [Explanatory Dictionary of the Russian Language in Four Volumes], 1086).

65. Acts 2:42a; 1 Cor 14:3, 19, 31; 1 Thess. 5:11. Along with 'edification,' Paul uses terms such as 'admonish' or 'encourage' one another.

66. Q, 2008; QM, 2008.

67. *Pesn' Vozrozhdeniya*, no. 1–20.

68. "O, Spasitel'! Blagodat' Na blaguyu vest' izley" [O Savior! Pour out Your Grace on the Good News], *Pesn' Vozrozhdeniya*, no. 5, first and second stanzas.

Calm and peaceful, now we leave this place,
Going home, we treasure dearly all the words of grace.[69]

The instructive value of traditional worship was shaped as part of the agenda of returning to the roots, to New Testament Christianity and the Apostles' teachings,[70] and through the adoption, through Western channels of influence, of the Reformation approach to the dominance of the Word and "greater verbal freedom in worship."[71] The edifying tone of public worship in Baptist churches owes its special prominence to the religious context in which this tradition has fought its way forward. Juxtaposing Baptist worship with Orthodox liturgy, Russian-speaking Baptists emphasize that "our worship has no room for some archaic incomprehensible language or complex symbolism which is only clear to the elect."[72] To answer people's spiritual questions an emphasis is placed on the communication of Bible knowledge in a simple and understandable way, primarily through preaching.

In the recent years, emphasis on edification has acquired a more Western touch due to the influence of figures such as John McArthur[73] and Alexei Kolomiytsev.[74] In their books, sermons, and conferences they promote the idea of the teaching pastor and expository sermons, and have drawn more attention to the teaching task of the church in general. As with the emphasis

---

69. "My okonchili uchen'ye I domoy poydem" [We Have Had a Time of Learning, Now We Leave This Place], *Pesn' Vozrozhdeniya*, no. 712, first and third stanzas and refrain.

70. 1 Cor 14:5, 12, 19; Eph 5:19. See Karev, "Svyashchennodeistviya tserkvi," p. 36.

71. Wainwright, *Doxology: The Praise of God in Worship, Doctrine and Life*, 114.

72. Ivanov, *Dukhovnost' evangel'skikh khristian-baptistov*, 18.

73. John Fullerton MacArthur, Jr. is a popular pastor-teacher of Grace Community Church in Sun Valley, California. He is a radio preacher, speaker, author, and the president of The Master's College in Santa Clarita and The Master's Seminary in Sun Valley, California. MacArthur has authored or edited more than one hundred books. The MacArthur Study Bible, and his series of commentaries on the New Testament, are very popular among Russian-speaking preachers. He is held in high regard due to his conservative views about the Bible and creation. See Grace Community Church, official website, https://www.gracechurch.org., last accessed 16 May 2019. MacArthur is also famous as a strong proponent of expository preaching. His views are popularized in various ways, including through the School of Preachers in Samara, Novosibirsk Bible Seminary in Russia, Irpen' Bible Seminary in Ukraine, conferences, and publishing. Almost all the pastors in Belarus are in possession of the MacArthur Study Bible and his other books as gifts from the Slavic Gospel Association mission.

74. Alexei Kolomiytsev is a pastor-teacher at Bible Church "Word of Grace," Battle Ground, Washington, USA. Kolomiytsev is a graduate of The Master's Seminary in Sun Valley, California. Kolomiytsev's focus is on thorough exegesis of the text, the doctrine the text teaches, and its application. See "Word of Grace" Church, official website, http://www.slovo.org., last accessed 16 May 2019.

on the Bible, "the word of edification"[75] is primarily equated with preaching, and as such it represents the corner stone of the worship service. Church members speak about the paramount value of sermons ("good edifying sermons," "sermons that touch the heart").[76] In church buildings nothing should distract the congregation from hearing the Word. For better absorption of biblical teaching in the Baptist Slavic tradition, it is recommended that one stays seated so that an "overtired body would not interfere with perception."[77] Open Bibles in many people's hands and the constant flipping of pages make the parallels between church and school even more evident.

Other components of the service serve the same task. Alexander Karev wrote that "just like preaching, [spiritual singing] should include spiritual edification, i.e. instruction and doctrine."[78] Thus, singing is to edify, and the hymnbook is to be "the first theological textbook."[79] Karev described singing as "preaching in music," "a source of deep instruction."[80] Certainly, the purpose of songs is not only edification, praise and thanksgiving are also important aspects. Yet, an authoritative figure in AUCECB, musician and composer Nikolai Vysotsky has sought to draw the pastors' attention to the edifying role of singing, arguing that mere inspiration, "spiritual enjoyment" and "meeting aesthetic needs" is not enough. Rather, it is necessary to strive to maintain a clear edifying, teaching, and correcting focus in singing. In Vysotsky's words, "spiritual singing should be an effective tool for improving the spiritual condition of believers' lives and work."[81]

Singing is typically used for augmenting the lessons of faith taught through preaching. Toivo Pilli comments that in Baptist and Evangelical Christian traditions singing and music provide a commentary on the preaching and biblical texts.[82] The person in charge of singing selects and offers hymns

---

75. From the report by M.A. Orlov on his trip to Belarus, *Bratskiy Vestnik*, no. 3 (1948): 47–48.

76. QM, 2008.

77. Ivanov, *Dukhovnost' evangel'skikh khristian-baptistov*, 19.

78. Karev, "Svyashchennodeistviya tserkvi," 38.

79. Goncharenko, *Muzyka i dukhovnoe vozrastanie tserkvi* [Music and the Spiritual Growth of the Church], 4.

80. Goncharenko, 39.

81. Vysotskiy, "Znacheniye i sila dukhovnoy muzyki," 57.

82. Pilli, "Evangelical Christians-Baptists of Estonia: The Shaping of Identity, 1945–1991," 157.

that resonate with the message of the sermon, and that can help embed these truths in people's hearts. For example, after a sermon about Jesus as the light of life, a song may be offered which has the following chorus, "But Jesus Shines There Like the Sun."[83]

Prayers which follow a sermon often play a similar role. A sermon about the person of Christ based on the text of John 7:11–17 may be followed by a sister's prayer about getting to know Christ, following Him, and serving Him. The second preacher may speak about a Christian attitude to work, and in the following prayer one of the brothers expresses his desire to glorify God by his attitude to work and by his passionate labor.[84]

"Truth and beauty can work together"[85] in the recitation of poems as well. On average, one or two poems are recited from memory or read in every worship service. This "poetic spiritual edification,"[86] or "spiritual edification in poetry,"[87] is intended to facilitate the involvement of more worship participants in active ministry, bring variety to the spiritual diet, and strengthen the foundations of faith. As spiritual gifts are given to brothers and sisters for edification,[88] many people can mutually edify one another in different ways.

6.2.2. Towards a Better Theology of Edification

All worship components contribute to edification. Yet how successful each particular meeting is in this can be questionable. The content of a specific sermon, prayer, or poem may be a surprise,[89] which then puts the edifying nature of worship at risk as it may become the subject of complaints and grievances among worship participants.[90] If they are to edify those who sing,

---

83. "Vot putniki k rodine slavnoy idut" [Here the Pilgrims Come to the Glorious Fatherland], *Pesn' Vozrozhdeniya*, no. 513.

84. Church in Borovliany, Minsk region, Personal visit of the author to the church service, 22 September 2019 (Personal notes, 65b). There are two sermons in this rather small congregation (27 members), and they are followed by a congregational prayer.

85. Harris, *Toward an Understanding of Russian Baptist Worship*, 6.

86. *Bratskiy Vestnik*, no. 6 (1946), 35.

87. *Bratskiy Vestnik*, no. 5 (1946), 54.

88. 1 Cor 12:14, 26.

89. Since the theme of the worship service is not always planned, and is not necessarily discerned by contributors, the themes of individual components can vary significantly, forcing the worship participants to be able to switch between various themes.

90. In 1981, the President of AUCECB, A.E. Klimenko, remarked that "Unchecked poems and the ones sometimes clearly contradictory to the spirit of our doctrine are recited

some songs from the *Song of Revival* Songbook need stylistic corrections and the replacement or explanation of archaic words and expressions, especially in the case of new visitors.[91]

Regarding the effectiveness of edification through preaching, a common criticism voiced concerns the shortage of capable preachers, or the lack of education and training among preachers, as well as their unwillingness to prepare for preaching in advance.[92] An instructive tone,[93] which is typical of many preachers, also causes congregational resistance, especially among young people.[94] They are not content to only receive instruction because, as expressed in the qualitative research, they also need "cordiality," "sincerity," and "intensity of feeling."[95] On the whole, young people no longer take the authority of the pulpit for granted and want the preachers to catch their attention and lead. The sermon would be able to meet its goal of edification if those who assign the preachers were to consider the teaching about gifts,[96] if churches became more aware of the value of educating and training preachers, and if the preachers, based on understanding the sermon as a gift and an art, were to be aware of the importance of sermon preparation. Public prayers are not always edifying either. They can suffer from a lack of depth and other aspects of prayer delivery, the most serious of which is poor audibility due to indistinct speech, weakness of voice, and/or the large size of the room. The congregation can also be dispirited by long and identical prayers,[97] when the same words or phrases are repeated by the same people at every meeting, regardless of the context or the topic of the worship service.[98] Bearing this in mind, the author of the article in *Bratskiy Vestnik* says that in worship

---

in worship" ("Materialy Plenuma AUCECB, Iyun' 1981 Goda" [Materials of a Plenum of the AUCECB, June 1981], 59).

91. See *Pesn' Vozrozhdeniya*, nos. 2, 13, 50, 68, 158, 184, 187, 220, 395.

92. QM, 2008. Also, Marat Nursultanov, A poll among the members of the Baptist church in Orsha, Vitebsk region (March 2008). Available through the author.

93. As a secular author observed, specific theological issues in Baptist preaching take a back seat to moral and edifying topics (Mitrokhin, ed., *Protestantizm. Slovar' ateista* [Protestantism. An Atheist's Vocabulary], 7).

94. Q, 2008.

95. QM, 2008.

96. 1 Cor 12, 13.

97. SI, 2012.

98. A nickname for such prayers is "tape-recorded" (Slutsk, SI, 2012).

only prayers which edify the whole congregation should be pronounced. However, even though these suggestions were expressed over fifty years ago, the churches are still struggling with the same issues at the beginning of the twenty-first century.

> Such are prayers about God's work in the whole world, God's workings in our country, the needs of the whole church, needs of this particular community of believers, asking God to bless this worship service, spiritual needs and requests generated by the sermon that has just been delivered, etc.[99]

Poor quality or irrelevant topics are not the only problem. An exaggerated emphasis on edification as instruction may neglect other aspects of worship, or create an imbalance between worship (believer-to-God activities), fellowship/edification (believer-to-believer activities), and evangelism (believer-to-unbeliever activities).[100] When the church puts too much emphasis on instruction, worship may be reduced to a class, to intellectual exhortations, or to teachings on ethics.[101] Yet "the classroom is not a viable substitute for sanctuary."[102] The pedagogical value of worship cannot replace the spiritual experience of an encounter with God. Authentic worship is not only growth in biblical knowledge and understanding, nor even just the application of Bible lessons in everyday life, rather it is also growth in a relationship with the God whom believers worship.

An analysis of the edifying function of public worship, and the evaluation of its strong and weak dimensions, allows two aspects to be singled out and addressed that could enrich public worship. First, there must be an acknowledgement of the value of edification and an appropriately contextual improving of its standard. Second, there must be an acknowledgement that the current need to improve the quality of instruction in Belarusian churches should go hand-in-hand with considerations of other public worship aspects, such as the worship itself, fellowship, and evangelism. After all,

---

99. V. S., "Voprosy dukhovnoy zhizni" [Issues of Spiritual Life], 23.

100. Here we take into consideration Cottrell's definition of worship. Cottrell, *The Faith Once for All: Bible Doctrine for Today*, 443.

101. Borchert, "The Lord of Form and Freedom: A New Testament Perspective on Worship," 13.

102. Resner, Jr., "To Worship or To Evangelize? Ecclesiology's Phantom Fork in the Road," 78.

"even edification – certainly a worthy purpose – is only a minor part of what worship is all about."[103] Paying attention to adoration as part of public worship, to fellowship, and to evangelism, would bring balance to the nature of worship. Enrichment of the practice through various elements will not only edify the mind, but will also make use of the imagination and emotions of worship practitioners, leading to worship in which "gesture and object allowed the Word to be seen – and indeed handled (1 John 1:1) and tasted (Heb 6:4f. and 1 Pet 2:3) – as well as heard."[104]

6.3. Evangelism

6.3.1. Evangelism in Life and Worship

Whereas edification focuses on worship in its relation to "insiders," evangelism focuses on worship in its relation to "outsiders" and plays an equally important role. The joy of proclaiming the gospel, the Good News, has been central to the activity of Russian-speaking evangelicals.[105] The Good News was spread during times of both persecution and relative freedom, in public and in secret, in large assemblies and privately. Modern Baptist scholar Mikhail Cherenkov claims that mission, together with personal godliness and conservative theology, is one of the main characteristics of evangelical Christians.[106] Spreading the Good News has been a sacred duty;[107] the principle of the priesthood of all believers allowed every believer to be a witness, an evangelist, or a preacher. One of the many hymns on this expresses the desire to win at least one "lost soul" for the Lord thus:

> I would not like to come fruitless
> To the throne of the Lord,
> I would like to carry at least
> One sheaf in my hands.[108]

---

103. Liesch, *People in the Presence of God. Models and Directions for Worship*, 22.
104. Wainwright, "Renewing Worship: The Recovery of Classical Patterns," 46.
105. Bortkovsky, "Shtundobaptizm" [Stundobaptists], 117.
106. Cherenkov, *Evropeis'ka reformatsiya ta ukrains'kiy evangel's'kiy protestantizm*, 64.
107. See section 7.2.
108. Originally written as "Must I Go, and Empty-handed?" *Pesn' Vozrozhdeniya*, no. 656, first stanza.

The message is especially clear in hymns sung during the Feast of Harvest which reflects on the theme of fruitfulness. The saved souls are regarded as the most important fruit:

> Would I bring no fruit at all when I answer Jesus' call
> On the day when He invites me to come home?
> When He asks about my sheaf, what would I have then to give?
> How can I come empty-handed when I go?
> > Filled with thankfulness to Him who redeemed my soul from sin,
> > I would like to work for Jesus all day long,
> > So my Master will receive from my hands at least one sheaf
> > When He comes again to meet and take me home.[109]

Such eagerness frequently triggered negative responses from both Orthodox and secular circles. At the beginning of the twentieth century, Orthodox writers warned that "our Orthodox Church is being attacked by a large horde of trained and experienced missionaries,"[110] and that "Shtundobaptists are the most dangerous group, in terms of their missionary organizations."[111] At the end of the twentieth century, a Belarusian researcher, referring to such groups as Baptists, speaks of "religious expansionism" and "aggressively militant mission."[112]

Evangelistic activity has been tightly linked to eschatological expectations, or looking forward to Christ's imminent Second Coming, to which persecution added special color. A sense of the brevity of time contributed to the desire to place all of life on the altar of Christian witness. In the light of the strong belief in salvation in Christ alone, each believer had to do their best in their duty of saving people, especially family members and neighbors:

> We live to share the Holy Word with others
> Who are dying in sin, despair, and hopelessness.
> Let us equip ourselves and one another
> To serve our Lord in trials and distress.

---

109. "Neuzheli bez plodov," *Pesn' Vozrozhdeniya*, no. 744, first and third stanzas.
110. Bortkovsky, "Shtundobaptizm," 117.
111. *Mogilevskie eparhial'nye vedomosti* [Mogilev Diocese Gazette], no. 21 (1910), 341.
112. Rekuts, *Protestantizm i khudozhestvennaya kul'tura Belarusi*, 3.

> This life is difficult and offers little comfort,
> But we are here to labor, not to feast -
> We see this world and so keep pressing onward
> To save the lost and bring them love and peace.[113]

The key motive for sharing the Gospel was one's personal conversion experience and its contrast with life before conversion. Generally, a transformed life as a result of conversion is a key concept in the Baptist tradition. When the Council of ECB Churches published a hymnal in 1978, which became especially popular in the Soviet and post-Soviet times, it was named *Pesn' Vozrozhdeniya*, or "Song of Rebirth" or "Revival." Evangelical Christians saw the Good News as a power that could transform lives, and their personal experience pushed them to lead others to repentance and salvation. They understood the Great Commission as their personal duty. As "New Testament Christians," they preached salvation, believing they were following the model of early Christian churches, because the call to "repent and believe in the Gospel"[114] "was constantly heard in the worship of the first Christians."[115] Their worship reflected the desire to "save the lost," not just to spread the Baptist faith. Indeed, if the structure of a traditional worship service is more a reflection of the principle of edification, the spirit of the service is marked by a "distinct revivalist flare."[116]

The evangelistic focus of Baptist worship was particularly dominant in many churches in the first decade after *perestroika*. Following the example of Luke 14:23, the evangelistic activities of church members may involve inviting family, friends, neighbors, and others to the house of prayer.[117] Evangelism and worship are believed to be tightly interwoven. In the words of Rick

---

113. "Nam zhizn' dana ne dlya pustykh mechtaniy" [We Are Not Granted This Life for Day Dreaming], *Pesn' Vozrozhdeniya*, no. 792, third and fifth stanzas.

114. Mark 1:15.

115. Somov, "Tserkov' Khrista i ejo Svyashchenstvo," 54.

116. Nichols, "Evangelical Spirituality and Russian Baptists," 206. According to Nichols, the evangelistic spirit was largely shaped by "the early influences of the Keswick Holiness movement and the Evangelical Alliance on the early leaders of baptistic communities in the Russian-speaking world" (Nichols). This point of view is also shared by Walter Sawatsky, a researcher of the Russian-speaking Baptist movement: *Evangelicheskoye dvizheniye v SSSR posle Vtoroy mirovoy voyny*, 396.

117. "And the master said to the slave, 'Go out into the highways and along the hedges, and compel *them* to come in, so that my house may be filled."

Warren, whose books have gained significant popularity in Belarus, "evangelism "produce[s] worshipers of God," and worship "provides the motivation for evangelism."[118]

6.3.2. Worship as Evangelism

When examining the relationship between worship and evangelism, it is worth mentioning the tradition of evangelistic services. These can be further divided into specialized meetings held in specific places at certain times, and meetings in place of regular worship services. As early as 1910, an Orthodox magazine reported the methods of sectarians, noting that one might open a small shop "and then stop everyone entering by talking about faith or reading from the Gospel that which would be especially eye-catching for those without deep understanding in religious questions... Another arranges a prayer meeting with the preaching and reading of the Gospel near his house in the open air in summer."[119] The article continues:

> In recent times, sectarian missionaries make their trips with well-organized choirs and dozens of young men preparing for preaching. Live improvisations by fanatics are abundantly interspersed with biblical texts, and their simple, touching, sad, melodic tunes produce compelling, deep impressions upon people. To this must be added that sectarians sing their psalms and cantatas with great religious enthusiasm, with a nervous tremor in their voices and tears in their eyes. This is a secret of their success and extraordinary influence on people.[120]

Depending on opportunities, meetings for evangelistic purposes have been held outside church buildings, in the street, in church grounds, in parks, clubs, and stadiums, as well as on public transportation. Iosif Bondarenko, a Baptist evangelist who spent a total of nine years in prison between 1962 and 1981, reports the activities that led to one of his charges:

---

118. Warren, *Purpose Driven Church: Growth Without Compromising Your Message and Mission*, 242.

119. *Mogilevskie eparhial'nye vedomosti*, no. 21 (1910), 717.

120. *Mogilevskie eparhial'nye vedomosti*, 716.

Believers gathered together in large groups in the woods near the city and in public places of summer recreation. Led by the defendants, they put up banners with Bible passages, engaged in loud readings and choir singing of hymns accompanied by an orchestra. They were involved in similar activities at railway stations and in electric train carriages.[121]

Even weddings and funerals can be turned into occasions for evangelism. As the critics of Baptists have pointed out, "In order to promote their religious activities, sectarians also use their baptisms, weddings, funerals, etc., making them as solemn as possible. People come to such events as spectators and they propagate their teaching among them, 'hunting for people's souls.'"[122] Similarly, Baptists were also accused of "turning their funeral processions into evangelistic prayer meetings" as a tool to witness. For example, under the act of Zelva town council of April 1986, a member of an unregistered Baptist community, P.V. Mosko, was held administratively liable for "organizing a funeral procession with singing in the town of Zelva [Grodno region]."[123] The practice, particularly common during the Soviet times, is still sometimes observed today.[124]

Evangelistic purposes were also served by special meetings in the houses of prayer. In 1911, an Orthodox missionary asked, "Do we need to say how strong and lasting is the impression produced on the souls of visitors by such celebrations with prayer, kneeling, choral singing and inspirational preaching?"[125] A circular of the Tzarist Ministry of Internal Affairs reported that "under the guise of worship and prayer meetings, sectarians hold public meetings for fellowship, reading and discussion of religious topics, which do

---

121. Bondarenko, *Tri prigovora*, 174.

122. Garkavenko, *Khristianskoe sektanstvo v SSSR. Avtoreferat dissertatsii na soiskanie uchenoi stepeni kandidata philosophskikh nauk* [Christian Sectarianism in the USSR. Dissertation for the Degree of Candidate of Philosophical Sciences], 14.

123. Report of an inspector of the Council for Religious Affairs, 16 April 1986, NARB, Stock 136, File 1, Case 88, 120–122.

124. On March 12, 2011, the author was informed by his mother that in the village of Lipniki, Brest region, evangelicals organized a solemn funeral procession for one of the local people; as they passed through the village, they sang and preached in the backyard of a private house and at the cemetery (Personal notes, 47).

125. Bortkovskiy, "Shtundobaptizm," 116.

not function as worship services or devotional meetings."[126] Soviet observers in Vitebsk later described an example of "evangelicals and Baptists organizing evenings, which they call 'literary soirees,'" where there are

> individual and collective recitals of religious poetry, solo, choir and group singing, and speeches by pastors and some sectarians, etc. These sects also use other forms and methods of propaganda and agitation, such as religious drama (passion plays), music and choir. They even have a piano in their houses of prayer. Following the orders of their leaders, sectarians invite youth and adults to these evenings.[127]

Evangelistic meetings are different from regular ones, not just because of their special focus, but also because they are marked out by better preparation, orderliness, careful selection of contributors and songs, and altered structure (more music, less preaching and prayer, and an inclusion of testimonies). However, regular meetings also have an evangelistic aspect and are conducted in an evangelistic spirit. All the aspects of public worship, from the space itself to a call to repentance, could fulfill an evangelistic purpose. The walls of prayer houses decorated with Scriptures announce the closeness and inevitability of the Second Coming and the need for repentance.[128] Other passages may be warning that the time to repent is today,[129] or speak about God's love, Christ's death, and faith through which salvation is made possible.[130]

Congregational singing also becomes an intentional tool for evangelism. "Call to Repentance," the largest of the thematic sections in *Pesn' Vozrozhdeniya*, includes ninety songs. In comparison, sections such as "About the Church" and "Call to Work" contain only eleven and thirty-two songs, respectively. Evangelistic aspects are strongly expressed in other sections

---

126. NHAB, Stock 295, File 8462, Case 1, 6, July 10, 1913 – November 11, 1914.

127. Khaytun and Kapayevich, *Suchasnae sektantstva na Belarusi*, 44.

128. "And behold, I am coming quickly. Blessed is he who heeds the words of the prophecy of this book" (Rev 22:7); "The time is fulfilled, and the kingdom of God is at hand; repent and believe in the gospel" (Mark 1:15); "He who has believed and has been baptized shall be saved; but he who has disbelieved shall be condemned" (Mark 16:16).

129. "For it is time to seek the LORD" (Hosea 10:12b).

130. "God is love" (1 John 4:8b); "For God so loved the world, that He gave His only begotten Son, that whoever believes in Him shall not perish, but have eternal life" (John 3:16); "So faith *comes* from hearing, and hearing by the word of Christ" (Rom 10:17); "Christ died for our sins according to the Scriptures" (1 Cor 15:3b). Information gathered from Q, 2008.

too, particularly in the "Youth Songs." It is assumed that hymns sung before preaching are to "soften hearts of stone" so that people may receive the Word of truth. When a sermon is followed by a call to repentance, a "call song" which elicits tears of repentance is often sung while penitent sinners are invited to come forward and repent. Such popular "call songs" include "Neuzheli uydesh', ty ne prinyav Khrista" (Are You Really Going to Leave Without Accepting Christ?), "Chto ty medlish' na greshnom puti" (Why Are You Lingering on Your Sinful Way?), "Put' ko spasen'yu novyy, zhivoy," (Way to Salvation, New and Living), "Khochet vsekh lyudey Gospod' blagoslovit'" (The Lord Wants to Bless All People),[131] amongst others. Along with congregational singing, "choral singing is called not only to affect people's feelings, but also to make them think, analyze their life, draw conclusions, and confess their sins before the Lord."[132] Furthermore, "if choral singing does not affect a listener's deep and secret feelings, but only pleases their ear, it does not fulfill its purpose and brings no glory to God."[133] Such "heartfelt" singing is to resonate with worship participants present in the house of prayer as well as with occasional passers-by.[134]

Even the opponents of Baptists, in various periods of time, acknowledged the power and effect of their singing and rightly stressed the value of singing as an art:

> A believer's esthetic feeling is given a special direction during public worship; it serves as one of the ways of perceiving religious ideas and images. Esthetic feelings and esthetic perception foster and strengthen religious faith, drawing it into the domain of influence of a preacher's ideas. As A.M. Gorky stated at the 2nd National Congress of the Union of Militant Atheists (1930), "Undoubtedly, many people convert to religion for esthetical reasons because churches have good singing."[135]

---

131. *Pesn' Vozrozhdeniya*, nos. 956, 381, 295, 346.

132. B. K., "O muzyke i penii" [On Music and Singing], 69.

133. B. K., 68–69.

134. Typical testimonies would go along the following lines: "I was walking by the house of prayer and heard some singing, so I came in . . ."; "I heard young people sing in a square. I was so impressed by their songs that I came to their worship service and repented a few months later."

135. Fedorenko, *Sekty, ih vera i dela* [Sects, Their Faith and Acts], 340; Gorkiy, *O religii* [On Religion], 186.

Testimonies, typically about significant episodes of life that illustrate how God has worked in a believer's life, are less customary in traditional Baptist worship. The testimony of conversion is the most common kind of testimony, and it is a powerful tool to attract others through the experience a former sinner who "was a bad person, had no happiness in life, but repented and received joy and happiness in life with God."[136]

However, preaching is regarded as the most important tool of evangelism, both by the Baptists themselves as well as by less-than-sympathetic critics.[137] In an analysis of sermons for the communities in Brest, Pinsk, Baranovichi, Pruzhany, and Ivanovo, Brest region in 1986, the Deputy Commissioner for Religious Affairs highlighted the fact that "sermons had a clear missionary vector, and the speakers devoted most of their time to brainwashing people who 'still do not have Christ in their hearts.'"[138] Sermons would frequently underline the danger of delay. "The last invitation" is announced;[139] "now," "today" is the time to come to Jesus because it may be too late tomorrow; the "grim reaper" may come, or Jesus Christ may return.[140]

The final sermon may include a call to repentance, or it may be used as an independent element at the end of the service. The preacher may invite those who want to repent and confess their sins before God and the church to come forward to the pulpit and to pray, confessing their sins and asking that God forgive them.[141] Next, a church minister prays and the congregation sings a stanza and the refrain of "Radostnuyu pesn' vospoyte v nebesakh! Bludnyy

---

136. Q, 2008.

137. Cf. the English Separatist tradition (McKibbens, "Our Baptist Heritage in Worship," p. 64).

138. NARB, Stock 136, File 1, Case 88, 150–155.

139. "Posledniy prizyv razdayetsya yeshche" [Last Call Is Still Given], *Pesn' Vozrozhdeniya*, no. 375.

140. The words of a well-known hymn which calls sinners to repentance confirm this idea:
The Sun will cease to give its light one day,
And darkness comes to sweep all things away,
When night falls down, the gate will soon be closed,
And you will hear a cry behind the doors:
There is no place! No place, the gate is closed! "Yest' mesto, yest'! Gospod' v chertog zovet" [There Is a Place, Yes Indeed! The Lord Is Calling to the Chamber], *Pesn' Vozrozhdeniya*, 298, fifth stanza.

141. The practice of public repentance (*pokayaniye*) is quite specific to the Russian-speaking Baptist life. It is an important step on the way to baptism and church membership. For more about repentance as a public event see Khrapov, *Dom Bozhii i sluzhenie v nem*, ch. 4.

syn naveki vozvrashchen" (Sing a Joyful Song in Heaven! The Prodigal Son Is Back Forever).¹⁴² When a woman publicly repents, a different stanza is sung, which refers to "The Lost Sheep" rather than the prodigal son. Sometimes repentance is made without a call, when a person comes to the front during the singing or even after the closing pastoral prayer and says they would like to pray a prayer of repentance. There are also, as one pastor put it, "arranged repentances" in which a person who wants to repent may inform the pastor before worship and ask the pastor to make a call.¹⁴³

Calls to repentance were particularly emotional at the beginning of *perestroika*. Repeating the same verse or singing several hymns at the time of the call was a common practice in order to build up emotion and encourage public repentance. Every so often the preacher would repeat the words of the call and the choir or the congregation would echo the call:

> Will you leave at this hour,
> Will you leave at this hour,
> Will you leave at this hour and reject Jesus' call?
> Will you leave at this hour?¹⁴⁴
> Your time is now, your time is now,
> Jesus' arms are open for you!
> Your time is now, your time is now,
> Come before night comes into view.¹⁴⁵

Such persistence was often followed by large groups of people coming to the pulpit or onto the stage. However, preliminary research in Belarusian churches confirms the insignificance of public events in terms of their contribution to church growth.¹⁴⁶ However, it is still possible that negative

---

142. *Pesn' Vozrozhdeniya*, no. 389.

143. Alexander Gelement, Personal interview by author, Pinsk, Brest region, 30 October 2016 (Personal notes, 47).

144. "Neuzheli uydesh', ty ne prinyav Khrista," *Pesn' Vozrozhdeniya*, no. 956, refrain.

145. "Chto ty medlish' na greshnom puti," *Pesn' Vozrozhdeniya*, no. 381, refrain.

146. Sergei Luk'yanov, pastor of "New Testament church" in Minsk, conducted a survey among the participants of youth conferences in Minsk from 2017–2018. He claims that approximately 80% of people have come to the ECB church in Belarus from parachurch environments or through parents or Christian grandparents. About 10% of people have Christian relatives, neighbors, and coworkers. And only 8.4% came "out of the world." According to Luk'yanov, only "friendly evangelism" makes sense. People come to Christ through friendly, long-term relationships, and only a very small number come as a result of various public events

evaluations of evangelistic events may result from having unrealistic, lofty expectations about them and from a lack of understanding about their role in peoples' spiritual lives.[147]

By the end of the first decade of the twenty-first century, calls to repentance have diminished, and the evangelistic activity of Baptist churches has lessened. Accumulated over sixty years, from the reinforcement of persecution in 1928 to the celebration of the Millennium of Christianity in Russia in 1988, this evangelistic energy expanded with great force in the early 1990s, but twenty years later its power has declined. Calls to repentance are made less frequently, usually at special services or during traditional Christian holidays, and they tend to be gentler. The call may not require going forward to the pulpit and public prayers. Sometimes it is sufficient to raise a hand or pray silently and then, after the meeting, to meet and talk to the ministers.

The weakening of evangelistic motivation is related to several factors. First, the absence of persecution has diminished eschatological expectations. The feeling of shortness of time has subsided, and so has the understanding of the need for urgency in the salvation of the lost.[148] Second, the church, and especially ministers, have needed to resolve many new problems which has taken away their focus from evangelistic ministry. These problems include: organizational and legal issues related to the registration of churches and related organizations, issues relating to the construction of houses of prayer, struggles resulting from a lack of funds caused by a decrease in support from Western churches, and a sharp increase in the cost of the construction and maintenance of church buildings.[149] Third, churches seem to be losing confidence as they are confronted by the decreased effectiveness of evangelism

---

(Personal interview with author, Minsk, 21 May 2019 [Personal notes, 47]). The Board of the Baptist Union discussed this issue at its meeting on 21st May 2019 (Minute of the Council of the ECB Union in Belarus, no. 141 (21 May 2019).

147. About different approaches to evangelism in Slavic culture late 20th – early 21st centuries, including mass evangelistic meetings, see Komisarenko, "Osobennosti blagovestiya v russkoy kul'ture" [Special Characteristics of Evangelism in Russian Culture], 60–87. In 2004, Komisarenko, a graduate of Moscow Theological Seminary, expressed the opinion that the time "of loud evangelistic crusades" had passed. (Komisarenko, 86.) For better understanding of the mission see Bosch, *Transforming Mission. Paradigm Shifts in Theology of Mission.*

148. In recent years preachers have spoken less of the Second Coming (QM, 2012). Cf. sections 4.3.2 and 4.3.3.

149. See footnote 616.

in the twenty-first century and the loss of the "sheaves" gathered before.[150] Fourthly, the human resources accumulated before *perestroika* have been extensively exhausted, and the training of new leaders has become a daunting task which cannot be solved solely within the walls of theological schools. Of course, the situation would be even worse without the 1,465 graduates of Baptist schools of the Union, who underwent theological studies between 1991 and 2017.[151] Fifthly, many members who were active in the past as evangelists and missionaries have transferred to work in educational institutions or Christian mission organizations. These may participate in evangelization indirectly, but they lack time for personal contact with unbelievers. Furthermore, as the 'effectiveness' of the call to repentance in the house of prayer has decreased, the lack of response disappoints the congregation and preachers who simply do not want to take chances again. For a preacher, it is safer to replace calls to repentance with calls to holiness and faithfulness in following the Lord since they do not require an open response in a meeting. These kinds of changes are evident from my own ministry experience of the past thirty years. Moreover, a new generation of preachers who emerged after

---

150. Konstantin Teteryatnikov, former Dean of the Bible College in Kremenchug, Ukraine, lists the reasons for lack of effectiveness. They include the Eastern Orthodox influence, but also rationalism and pragmatism, which characterize Western culture (Teteryatnikov, 'Blagovestiye: vchera i segodnya' [Evangelism: Yesterday and Today] https://www.christianmegapolis.com// благовестие-вчера-и-сегодня/, 01.02.2011, last accessed 30 September 2019.). Oleg Turlac suggests that the arrival of new people in church was influenced by a change in the religious climate (the spiritual hunger, characteristic of the 1990s, has dried up), and by the increasing role of the Orthodox Church in cultural, political, and social life. (http://www.bethel.md/view_post.php?id=26, last accessed 2 September 2010.) In turn, some churches were not ready to assimilate new people. The case of the Baptist Church in Kopyl, Minsk region, cannot be called typical but it provides an idea of the problem. By 2010, this church had only twelve members. At the same time, according to the pastor, for a decade the same number of people had been excommunicated for "unchristian behavior" and disregarding meetings, i.e., almost all the people who came to the church after the *perestroika* have been lost (Alexander Vislaus, Personal interview with author, Kopyl, 22 April 2012 [Personal notes, 47]).

151. In speaking about potential ministers, we should note that many gifted ministers emigrated to the United States. As the pastor reports show, from 1990 to 2005 about one hundred fifty families from the church on Fortechnaya 61/1, Brest, emigrated to America (Viktor Zdanevich, Personal interview with author, Brest, 4 October 2019 [Personal notes, 47b]). From 1990 to the present, about two hundred persons, including small children, have emigrated from the church on Moprovskaya in Pinsk (Anatoliy Filanovich, Personal interview with author, Pinsk, 12 July 2018 [Personal notes]).

perestroika lack the skills for evangelistic preaching, they have neither the experience nor the involvement, nor strong examples to follow.[152]

In its historical context, an evangelistic focus on public worship has contributed to a reductive understanding of mission. It has encouraged a theology of evangelism as proclamation. Social ministry, small group ministry, the cultivation of friendships and personal relationships (already limited due to the clear distinction between Christians and non-Christians in Soviet times), and even more so working for societal transformation, education, and awareness raising, have generally remained beyond the view of the church.[153] As Keith Jones has pointed out, "there is a grave temptation for us to mix up the worship of believers in Spirit in Truth with the pre-evangelism or evangelism of Paul on Mars Hill, rather than the synagogue at Capernaum, or the Basilica in Alexandria."[154] So the way to balanced and integrated public worship begins with rethinking the purposes of worship and the place of evangelism in community meetings. Evangelism can be one of the aspects of public worship and not its purpose; it is a natural consequence of the worship of the faithful. It can be argued that the worship meeting is directed to God, and relationship dynamics and dialogue between the Lord and Christians awaken faith in those present and encourage them to join the dialogue.

---

152. Now, "coming forward" in the meeting is being replaced by other forms of repentance. Teenagers and young people more often "make confessions" in children's and youth camps. This is also associated with "coming forward," but it usually happens in a group when dozens come to repent, and the number of observers is smaller than in the regular worship in the house of prayer. Repentance in small groups, or at home, is usually reported to ministers later. Such new trends may have positive outcomes because many people find it difficult to overcome psychological barriers and come forward during public worship in church. Also, ministers now "pressure" people less, wishing to avoid excessively hasty, emotional decisions.

153. Lina Andronoviene and Parush R. Parushev discuss the reasons for such a "mentality of seclusion and secrecy" in their very helpful article "Church, State, and Culture: On the Complexities of Post-Soviet Evangelical Social Involvement," 161–213. In their opinion, social activity in church could be regarded as a threat to holiness (Andronoviene and Parushev, 199). However, if we talk about the involvement of Belarusian churches in society in the second decade of the 21st century, it should be noted that churches are beginning to rethink their mission, and as a result mercy ministry outside the houses of prayer is gaining momentum. Some churches develop ministries with the disabled, the homeless, or orphanages. In 2019 there are five functioning rehabilitation centers for alcoholics at the Baptist Union of Belarus.

154. Jones, "On Abandoning Public Worship," 8.

6.4. Simplicity

6.4.1. Pursuit of the "Gospel Simplicity"

The last of the determinative principles of traditional public worship is simplicity. Belarusian Baptists believe that "God wants to see decency, modesty, and simplicity in worship."[155] When a Soviet researcher compared the worship of the Baptists and the Orthodox, he noted that Baptists had adapted it more to the masses "by simplification and reduction of rites." In his opinion, this was done in order to attract more believers by its "democratic style and availability."[156]

This comparison is a good way to understand the idea of simplicity from a Baptist point of view. Radical differences can be noted beginning with the space of worship. This was especially conspicuous in the early origins of the Shtundo-baptist movement in the Russian Empire. At the end of the nineteenth century, Orthodox priest A. Rozhdestvensky, who studied the origin of Shtundism, noted that services are held in houses, "which from the outside are not different from regular ones," and "the furniture of the facilities in which the sectarians gather for prayer, is very simple: benches, wooden chairs, and a table with the Bible and the spiritual song books on it."[157] In small Baptist churches, the worship space has not fundamentally changed in over a hundred years. Only a few new things have been introduced such as electricity and sometimes central heating and water facilities.[158]

Emphasis on simplicity is especially evident in contrast to the Orthodox tradition and its "synthesis of ritual, art, church, design, and symbolic structure"[159] which gives birth to icons, holy vessels, and devotional articles which, together with sacred garments, their colors, and the structure of the sanctuary, are filled with deep meaning and significance. On the other hand, in Baptist churches the primary verbal components are sermons, songs, prayers, and poems. If choir members wear special robes, their colors and

---

155. Q, 2008.

156. Belov, *Sekty, sektantstvo, sektanty*, 88.

157. Rozhdestvensky, *Yuzhnorussky Shtundism*, 243.

158. Churches in Osovo, Starye Terushki, Zabashevichi, Kopyl', Minsk region; Svyatopolka, Gantsevichi, Brest region; Braslav, Vitebsk region.

159. Taft, "'Eastern Presuppositions' and Western Liturgical Renewal," http://www.archeparchy.ca/documents/Taft%20Eastern%20Presuppositions.pdf., last accessed 30 January 2011.

design reflect a certain aesthetic expression, comfort and decency, and have no sacral meaning. Even though objects such as a cross bear symbolic meaning, they do not play any specific role in the worship itself.

Some Baptists apply the idea of simplicity to the content of the worship components. They defend the idea of an "uneducated faith" which stems out of an assumption that only a simple-hearted, naïve, and therefore completely sincere person can come to Christ and know his love. One popular poem expresses this idea:

> You have studied serious questions,
> You have achieved much in your meditations,
> But it should only take a simple joyful step of faith
> As a child, run to Jesus, and get on His path.
>> You will see the rugged cross
>> And hear a groan of the Son of God,
>> Then you will understand how sinful and insignificant you are,
>> Standing before eternal and holy love.[160]

Thus, to approach and comprehend God's Word requires humility and putting aside one's reason and intellect. As Toivo Pilli puts it: "In a somewhat naive but sincere way [Baptists] believed that obedience to this 'plain meaning' is of prime importance, and they paid much less attention to the process of interpreting the text."[161] More than that, such an approach was accompanied by the fear that mystical or aesthetic experiences, or rationalism, might endanger true spirituality.

An emphasis on simplicity has been conditioned by the evangelical heritage, an opposition to the Orthodox Church and its practice, and the context of persecution. Russian-speaking Baptists are part of a broad evangelical tradition into which, in the context of opposition to traditional or state churches, was planted the idea of returning to "the original simplicity." Russian-speaking author, Victor Leahu, justly criticizing the theological and aesthetic poverty of some evangelical churches, looks for reasons in its historical development. He notes: "As it seems to me early Protestantism, possessed by reforms and

---

160. Galina Vezikova, "V poiskakh puti" [In Search of the Way], http://www.blagovestnik.org/books/00430/db/v4599835.html., last accessed 16 May 2019.

161. Pilli, "Evangelical Christians-Baptists of Estonia: The Shaping of Identity, 1945–1991," 164.

perfectionism, unconsciously set a precedent for public worship simplification as a foundation of its experience of faith."[162] Simplicity in worship was promoted by influential leaders such as Ivan Prokhanov and Vasiliy Pavlov, and, before them, simplicity was the hallmark of the aristocratic evangelical community in St. Petersburg because it represented their understanding of New Testament worship.[163]

Striving toward simplicity can be better understood by examining the religious context in which the Russian-speaking evangelical Baptist movement developed. The early evangelicals in Belarus were converts from the Orthodox Church. Magnificent buildings, paintings, icons, and elaborate costumes impressed them, although perhaps only as aesthetic and cultural achievements.[164] An author of a popular research among Russian-speaking evangelical Christians, In arguing that the Orthodox and Catholic Churches have drifted away from the Gospel, an author of popular research among Russian-speakers put it this way:

> Modest evangelical public worship, the main purpose of which is reading the Word of God, singing Davidic psalms, and common prayer, was gradually enforced by the pompousness of the rituals and rites set by the [official] Church.[165]

Or, as expressed by a Russian Baptist historian, in the Orthodox tradition "the Bible was relegated to the background, for there was no time to do a deep study of it at public worship, ceremonial ritual became too complicated, and only some Scripture passages were read for the edification of believers."[166] It then follows that in order to overcome the gap between worship and life, elaborate liturgical practice should be dismissed out of hand in order to go back to "gospel simplicity," while rituals and ceremonies must be removed.

Adverse circumstances have also influenced worship in Belarus. Here a parallel can be drawn with the Puritan worship of early Baptists in England, and the simplicity of their worship which was impacted by the persecution

---

162. Leahu, "K voprosu o vzaimodeistvii teologii bogosluzheniya i teologii kul'tury," 49.

163. *Novoe vremya*, no. 802 [The New Time, no. 802], 38.

164. On the complexity of differentiating between the religious and the aesthetic, see MacIntyre, *After Virtue: A Study in Moral Theory*, 38.

165. Rogozin, *Otkuda vse eto poyavilos'?* [Where Did It All Come from?], 144.

166. Somov, "Tserkov' Khrista i ejo Svyashchenstvo," 61.

they experienced between 1660 and 1688. Having to worship in secret contributed to focusing on just the essential aspects.[167] In the same way, times of severe persecution and repression, for example of Christians in the Soviet Union beginning in 1928, have resulted in a very simple form, as well as environment, of worship. There were few opportunities (including financial ones) for a conscious enrichment of the tradition or for developing forms.[168] The meeting place itself did not encourage splendor or elaborate rituals, since people were gathered in private houses or small church buildings, sometimes in secret or having to keep changing the location of their gatherings. In this context of repression and persecution, sophistication, elegance, and rich finish were seen to be in contradiction to "the way of suffering" and the essence of faith as it was understood by the Baptists. The agenda was simply to *have* a communal experience of worship. Thus, the context of persecution, as well as opposition to Eastern Orthodoxy, shaped the style of Baptist public worship, fostering an emphasis on modesty and simplicity.

6.4.2. From Oversimplification to Creditable Simplicity

Strong emphasis on simplicity can lead to a loss of the depth and wealth of meanings inherent to a communal act of worship. In the desire to be simple in its elements, worship may not make full use of all the sensory and symbolic resources that are available, nor harness the potential for exploring diverse and creative ways of expressing faith within a worship service. In essence, the "gospel simplicity" principle becomes a defense of impoverished practice from a theological, literary, or aesthetic point of view. Therefore, it may not be surprising that Andrey Kuraev, an Orthodox theologian, missionary, and

---

167. Ellis, *Gathering*, 32.

168. Alexander Schmemann gives an illustration of the influence of difficult circumstances even on Orthodox worship as he considers his early worship experience in Paris: "In the first years of the Russian emigration, when worship had to be celebrated in cellars and garages converted into churches, we became aware of the complete impossibility of celebrating it "as it should be," according to all the canons of elegance and solemnity proper to the synodical style of Russian Orthodoxy" (Schmemann, *Introduction to Liturgical Theology*, 118–119). He discusses the issue of the relationship between worship and the place of worship and comes to the conclusion that abandoning simplicity was, in fact, inevitable: "But in the great, magnificent and indeed solemn basilicas the complication and 'decoration' of worship was inevitable, if only because if it had been celebrated in the old way it simply would not have reached the eyes and ears of those assembled." (Schmemann, 119.)

former professor at Moscow Orthodox Theological Academy, has accused Protestants of replacing:

> an ancient and aesthetically beautiful Roman Catholic rite by a poor, cold, commonplace equivalent. . . . So our sectarians replace the divine beauty of Orthodox liturgy by boring and vapid 'psalms' and bare protestant ritual.[169]

Different components of worship can suffer from an unreflected pursuit of simplicity. The very popular practice of reciting poems can serve as an example. Along with profound creations by famous Russian poets[170] and evangelical Russian classics[171] one can also hear poems of very poor quality in terms of their literary value or theological merit.[172] Secular researchers on Russian-speaking Baptists have also observed that the poems created by ordinary Christians reflect their views and emotions with "primitivism, naivete of 'philosophizing,' and poor composition."[173] To illustrate their point they mention poems with such titles as "Tri schastlivtsa" (Three Lucky Men) and "Mne mama v detstve govorila" (My Mom Told Me When I Was a Child).[174]

The key element, the sermon, also often suffers from "the lack of illustrations from life, the lack of practical applications, poor interpretation, monotony, the lack of oratory skill, preparation, etc."[175] In the words of a

---

169. Kuraev, *Protestantam o pravoslavii. Nasledie Khrista* [To Protestants on Orthodoxy. Legacy of Christ], 241–242.

170. M.V. Lomonosov, G.R. Derzhavin, N.M. Karamzin, I.A. Krylov, V.A. Zhukovsky, A.S. Pushkin, K.F. Ryleyev, A.I. Polezhayev, F.I. Tyutchev, M.Y. Lermontov, I. Nikitin, S. Nadson, K. L'dov, D. Merezhkovsky, O. Mandelstam, A. Akhmatova, M. Voloshin, Y. Yevtushenko.

171. I.S. Prokhanov, Y. Pushkov, L. Boleslavsky, Y. Buzinny, V. Kushnir, A. Savchenko, R. Beryozov, A. Lukashin, and others. Special collections of poems on Christian themes written by famous poets of the 18th–20th centuries are available, as well as anthologies of Christian poets. Manuscript collections are also used.

172. See an interesting analysis in this field by Vladimir Nesteruk, *Khristianstvo i estetika*, Diplomnaya rabota [Christianity and Aesthetics, Diploma Thesis] (Minskaya bogoslovskaya seminariya, 2003, Unpublished).

173. Mitrokhin and Lyagushina, *Nekotoryye cherty sovremennogo baptizma* [Some Features of the Modern Baptists], 65.

174. The poetic value of the first poem (the author is unknown) is indeed poor but the second one (presumably written by Prokhanov) arguably has a deep meaning and harmony. These words have been put to music. See *Pesn' Vozrozhdeniya 2500. Sbornik dukhovnykh gimnov i pesen evangel'skih tserkvey* [The Song of Revival 2500. Collection of Hymns and Songs of Evangelical Churches] (Moskva: Mezhkonfessional'nyy khristianskiy tsentr, 2001), no. 937.

175. QM, 2008. Members in a church in Orsha have complained that the main idea of the sermon is not always clear, that the sermon is merely a paraphrase of the Scripture they have

school teacher who is a member of the Baptist church in Berezino, Minsk region, "you want to listen to properly composed and developed sermons, not to mention their content."[176] One might also accept valid criticisms of the architectural space of the worship hall and its less than skillful design, as well as of the order and the course of the worship service itself.[177] Of course, the reason for that may not simply be an insistence on simplicity, but, also, as has been noted previously, the result of the general low level of education, as well as the low level of theological training ministers received as a consequence of the discrimination endured by the evangelicals during the Soviet times.

Therefore, it is important to continue clarifying the nature of "gospel simplicity." At this point, insights from other Christian traditions can be of help. Simplicity should not be "confused with baldness, negligence of forms or a docetic impatience with regard to forms . . . It is rather a matter of concentration, a determination to base worship on the central issues."[178] The *Sacrosanctum Concilium* uses the helpful expression of "a noble simplicity." According to the authors, the rites "should be short, clear, and unencumbered by useless repetitions; they should be within the people's powers of comprehensions, and normally should not require much explanation."[179] True simplicity requires conciseness, accuracy, careful selection of words or gestures, and also considers the degree of perception, education, and preparedness of the audience and other participants. Such simplicity may involve serious preparation for the sermon (including its outline) and for prayer (reflection on content), and requires teamwork in preparing for the worship, and the evaluation of participants' reaction and feedback.

Of course, to a considerable degree, the worship format and contents can also reflect the abilities, experience, and knowledge of the person conducting

---

read, that there is insufficient or poor preparation of the sermon, a lack of contact with the audience, dull presentation, and sermons which are frequently too long. (Marat Nursultanov, A poll among the members of the Baptist church in Orsha, Vitebsk region [March 2008]. Available through the author.)

176. Personal visit of the author to the church service, 7 January 2009 (Personal notes, 51.)
177. Nesteruk, *Khristianstvo i estetika*.
178. Allmen, *Worship: Its Theology and Practice*, 102.
179. Ch. 1.3.34. *Sacrosanctum Concilium*, the *Constitution on the Sacred Liturgy* is one of the constitutions of the Second Vatical Council (1962–1965). It was promulgated by Pope Paul VI on December 1963 and can be found at http://www.vatican.va/archive/hist_councils/ii_vatican_council/documents/vat-ii_const_19631204_sacrosanctum-concilium_en.html., last accessed 6 November 2019.

the worship. They are also shaped by the participants' tastes, preferences, and wishes.[180] If theological reflection on worship forms and traditions is rejected, and/or there are few materials available at the minister's disposal, then much may depend on the minister's resourcefulness, quick wit, and level of biblical and theological education as he attempts to lead worship in an appropriate, effective and contextual manner.[181]

In this regard, evangelical simplicity needs to be freed from being presented in contrast to the quality of education of the main shapers of the worship service, particularly the minister.[182] The level of theological education in Belarus still lags behind the secular educational standards. One of the reasons is the young age of the theological schools themselves and the rather limited development of Russian-speaking Baptist theological thought. As a result, the pastor's level of education can be lower than that of the church members and guests. Yet an appreciation of theological resources for worship and ecclesiastical heritage would significantly enrich the genuine 'gospel simplicity' of traditional Baptist worship. Whilst modern worship styles are frequently presented as an alternative to the traditional worship service, understanding the richness of the Christian tradition would open avenues for more contextual development of the practice of worship in Belarusian Baptist churches. For example, the use of some form of a lectionary would prevent a pastor from only preaching on their favorite themes and would rescue the church from their personal preferences.[183] Improving the general education and cultural

---

180. Perhaps one can use the term "bricolage" to describe such a ritual, activated and actualized "in a specific local and temporal context", and taking "a particular, more or less random, shape." (Barnard, Cilliers, and Wepener, *Worship in the Network Culture. Liturgical Ritual Studies. Fields and Methods, Concepts and Metaphors*, 4.)

181. Aidan Kavanagh speaks about this role of the leader under the heading of "consumer mentality, supply and demand: the latest gimmicks for a bored and jaded people", in his article "Liturgical Needs for Today and Tomorrow," 493.

Some experienced Russian-speaking Baptist ministers have published a few textbooks, including sections on worship, but these books are not widely used, and personal experience as well as oral tradition still dominate in the practice of worship in comparison to the transfer of experience and accumulated knowledge. E.g. see Kolesnikov, *Khristianin! Znaesh lit y kak dolzhno postupat' v dome Bozhiem?*; Matviiv, *Svyashchennodii pastora* [Pastor's Sacred Rites]; Khrapov, *Dom Bozhii i sluzhenie v nem*. The first edition of the latter was prepared as *samizdat* in 1972–1974 and was not in widely available.

182. Leahu, "K voprosu o vzaimodeistvii teologii bogosluzheniya i teologii kul'tury," 46.

183. Quill, "Liturgical Worship," 40.

conversance of the pastor would assit in expressing the simplicity and sincerity of faith at the appropriate literary and aesthetical level.[184]

Finally, it is also essential to develop a contextual traditional Baptist theology of worship, which is practically non-existent in Russian-speaking evangelical churches, and evaluate, from the Baptist standpoint, an ancient principle *lex orandi lex credendi*.[185] It would require paying greater attention to the relationship between public worship and faith in order to understand how "the liturgical holds the ethical and the aesthetic together,"[186] how the spiritual is embodied in the material, how worship and space, theology and time, worship service and art, and worship and life are related to each other. As a result of such theological work, traditional Baptist worship could offer "a wonderful combination of simplicity and dignity in its form."[187]

Part Two has sought to analyze in depth the form, content, space, and emphases of traditional Baptist worship in Belarus against the background of the historical, socio-political, and religious backgrounds (as discussed in Part One). This was done to bring to light the intimate connections between the two, and to demonstrate that any theology of Baptist worship needs to seriously consider the way the wider context in which that worship happens influences its formation and values. The intention of the thesis in making such an examination of traditional forms of Baptist worship in Belarus is to seek a way whereby in facing the challenges of changing circumstances and situations, such traditional worship may still make a significant contribution to the ways in which public worship can continue to develop contextually, keeping its emphases as well as its Baptist identity. It is to this issue that Part Three now turns.

---

184. Quality also depends on church members, who do not always have corresponding gifts and training for their involvement in ministry. Taking preparation seriously, as well as adopting a certain degree of "liturgy," without encroaching on the aspect of freedom, could protect worship from church members who do not have a clear biblical understanding of worship and who are guided by their preferences, suggesting a change or wish to participate in the service without having the ability to back up that desire (Quill, 40.).

185. "The law of praying [is] the law of believing," abbreviated form of Latin *Ut legem credendi lex statuat supplican*, the expression ascribed to Prosper of Aquitaine (390–455), a disciple of Augustin of Hippo. See Irwin, "Lex Orandi, Lex Credendi – Origins and Meaning: State of the Question," 57–69.

186. Pickstock, "Liturgy and Modernity," 24.

187. Motorin, "O bogosluzhenii v dni apostolov i v nashi dni," 8.

Part III

Tensions in Worship

CHAPTER 7

Identifying Tensions in Public Worship

Belarusian Baptists originated at the juncture of the West and East, in a climate of persecution by the state and in conflict with the dominant religious tradition represented by the Orthodox Church. In turn, the variety of historical links and contexts resulted in a unique set of characteristics. However, due to the radical changes in social life after communism, Belarusian Baptist churches are still uncertain of their identity, and this theological uncertainty manifests itself in tensions present in the practice of worship.

The notion of tensions can be illustrated by the example of public prayer. The *ad hoc* nature of such prayer is associated with the free nature of traditional Baptist worship, yet it raises both theological and practical questions. It is a collision point between the principle of universal priesthood and the principle of church edification. Everybody can pray, but not every prayer edifies the church. The communal and the personal aspects of public worship are also in conflict here. Personal interests or needs expressed in prayer may be not in line with the general tone of the worship, and one member of the church may be given much more public attention than others regardless of their real needs. There are also questions regarding freedom and the formal organization of public worship. Inspiration and the desires of individual church members expressed in overlong prayers can clash with the topic of worship and time management if this time was meant to be used for other components of worship.

It should be acknowledged that, to some extent, tensions are naturally an integral part of the practice of worship, arising out of the dual citizenship and nature (physical and spiritual) of those who worship; their "true life is neither that of heaven nor of earth exclusively, but of both compounded."[1] In fact, Christian life can be described in terms of contradictions, collisions, and tensions between the analytical and intuitive ways of knowing God, the active and devotional approach to ministry, the objective and subjective understanding of conversion, the intellectual and emotional expression of faith, and so on.

This chapter reviews some of the tensions that characterize traditional worship: namely, the tensions between freedom and forms expressed in the structure and content of worship; between the individual and communal aspects of worship; and between the sacred and secular perspectives of worship in its relation to the world and to culture. Evangelicals may wish to believe that their theology determines their worship,[2] but the actual practice of worship often preaches a different message and teaches a different theology. Especially for those new to the faith, public worship becomes the primary teacher of theology.[3] They may know little about denominational theology, creeds, and confessions despite attempts to teach them the basics of faith before baptism.[4] So as "worship both *expresses* and *nurtures* certain values,"[5] these values can be in conflict with official written or unwritten dogmas and doctrines of worship.

7.1. Freedom and Forms in Tension

7.1.1. Freedom in Worship

In James White's taxonomy, the Protestant church is divided into nine categories, represented in a chart from left-wing to right-wing in the following order: Quaker, Pentecostal, Frontier, Anabaptist, Puritan, Reformed, Methodist,

---

1. Peck, *Living Worship*, 21.
2. Ellis, *Gathering*, 18.
3. Thus Maria Cornou wisely assumes "that the relationship between theology and worship is reciprocal" and worship "both shapes and expresses the theology of a particular community or congregation." (Cornou, "Worship as a Formative Practice: The Worship Practices of Methodists, Baptists, and Free Brethren in Emerging Protestantism in Argentina (1867–1930)", 24.)
4. Cf. Bradley, "Congregational Song as Shaper of Theology: A Contemporary Assessment," 357–358.
5. Ellis, *Gathering*, 98.

Anglican, and Lutheran.⁶ Traditional Baptist worship in Belarus, with its rejection of service books, potential for the introduction of new elements, and its lack of set ritual and ceremony would represent the left-wing of the spectrum, between the Frontier and Puritan worship. Ellis uses the term "free worship" to describe evangelical gatherings, where he defines freedom as:

> the freedom of local congregations to order their own gatherings for worship; it is the freedom of spontaneity which is open to the extempore guidance of the Holy Spirit; and it is the freedom of a particular worshipping community to respond to the reading and preaching of scripture addressed to them as God's living Word.⁷

"Concern for simplicity and freedom"⁸ has always been a "trademark" of Baptists. As McKibbens put it, "our Baptist tradition of freedom in worship is a valued part of the denomination's heritage."⁹ Prescribed forms and authentic worship are seen to be mutually exclusive.¹⁰ "The Spirit blows where He wishes,"¹¹ so it would then be wrong to limit his actions by certain formulae. Alluding to the Orthodox Church, where liturgy is the center of church life,¹² Baptists would conversely say, "Evangelical Christians-Baptists have neither

---

6. White, *Protestant Worship: Traditions in Transition*, 21–24. Cf. Ross, "Lefts and Rites: One Evangelical's Perspective," 36.

7. Ellis, *Gathering*, 27.

8. Ellis, 68.

9. McKibbens, "Our Baptist Heritage in Worship," 67.

10. Cf. Prokhanov, *V kotle Rossii*, 20; Rogozin, *Otkuda vse eto poyavilos'?* 145; Lensu and Prokshina, *Baptizm i baptisty*, 17.

11. John 3:8, literal translation from Russian Synodal Bible.

12. "An Orthodox is '*homo liturgical*'" according to Tatiana Goricheva, "Freid i *homo liturgikas*" [Freud and the '*homo liturgikas*'], 77.

rituals nor liturgy."[13] The suspicion of "ceremonial overgrowth,"[14] forms and rituals, which were associated with traditions of the "Established Church," only strengthens the anti-liturgical frame of mind.[15]

Historical circumstances have also not been conducive to the development and preservation of ceremonies and rituals. Persecutions, shortages and restrictions around worship spaces, limited opportunities for the written transfer of tradition, and, until recently, practically no theological literature about worship has left a deep mark. For a long time, apart from Eastern Orthodoxy, there were no other models of appropriate forms of worship which could be adapted.

As with the wider Baptist tradition, Belarusian Baptists pay particular attention to the spirit and mood of worship, or, in the words of Ellis, "the sincerity of the worshippers rather than when particular parts of worship [take] place."[16] The "Principles of Christian Life" in the 2003 "Doctrine of Faith of Evangelical Christian Baptists in Belarus" establishes the following principles:

---

13. Words such as "liturgy" and "liturgical" may have various meanings and may describe worship of a congregation in its entirety or refer to the interrelation and implication of components in worship. Alexander Schmemann, an Orthodox liturgist, attempted a broad definition, fighting against the reduction of the term (Schmemann, *For the Life of the World*, 25). Schmemann's definition is in unison with a common understanding among theologians of the word "liturgy" when they examine it from an etymological perspective: "In the singular the word 'liturgy' denotes an act of worship, more specifically the Eucharist. Derived from the Greek *leitourgia*, it was used in Hellenistic Greek of an act of public service. In the New Testament it is employed to describe an act of service or ministry" (Davies, *A Dictionary of Liturgy & Worship*, 222.). However, the term "liturgy" also has a narrower meaning, mainly relating to the words used in a service, which is why Paul Basden speaks about "liturgical churches," which include the Russian Orthodox Church (Basden, *The Worship Maze: Finding a Style to Fit Your Church*, 36, 54.). In the Orthodox liturgy, true meaning is revealed in the proportion, fullness, order, and relations of elements. As Gordon Lathrop points out, "Meaning occurs through structure, by one thing set against another" (Lathrop, *Holy Things: A Liturgical Theology*, 33). If the understanding of "liturgy" is narrowed to a certain developed form of worship, with a fixed structure and invariable content, primarily but not limited to the ordered commission of the Lord's Supper, traditional services in ECB churches in Belarus would not be considered liturgical. Secondly, despite the fact that there are some familiar traditions of holding worship and common elements for the service, there are no officially approved or required forms in regard to worship, with no such decisions adopted either at church level, or at the level of a council of churches in Belarus. And thirdly, no theological meaning would be attached (at least explicitly) to the relationship and sequence of elements of worship. In that sense, 'non-liturgical worship' would be worship that is characterized by the absence of fixed forms in which the relationship and sequence of the elements has theological meaning.

14. Chambers, "The Renaissance of Worship," 13.

15. In the Orthodox Church "all this lofty and beautiful liturgical life is regulated by very stiff and clear regulations" (Krasovitskaya, *Liturgica*, 9.)

16. Ellis, "Understanding Worship: Trends and Criteria," 36.

12.4.3. Public Worship in a House of Prayer should be done in atmosphere of reverential worship in spirit and in truth, and in holiness and purity *(Ps 5:7; Ps 33:8; Ps 111:10; Ps 119:38; Prov 22:4; Isa 30:15; Neh 1:11; Eccl 8:11–13; Mal 1:6; 4:2; Acts 9:31; John 4:23, 24; 2 Cor 5:11; 2 Cor 7:1; Eph 5:21; Phil 2:12; Heb 5:7; Heb 12:22–28).*

12.4.4. We understand that music ministry and singing in church should be spiritual, edifying and aim at glorifying the Lord, without contradiction to the spirit of the Scriptures, without bringing a spirit of this world, worldly manner of performance and dancing *(Ps 47:6, 7; Ps 67:1; 1 Cor 10:7; 1 Cor 14:33; Eph 5:19, 20; Col 3:16; Rev 18:21, 22).*[17]

The foremost, and most obvious feature is the absence of a strict and explicit plan or prepared content for public worship. In traditional Belarusian Baptist worship, the program of the service only exists in the mind of the pastor, and often during the sermon he decides which song the congregation will be singing next. The way the offering is collected, making announcements, and giving greetings can be arranged in an entirely new format if the service is directed by another minister. Quite often the issue of someone's involvement in the worship is addressed during the course of the service. In the middle of the service a person may send a note to the pastor volunteering to recite a poem or sing a hymn. In small churches the worship service leader may ask, "Who else is ready to take part in praising the Lord?" Or they may encourage people to sing, share a testimony, or recite poetry, inviting the ones "who are led by the Lord." A pastor also may invite church members to participate by a slight nod or gesture.[18] Few pastors in Belarus are full-

---

17. *Verouchenie evangel'skikh khristian baptistov v Belarusi, prinyatoye na s'ezde EKhB v Belarusi 15.03.2003 goda.*

18. Nursultanov, A poll among the members of the Baptist church in Orsha. The same can be seen in other churches. For example, on 12 August 2012 in a worship service of the Russian-speaking church "Bethany" in Tallinn, Estonia, whose pastors along with some members are originally from Belarus, the pastor asked the musicians during the worship service: "What else can you sing?" "There is a song, but we will do it after the sermon," the musician responded. In the same meeting, while the congregation was singing, one guest was told that he must also preach the final sermon immediately after this song (Personal notes, 59). In some churches or on special occasions such as Christmas or times of evangelism, written programs can be used but they usually represent a half-page general scheme. (Churches in Slutsk, Minsk region;

time and they do not have enough time, intellectual resources, or financial resources to plan and prepare for worship gatherings as an essential part of their responsibilities. There are few resources or guides in the Russian language, and many pastors lack finances and equipment to print new programs every Sunday. It is less complicated and expensive to rely on members' spontaneous inspiration during the time of worship.

The most popular pattern for public worship preparation is as follows: sermons are planned a month,[19] a week,[20] two or three days before worship[21], or right before worship.[22] In some churches the music element is usually planned and prepared three to four days in advance,[23] or the day before[24] (the choir schedule might be planned a quarter in advance).[25] In the five to fifteen minutes before the worship service begins, the brothers define the order of sermons, the order of guests, and the involvement of musicians. During public worship the church members can suggest reciting poetry, singing, or sharing their testimony if they feel led to it. In "House of Gospel," Vitebsk, the leaders define a general pattern based on preaching and singing; information about the participants is collected right before the worship starts in Slutsk, Minsk region and they print out a schedule on the spot.[26]

"Golgotha" and "Light of Truth," Minsk; churches on Fortechnaya 61/1 and Voolka, Brest; "Grace of God," Bobruisk, Mogilev region [Personal notes, 66].)

19. "Good News," Minsk; churches in Borovliany and Stolbtsy, Minsk region; church "Emmanuel" in Mogilev (SI, 2012; Q, 2013).

20. "Bible Church" in Borisov and church in Slutsk, Minsk region. Q, 2013.

21. Church in Zhdanovichi, Minsk region. Q, 2013.

22. The traditional practice in one of the churches in Polotsk, Vitebsk region ("Piety") at least till 2005, was that before the meeting, five to seven men who had "the gift of teaching," presented their messages and outlines of their sermons to the pastor. All of them should have their messages ready, but only two of them will actually be asked to preach. This practice is repeated the next Sunday, except that each man should have prepared a new message this time. (Personal notes, 65b.)

23. SI, 2012; Q, 2013.

24. Central Baptist Church in Gomel. Q, 2013.

25. Church in Voolka, Brest. Q, 2013.

26. Personal notes, 65b-66; SI, 2012. It is important to observe that, despite seemingly neglecting planning, believers have a very high view of worship and the strict requirements concerning attending worship which they respect very much. One of the key characteristics of traditional public worship in Belarus is "awe," "deep concentrated worship of a human soul to God while contemplating by faith His majesty, His power, holiness and love for a human being" (Shchavelin, "O blagogovenii v dome molitvy," 41). This characteristic is accompanied by humility, which expresses itself through restrained behavior in a house of prayer, a strict dress

Still, the spiritual preparation of mind and heart plays a significant role and includes prayer, reading, and fasting, especially before the Lord's Supper. In many churches, on entering the sanctuary, church members kneel to pray, after which they greet each other saying, "Peace be with you." As soon as the ones able to lead the singing arrive, the congregation starts singing hymns even without waiting for the formal beginning of the worship service, preparing themselves to participate in it.[27] In some other churches, members read Christian articles and sermons before the service starts in order to lead the congregation away from worldly thoughts and conversations.[28] An author of an article in *Bratskiy Vestnik* recommended that, "Coming into the house of prayer, let us take our seat quietly, so that we may not break the silence, and let us read the Word of God or pray silently before the service."[29] Thus, in the best cases the lack of planning is not negligence around worship but is rather an expression of the understanding of the inspiration and activity of the Holy Spirit.

> Aspiration for freedom is also reflected in the preaching. The absence of planning in *preaching* was almost universally practiced until the turn of the millennium. Out of the fourteen churches covered in the research questionnaires[30] eight, primarily small and middle-sized, do not have a sermon schedule. Preachers would be appointed by pastors before the service or some brothers, "inspired by Spirit," may just volunteer to preach. Moreover, even in the middle of the service a brother from the congregation could be called out to do "the ministry of the word." This would be especially true when the congregation

---

code, and kneeling (Gnida, "Poryadok provedeniya bogosluzheniy v tserkvakh evangel'skikh khristian-baptistov," 72.).

27. Rechitsa, Svyatopolka, Brest region; Kopyl', Minsk region; "Grace of God," Bobruisk, Mogilev region. In the church in Luninets, Brest region, they turn on classical music ten minutes before worship starts (Personal visits of the author to the church services [Personal notes, 50].).

28. "Emmanuel," Mogilev, 2008. Until 2005 "Light of Gospel" church had a similar practice. In Church "Golgotha," Minsk, in the evening they read articles from *Bratskiy Vestnik* (Personal notes, 50.).

29. Shchavelin, "O blagogovenii v dome molitvy," 42

30. Q, 2008.

had the privilege of having a welcome guest in attendance such as a preacher or a minister from another church.[31]

Large churches began to change this practice of scheduling in 2000, usually preparing a schedule a month ahead.[32] Some of these large churches have fifteen to twenty preachers available, so scheduling helps to order worship. The sermon schedule has already found wide use among younger preachers who are strong supporters of greater preparation before delivering a sermon. In fact, this approach is not new within the Russian-speaking Baptist tradition. Back in 1988, AUCECB leaders supported the idea that it is good to inform a preacher of the time when he is going to speak so that he may have time to prepare a biblical message and meditate over God's Word.[33] The understanding was that a sermon should not only be inspirational, but also well-prepared. However, this practice does not go unchallenged even today. For example, in January 2013 the senior pastor in "Light of Gospel," Minsk initiated the discussion about canceling the schedule of sermons. Most preachers were not very enthusiastic about the idea, but later in 2014 the practice of planning was cancelled, and preachers have since been appointed right before worship. In 2012 the schedule was cancelled in Slutsk, Minsk region, too.[34] The reasons expressed were the fear of limiting the Holy Spirit and depriving worship of

---

31. In church "Gethsemane" in Machulishchi, Minsk region the pastor asks before worship begins: "Who is ready to preach the first sermon?" (The second sermon has been reserved for the guest preacher). The brothers give a shy and uncertain response. The pastor's question is more a formality. In reality he is ready to preach himself and he only wants to be respectful of other preachers. (Personal visit of the author to the church service, 12 May 2013 [Personal notes, 65b].) In the church in Rubel', Brest region, the pastor gives notice to the preachers two to five days ahead. At times the issue is solved right before worship. Somebody is ready and somebody is not, but when the church has twelve preachers, at least three of them, including the pastor, are always ready to preach (or more or less ready). (Anatoliy Filanovich, Personal interview with author, Minsk, 18 January 2016 [Personal notes, 66].)

32. "Light of Gospel," "Golgotha," "Bethlehem," Minsk; central Baptist church in Kobrin, church on Fortechnaya 61/1, Brest; church in Luninets, Brest region; "Grace of God," Bobruisk, Mogilev region; "House of the Gospel," Vitebsk (for two-three months ahead). At "Light of Truth" the issue of sermon topics is determined two to three months ahead of time and they make a decision about singing just before worship. (SI, 2012; Q, 2013.)

33. Gnida, "Poryadok provedeniya bogosluzheniy v tserkvakh evangel'skikh khristian-baptistov," 72. When I preached in Moscow central Baptist church (1993–1997), the senior pastor usually called me three to four days before the occasion to let me know that I should be preaching, and that as the preacher, I was to determine the topic.

34. Personal visit of the author to "Light of Gospel" church service, Minsk, 31 August 2014; Gennadiy Ralko, Personal interview with author, Minsk, 11 February 2014 (Personal notes, 65).

its authenticity and sincerity. It is still expected that being filled by the Spirit, which is especially important for a sermon, is characterized by spontaneity, ingenuity, and unpredictability (cf. Acts 2:4; 4:31; 1 Cor 14:29–30), and that planning sets limits for God's work in worship. The opponents of the schedule also suppose that the obligation to preach (according to the schedule) could conflict with the spiritual condition of a person (lack of inspiration) in that moment, and therefore the preacher would not have the appropriate influence.[35]

Prayers in churches are examples of what may be called "free" or "extempore" prayer, in which spontaneously articulated prayers are offered by one person, or several persons, on the behalf of the congregation,[36] or, as they are often called, prayers "using your own words," prayers which express unfeigned feelings, from the bottom of the heart.[37] The idea of composing prayers in advance is foreign to the Baptists in Belarus, primarily due to a negative reaction to the ritualistic liturgy of Orthodoxy, along with a desire to preserve their Baptist identity and keep prayer as a real-life conversation or communication with God.[38]

Some theologians from other traditions, like Evelyn Underhill, an English Anglo-Catholic writer, would also advocate freedom, spontaneity, and enthusiasm in worship, as a protest against formality, and routine, and as an expression of the manifestation of the Spirit.[39] In the context of traditional Baptist worship this is expressed in flexibility, encouragement, greater involvement, and the possibility of spontaneous participation. In this way, the invisible Holy Spirit manifests Himself through believers for the benefit of members in various spiritual gifts, and first of all, gifts of speaking.[40]

---

35. Pavel Obrovets, Personal interview with author, Minsk, 17 February 2015 (Personal notes, 65).

36. Ellis, *Gathering*, 104.

37. Gnida, "Poryadok provedeniya bogosluzheniy v tserkvakh evangel'skikh khristian-baptistov," 72.

38. Arguments against written prayers and a focus on prayer "from the heart," "living prayer," remind us of arguments brought forward by Congregationalists in England against the set, formal, structured prayers established in the Book of Common Prayer. (See Webber, *Worship Old & New: A Biblical, Historical, and Practical Introduction*, 115.)

39. Underhill, *Worship*, 87–90.

40. 1 Cor 12:7–12

In practice, this approach, which could be identified as "the Cult of Spontaneity," can result in a number of problems, like unsystematic teaching.[41] Indeed, as William Abernethy, who served in Congregational churches in the United States, has observed, "The content of a service which emphasizes spirit over order is often shaped [. . .] not so much by the full biblical story as by our own experience."[42] This often proves to be the case because the topics of the sermons are determined by the interests of the preacher, and not by the church calendar, or by the Bible text, or by the needs of the congregation. Russian researcher, Seventh Day Adventist Viktor Leahu, warns that:

> in the absence of the latter [a planned and prepared order of worship], the Church may come under the power of destructive forces, and, particularly pantophagy [the assimilation of elements of different traditions of worship, as well as elements of secular culture] and arbitrary rule of taste.[43]

Paradoxically, unpreparedness may result in less flexibility and variety in worship[44] but planning may schedule more components, involve more people, and make worship more diverse and meaningful.

Lack of planning may also result in low quality elements and low quality worship as a whole, and it may even lead to disorder. As a result of the emphasis on spontaneity, some people who like to preach, teach, or sing but have no gift to do so may take on a large role in worship; some components such as a very long poem or a "prayer-sermon" may not be appropriate, or the content of some components may simply be irrelevant. Amateurish singing and unprepared preaching may increase a congregation's discontent.[45]

---

41. Some preachers do not follow the generally accepted custom of keeping to the topic when churches celebrate the Lord's Supper or some Christian holidays. For example, March 28, 2010, on Palm Sunday at "Bethlehem" Church in Minsk, during evening worship the first preacher neither mentioned how Jesus entered Jerusalem nor about the meaning of the celebration, but preached, instead, about ethical issues of Christian life. February 5, 2012, before the Lord's Supper, a preacher at Borovliany spent his time exposing evolutionary theory and paid no attention to the suffering and death of Christ (Personal visits of the author to the church services [Personal notes, 65]).

42. Abernethy, *A New Look for Sunday Morning*, 53.

43. Leahu, "K voprosu o vzaimodeistvii teologii bogosluzheniya i teologii kul'tury . . .," 46.

44. Cf. Segler, *Christian Worship, Its Theology and Practice*, 180. Segler, a Baptist theologian, says that when Baptists "do not plan some order or ritual, they usually drift into a rut which they follow as slavishly as the more liturgical churches follow their liturgies."

45. QM, 2008.

Such lack of preparation may also result in a sense of disorder if musicians become distracted by searching for songs or tuning their instruments, and there may be tedious pauses between the components, which lessens the sense of awe.[46] The results from the research questionnaires highlight the failure of amplifiers, projectors, sound-tracks, faults of stage arrangement, and poor attempts to fix the microphones during public worship among common problems.[47] Church members acknowledge with a heavy heart that such lack of preparation and poor organization has a negative effect on the reputation of their church. Church members may feel embarrassed if unbelievers are present at the meeting.[48] Therefore, it is not surprising that church members report more interest in organization than in unplanned freedom, or in other words that they prefer organized freedom,[49] knowing that freedom in worship may bring both blessings and problems. Thus, freedom in worship must be handled wisely, and must be balanced with planning and preparation in terms of both the structure and the components of worship.

7.1.2. Forms in Worship

Worship in Baptist Churches is distinguished not only by freedom but also by certain structures and forms which are repeated each Sunday. In fact, any repeated activities take on a kind of form, which also becomes repeated, especially when these activities are practiced in some churches three times a week and about two hundred times a year. Thus, in Belarusian churches some invariable forms such as "the ritual of non-ritualistic churches"[50] have gradually developed: a traditional structure of worship, established formulae for the Lord's Supper, the methods of receiving the offering, the prayer of blessing, and dismissal when the meeting ends, and so on. It is not surprising, then, that secular Belarusian sociologists noted in 1969 that Baptists observe "strict regulation, a certain system of actions at prayer services, and obeying

---

46. SI, 2012.
47. Q, 2013.
48. Q.
49. QM, 2008.
50. Hoon, *The Integrity of Worship*, 217.

rituals," and, on this basis, they claimed that "Baptists also have a cult."[51] Thus we speak of "non-ritualist churches" tentatively; the issue is not the presence of forms but rather the meaning and role that they play in worship.

Forms or some structures are essential for the survival, retention, and transition of meaningful customs of a group of people. In the opinion of theologian and Methodist minister Paul Hoon, "This helps maintain and communicate the content of worship to other people and generations."[52] As such, forms or traditions are valuable carriers of information that is memorized by the participants of worship due to regular repetition. Geographical dispersion and the number of believers who have experienced these repeated forms allows information to be saved when any written documents might be destroyed or do not exist.

Forms also help (new) ministers to lead worship, as they have some ready and time-tested forms to refer to. Without inherited forms, leaders or groups invent them anew every Sunday, and experiments of this kind are usually a distraction as people are unable to concentrate on content when they are busy with negotiating forms. The authors of AUCECB's *Presbyters' Handbook* warn: "As far as church members get used to the set order of worship and church statutes, any deviations may cause distress."[53]

Furthermore, and this is very highly appreciated by Belarusian Baptists, forms control and bring order to the energy of freedom. Baptists often repeat that "God is not a God of confusion but of peace,"[54] and that God's nature calls us to order in worship which means some structure, discipline, and form.[55] This issue was vital in terms of past relationships with the Pentecostal church.[56] To avoid some extremes such as uncontrolled prophesies, speaking

---

51. Lensu and Prokshina, *Baptizm i Baptisty*, 76. They add that "Baptist ceremonies are cleansed from clearly magical acts which are so characteristic of Eastern Orthodoxy or Roman Catholicism" (Lensu and Prokshina, 77).

52. Hoon, *The Integrity of Worship*, 216.

53. *Nastol'naya kniga presvitera*, 2d. edn. [The Pastor's Handbook], 76.

54. 1 Cor 14:33.

55. SI, 2012.

56. Pentecostals were part of AUCECB from 1945 to 1989. See section 1.1.

in tongues, or outcries, "the Spirit-emphasis ... was marginalized during the decades after the [Second World] war."[57]

In addition, through public worship, Baptists tried to express their denominational affiliation and their understanding of faith, which influenced the leading role of the sermon and the place of common singing. The Baptist movement needed new forms to distinguish itself and consolidate its followers. Among such forms one can list the traditions which regulate yearly, monthly, and weekly cycles of worship.[58] In fact, this commitment to differences in personal devotion, public worship, and interchurch relations helped Baptists to survive and spread their beliefs better than the unorganized and unstructured Molokans and Stundists, many of whom joined the Baptists or were absorbed by them.

The above suggests that forms which have developed over time in Baptist worship are important in the passing on of tradition, in preventing confusion in worship, and in keeping the identity of a particular religious group. On the other hand, forms, or a rigid attitude toward forms, can act to hinder the expression of gifts, limit the sense of freedom in Christ, and not be sensitive enough to the flow of the Spirit if these limit the freedom in Christ and quench the Spirit and the expression of gifts. Forms may also be irrelevant in particular situations and contexts and may prevent the adaptation of better forms from other traditions. "Sanctified by time" forms, which are difficult to change, can damage worship. Thus, as in the case of freedom, balance is needed to allow real blessing from worship to emerge. As William Abernethy concluded:

> Spirit then is related to the vitality of worship, yet too much raw spirit can lead to chaos or unwanted excesses. Some order is necessary to channel that spirit in beneficial ways. Yet too much order can be a problem, too, in that such order can stifle living spirit and lead to rigid, cold, and unfeeling worship.[59]

---

57. Pilli, "Evangelical Christians-Baptists of Estonia: The Shaping of Identity, 1945–1991," 163. The Pentecostals were forcibly united with AUCECB in 1945, and they formed their own Union in 1989. Thus, they really were part of the same worship tradition. (See section 1.1.)

58. Zhidkov, "Nashi prazdniki" [Our Festivals], 13–20.

59. Abernethy, *A New Look for Sunday Morning*, 48.

This evaluation could be a good description of worship in Belarus, where the balance is tilted to one side. As worship inevitably uses some forms, regulations, and schemes, there is some tension between form and freedom, order and spirit, "structure and liberty,"[60] between "freedom and tradition, spontaneity and order, the extempore and the liturgical, the charismatic and the formal, the prophetic and the sacramental."[61] Just as Scylla and Charybdis we seem to be either waylaid with lifeless ritual or with destructive freedom, either "unstructured spontaneity that creates bedlam," or "a well-regulated order of worship that often creates boredom."[62]

The churches enjoy the fruit of 'freedom in the Spirit' in worship, but at the same time they suffer from poor organization and superficiality, which is often an end result of aspirations for freedom. They might enjoy order in worship, yet also suffer from formality and coldness, which are often the end result of aspirations for structure and arrangement. Aware of that, Baptists are looking for ways to reconcile spirit and order in worship. The search is not always successful, yet each time church members come for public worship hoping that freedom will build and edify, that forms will serve a real freedom, and that the combination of order and spontaneity will lead them into God's presence and allow them to experience God's Spirit at work in their life.

7.2. The Priesthood of All Believers Versus the Corporate Nature of Worship

7.2.1. "Each One . . . Has a Revelation" (1 Cor 14:26)

Tension between individual and communal aspects of worship, arising out of a particular understanding of the priesthood of all believers and their direct involvement in worship, is another feature of public worship. Quoting 1 Peter 2:9, Russian-speaking Baptists often talk about "the holy nation," and "the priesthood of all believers," and they especially stress this feature when talking about the differences between Orthodox and Baptist beliefs and practices.

---

60. Wainwright, *Doxology: The Praise of God in Worship, Doctrine and Life*, 114.
61. Segler, *Christian Worship, Its Theology and Practice*, 178.
62. Chafin, *1, 2 Corinthians. The Communicator's Commentary*, 173.

Baptists emphasize that all believers are priests who have personal access to God through prayer and the Word of God.[63]

The legacy of the Reformation and common Baptist roots may help explain this "emphasis on a personal faith experience" in worship.[64] Yet what is more important for Russian-speaking Baptists in their approach to participation in worship, is the way they link it to their understanding of New Testament Christianity. Along with 1 Peter 2:9, they quote the Apostle Paul, who uses the term "everyone" and "all" when speaking about gifts (1 Cor 12:7, 13; 14:26).[65] Since there was no separation between clergy and laity in the apostolic church and everyone could participate in some way, it is argued that it should be like that in a church that seeks to follow the New Testament Way.[66]

In fact, it can be argued that the responsibility and capacity of each soul, the priesthood of all believers, and the universal call to sanctity, are the central truths governing worship.[67] In the words of James and Susan White, participation "is [the] central [word] in our thinking about worship today."[68] Everyone has the opportunity to speak, not based on some vague egalitarian or democratic principles, but because everyone has been gifted and therefore has something to bring to the conversation.[69] Historically, the practice was not unique to Belarusian Baptists. Describing Baptist development in Poland, to which Western Belarus belonged from 1921 to 1939, Zbigniew Wierzchowski writes that "everyone was encouraged to pray aloud [one by one] during the services."[70] Joining in the weekly worship is essential in the

---

63. "Seven Baptist principles," website of the Union of ECB in Belarus, http://baptist.by/principy-baptizma/, last accessed 16 May 2019.

64. Pilli, "Evangelical Christians-Baptists of Estonia: The Shaping of Identity, 1945–1991," 137.

65. Rees, "The Worship of all Believers," 176; Liesch, *People in the Presence of God*, 73.

66. In the Orthodox context, this teaching played a special role in the self-determination and preservation of Baptist identity.

67. Underhill, *Worship*, 299.

68. White and White, *Church Architecture. Building and Renovating for Christian Worship*, 17.

69. Freeman, McClendon, Jr., da Silva, *Baptist Roots. A Reader in the Theology of a Christian People*, 9.

70. Wierzchowski, "Between the Wars: Golden Years for Polish Baptists," 89.

Baptist practice of traditional worship, because Sunday should be devoted "to the Lord, Bible study, abiding in prayer and public worship involvement..."[71]

In worship practice the "priesthood of all believers" is manifested in a variety of participants: both "ministers" and congregation members take part in worship, and those who are not members of the church but attend worship services regularly such as children, youth, and *priblizhionnye*.[72] Unbelievers may also participate in public worship by singing with the congregation and participating in the offering.[73]

Women dominate in every aspect in many congregations, except in preaching and leading public worship where their participation is not allowed.[74] Poetry is recited almost exclusively by children and women in most churches; this, with singing, seems to be sui generis compensation for the ban on sisters' preaching. Prayer services are generally considered to be predominantly women's meetings. In special prayer services women usually outnumber men by a ratio of 3:1 or 4:3.[75] Pastors strongly encourage men to join prayer services, but the situation is slow to change, and men's prayer groups are more rarely observed than women's prayer groups.[76]

The dominance of women in prayer and other public worship components is related to the fact that they outnumber men in churches. In some communities, such as Lesovnya, Starye Terushki, Kopyl, Slutsk, Minsk region, women

---

71. *Verouchenie evangel'skikh khristian baptistov v Belarusi, prinyatoe na s'ezde EKhB v Belarusi 15.03.2003 goda*. 9.3.

72. See footnote 133 on page 163.

73. Participation of unbaptized believers periodically provokes arguments in churches. Yet most of the time the sides agree that the unbaptized people, and even children yet to make a decision, can participate in public worship (except for preaching), especially if they come from Baptist homes, "for the kingdom of heaven belongs to such as these" (Matt 19:14). As to "unbelieving" adults they should not participate in public worship individually or in groups in front of the congregation. However, the practice may vary across churches. For example, in "House of the Gospel" in Vitebsk an unbaptized visitor does not have the right to recite poetry and children can participate in public worship only under the leadership of their teacher (Timofei Egorenkov, Personal interview with author, Minsk, 26 November 2015 [Personal notes, 68].).

74. Cf. "Vzglyad nazad," 7.

75. Q, 2008.

76. On women's roles and involvement in the life of Baptist churches and unions of the European Baptist Federation see also the article by Andronovienne and Jones, "Women in Baptist life," 529–531.

(mostly elderly) make up almost ninety per cent of believers,[77] or even one hundred per cent,[78] which is in turn explained by a higher degree of religious activity on the part of women in Belarus as well as women's longer lifespan.[79]

The participation of many people in worship brings dynamism and can create the feeling of informality and ease. Since this expresses the non-liturgical nature of worship, to a certain extent it leaves room for freedom of worship, and a quick change of components helps the congregation engage throughout this long time of worship. The diversity of components enriches Baptist worship and adds some color to it. Poetry read by good reciters often produces an effect comparable to that of a good sermon. Testimonies bring a realistic touch to the Baptist religious experience and appeal to their feelings as well as to their minds. Testimonies touch hearts, arouse emotions, and are powerful tools for witnessing to unbelievers because they make it easier for people to understand how others have been drawn into God's saving activity.

As participants use their talents and gifts, which is especially true for singers, musicians,[80] and poets, a sincere individual's worship encourages others to come into the presence of the Lord and it edifies them.

---

77. Data for 2012 is as follows: up to 85% in Molodechno, Minsk region; 70–80% in Liadno, Volozhin, Berezinskoe, Mar'ina Gorka, Machulishchi, Minsk region. 60–70% in Borovliany, Kolodishchi, Gatovo, Soligorsk, Shatsk, Minsk region; "Light of Truth," "Bethlehem," "Resurrection," Minsk (Personal notes, 68b.). The data for 1979 shows that men made up to 20.4% of the membership in ECB churches of Vitebsk area and 36.5% in Brest area. (Baltrushevich, *Uzajemadachynienni dziarzhavy i pratestanckich cerkvau u BSSR u 1965-1985 hh.* [The Relations of State and Protestant Churches in the Byelorussian SSR in 1965–1985], 227.)

78. In Ruzhany, Brest region, there are only women in the congregation, and in order to have public worship and preaching they invite a brother in Christ from another church (Valeriy Okhrimuk, Personal interview with author, Minsk, 27 November 2013 [Personal notes, 68b]). The situation was the same in a congregation in Liubiacha, Minsk region, until August 2013 when the church merged with the neighboring church in the village of Volok (Okhrimuk).

79. In her dissertation, Lina Andronoviene explores the position of women in the wider evangelical Post-Soviet context, expanding on the problem of singleness ("Transforming the Struggles of Tamars: Singleness in Intentional Baptistic Communities"). She also addresses the subject of women in church ministry in *Involuntarily Free or Voluntarily Bound: Singleness in the Baptistic Communities of Post-Communist Europe.* The book by Belyakova and Dobson, *Zhenshchiny v evangel'skikh obshchinakh poslevoyennogo SSSR. 1940-1980-ye gg. Issledovaniye i istochniki* is dedicated to the history of the life of women in Baptist and Pentecostal churches, and their role in the community and family.

80. Zbigniew Wierzchowski noted the importance of this practice in the 1920s, arguing that "Various types of singing and music forms such as orchestras, multiple choirs, soloists, and duets also make it possible to utilize the different talents of the believers" (Wierzchowski, "Between the Wars: Golden Years for Polish Baptists," 97).

> If a person who prays a public prayer, tells the Lord sincerely, with great passion about different requests and gives thanks to Him, these requests and thanksgiving are put on the hearts of all people in the congregation and their hearts begin to burn with the desire to pray about these things, also.[81]

The presumption is that meaningful and deep prayers or songs teach and instruct others in the same way that prayers and songs recorded in the Scripture continue to teach believers.

Individual prayer allows every believer to express religious feelings and desires. In fact, an individual prayer may soon become a congregational prayer because "Every worshipper has the duty to act as priest for his fellow worshippers."[82] If believers agree with the content of a prayer, they often murmur words of assent, "Hear this prayer, Lord," "Yes, Lord," and speak a loud "Amen" at the end of the prayer.[83] In large gatherings, Christians are not usually very personal in their prayers, and their words express the desires of many believers with some individual features.

Public worship involvement enables people to become aware of their importance and value in church. Thus, pastors and Sunday school teachers give children opportunities to sing or recite poems. Sometimes it is difficult to understand them, but their participation and joy are more important in this case than the goal of edification. If everyone is encouraged to bring themselves to the worship, then those who might otherwise view themselves, or be regarded by others, as "those without strength"[84] find a place amongst the willingness of others to bear with their weaknesses.[85]

Of course, paying exaggerated attention to individual participants can underestimate the significance of the church as a body of believers. However, the emphasis is on every member being essential for public worship because,

---

81. V.S., "Voprosy dukhovnoy zhizni," 22.

82. Hoon, *The Integrity of Worship*, 105.

83. In most churches, besides "Amen" members exclaim "praise the Lord" or give thanks (they say *blagodarim* – "thank you") after singing and reciting a poem. (Q, 2008.)

84. Rom 15:1.

85. Some Baptist ministers and members think it is very important to maintain and encourage individual participation for the benefit and spiritual growth of members (SI, 2012.). For example, preaching causes younger members of the congregation to discipline themselves, study the Bible, and pray regularly. Church leaders therefore encourage every individual to discover some gift with which to minister in worship.

without bringing to the meeting the fullness of our private or personal characters, or our personal relationship with God, real worship cannot happen.[86] Yet, these individuals worship in corporate spirit since personal religious experience cannot be separated from the communal life of believers.

Certainly, styles of worship change over time, and one can observe a shift toward professionalism, especially as/since evangelicals in Belarus now have the opportunity to study in theological schools and secular universities. Therefore, in large churches, some elements of worship are reserved for certain people; for example, the stage may be occupied by trained musicians. The process of professionalization is gaining momentum, with the result that only congregational and group singing, and applause in less traditional churches, remain available to the majority of members. Professional and corporate participation better meet the modern trends in culture and the demands of many believers, especially from the point of view of quality. Still, Belarusian Baptists are trying to maintain active participation because of the reasons set out above, and because human resources in small churches are limited. Without individual participation, public worship might not take place. This situation is a good illustration of the tension between the individual and the corporate aspects of worship.

7.2.2. Individual and Corporate Aspects in Conflict

Before discussing the nature of the tension between the practice of "universal priesthood" and corporate expression of worship, the following question could be asked in any typical traditional Baptist worship: How many of those present genuinely take an active part in the worship? In fact, few individuals take a lead or are involved in direct participation, which suggests that what is really happening is better described as a separate "group of the priesthood" rather than a universal priesthood.[87] For example, the number and composition of people praying provides sufficient grounds for the critique of the very term 'congregational prayer' as it is usually the same group of people that take part in the prayer of the church. Depending on the effect of the preaching and its inspirational power to encourage prayer, or on the tradition

---

86. Kay, *The Nature of Christian Worship*, 54. See also Walter B. Shurden, "The Baptist Identity," 329; Newman, "The Priesthood of All Believers and the Necessity of the Church," 53.
87. SI, 2012.

established in a particular church that five to eight people pray every service and another five to eight pray occasionally, there may actually be no more than five to fifteen per cent of the total number of church members actively participating. Thus, the element of congregational prayer actually involving the whole congregation is only "Amen" at the end of each prayer (although this element of participation is not to be underestimated, since their "Amen" shows "their acceptance of the prophetic and apostolic Word."[88])

About the same percentage of members regularly take part in preaching and reciting poems, and fewer members sing solos or duets. Up to twenty five percent sing as a part of choirs and ensembles,[89] but the majority of members come to the house of prayer as listeners. This is true for many Baptist churches. "The observer model"[90] is becoming increasingly common, in which worship is perceived as some event reaching the audience, rather than something done by a congregation. The participants of worship become listeners and spectators of a performance.[91] It is noteworthy that the front of the sanctuary is becoming more like a stage in a theater, and, as Mark J. Harris claims, "Passive observation, the norm in Orthodoxy, also became a general (though less pronounced) feature of Baptist worship."[92] The house of prayer is not now a meeting place for corporate worship, but a place where the audience watches a group of professionals worshipping God (the members are blessed if these active participants are really professionals and if this is not a one-man show). Regrettably, this situation satisfies many church members, who have little or no interest in participation. Some members do not want

---

88. Allmen, *Worship: Its Theology and Practice*, 164.

89. Q, 2008. In the church in Borovliany, Minsk region, twelve out of twenty-seven members sing in the choir. More examples of the percentages or numbers of those actively involved are as follows: In Voolka church, Brest, 5–8% of the church members preach, about 5% recite poetry, up to 10% pray, and 20% are involved in choir ministry (Q, 2008). At "Light of Gospel" church in Minsk (446 members in 2018), preachers – twelve, prayers – about twenty (some preachers are included); singers (solos, duets, small groups) – ten; choir (adult and youth) – fifty-five (including the same singers); musicians – ten (half of them also take part in singing); regular poem reciters – five (not including children, who are not formally members of the church); children's choir – up to fifty (they are not members, and sing in worship sporadically). Here up to a hundred members take part in worship at least once a month and around seventy do it every Sunday (Personal notes, 68).

90. Jones, *A Shared Meal and a Common Table: Some reflections on the Lord's Supper and Baptists*, 22.

91. Shepherd, Jr., *The Worship of the Church*, 55.

92. Harris, *Toward an Understanding of Russian Baptist Worship*, 9.

to preach, preferring not to have the responsibility or the requirement or preparing sermons. Others cannot overcome fear or psychological barriers, especially regarding spoken prayers or sermons. However, some may desire to participate but, as the quality improves, do not want to take part in worship, thus avoiding comparison with the "real professionals."

Of course, practices differ in various churches. On the one hand, in small churches with ten to twenty-five members, more than half of the members may be involved in directly leading worship. On the other hand, large churches also have a variety of options for individual participation since they schedule a number of public worship occasions. Thereby, each have opportunities to be involved, but these may arise for different reasons and it is difficult to judge what might be truly classed as the priesthood of all believers in terms of looking at the active and direct participation of individual members. In small churches participation may arise out of necessity to ensure the worship time is filled rather than from a deep interest in every member participating.[93] Similarly, the more performance orientation of large churches may again be out of necessity, and they do offer a high level of opportunity to be part of orchestras, ensembles, choirs, and other music groups. At least across the range of churches, worship does provide every believer with the potential opportunity to participate either individually or through a group activity.

Unfortunately, the participation of individuals can collide with the 'fitting and orderly way' of doing things in public worship. In such cases, individual ministry does not fully become an integral part of communal worship. Prayer, for example, may illustrate this problem.[94] As a writer in *Bratskiy Vestnik* observed, "Some simple souls quite often publicly share with the Lord (or, more exactly, with all people attending the house of prayer) all details about their feelings and experiences," and they do it with tears, which does not edify listeners, but, on the contrary, becomes "a temptation and a stumbling block" for them.[95] Prayer allows individuals to express their desires before God, but extreme individualism in prayer can conflict with the desires and expectations of other worshippers, when an individual does not have a good understanding of what public worship is and the role of each member of the Body.

---

93. QM, 2008.
94. Q, 2008.
95. V.S., "Voprosy dukhovnoy zhizni," 23.

The challenge of worshipping as a body whilst making space for its members to participate individually is perhaps particularly acute as churches grow their numbers. If this is coupled with either a low level of organization and planning, or a negative attitude toward those, it can be difficult as an increasing number of participants each determine their own place and role in the meeting, as well as the length of their involvement and the topic. As a result, the rhythm and structure of worship are disturbed. Too many songs and too long a sermon or prayer, along with too many topics, is exhausting and frustrating for the congregation.[96] Nathan Nettleton, an Australian Baptist, aptly comments that such a meeting, "instead of becoming a community's corporate offering to God, . . . will remain merely the sum of its parts, a group of people each offering their own individual worship while just happening to be in the same place."[97] Individuals may enjoy their participation, but being aware of the church as one body[98] requires holistic worship where horizontal ties (between church members) are not overlooked for the sake of vertical (between Christians and God). This tension lies in the fact that the latter are effective only if the former are present and being developed.[99]

The sense of "lawless individualism"[100] that is apt to prevail when individual contribution is valued more than the process of weaving these into a communal exploration of a particular theme or aspect, is exacerbated by the fact that desire and willingness to take part in worship often prevail over the importance of thinking through what is said or contributed. This is further exacerbated by the continuing belief that dedication and maturity, rather than preparation, is the best channel for the free activity of the Holy Spirit in worship. This is complicated even more by the difficulty of discerning motives or motivation. The necessity to express the self runs the risk of arising from narcissism, and if this then becomes the foundation of participation, the church is "optional, secondary to the individual."[101] Music ministry is especially vulnerable, particularly where individual singing prevails over

---

96. SI, 2012.
97. Nathan Nettleton, "Making Meaning in Worship," 85.
98. 1 Cor 12:13.
99. Eph 4:16.
100. Underhill, *Worship*, 235.
101. Newman, "The Priesthood of All Believers and the Necessity of the Church," 54.

congregational singing,[102] and worship resembles a concert and talent parade. David Fagerberg criticizes such an approach, reminding us that "There is a great therapeutic value in expressing ourselves, but this is not the service commanded of us at the altar of the Lord."[103]

When personal desires and demands prevail in worship, the edifying element suffers, and, perhaps more seriously, worship faces the danger of becoming anthropocentric and it is not easy to find Christ where two or three are gathered together in His name.[104] The blessings of the worship become heavily dependent on particular persons who preach, sing, play music, witness, or pray. Famous singers attract people and enjoy popularity but the church gathering loses its "radical Christocentrism,"[105] which was always inherent in free worship. Building a time of integrated collective worship and a strong sense of direction is not without certain vulnerabilities either, including: the inappropriate exercise of control, the concentration of the process into too few hands, and the exclusion of those who do not 'fit' comfortably into the looked-for quality.

Since churches consists of individual believers, some tensions are inevitable in any kind of worship. Certainly, the problems and disadvantages of individualism can be partly solved by planning, teaching, and appropriate limits, but it is this area where church members can grow and learn how to serve each other in the best way. Overall, the tension between individual and communal aspects of worship will remain until the Lord comes. Worship on this earth is a rehearsal, a preparation for worship in Heaven, where all tensions and discrepancies will be removed by the perfect worship Leader.

7.3. Public Worship in the Secular Environment
7.3.1. Traditional Forms and Culture in Conflict
If the relationship of Baptist beliefs in the priesthood of all believers is important within the church, the relationship of Baptists to secular culture beyond the house of prayer is equally important. Worship, as a meeting of Christians,

---

102. Church in Orsha. Personal visit of the author to the church service, 7 June 2009 (Personal notes, 53b).
103. Fagerberg, "A Theology of the Liturgy," 174.
104. Merton, "Liturgy and Spiritual Personalism," 505.
105. Hughes, "Free Church Worship: The Challenge of Freedom," 154.

marked with special terminology and a special worldview, is also open to those unfamiliar with the Gospel and church culture, to, as Paul terms it in 1 Corinthians 14:23, "ungifted men and unbelievers." Also, as expressed in verses 24 and 25, the sermon's songs should convict them and call them to account, so they will fall on their faces "and worship God, declaring that God is certainly among you."[106] Tensions arise at the junction of worship and mass (or multi-media) culture, since it is difficult to reconcile the needs of representatives of the church with secular culture, the wishes of experienced believers with young believers or "outsiders,"[107] and "good old traditions" with popular elements of contemporary culture.[108]

These issues were not much discussed in the twentieth century. As has already been demonstrated, Christians were primarily interested in the occasion of worship rather than its form. Secondly, during the Soviet era, especially with the severe persecution at the end of 1920s, there was almost no contact between worship and secular culture because boundaries between the church and the world, as well as between believers and non-believers, were clearly defined. The great majority of those attending worship were

---

106. 1 Cor 14:24–25.

107. 1 Cor 5:12.

108. H. Richard Niebuhr defines culture as "that total process of human activity" that "comprises language, habits, ideas, beliefs, customs, social organization, inherited artifacts, technical processes, and values" (H. Niehbuhr, *Christ and Culture*, 32). Frank C. Senn makes our task difficult, pointing out that "In complex modern societies people actually participate in several cultures simultaneously: a national culture, a regional culture, a local culture, an ethnic or racial culture, a family culture, and a religious culture" (Senn, *Introduction to Christian Liturgy*, 38.). Similarly, Gerard Lukken points out that "the culture is not univocal. Therefore one should never speak of only one culture, but there are always many cultures, both in succession to one another (diachronic) and simultaneously (synchronic). No one culture thus has absolute value, and every culture is only relative" (Lukken, *Ritual in Abundance. Critical Reflections on the Place, Form and Identity of Christian Ritual in our Culture*, 171). Martin Stringer highlights the same issue from an anthropological point of view. "As an anthropologist, therefore, I find the concept of 'culture' far too vague and much too slippery for the kind of purposes that I am trying to engage with in this text. Perhaps equally problematic is the relationship between 'culture' and 'religion'" (Stringer, *A Sociological History of Christian Worship*, 9). Yet for our purposes we do not need to have too narrow or specific a definition. Anscar J. Chupungco lists values, cultural patterns, and institutions among the components of culture, here I concentrate on the cultural patterns (thought patterns, language patterns, rites and symbols, literature, music) (Chupungco, "Liturgy and the Components of Culture," 156–164). It is possible to speak about pop culture, the world of ideas and images of an average Belarusian, including pop music, films, and popular entertainment. This world is largely formed by the media, especially television, and, for the younger generation, by the Internet. Lukken puts it in this way: "Popular culture is rather the culture which people unconsciously share with one another" (Lukken, *Ritual in Abundance*, 373).

raised in a Christian environment; few neophytes adjusted to evangelical subculture. Later, approximately ten to fifteen years after the celebration of the Millennium of the Baptism of Rus' in 1998, when the world became more "friendly," churches were busy with evangelism and the construction of houses of prayer. They lacked time for analyzing and understanding public worship, and they did not see any need to do so.

The debates began in the first decade of the twenty-first century. A new situation arose as many people who had been raised in secular culture came to worship, and, on the other hand, there were significantly more opportunities for ministries outside the house of prayer and more opportunities for believers to become involved in social and cultural life. Nowadays, large numbers of young Baptists receive education in higher schools and enjoy more of the fruits of secular culture, whereas this was rarely possible thirty or forty years ago. Connections to all parts of the world through the Internet also overcomes many barriers. As a result, a generation and a cultural gap has arisen even within the church, and many believers are attracted to adopting forms of worship that reflect what they experience in the new culture. Positive perceptions of elements of secular culture have resulted in the fact that the church and state boundary has shifted, and it is now inside the church.

Once the waves of people coming into churches ceased, the search for a new method of evangelism also contributed to this tension.[109] Some Baptists began to adapt popular forms and styles from theater and popular music in an effort to attract non-believers and to interpret the Gospel in forms relevant for outsiders and young churchgoers.[110] Christopher Ellis describes it as the tension between "a desire for 'holy' worship for a 'holy' people and the missionary urge to offer 'relevant' worship for a consumerist generation."[111]

Indeed, during the period of their formation, Belarusian Baptists had already made use of the cultural elements of their day while attempting to attract people and make public worship more accessible. In the 1920s, when

---

109. In some cases, this search led to the splitting of youth groups from traditional churches and the formation of new ones, such as the youth-oriented churches "Pure Heart" in Brest, "Reconciliation" in Bobruisk, Mogilev region, and church "Without Walls" in Pinsk, Brest region which were formed between 2007–2013.

110. For example, "Light of Gospel" church in Minsk, which practices a traditional style of worship, does not countenance electronic music but it does put on theater performances at Christmas.

111. Ellis, "Who is Worship For? Dispatches from the War Zone," 179.

evaluating evangelical public worship from an Orthodox perspective, some critics accused Baptists of such unprecedented innovations as putting pianos in the sanctuary.[112] Now a piano is considered an essential attribute of traditional worship, and it is electronic instruments and pop-music that have become points of contention instead. It is important to note that even though electronic instruments were widely used in the Council of Churches[113] in the 1970s and 1980s as a means of attracting young people (primarily from Christian families) to church, they were of limited use, and the traditional worship structure was not under pressure to change. Pop-songs were an addition to traditional singing. However, the early twenty-first century is special in the intensity and scale of the introduction of new music styles.

7.3.2. Cultural Gap

Music styles provoke most of the debates, but they seem to be only the tip of the iceberg. The issues of preaching and the use of Bible texts in public worship appear to be even more serious. In traditional worship services, preachers use the Russian Synodal translation. Even young churches stay faithful to this, although they may sometimes use a new translation by the Russian Bible Society from 2011,[114] or a translation by the International Bible Society from 2007.[115] The Synodal translation was published in 1876. In this translation there are many archaisms and transliterated loanwords from the Hebrew, Aramaic, Greek, and Latin languages, requiring translation or explanation,[116] as well as many Slavonicisms.[117] The pronunciation of some Slavonicisms is

---

112. Khaytun and Kapayevich, *Suchasnaya sektantstva na Belarusi*, 44.

113. See footnote 26 on page 8.

114. "New Earth," Minsk (Dmitriy Mamoiko, Personal interview with author, Minsk, 21 November 2014 [Personal notes, 73].). "New Testament" Church from its outset (March 2015) uses a new translation of the Russian Bible Society as a liturgical text (Sergei Luk'yanov, Personal interview with author, Minsk, 12 September 2017 [Personal notes, 73].).

115. "Light of Hope," Minsk; "Church 'Without Walls'" in Pinsk (Mikhail Stepnov and Dmitriy Polukhovich, Personal interview with author, Minsk, 21 November 2014 [Personal notes, 73].).

116. They are words such as the Jewish "Amen," "kidar" (turban, Exod 28:4), and "Osanna" (Hosanna, Matt 21:9);" the Aramaic "Avva" (Abba, Mark 14:36)," "Maran-afa" and "anathema" (1 Cor 16:22), "raka" (good-for-nothing, Matt 5:22); the Greek "akridy" (locusts, Matt 3:4), "diadema" (diadem, Isa 28:5), "ipostas'" (hypostasis, Heb 1:3), "phelon'" (the cloak, 2 Tim 4:13); the Latin "legion" (Matt 26:53) and "pretoria" (the Praetorium, Matt 27:27).

117. Loanwords from Church Slavonic language include: "Biytsa" (pugnacious, 1 Tim 3:3), "blagoutrobnyy" (the tender mercy, Luke 1:78), "breniye" (clay of the spittle, John 9:6),

similar to well-known Russian words, but the meaning is different.[118] Also titles, plant and animal names, units of measurement and coins/currency are unclear for many readers.[119] In 2000, the Russian Bible Society published a Bible edition with a dictionary of five hundred and seventy words that needed to be explained, and there were about three hundred Slavonicisms among them. Archaism characterized the first edition of the Synodal translation, yet the difference between Church Slavonic and the Russian language was not so great at that time. However, experts did call attention to this issue in the early twentieth century when I.E. Yevseyev wrote,

> It is much more important that the Synodal translation is outdated as literature. The language of this translation is difficult, out-of-date, and artificially drawn close to Slavonic. It is a century behind common literary language and is totally unacceptable to be used in literature because it came from the period before Pushkin.[120]

Yet the lack of alternatives for many years, the influence of the Synodal translation on Christians, and the significance of the translation for the origin and development of the evangelical movement, put it in a unique position and attributed a special aura to it and the status of "the inspired by God translation."[121] At a pastors' conference for the churches of Minsk region on February 23, 2013, Nikolai Kolesnikov, an authoritative teacher in traditional Baptist circles and a writer of a number of books, warned ministers against

---

"vezhdy" (eyelids, Psalm 11:4), "vozglaviye" (the head, Gen 47:31), "vyya" (neck, 2 Kings 17:14), "glagol" (the word, Luke 3:2), "gorlitsa" (turtledove, Gen 15:9), "dlan'" (hand, Prov 31:20), "dshcher'" (daughter, Matt 9:22), "igo" (yoke, Matt 11:29), "lanity" (cheeks, Song of Sol 1:10), "odr" (bedstead, Deut 3:11), "chado" (child, Luke 16:25), among others.

118. For example, "bran'" (struggle, Eph 6:12), "koleno" (the tribe, Num 2:5), "okopy" (barricade, Luke 19:43), "pozorishche" (spectacle, 1 Cor 4:9), "tochilo" (a wine press, Matt 21:33), "t'ma" (myriads, Num 12:22), "khudozhnik" (architect, Heb 11:10), "yazyk" (tongue, Rev 5:9), and "yasli" (manger, Luke 2:7). Now these words mean correspondingly quarrel or strife, knee, trench, shameful event, grindstone, darkness, artist, tongue or language, nursery.

119. Like "Augustus," "air" (calamus, Song of Sol 4:14), "yavor" (plane tree, Gen 30:37), "anaka" (the gecko, Lev 11:30), "aspid" (cobra, Psalm 91:13, "gomor" and "yefa" (omer and ephah, Exod 16:36), "lokot'" (a cubit, Gen 6:16), sikl'" (shekel, Gen 23:15), "lepta" and "kodrant" (copper coin and a cent, Mark 12:42), etc. See *Bibliya. Knigi Svyashchennogo Pisaniya Vetkhogo i Novogo Zaveta. Kanonicheskiye* [The Bible. The Books of the Holy Scriptures of the Old and New Testament. Canonical], Slovar' and Vvedeniye [Glossary and introduction].

120. Yevseyev, *Sobor i Bibliya* [The Council and the Bible], 5.

121. Compare with the position of the King James Version in English.

making use of new translations, and called them to stay faithful to the Synodal translation, stressing its special value in the church's history, its effectiveness, and its life-changing power. He added that giving up the Synodal translation would lead to biblical illiteracy, since Bible cross references and commentaries in Russian are based on the Synodal translation.

A terminology and style from more than one hundred and thirty years ago appears not only in Bible translations but also in sermons, prayers, poems, and the language of worship. For example, public worship often begins with the greeting "I extend my greetings to you, dear brothers and sisters."[122] Such a greeting is not usually used in everyday life, particularly by those who do not attend church, and, in a church using a modern worship style, it is often replaced with neutral phrases such as "good morning," "good evening," or "hello." Archaic lofty adjectives such as "blessed," "glorious," and "didactic/edificatory" are often used in traditional worship although they are rarely heard in everyday speech.[123]

Although this is not a typical case, one incident illustrates the difficulty well. The pastor of "Salvation" church in Kolodishchi, Minsk region, told of a woman who attended their public worship for the very first time in her life in May 2013. On her way back home, she was asked if she understood the message. She responded, "Well, the preacher was speaking in Church Slavonic language, so how could I understand it?" The preacher had used the Synodal translation and preached in Russian, referring to terminology familiar for regular attendants, such as "umilostivleniye," "osvyashcheniye," "blagodat'" ("propitiation," "sanctification," and "grace") but that would not necessarily be familiar to the general public.[124]

The cultural gap is particularly evident in the use of musical forms that are not characteristic of the mass culture of the early twenty-first century. In

---

122. Forty years ago, N. Khrapov insisted that "it is a sin to use a greeting synonymous to the one the world uses – 'Hello!'" *Dom Bozhiy i sluzheniye v nem*, ch. 60.

123. Other typical expressions ("Canaanite" language) which are heard only in public worship include "bless each heart," "let us bow down our hearts," "speak to each heart," "put something on the heart," "young hearts," "be washed in the blood of Jesus," "grant eternal life," "draw strength," "cover with grace," "contemplate with the heart's eyes," "kneel down with the heart," "feed on the word of God," "may the Lord grant you abundant blessings," "ministry of the word," "a lost sheep," etc.

124. Nikolai Sinkovets, Personal interview with author, Minsk, 28 May 2013 (Personal notes, 73.)

addition to choral singing, some churches enrich worship by a wind and folk instrument orchestra.[125] These forms, especially popular in the first third of the twentieth century, are now associated with military music and folklore, and they do not play a significant role in secular culture. Besides, traditional worship usually uses hymns written and translated in the nineteenth century and the first third of the twentieth century, such as "Blizhe, Gospod', k Tebe" (Nearer, Lord, to Thee), "Bud'te bodry i vsegda molites'" (Be Cheerful and Always Pray), and "Tverdo ya veryu" (I Firmly Believe).[126] They reflect the language of their own day, and in just the first ten hymns of the *Song of Revival* hymn collection, it is possible to find plenty of words that could be considered outdated, bookish, and/or religious terminology.[127]

Other aspects of the cultural gap include the appearance of Christians. Especially in the ICCECB, women are expected to cover their heads, wear long skirts, avoid jewelry such as chains, rings, earrings, and even wedding bands, and to wear their hair long. Under no circumstances would women in these churches come to public worship wearing trousers (sisters keep this rule in other public places as well as in their own home). Brothers, especially preachers, could be singled out for wearing a shirt with no tie. So, it is easy to identify people who belong and those who are strangers, both in the house of prayer and even outside it. However, in the Baptist Union churches, the requirements around appearance are not as strict, and the women experiment with make-up, jewelry, and haircuts, even though in a moderate manner, so the external differences from the "world" are less obvious.

7.3.3. From Culture to Subculture

Traditional worship reflects Niebuhr's model of "Christ against culture."[128] Its form and content are evidence of a separation from the world, and the

---

125. Churches in Voolka and on Fortechnaya 61/1, Brest; church in Kobrin, Brest region.

126. *Pesn' Vozrozhdeniya*, nos. 22, 25, 184. "Tverdo ya veryu" originally written as "Blessed Assurance."

127. "Divnyy, osenyat', l'nut', mol'ba, svyashchennoye obshchen'ye, lik, chada, vnimat', molen'ye, otrada, nisposylat', obremenennyy, uzret'," which mean "amazing, overhang, cling, plea, holy fellowship, face, children, listen, prayer, delight, grant, burdened, and behold." These words are not currently in everyday use. Outdated words give the songs loftiness and an air of solemnity, but the aesthetic component dominates the semantic, and they do not meet the principle of edification (section 6.2).

128. H. Richard Niebuhr, in his book *Christ and Culture*, explores five different approaches that Christians may take to culture: opposition, agreement, Christ above culture, tension, and

rejection of secular culture. In the words of Tatyana Nikol'skaya in relation to the life of Baptist churches in the Soviet Union in the second half of the twentieth century, "Reticence, a special life style and clothes and even unique vocabulary, rather obscure for the people around, are characteristics of such subculture."[129] For this type of worldview, self-preservation and survival was the main goal,[130] and it was only natural that the desire to separate from the "sinful world" was expressed in worship in a concentrated form.

It should be noted once again that, for the most part, the character of traditional worship has been defined by historical and political contexts, by hostility and persecution from the state that excluded the believers from social and cultural life. On the other hand, this situation stimulated the creation of their own world and public worship as a shelter. The world could do nothing but harm; dialogue and being open would make the church vulnerable to sinful influence. The impact of the Orthodox environment, with its adherence to the archaic and old, even though mysterious and incomprehensible, contributed to such an approach to worship as well.

Using Henri Bergson's terminology, Mikhail Cherenkov refers to "a closed type of Christianity" to describe evangelicals living in a similar context in Ukraine, where he noted such characteristics as:

> a demonstrative rejection of dialogue with modern culture, faith which is associated with birth and upbringing and which corresponds to the understanding of religion as moral and culture-forming, submission of values of freedom to the value of church authority, church autarky, and hostility to the secular world.[131]

In fact, staying active and open to the world characterized many Christians, but their active position was related only to preaching the Gospel. These

---

reformation. Here I refer to the first attitude – opposition. D.A. Carson, in his book *Christ and Culture Revisited*, criticizes Niebuhr's position for simplification and primitivism. He believes that the concept of dialogue between Christ (Christianity) and culture holds intrinsic controversy, since all kinds of Christianity are inherently an expression of culture. It is possible that Niebuhr's classification presents some difficulty on the level of terminology and cultural studies, but it is still a handy tool with which to compare the approaches of various Christian groups to mass culture.

129. Nikol'skaya, "Uroki istorii dlya EKhB," 10.
130. Nikol'skaya.
131. Cherenkov, *Evropeis'ka reformatsiya ta ukrains'kyi évanhel's'kyi protestantyzm*, 271–272.

communities called for a high degree of commitment, and there was an initiation process which introduced the newcomer to a community marked by strong self-awareness and the maintenance of a countercultural rhetoric.[132] An application for church membership through baptism was a heroic action in Soviet days, and points to this this kind of stance, as can be seen in this application from Maria Shakhlevich in 1979:

> I ask Lesovenskaya church to accept me as a member through water baptism, as I wish to become a member of the church of Christ and to proclaim the teachings of Christ to all people ignorant of Him. I promise to be a fearless witness of the Gospel in the world around me.[133]

Thereby, an active stance regarding preaching the Gospel was combined with a hostile attitude to secular culture, and this situation contributed to establishing a special evangelical microclimate, subculture, or "cultural enclave,"[134] evident in many areas, including in the content and style of worship. Meanwhile, the desire for worshipping God in spirit and in truth, a growing understanding of the relativity of worship forms and their historical development, along with attempts to attract young people and pronounced evangelical motives, led many ministers to adjust public worship to the way of thinking of the twenty-first century listener. Cherenkov has remarked that "isolationism, radical conservatism and separatism were replaced by the acknowledgement of secularization of the world as an objective fact, which requires modernization and church reform."[135] In Baptist churches there have been moves towards change and adaptations for particular situations and special events such as concerts, festivals, holiday performances, nights of questions and answers, evangelistic meetings with a musical style similar to popular music, and sermon language appropriate to those who are relatively unacquainted with the Bible. Nevertheless, a bolder move, that involves reforming theology at a broader level, is required if this cultural gap is going to be overcome. The following chapter focuses on the types of theological and practical steps that this thesis proposes are needed to overcome

---

132. Lathrop, *Holy Things: A Liturgical Theology*, 92–93.
133. 1 July 1978. Archive, Church ECB in Lesovnia, Soligorsk district, Minsk region.
134. Cherenkov, *Evropeis'ka reformatsiya ta ukrains'kyi évanhel's'kyi protestantyzm*, 453.
135. Cherenkov, 415.

the conflict between traditional forms and culture, particularly with respect to the three major areas outlined above: the expression of freedom and the order in worship, the tension between the public character of worship and the participation of individual members, and the cultural tensions within worship and between worship and wider society.

CHAPTER 8

Overcoming the Tensions

An analysis of the tensions in traditional worship identified several problems concerning organizational quality, content, the conflict of individual with communal aspects of worship, and dangers of social and cultural isolationism. In order to address these tensions, inner resources can be employed – for instance, worship practices in other Baptist churches in Belarus, acquaintance with the history and formation of Russian-speaking worship, development of a theology of worship within the framework of spiritual education, etc. However, it is also helpful to set the discussion against the experience of other worship traditions in the local context. Even a brief engagement holds the possibility of suggesting some principles and practices that might be borrowed by and implemented in traditional Baptist worship.

Orthodox worship is a clear model of the service structure, order, and organization, that is sometimes lacking in Baptist worship. Of special interest are Orthodox sermons at the level of particular components, examples of which can be found not only in churches, but also online. Orthodox worship also suggests options for engaging various senses, not just hearing. However, the main difficulty in borrowing from Orthodox worship stems from the history of relationship conflicts between the Baptist and Orthodox, as well as radical differences in approach to the worship service.

Interestingly, Roman Catholic worship in Belarus is much closer to traditional Baptist worship in its content and form, and even in the way it looks. For example, the majority of the congregation sits during worship; some aspects of modern technology, like multimedia projectors, are employed; and much attention is paid to the verbal component, including preaching, and congregation participation, such as singing, saying Psalms, the Lord's

Prayer, and the Creed. The Belarusian language is actively used in worship, along with Polish and Russian.[1]

The comparison with the Catholic church could be interesting since it is a minority religion in Belarus and, in popular understanding, it is defined as a 'foreign' church ('Latin,' 'Polish,' or 'Roman'). The same would be true of Baptists, who are also considered to be of a foreign nature.[2] In addition, Catholic worship has experienced reform after the Second Vatican Council. Martin Stringer reminds us that:

> The *Constitution on the Liturgy* that was produced as a consequence of the Council was one of the most far-reaching documents in the history of Christian worship, as it enabled a revolution in liturgical thinking and practice, not just within the Catholic Church but across all the mainline churches.[3]

---

1. The use of the Belarusian language in Belarus is an ambiguous and controversial question. Perhaps, in terms of the future (largely depending on the political development of the country), this can be effective, but currently the vast majority of people speak Russian. The Russian language is also the main language of the media, politics, science, and education. At the beginning of the twenty-first century there was not a single higher education establishment with a curriculum in Belarusian. Office work and legal proceedings are almost absent in Belarusian. The Belarusian language has a symbolic rather than communication function. See Koryakov, "Yazykovaya situatsiya v Belorussii i tipologiya yazykovykh situatsiy. Dissertatsiya na soiskaniye uchenoy stepeni kandidata philosophskikh nauk" [Language Situation in Belarus and the Typology of Language Situations. Thesis for the Degree of Candidate of Philosophical Sciences], see especially 57–61. Also, Sevyarynets, *Lyublyu Belarus': 200 fenomenau natsyyanal'nay idei* [I love Belarus: 200 Phenomenon of National Idea], 302–304. See also an article that explores the linguistic identity of the country by Bekus, "'Hybrid Linguistic Identity of Post-Soviet Belarus," 26–51. In some churches, hymns may be sung in Belarusian, as is done on a regular basis in churches "Grace of God" in Bobruisk, Mogilev region and in Orsha, Vitebsk region (Personal visits of the author to the church services, 30 December 2012 and 25 August 2013, respectively [Personal notes, 15]). There are two sermons during worship in "Grace of God" church in Bobruisk, and the second one (in the evening) has been preached in Belarusian since 2014 (Sergei Gormash, Personal interview with author, Minsk, 11 December 2017 [Personal notes, 73b].). Baptist church "Ascension" in Minsk, consisting of nearly twenty members, does worship in Belarusian and it also makes use of folk culture elements, including ancient national music instruments and songs. At the moment, the suggested form looks somewhat exotic and cut off from everyday life.

2. Cf. Chapter 3.2. The Reform of the Sacred Liturgy.

3. Stringer, *A Sociological History of Christian Worship*, 220. Anderson, writing in the 1980s, confirms this claim and comments in this respect that the notable thing about "Protestant worship today is that it is in dialogue with more than its own tradition" (Anderson R., "Protestant Worship Today," 64).

Comments on the meaning of Scripture, and its relation to worship,[4] and the demand for varied and suitable Bible reading,[5] are very valuable and relevant. Recommendations to maintain a balance between adherence to sound traditions and openness to legitimate changes which are preceded by "theological, historical, and pastoral" reflection,[6] are still relevant, given the tension between traditional and new forms of worship in the Baptist churches of Belarus. Acquaintance with the experience of adapting Catholic worship services in Belarus can indeed be useful.

Nevertheless, the perception of fundamental theological differences does not encourage the exchange of experience or interaction. In the *Constitution on the Liturgy*, the main role in building liturgy is played by the hierarchical structure,[7] which differs from the Baptist structure that relies on a horizontal network of churches. In addition to restricting the rights of local priests, the *Constitution* also prescribes the priority of the Latin language (in Latin rites) and the restriction of local languages.[8] Such statements demonstrate how closely worship is tied with theology and church structure, so any mechanical transfer of form will not always be productive if it does not consider the principles underlying the changes.

The Reformed or Methodist traditions, placed between "left" and "right-wing,"[9] and with a focus on spending time in reading, studying the Bible, and singing, might be a helpful reference point. Although they are not developed enough in Belarus,[10] studying their practice and heritage may be useful as their approach could enrich Baptist worship in terms of the interaction of freedom and form as well as a reinforcement of the corporate element in worship. Section 8.2.3. of this chapter *(Inculturation: A Theological Model for*

---

4. *Sacrosanctum Concilium*, ch. 1.3.24.
5. *Sacrosanctum Concilium*, ch. 1.3.35.
6. *Sacrosanctum Concilium*, ch. 1.2.23.
7. *Sacrosanctum Concilium*, ch. 1.2.22.
8. *Sacrosanctum Concilium*, ch. 1.3.36.
9. White, *Protestant Worship: Traditions in Transition*, 21–24. Also see section 7.1.1. of this thesis.
10. According to the media source, religia.by, which covers the main spheres of religious life in the Republic of Belarus, as of 16 May 2019 there was one officially registered Evangelical reformed church, two Lutheran churches and there was neither a Methodist nor Presbyterian Church in Minsk. (http://religia.by/religioznye-organizacii/svodnyj-perechen-zaregistrirovannyx-religioznyx-obshhin-v-g-minske, last accessed 16 May 2019.)

Traditional Baptist Worship) utilizes the model from reformed theologian John Witvliet to analyze the relation between worship and local culture.

The Pentecostal church is wide-spread in Belarus, which represents the "left-wing" category as defined earlier in chapter six.[11] In some areas of worship Pentecostals may be even more suspicious of planned forms of services.[12] However, in the same manner as Baptist worship, their pursuit of freedom has a negative effect, so they state in a recently published Confession that "conducting worship in any group of believers always requires prayerful preliminary ordering of worship elements. It is especially true when worship takes place in a local church with many people."[13] The authors of the Confession refer to 1 Cor 14:26–40, but they also warn that:

> These words do not imply that God's grace in public worship should be limited. On the contrary, when we avoid chaos and spend time in organizing worship and looking forward to the revelation of the Holy Spirit, we promote the Lord's work in the hearts of Christians."[14]

Being aware of the shortcomings of over-stressing the aspect of freedom, traditional Baptist worship could be enriched by the dynamics, vivacity, and emotionality of the Pentecostal worship. The concern about the future of traditional public worship prompts the search for ways in which worship might be renewed in order to satisfy the spiritual demands of Christians and attract seekers, positively influencing all the worshippers.

The experience of various traditions may indeed offer helpful insights for addressing the tensions in worship and enabling the search for a healthy balance in worship. However, it must also be kept in mind that there is no

---

11. See this thesis, section 6.1.1. Freedom in worship. I should remind the reader again that for much of the Soviet period the Pentecostals were forcibly united with AUCECB, and thus really part of the same worship tradition (see section 1.1.).

12. The pastor of the Pentecostal church in Minsk region, Pavel Kalosha, admitted in a homiletics class that over the number of years of his ministry in Pentecostal churches in Minsk and Minsk area he had never encountered someone preaching a series of sermons. He had not preached a series of sermons himself either. He chose topics as other Pentecostal ministers did, "by inspiration." (Personal interview with author, Minsk, 22 March 2013 [Personal notes, 65].)

13. Verouchenie Ob'edinionnoi tserkvi khristian very evangel'skoi v Respublice Belarus', izd. 2, 167.

14. Verouchenie Ob'edinionnoi tserkvi khristian very evangel'skoi v Respublice Belarus'., 167.

need for a final solution because "healthy tension"[15] can make a significant contribution to the wholeness and vitality of worship. The following sections examine more closely the three key areas of freedom and forms, the personal and public aspects of worship, and cultural gaps to see how the tensions inherent in them might be addressed, whilst acknowledging the necessity of those tensions for bringing full value to the nature of worship in Belarusian Baptist churches.

8.1. Freedom and Forms

8.1.1. Striving for Balance

Some of the tensions can be eliminated or reduced with a proper understanding of the opposites and their reciprocal concessions to each other. In this case, the approach to worship taken by the Apostle Paul and his advice in 1 Corinthians 12–14 (especially 14:26–33) are crucial regarding the free worship tradition and may help evaluate the relationship between form and freedom in worship. As William Abernethy notes, Paul maintains a delicate balance between spirit and order in worship, by keeping worship "open to the power of the spontaneous life of the Spirit" and recognizing "that people can be carried away into divisive and unhealthy excesses when they open themselves in an undisciplined, unknowing way to that life of the Spirit."[16]

Paul's understanding of spirit and order reflects the whole biblical teaching. Despite freedom and form occupying different places in the continuum of the Old and New Testaments, neither the Old nor the New Testament rejects forms and freedom;[17] we build our worship on the twin pillars of Jachin and Boaz, which symbolize freedom and order.[18] Liberty and structure do not necessarily confront each other, as they may be two sides of the same. In fact, all formal elements can be practiced in a spirit of freedom; reading a Bible passage should not be read in any other way than in the spirit of freedom.[19]

---

15. Kauflin, *Worship Matters: Learning Others to Encounter the Greatness of God*, 156.
16. Abernethy, *A New Look for Sunday Morning*, 48.
17. Segler, *Christian Worship, Its Theology and Practice*, 12.
18. 1 Kings 7:21. S.F. Winward uses this image in his book *The Reformation of Our*, 74.
19. It is also possible to choose texts in the spirit of freedom. McGowan states, "The early references to Christian communal reading suggest texts chosen according to occasion or opportunity, in keeping with more charismatic aspects of the communal discourse, rather

This prerequisite lays the foundation for further discussion because it pays tribute to both form and freedom, and yet it also limits freedom, with the understanding that forms must not quench the Spirit.[20]

A more "excellent way"[21] requires adapting freedom and structure to each other. Freedom may be limited, or better, regulated, and the structure may be adjusted to particular situations. As with the first Baptists in England, in the midst of desire for freedom and flexibility in worship, a church can look for order while still leaving room for spontaneity,[22] because "successful, ongoing worship depends in part on the creative pull from both extremes of spontaneity or order."[23] Order may be expressed by limiting the time for participation or the number of participants; freedom may be expressed in the content of components and their diversity. Evelyn Underhill notes that

> the great Protestant churches of Germany, Scandinavia, Scotland, and Holland have each developed a type of worship which retains a sufficient traditional and liturgical element to ensure stability, and even some continuity with the historic Christian cultus; whilst leaving room for the expression of that prophetic, ethical, spontaneous element in the primitive Christian response to God, which every reform and revival seeks to restore.[24]

Striving for balance, freedom in worship is especially important in large churches that put more emphasis on quality and a limited number of professional "performers." Involving guests from other churches in their program, enabling youth participation, and including personal testimonies of spiritual experiences during the week can open doors to the breathing of the Spirit. Organization is not an encroachment on the work of the Spirit and the participants' inspiration; rather it is the wise stewardship of freedom, resulting from understanding its purpose in worship.

---

than set patterns such as lectionaries" (*Ancient Christian Worship*, 99). This practice could be justified in the free worship tradition.

20. 1 Cor 14:32–33; 14:30.
21. 1 Cor 12:31.
22. McKibbens, "Our Baptist Heritage in Worship," 60.
23. Longhurst, "Worship Music: Varied Styles, A Common Goal," 28.
24. Underhill, *Worship*, 298.

Yet, in the context of 1 Corinthians 12–14, spontaneity and freedom do not serve to express individuality or create an informal atmosphere. Paul speaks about the edification and benefit of the church, and the principle of edification may require the restriction of individual freedom. If forethought serves the content better than improvisation, freedom must give way to a certain form and a plan prepared in advance. Paul Hoon argues that "form can provide wings without which aspiration would remain limp and unalive. It can also chasten and channel aspiration in its freedom."[25] Through form, Baptists might add depth to their level of worship, overcoming "a deep-rooted suspicion of 'formalism'"[26] and using a "supportive, constructive role"[27] of liturgical elements in the life of the church.

Freedom, like a powerful stream of water, should be controlled in order to bring blessings and encouragement, lest it be devastating. Thomas McKibbens phrases it as "an orderly openness to the Spirit."[28] In terms of frameworks for worship, a more serious attitude toward the Christian calendar in new Baptist churches may help to focus the attention of both preachers and congregations on Christ and God's provision in salvation. Organization and planning can be good mediators for the spiritual gifts of Christians, so that they might be used in order to build up the church. As various commentators have argued, freedom works best within structure[29] and "spontaneity operates within some ordered framework."[30]

This thesis likewise proposes that the practice of worship in Baptist churches should also reflect this rule. Firstly, prayerful work is needed/required in planning the service in terms of the sermons, singing, poems, and testimonies, and ideally this should be done a week or a few days before the service.[31] Planning certainly does not have to be final in that it is open

---

25. Hoon, *The Integrity of Worship*, 218.
26. Segler, *Christian Worship, Its Theology and Practice*, 178.
27. Segler.
28. McKibbens, "Our Baptist Heritage in Worship," 57.
29. Erickson, *Participating in Worship. History, Theory, and Practice*, 25.
30. Rowe, "1 Corinthians 12–14: The Use of a Text for Christian worship," 120.
31. For example, it is rather typical of the public worship at "Light of Gospel" Church in Minsk that the pianist must search quickly for the music immediately after the pastor announces the forthcoming congregational song. Although the pastor usually announces the song twice and refers to two hymnals, which provides the pianist with additional time to find the music, delays sometimes occur. In the churches "Grace of God," Bobruisk, and "House of the Gospel,"

to the possibility of a change in plans at any time in any worship situation. As Bob Kauflin reminds us, "Planning can't replace dependence on the Holy Spirit ... Our goal should be to plan wisely, humbly, and prayerfully, fully expecting that God may provide fresh and unexpected guidance during the meeting."[32]

Special attention should be given to the concept of a "team," which is sometimes lacking in traditional churches. A variety of team members may serve to boost the level of diversity in public worship, and the combined wisdom will reduce the risk of errors and compensate for the shortcomings of one person. For example, discussing the plan and content of sermons will help the preacher avoid subjectivity and personal preferences in choosing a topic, and will help them see the sermon as a part of the whole ministry of the Body. Interestingly, the churches that have adopted a contemporary style of worship pay more attention to teamwork and planning worship, which can take place a quarter or even half a year prior to the meeting.[33]

Limitations on freedom may even be required during public worship if the church has previously had negative experiences of a particular person's involvement, or when the time or topics of some components do not fit the worship very well.[34] Moreover, in an emergency, the leader may even interrupt someone's prayer or witness. The former senior pastor in church in Fortechnaya 61/1, Brest, who ministered in the 1980s and early 1990s, used to cut short some particularly clumsy repeated prayers by his prayer or by prayerful singing.[35] In "House of the Gospel," Vitebsk, the pastor says "Amen" in similar situations and concludes with his prayer.[36] Undoubtedly, it is preferable to settle these issues in advance at the stage of planning by

---

Vitebsk, the songs are selected in the moment. In the latter church, if the musician does not know the music for the song that the pastor has suggested, then the congregation sings it a cappella (Personal notes, 66b).

32. Kauflin, *Worship Matters: Learning Others to Encounter the Greatness of God*, 182.

33. "Pure Heart," Brest; "Light of Hope," "Light of Truth," Minsk. The pastor of "Light of Hope" Church in Minsk might invite someone to be part of a certain worship service with a specific topic three to four months before the event (Personal experience of the author [Personal notes, 66]).

34. In the practice of "Light of Gospel," Minsk, the pastor occasionally does not pay attention to some requests to recite poems, especially when several people ask to do it.

35. Personal notes, 64b.

36. "House of the Gospel," Vitebsk (Timofei Egorenkov, Personal interview with author, Minsk, 26 November 2015 [Personal notes, 64b]).

regulating and directing the energy of the people involved. However, the openness of public worship to all church members can create situations that require decisive intervention.

A proper understanding of this notion of orderly freedom reduces tension in worship. Yet this is not a one-way street. To achieve harmony in worship we can also reduce the emphasis on structure. An important assumption behind loosening structure is the supremacy of content (which is focused on Christ in the Baptist churches of Belarus – see section 5.2). Reformed theologian Robert Webber argues in his book, *Worship Old & New*[37] that "The primary factor in worship concerns not the structure, nor the style, but the content. Judgment about a particular style of worship must be concerned chiefly with the content of the worship."[38] J.J. von Allmen, who writes from a liturgical perspective, also points out that "liturgical forms are limited by the second commandment: "You shall not make yourself a graven image . . . ."[39] He continues,

> [liturgical forms] are limited by their inherent justification; they cease to be valid as soon as they seek their meaning and their justification in themselves, as soon as they are no longer content to be an echo of the offense and the appeal of the incarnation and seek to become a continued incarnation, to be in themselves as salvation rather than a means of transmitting a salvation accomplished once for all.[40]

Thus there is no need to be bound by forms in planning and preparation, and it is possible to change and even reject some forms just as Christ "refused to put the new wine of the gospel into old wineskins of tradition."[41] Following the example of the reformers, the special sacramental connection between a specific ritual and God's presence can be rejected.[42] If the three or four sermon tradition quenches the Spirit, especially in the evenings or on

---

37. Webber, *Worship Old & New: A Biblical, Historical, and Practical Introduction*, 149–151.
38. Webber, 149.
39. Exod 20:4.
40. Allmen, *Worship: Its Theology and Practice*, 82–83.
41. Segler, *Christian Worship, Its Theology and Practice*, 177.
42. Barnard, Cilliers, and Wepener, *Worship in the Network Culture. Liturgical Ritual Studies. Fields and Methods, Concepts and Metaphors*, 128.

holidays, it is possible to change the structure and miss one or two sermons and fill a service with singing in the Spirit. A Bible-study format could replace part of public worship if some sermons do not edify Christians, and indeed some churches are taking steps in that direction.[43]

However, a proper attitude to structure should offer something more than some external changes. Structure must be understood as an implicit agreement between the main group of worship participants and an internal logic of worship. It is the idea hidden behind the scenes which becomes clear to worship participants and which directs and defines the following steps and inspires the content of worship. This thinking usually works well in special evangelistic meetings which are aimed at "the conversion of sinners." These meetings are characterized by the unity of topic, the logical relationship of the elements, the psychological chain from bad to Good News, the development and progress of the topic, a climax which calls to repentance, and every active participant understanding the ideas and meaning behind the structure. The experience of thematic and festive worship also proves that understanding the purpose and topic of worship, its internal logic (along with thorough preparation) helps to achieve unity, purpose, and a balanced combination of worship components, preserving the elements of improvisation in sermons, prayers, or short testimonies.[44]

Another element where it is particularly important to combine form and freedom is that of prayer. Raymond Abba says that:

> "free prayer does not necessarily mean extempore prayer, which is spontaneous and unpremeditated, springing directly out of the occasion (*ex tempore*). It may equally well mean what Isaac

---

43. Thus "Bethlehem" Church in Minsk reduced the morning worship service to 40–50 minutes by offering Bible studies in groups to supplement the shorter service. Church members are divided into three groups in Bible studies according to age: younger than 28, 28–50, and 50 and older. Children and teenagers have separate classes (Jacob Timofeev, Personal interview with author, Minsk, 16 October 2015 [Personal notes, 64]).

44. In this regard, Morgan Noyes also points out the danger of a representation of the theme that is too narrow, as "if every hymn and every prayer center too directly in the same thought, the service as a whole loses a richness which it may rightfully claim" (Noyes, *Preaching the Word of God*, 179). Paul Hoon also warns that topical ties of the elements that are too close lead to a state where "the worshipper is theologically and psychologically overwhelmed" (Hoon, *The Integrity of Worship*, 279).

Watts calls 'conceived prayer,' that is, prayer which is carefully prepared by the minister in advance."[45]

For this reason, Isaac Watts recommended that two extremes in prayer should be avoided. "On the one hand, we should avoid 'confining ourselves entirely to pre-composed forms of prayer' and, on the other, we should be wary of 'entire dependence on sudden motions and suggestions of thought.'"[46] He interprets "extempore prayer" as what happens "when we, without any reflection or meditation beforehand, address ourselves to God, and speak the thoughts of our hearts, as fast as we conceive them."[47] From this he makes the following distinction between "conceived" and "free" prayer:

> When we have not the words of our prayer formed beforehand, to direct our thoughts, but we conceive the matter or substance of our address to God, first in our minds, and then put those conceptions in such words and expressions as we think most proper.[48]

Ellis, commenting on Isaac Watts' ideas of conceived prayer, observes that "conceived prayer may not involve a detailed working out of what will be uttered in public, but should include what he describes as 'premeditation' involving the preparation of the heart as well as a reflection on the subjects for prayer."[49]

Carefully thought-out prayer may represent a middle ground between written prayer and the kind of extempore prayer that may not edify the congregation. Meaningful and rich prayers, recorded in Psalms, together with the prayers of David (1 Chron. 17:16–27), Solomon (1 Kings 8:23–53), Isaiah (25:1–5), Paul (Eph 3:14–21), and Christ (Matt 6:9–13; John 17) become a model of depth and motivation to serious preparation for the prayer ministry. *Prayer*, a book by Karl Barth which has been translated into Russian and consists of a lot of his prayers may also act as a model for ministers' prayers

---

45. Abba, *Principles of Christian Worship*, 115.
46. Watts, "A Guide to Prayer," 125.
47. Watts, 125
48. Watts.
49. Ellis, *Gathering*, 107–108. This resonates with Harold Best's idea, when he proposes a "composition and improvisation" model for worship instead of a "fixity-spontaneity dilemma" (Harold Best, "A Traditional Worship Response," in *Exploring the Worship Spectrum*, 37–38).

in worship.[50] Preliminary meditation would enrich the themes and content of prayer, which would in turn contribute to the edifying function of prayer and the general improvement of prayer quality within the church. As with the advantages of conceived and freely delivered sermons, meditation and preparation help to put prayer in the most appropriate forms as "the spirits of prophets are subject to prophets,"[51] and freedom allows the context to influence the content of a prayer to make it more relevant and natural.

Combining freedom and form in prayer is also possible in a local context by suggesting topics for prayer. The Union of Evangelical Christian Baptists in the Republic of Belarus sends out a monthly prayer letter to churches, calling for prayer both in corporate worship and in homes on certain topics (about peace, church, faithfulness, etc.), presenting the needs of churches and departments of the Union (prayer for children's camps, youth conventions, thankfulness for baptism services, etc.), and of Baptist churches in other countries. The wording of the topic focuses the prayer, yet, at the same time, each prayer expresses gratitude and request in a free manner.

The unique role of worship from a historical point of view, the respect of older believers for traditions and forms, and the continuing confrontation between the Orthodox context and Western sources remain important factors in sustaining the present tensions and complicating the process of change. However, understanding the paramount importance of content and the consideration of theological emphases, especially the focus on Christ and evangelism, enables going beyond form. Thus, striving for balance, expressed in mutual concessions of form and freedom, or through controlled freedom, can provide meaningful content to the entire congregation.

8.1.2. Freedom and Forms in a Creative Tension[52]

However, the problem of the relationship between freedom and form in traditional public worship cannot be solved once and for all because it originates in the very nature of public worship itself. Since "God is spirit,"[53] Christian, or at least Baptist, worship is essentially free, and forms may from

---

50. Barth, *Molitva* [*Prayer*].
51. 1 Cor 14:32.
52. See Ellis, "Gathering Struggles: Creative Tensions in Baptist Worship."
53. John 4:24.

time to time come into conflict with freedom in houses of prayer. This is only the continuation of an ancient dispute. Evelyn Underhill reminds us that "ordered" and "free" worship "both present in the primitive Church." Underhill goes on to argue that "both are needed if the full span and possibilities of Christian worship are to be realized; and it is one of the many tragedies of Church history that they have so often been regarded as hostile to one another."[54]

Yet, both are related to the nature of worship, and both are needed for a "mature worship."[55] Both traditions can be found in the history of Russian-speaking Baptists (although their encounter in worship was not always peaceful) and they are now represented to various degrees in Baptist churches in Belarus.

However, even if they may not be regarded as openly hostile to each other, in the light of our imperfect understanding and practice, these concepts remain in constant tension, a tension that is not necessarily fully soluble. These kinds of tensions in religious life involve "the dialectic of the sacred and the secular, of the supernatural and the natural, of the eternal and the temporal, of the trans-historical and historical."[56] In terms of freedom and forms, when they operate with mutual respect, they can choose the direction together. Forms are needed for overview and stability,[57] to provide solemnity and ceremony, as with weddings and the blessing of children, and to combine the religious and aesthetic.[58] At the same time spontaneous and extempore elements must not be excluded from Christian worship, because the Spirit can act in a special way at a particular time. Here we turn again to prayer as illustrative.[59] Ellis highlights that "The *ad hoc* nature of this [extempore] prayer enables it to be the prayer of *this* local church, the needs and aspirations of

---

54. Underhill, *Worship*, 110–111. Here we could once again remember the negative and even hostile attitude of the Evangelicals to the Orthodox Church in the early stages of worship formation (See this thesis, section 4.2.2. The Shaping of Worship in Opposition to the Orthodoxy).

55. Abernethy, *A New Look for Sunday Morning*, 50.

56. Hoon, *The Integrity of Worship*, 125.

57. Gnida, "Poryadok provedeniya bogosluzhenii v tserkvakh evangel'skih khristian-baptistov," 71.

58. On necessity of forms see Peck, *Living Worship*, 22; Shepherd, *The Worship of the Church*, 51, 54; Segler, *Christian Worship, Its Theology and Practice*, 181.

59. See footnotes 45–48.

this group of people on *this* particular day."[60] Hence these contradictions and tensions can be called productive, "creative tensions;"[61] they are important for the viability of a public worship that is helpfully structured and directed but which contains sufficient diversity and flexibility in the forms it chooses so as to preserve the spontaneity and richness of prayer and worship.[62]

The tension can be regulated to some extent or even overcome in terms of some specific actions although it is impossible to achieve complete harmony. Yet surely the conflict of freedom and form in public worship is an area that should be worked on. Basic preparation, discussion, and organization done in the spirit of freedom, should make public worship more effective. Church ministers may not achieve ideal worship in their churches, but they might find a way of worship that is best suited to the needs of their particular church that would be able to embrace freedom and order, individualism and the communal nature of worship, and the openness and the mysteriousness of public worship.

At the same time, in public worship it is important that freedom and forms are not understood as rivals; rather they are allies, heading in one direction, and inseparable: "The paradoxical truth is that form assumes and fosters freedom as freedom begets and requires form."[63] The creative tension itself adds freshness and life into worship. This is a kind of perpetual motion in worship which helps to change, grow, transform, and develop worship. Embracing the tension keeps worship from solidification, from rigid tradition, and from confusion and the chaos of laxity. This blessing of uncertainty in the relation between freedom and forms, helps a worship service to adapt to context and situation, enriches it with new forms and components, and involves more participants in worship, all while key elements such as the centrality of the Bible, Christocentrism, and the principle of edification, keep us on track. "Worship benefits from modes of ritual and prophesy and enjoys predictability as well as surprise, composition and improvisation, familiarity and newness, the habitual and the fresh, corporate and individual creativity."[64]

---

60. Ellis, *Gathering*, 124. (Emphases in original.)
61. Ellis, "Gathering Struggles: Creative Tensions in Baptist Worship," 8.
62. Macquarrie, *Christian Theology*, 499.
63. Macquarrie, 218.
64. Erickson, *Participating in Worship*, 25.

Thus Paul's concept of worship as expressed in his prescriptions "Do not quench the Spirit," and "Let all things be done properly and in an orderly manner"[65] (two verses that are frequently quoted in the Belarusian Baptist context) is an invitation to the further development of this creative dynamic.

8.2. Individual and Communal Aspects of Worship

8.2.1. Priesthood of All Believers in Relation to Worship

Understanding the interaction of freedom and form in worship makes further work of reconciliation between individual and communal aspects of worship easier. Here we follow the method tested in the previous section, putting forward the following thesis: tensions between the individual and corporate character of worship may be alleviated by a proper understanding and clarification of the nature of the church and public worship, in conjunction with a number of practical ways of adjusting the concept of priesthood in regard to worship. An individual does not disappear within the community, because "each one has a psalm, has a teaching, has a revelation, has a tongue, has an interpretation"[66] and worship offers some orderly opportunity to serve each other for church edification and His glory.[67] At the same time, "[c]orporate worship is naturally communal, even though it may sometimes be corrupted by individualism, passivity or dysfunctional leadership."[68]

A variety of gifts enrich worship and invest in the spiritual growth of participants. Yet, the use of gifts is associated with certain risks. In light of the imperfection of the members of the body, some internal tension is unavoidable. Thus, the apostle Paul calls the church to maintain order in gathering together and shows how individuality can effectively participate in building the church. Key to this is the necessity that participants understand the nature of the Church as one Body. Elizabeth Newman warns:

> As long as the church is secondary to Baptist self-understanding, then the priesthood of the believer will remain a description

---

65. 1 Thess. 5:19. 1 Cor 14:40.

66. 1 Cor 14:26. Thus we reaffirm the "participation of the whole congregation" (Cherry, "Merging Tradition and Innovation in the Life of the Church," 22).

67. Col 3:17.

68. Ellis, *Gathering*, vii.

primarily of the individual, and worship will be understood primarily as that which takes places between an individual and God.[69]

Every member is to understand themselves as an interdependent part of the whole. Here in the church, it is not isolated individuals but a fellowship of believers; *sobranie* (congregational gathering) is how believers in Belarus often refer to the time of worship that comes into His presence, although, at the same time, each gives account of themselves to God.[70] This "indivisible and unmerged" state determines the relationship of the individual with the group and with God.

Understanding the church as one body helps us understand the essence of corporate worship. The whole body and its members worship the Lord. The subjective experience of individuals is tested and interpreted in the community. Even private worship is tested in the worship of the church. Brian Haymes' explanation of the Baptist way of doing theology is appropriate with respect to worship:

> The emphasis I have laid on enquiry 'together' is not without significance. The church is gathered by God, lives in and by the fellowship of the Holy Spirit and is nourished by word and sacraments. It exists as a community, a gathered community that together seeks the mind of Christ. A Baptist way of doing theology is therefore unashamedly confessional and collegiate. The corporate nature of the church questions any models that are individualistic and unaccountable, a fact that has implications for our understanding of ministry and ordination. We bring our theological reflections to the test of others, and not just other theologians, but the whole people of God. The Baptist theologian is accountable not only to her academic peers but also to the gathered church.[71]

Likewise, in worship every participant understands that they do not perform in a recital when they preach, pray, witness, or sing. Each component

---

69. Newman, "The Priesthood of All Believers and the Necessity of the Church," 63.
70. Rom 14:12.
71. Haymes, "Theology and Baptist identity," 4.

is an integral part of the symphonic orchestra of praise in which each individual has a part that is related to the overall score. Certainly, participants do not deny their individuality. In fact, each individual in corporate worship actualizes himself as "a corporate and social creature,"[72] and, what is more important, as a member of the one body. Without the body, a member cannot fulfill their destination in congregational worship, but the full participation of that one member does not contradict the complete corporate participation.

Bearing this in mind, participants comprehend the difference between public and personal worship, between communal prayer, such as in the house of prayer where dozens or even hundreds of people gather for worship, and personal prayer that might take place in a closed room. Belarusian pastors often encourage church members to pray during worship, but they very rarely explain that communal prayer requires social cooperation, or that there are certain limitations regarding opportunities for participation.[73] One of the past leaders of AUCECB, Zhidkov, recommended that:

> everyone say their personal prayers before God in their homes, while during worship, if such a prayer is said these days, it should be done by a worship leader, namely the pastor of the church, who will think over the words of his public prayer in front of God before saying it, so that it may have edifying value for the listeners who will pray along with this prayer, and comply fully with the apostolic directions.[74]

What, therefore, does it mean to participate in public worship? Baptists in Belarus speak about "participation in the service," referring to active and direct individual participation through preaching, singing, spoken prayers, and so on in order "to fulfill the Scripture, to follow the apostolic church, and to help people to grow in Christ."[75] Yet it is possible to make some initial evaluation of participation based on the level of the members' involvement. Some members have direct individual participation when they preach, pray aloud,

---

72. Aune, "The Corporate and Confessional Character of Worship: The Common Service Debate," 32.

73. Murphy, Kallenberg and Nation, *Virtues & Practices in the Christian Tradition, Christian Ethics after MacIntyre*, 33.

74. Zhidkov, "Nashi prazdniki," 15.

75. SI, 2008.

sing solos, play musical instruments, witness, or even provide decorations, symbols, or texts in the sanctuary to edify the congregation. Some members are involved in group participation through a choir, ensemble, or orchestra, or when a group of people perform drama or recite poetry. Corporate congregational participation occurs when the entire congregation has opportunities to respond and to praise the Lord, whether that is through congregational singing, or jointly affirming prayers, exclaiming "Praise to God," or repeating (occasionally) "Blessings."[76]

Yet participation is not limited to visible or verbal involvement in worship. As Simon Chan observes, "active participation is possible if the people understand what is going on, are inwardly prepared and are able to use their gifts in the worship service."[77] On the other hand, silent or immobile participation can be just as meaningful. Active listening or silent prayer are good examples of such participation. James White, a Methodist liturgical historian, suggests the term "passive participation" alongside the active. If active participation "refers to those worship activities in which the members of the congregation engage outwardly, such as singing, open prayer or the offering," then "passive participation refers to those activities in which the congregation is not observably 'doing' something, such as listening to the sermon or being led in prayer by a representative."[78] A similar idea was expressed by Mitskevich, one of the authors of *Bratskiy Vestnik*. He instructs believers in how they should listen to sermons:

> Be watchful, open the ears of your heart [to] hear and reflect. Be like Mary at Jesus' feet, place in your heart the seeds of eternal life. Do not sleep or doze, so that the evil one would not steal the seed planted in your heart (Matt 13:19). Do not let your heart become a transit road for various unclean or vain thought[s]. Find the pearl in what was said, wonderful truths, draw lessons

---

76. 2 Cor 13:14. One could refer here to the parallel that exists in the African-American tradition (or in Belarus in Pentecostal circles), where such exclamations (plus "Alleluia") are an even more significant part of the worship experience.

77. Chan, *Liturgical Theology*, 152.

78. White, "Protestant Worship," 17ff., cited in Ellis, "Understanding Worship: Trends and Criteria," 38.

not only for others, but also for your personal life. Do not set your heart for criticism or judgement.[79]

Participation is not limited to individual or group activities; it is also a ministry of the congregation as a whole. Such a definition does not exclude individual or group involvement, but instead gives value to communal activities as a whole and extends understanding of "listening" as a way to participate in public worship. Although the idea of silent participation is not developed in the churches of Belarus, we must pay tribute to the preachers who often urge members to be ready "to listen rather than to offer the sacrifice."[80]

A biblical understanding of the concept of priesthood is also essential here. In the context of the ministry of the Baptist churches in Belarus, the teaching of the priesthood of all believers comes primarily from denial of the teaching and practices of the Orthodox Church. Yet the positive aspect has not been developed deeply enough. Frank Rees, an Australian Baptist, draws attention to the difference between the priesthood of each believer and the priesthood of all believers. In the church we have a collective, communal priesthood.[81] This emphasis on the body does not deny individual participation in worship but encourages harmonizing personal activity with the corporate one. Yet priesthood may be attributed to every believer in terms of their relationship with God and personal access to God through a High Priest, Jesus. Thus, every person can come to God during worship through loud or silent prayer in an orderly manner.[82] "New Testament priests" are to offer up spiritual sacrifices, and the time of worship provides these opportunities. Of course the priesthood of all believers not only impacts worship, but all Christian life, "not only *leitourgia* but also *diakonia*," "sharing and loving deeds, – gifts of money, evangelistic endeavor, and holy living."[83] However, public worship

---

79. Mitskevich, "Vseobshcheye svyashchenstvo I sluzhiteli tserkvi" [Priesthood of All Believers and Church Ministers], *Bratskiy Vestnik*, 30–31.

80. Eccl 5:1.

81. Rees, "The Worship of all Believers," 179–180.

82. Rees identifies the priesthood as "the quality which enables a man to come before God to gain his grace, and therefore fellowship with him, by offering up a sacrifice acceptable to him." He continues with this statement: "The priesthood of all believers is about the life of the whole church as worship, in which we all have both a gift and a calling" (Rees, "The Worship of All Believers," 176.).

83. Rees, 180–181. Rees calls these "*the gathered life* of the church and *the dispersed life* of the church" (Rees, 183.)

provides a unique opportunity to express individual priesthood in the context of communal priesthood, when we remember that the priesthood of all does not imply equal participation or "autonomous individualism."[84] It should be understood in a wider ecclesiastical context.

A robust theology of gifts is fundamental in terms of communal involvement in public worship. Although the topic of gifts is occasionally raised in congregations, there is seldom any mention of the application of this teaching in the practice of worship. Yet, the Apostle's teaching about worship order in Corinth also applies today. Paul explains:

> All are not apostles are they? All are not prophets are they? All are not teachers are they? All are not workers of miracles are they? All do not have gifts of healings do they? All do not speak with tongues do they? All do not interpret do they?[85]

In a Belarusian Baptist community the question could be rephrased, "All are not preachers are they? All are not singers are they? All do not pray out loud in public worship do they? All do not lead the public worship, do they?" Of course, in small churches this argument is difficult to apply in the absence of potential preachers or musicians, where the audience welcomes any brother coming to the pulpit and leading worship. However, in such churches, members have moderate expectations for preaching or singing. In church, they are encouraged by the fellowship with brothers and sisters, the mere presence around His Word in the "house of the Lord," and the opportunity to be involved in worship and glorify the Lord. Yet the discussion of gifts is quite appropriate in most churches;[86] both big and small churches prefer edifying and inspiring involvement to "the blind, lame and sick."[87]

8.2.2. Towards a Disciplined Participation

A theological understanding of the worship of the church in relation to the priesthood lays a firm basis for holding a creative tension between individual and corporate aspects of worship. The concept of the "body" requires limiting or rather disciplining individuals and strengthening the corporate elements

---

84. Harmon, *Towards Baptist Catholicity*, 218.
85. 1 Cor 29:29–30.
86. SI, 2012.
87. Mal 1:8.

of worship, so that "the freedom of some does not destroy the worship of others."[88] As Christopher Ellis puts it, "we need to be clear that this freedom in worship is not our human freedom to assert our autonomy but God's freedom to direct our worship in proportion to our openness to the Spirit's leading."[89] There is something significant about bringing whatever each one has prepared for worship,[90] but all these "offerings" serve the building up of the church.[91] Individuality submits or adapts to the community, which is the first step to overcoming the tension between individual and communal aspects of worship.[92]

Thus, churches develop disciplined participation.[93] Those who participate follow standards in terms of time, topic, and content of worship. For this purpose, the apprentice preachers in "Light of Truth," Minsk, who have just begun their preaching career, provide full-text sermons ahead of time (a unique phenomenon in Belarusian churches); in some churches the texts of poems and songs are agreed with the worship leader.[94] Worship leaders should be aware of the level of skill and preparation of those who wish to be involved in preaching, singing, or reciting poetry.

Michael Green offers seven questions which may help churches and individuals to evaluate the components of worship: questions, rate, content, and manner of presentation, as well as the personal qualities of the participant. In the local context, this should be supplemented by an assessment of the quality of the material and preparation. The primary goal of such questions should be the improvement of quality, rather than looking to ban elements:

> 1) Does it glorify God rather than the speaker, church, or denomination? 2) Does it accord with Scripture? 3) Does it

---

88. Ellis, "Gathering Struggles: Creative Tensions in Baptist Worship," 13.
89. Ellis, "Understanding Worship: Trends and Criteria," 38.
90. 1 Cor 14:26.
91. Ellis.
92. At the same time, churches provide other opportunities for the implementation of gifts. Some new churches, which practice a contemporary style of worship, encourage members to gather into small groups in which brothers and sisters encourage each other with their gifts, and where they encourage developing their gifts in discipleship, counseling, evangelism, and charity ("New Earth," Minsk; "Pure Heart," Brest [SI, 2012]).
93. Chan, *Liturgical Theology*, 155.
94. "House of the Gospel," Vitebsk; "Hope," Gomel (Timofei Egorenkov and Igor Gritsenko, Personal interview with author, Minsk, 26 November 2015 [Personal notes, 79]).

build up the church? 4) Is it spoken in love? 5) Does the speaker submit him- or herself to the judgment and consensus of others in spiritual humility? 6) Is the speaker in control of him- or herself? 7) Is there a reasonable amount of instruction, or does the message seem excessive in detail?[95]

To overcome the tension between individual and communal character of worship, churches must also give adequate attention to corporate activities, in order to involve as many people as possible in active worship. Here Robert Webber's analysis of evangelical worship in the States may be helpful when we think about some Baptist services in medium and large sized churches in Belarus.

> [E]vangelicals will be challenged in the matter of participation. I find evangelical worship to be passive and uninvolving. The worshiper sits, listens, and absorbs. But seldom does the worshiper respond. As in the medieval period, worship has been taken away from the people. It must be returned. Participation will be recovered as the dramatic sense of worship is restored.[96]

Mark Dever and Paul Alexander turn to congregational singing in this regard and warn that:

> continual singing by soloists or even by the choir can have the unintended effect of underestimating the nature of communal musical worship in which everybody is involved. People can gradually come to believe that worship is a passive contemplation, while in the Bible we find no evidence for that.[97]

Congregational singing, as compared to all other elements except, perhaps, the Lord's Supper, serves to better reflect the communal nature of worship, to express more aptly the idea of a royal priesthood as well as "the catholic

---

95. Green, *To Corinth with Love*, 77–78.

96. Webber, "An Evangelical and Catholic Methodology," chapter 8, https://www.religion-online.org/article/an-evangelical-and-catholic-methodology/, last accessed 26 January 2011.

97. Dever and Alexander, *Produmannoye sozidaniye tserkvi: sluzheniye, osnovannoye na Evangelii* [Thoughtful Building of the Church: A Ministry Based on the Gospel], 113. Originally published as *The Deliberate Church: Building Your Ministry on the Gospel* (Wheaton: Crossway Books, 2005).

nature of the Church,"⁹⁸ to unite diverse believers into one Body, to connect different generations, and to eliminate conflict between the communal and the individual aspects of worship. Here I strongly support Ellis' emphasis on singing. He claims that hymns are an important form in articulating "corporate acts of praise, corporate prayer and corporate confessions of faith."⁹⁹ In congregational singing, believers "actively and concertedly" participate in worship.¹⁰⁰ Singing allows the community to express itself as a whole, unites in spirit, and "encourages a sense of belonging and community."¹⁰¹ Taking part in the congregational singing, everyone present feels and acts as a part of the worship.¹⁰² Therefore, congregational singing should be considered an integral part of the worship service, "for each redeemed soul coming to this Lord's church not only wants to listen, but also longs to sing themselves praising their Savior."¹⁰³

It must be acknowledged that a lot of attention is paid to congregational singing in traditional worship. However, this element can be strengthened by continually updating the repertoire. Other elements, such as corporate prayer (particularly the Lord's Prayer), or the joint public reading of the Bible or Creed will also enhance the possibilities of the entire church participating.

In addition, personal investment of time, energy, and thinking by those who lead worship is required. Peter Fink says that even "Christian prayer cannot be simply a public act without some personal investment on the part of the 'actors' in what they do, and without personal vulnerability to what they do."¹⁰⁴ Therefore, in caring for the communal character of public worship, it is important to preserve its individuality because individuality also has an appropriate place within the presence of God, and the individual and communal do not abolish or negate one another. As Geoffrey Wainwright says, "Christian religion is neither an atomistic affair of isolated individuals nor

---

98. Krasovitskaya, *Liturgica*, 6.
99. Ellis, *Gathering*, 152.
100. Ellis, 164.
101. Ellis.
102. B. K., "O muzyke i penii," 67.
103. B. K.
104. Fink, "Public and Private Moments in Christian Prayer," 492–493.

yet a totalitarian collectivism, in which individual identity and responsibilities are submerged. It is rather a case of members integrated into a body."[105]

These clarifications in teaching and in thinking (especially about the church as one body), as well as an emphasis on disciplined participation and corporate actions, can reduce the tension, but they can also affect spontaneity and introduce some formality into worship. An excess of discipline, orderliness, and predictability can produce monotony and boredom. To keep its openness and freedom, Baptist worship should not go too far in any direction. "The dialectic of the body and the individual member, of Church and person . . . must not be unbalanced nor collapsed."[106] Quality of performance and depth of content enhance edification, but edification is not the only goal of the meeting. The Church does not forget about the principles of simplicity or sincerity, which allow for non-professional, organic participation in acts of worship. In fact, spontaneous participation can be more inspirational and edifying than a prepared and rehearsed sermon.[107] The body is not a frozen structure, and better organization, planning, and preparation cannot solve all its problems. Such objective reasons as the lack of trained preachers or musicians, as well as limited talents, skills, experience, and education are reflected in the imperfection of sermons, singing, prayers, and poems; embracing these requires humility, patience, encouragement, and love towards each other. Progress in respect to these Christian virtues can also be interpreted as an unintended, positive consequence of the (imperfect) worship, where, in their interaction, individual and communal aspects produce viability, vitality, and openness.

8.3. The Relevance of Worship to the Secular Environment

8.3.1. Inculturation: Pro and Contra

Conflicts in relation to forms and participants are not the only aspects that are to be held in tension. Another point of tension, specified by the context of formation and which must also be overcome, is between the worship of

---

105. Wainwright, *Doxology: The Praise of God in Worship, Doctrine, and Life*, 142.
106. Hoon, *The Integrity of Worship*, 104.
107. 1 Cor 14:29–30.

the church and the culture within which the church lives. To describe this I use the term "inculturation" – "the dynamic relation between the Christian message and the culture,"[108] or "the Church's efforts to make the message of Christ penetrate a given sociocultural milieu, calling on the latter to grow according to all its particular values, as long as these are compatible with the Gospel."[109]

Inculturation does not necessarily require transformation of the currently established forms of traditional Baptist worship where those forms are in harmony with the local culture and traditions, for example, in some villages where there are almost no young people, and where the average age of residents and church members is nearing sixty or seventy.[110] Traditional forms also appeal to people of various ages who perceive the service as a refuge from the world and its culture (see section 2.2.). In David Brown's observation, "traditional worship has great value when it provides a safe haven from the pain and perils of an oppressive or confusing world."[111] Acceleration of the rhythm of life, information overflow, and the technification of society contribute to the popularity of disconnecting forms of worship from the present, seeing them then become places of rest from the noise and hurry of big cities.[112] In fact, the evangelical Baptist movement ensured its long life by hiding in subculture and by abstention from social and cultural processes.[113]

Moreover, it is vital to preserve traditional church culture in terms of outreach in the Orthodox context (see section 4.2.). Such forms allow churches to attract people who have been raised in the Orthodox understanding of the church, but who have not found answers there to their spiritual questions, and

---

108. Lukken, *Ritual in Abundance*, 182.

109. "Faith and Inculturation." International Theological Commission (1988), http://www.vatican.va/roman_curia/congregations/cfaith/cti_documents/rc_cti_1988_fede-inculturazione_en.html., last accessed 16 May 2019. For comparison with terms like "indigenization" and "adaptation" see Senn, *Christian Liturgy Catholic and Evangelical*, 677.

110. Churches in Liubiacha, Bol'shaya Ganuta, Zabashevichi, Lesovniya, Yakshitsy, Minsk region in 2012. (Author observation [Personal notes, 80].)

111. Brown, *Transformational Preaching*, 64.

112. Susan White points to an interesting phenomenon, when "recently evangelized people have been unwilling to allow their native culture to be incorporated into the practice of their new-found faith. They wish to put away all vestiges of their pre-Christian past, and embark upon a fresh course; they wish to practice a form of Christianity which is 'untainted' by elements of their culture" (White, *Groundwork of Christian Worship*, 188.),

113. Cherenkov, "Evangel'skaya vera v postateisticheskikh soobshchestvakh" [Evangelical Belief in Post Atheistic Communities], 14.

who are ready to be part of the evangelical tradition. In fact, various forms of service are relevant for various people; the relevance is not always related to novelty of language or the use of modern technologies. Ministers and church members alike indicate that the most important things they value are humility, openness, kindness, care and love for others, compassion, exemplary lives of believers, and the importance of revealing emotion, warmth, and simplicity in the presentation of the Gospel.[114]

One must also consider the situation of inculturation being reduced to primitive imitation and speculative reflection of culture.[115] This has been true in relation to some churches in Belarus, where, in attempts to overcome the communication problem faced by traditional public worship and make worship relevant, they have just copied popular culture. A worship meeting may take the form of a pop concert, where the worship participants imitate the conduct and appearance of artists on the stage, including styles of clothing which would be inappropriate in a traditional meeting, dyed hair for men, the use of youth slang such as "mega-cool" and "cool" replacing the archaic "blessed" and "edifying," and disco-type lighting.[116] Thoughtless, rather than creative borrowing, and reductionism in terms of the content and different layers of the worship service during the adaptation process, would impoverish rather than enrich the gathering of believers.[117] Thus, practice can lead to extremes, which James Hitchcock calls "the Harvey Cox syndrome."[118] He gives an example of such a radical secularization where "the most notorious cases were the coffee-and-doughnut or beer-and-pretzel Eucharists, the gatherings where *agape* moved aside to admit *eros*, and the groups who used marijuana to stimulate 'religious experiences.'" Hitchcock concludes:

> The more the Eucharist is secularized to make it relevant, the more it is robbed of its meaning and the less likely it is to endure,

---

114. SI, 2012.

115. White, "Worship and Culture: Mirror or Beacon?" 288.

116. Youth gathering in "Light of Truth," Minsk, 1 November 2012. I participated in the worship. (Personal notes, 80.)

117. For example, in the last ten to fifteen years, contemporary worship is becoming more common in Belarusian churches where there is one style of music, one form of praise band accompanying congregational singing, one kind praise and worship songs, and usually only *forte* and *fortissimo* volume. This kind of worship tends to be rather poor in terms of art and culture.

118. Hitchcock, *The Recovery of the Sacred*, 22.

except as a residual tie with tradition for persons who are reluctant to make themselves completely post-Christian.[119]

Christopher Ellis is similarly concerned that:

> if relevance becomes the dominant value, then church identity may be at risk which, in turn, will threaten its actual relevance. If identity is safeguarded at the cost of relevance, then even that identity is put at risk.[120]

"The so called Chimera of Relevance,"[121] a desire "of finding or inventing a worship more acceptable, more 'relevant' to the modern man's [sic] secular world view," could lead to worship turning to express "the needs and aspirations of the secular man [sic], or even better, of secularism itself,"[122] but it will be robbed of its essence, and worship finds itself absorbed by the culture.[123] Belarusian Baptists would also benefit from both positive and negative experiences of models of inculturation in the West. In the 1980s and 1990s, in churches such as Willow Creek, seeker-sensitive worship attracted nonbelievers, but it is questionable whether it brought the desired effect in the long run. "For all the money, time, and effort we've spent on . . . culturally relevant worship," Sally Morgenthaler, an innovator in worship practices and founder of Worship Evangelism Concepts, writes, "it seems we came through the last 15 years with a significant net loss in churchgoers."[124]

On the other hand, consistent rejection or fear of changes leads to the neglect of reality, escapes "from history into liturgy,"[125] and (going back to the theological emphasis on evangelism) surely impinges on the ability to communicate the Good News. Wainwright calls the consequence of such

---

119. Hitchcock, 28, 33.
120. Ellis, "Gathering Struggles: Creative Tensions in Baptist Worship," 6.
121. Hitchcock, *The Recovery of the Sacred*, 17.
122. Schmemann, "Worship in A Secular Age," 119.
123. Byars, *The Future of Protestant Worship: Beyond the Worship Wars*, 18.
124. Morgenthaler, "Worship Evangelism: Sally Morgenthaler Rethinks Her Own Paradigm," 50.
125. Wainwright, *Doxology: The Praise of God in Worship, Doctrine and Life*, 407.
David Peck states in this regard that as a result of the separation of worship and everyday life they both suffer: worship "becomes remote, disembodied," "and life becomes formless, without content, meaning or purpose, consumed but never consummated." (Peck, *Living Worship*, 21.)

an approach, as in the case of Orthodox churches, "liturgical escapism."[126] Catholic theologian Charles Davis defines such meetings as a "Ghetto."[127] Such danger also exists for traditional Belarusian Baptist worship practices when they react against any new appropriation of culture and turns itself into "a conservation area."[128] Yet the extremes must not serve as ground for rejecting the need to change. This need is recognized by a number of reputable ministers both in traditional Baptist churches in Belarus, and other Russian-speaking communities experiencing similar problems. At the Pastoral Conference of the Union of Baptist Churches in Ukraine, held in Kiev on March 15–16, 2012, while discussing the relevance of the sermon topic one elderly pastor admitted: "We were taught to speak from the heart. We speak from the heart, but the youth does not understand us."[129] Analyzing the situation, the leadership of the Baptist Union of Russia made this recommendation:

> It is no secret that the prayer meetings in many communities of Evangelical Christians-Baptists do not correspond to any needs either of believers or of contemporary life. Numerous shallow sermons, prolonged and sad songs, absence of spiritual enthusiasm repel rather than attract young people to Baptist churches. The search for new, effective, dynamic, contributing to an atmosphere of spiritual optimism forms of worship is not a charismatic deviation itself. Any new initiative to improve the quality of service should not be labeled as "charismatic." On the liturgical assembly there can and should be a place for healthy positive emotions. What matters is that everything should be done "in a fitting and orderly way" (1 Cor 14:40).[130]

---

126. Wainwright, *Doxology: The Praise of God in Worship, Doctrine and Life*, 407.

127. Charles Davis, "Ghetto or Desert: Liturgy in a cultural dilemma," 19–23.

128. As noted by James McClendon, "over long periods of time Christian worship missed its mark by seeking a nostalgic return to real or mythical past time." He continues with the statement: "But true biblical worship is never nostalgic and never mythical; its feet are firmly planted in the here and now of today, and its movement is forward, on to the beckoning end." (McClendon, *Doctrine*, 408.)

129. Personal notes, 80b.

130. "O kharizmatii" [On Charismatics]. Open letter of the Union Council of Baptist Churches in Russia to Baptist Churches, http://ehbtambov.ru/archives/2142, last accessed 16 May 2019.

Indeed, the traditional style of worship requires a rethink regarding adolescents and young people.[131] The outward expression of faith should be related to modern life and "expressed anew with every generation."[132] This statement is especially relevant in relation to the rapid changes in popular culture due to the widespread use of IT.

Yet church not only straddles a generation gap, but also crosses the boundaries of the subculture, making the gospel comprehensible for unbelievers, since they also constitute part of worship in a certain sense.[133] The Apostle Paul speaks of the presence of others at services and the positive effect they should gain from the service.[134] Such a result is achieved by adapting the language to a visitor level of understanding and omitting secret coded rituals, in favor of self-explanatory steps.[135]

Thus, if for certain groups of people and in certain communities, especially village churches, the issue of inculturation requires the preservation of the *status quo*, in the broad context, changes in the language and culture make this issue a crucial one both in terms of mission (relevance to outsiders, who come to public worship) and of edification (relevance to insiders, living in the world). The necessity of bridging worship and ethics (daily living) also promotes modification in worship, which does not come down to primitive copying and uncritical borrowing but is the result of a meaningful and reasonable strategy, appropriate in this context. In its turn, New Testament examples of culture transformation and overcoming national barriers[136] bring this demand beyond the limits of tastes and preferences and build a healthy biblical foundation for the need in inculturation.

---

131. Bria, *The Liturgy After the Liturgy*, 21.

132. Blosser, "Ritual Revival for Playful Protestant Preaching," 252.

133. See in this regard the definition by Keith Jones: "Rather than such concepts as 'Public worship' where the doors are open wide (it can almost be a civic requirement), everyone comes in, believer and unbeliever . . .", and "Private worship, where all but the elect . . . are locked out at the door" Jones prefers "'Porous worship,' where a core of covenanted believers engage together in worship, which is a meal, a narrative and a prayer. Yet others are welcome to 'taste and see' for 'even the dogs under the table get the crumbs' (Mark 7:27–28) as the Syro-Phoenician woman declares." ("On Abandoning Public Worship," p. 20.)

134. 1 Cor 14:23–25.

135. Pecklers states, that "The simple presence of four gospels rather than one already suggests something of the need to contextualize the message." (Pecklers, *Worship*, 127.)

136. Acts 10; 15:1–32.

8.3.2. Inculturation: A Theological Model for Traditional Baptist Worship

Inculturation is not a simple process. Here one takes into account the gospel itself, tradition, culture, and social changes.[137] "A way needs to be found to avoid either a slavish copying of the past or an inappropriate submission to the spirit of the present age."[138] This call for balance, prudence, evaluation of the cultural context, and thorough theological analysis is very relevant in Belarusian churches in order to avoid the extremes of inertness, reproduction of the usual order, or hasty and uncritical adaptation.

In light of the above, I next propose a pattern of inculturation which largely follows John Witvliet's work. Referencing some of the recent work in liturgical inculturation and with regard to the models outlined by Niebuhr and Bevans,[139] Witvliet offers a number of theses which can serve as a manual for the practical inculturation of worship. I list them below and provide comment regarding their application in the traditional Baptist worship context.

> *Thesis 1: All liturgical action is culturally conditioned.* No circumspect attempt at liturgical reform, liturgical inculturation, or cultural critique can glibly assume that liturgy is not shaped by its cultural environment.
>
> Thesis 2: The relationship between liturgy and culture is theologically framed by the biblical-theological categories of creation and incarnation. Inculturation is both possible and necessary because of the twin claims that "in the beginning God created the heavens and the earth" and that "the Word became flesh and lived among us."[140]

---

137. Stephen B. Bevans, *Models of Contextual Theology* (Maryknoll: Orbis, 1992), 1, cited in Witvliet, *Worship Seeking Understanding*, 109.

138. Ellis, *Gathering*, 16. Likewise, James Cox calls the church neither to be enticed away by the charm of the past nor by the novelty of the present (Cox, *Preaching*, 49–50). Raymond Balley puts it, "Let us not be hypnotized by the old nor fascinated by the new." ("The Changing Face of Baptist Worship," 57). Robb Redman goes even further, explaining that the key to "the worship awakening is not the opposition of new and old, but rather the fusion of ancient and contemporary forms, as well high and low technology." (Redman, "Worship Wars or Worship Awakening?" 39–40.)

139. Niebuhr, *Christ and Culture*; Bevans, *Models of Contextual Theology*.

140. "Contemporary scholars tend to speak of a four-fold theological foundation for inculturation: creation, incarnation, redemption through the paschal mystery and Pentecost." (Pecklers and Keith, *Worship*, 120).

Thesis 3: Liturgical inculturation requires theologically informed cultural criticism of one's own cultural context.

Thesis 4: The extremes of either complete identification with or rejection of a given culture are to be avoided at all costs.

Thesis 5: Liturgical action must reflect common elements in the Christian tradition through the unique expressions of a particular cultural context. There must be a judicious balance of particularization and universality.

Thesis 6: This balance of particularization and universality requires "a mediating strategy" for liturgical inculturation. Often such strategies are summarized in a single phrase: "transforming culture," "dynamic equivalence," "creative assimilation."

Thesis 7: The constituent liturgical actions of the Christian church – including proclamation of the Word, common prayer, baptism, and Eucharist – are among the "universal" or common factors in the Christian tradition.[141]

1. "*All liturgical action is culturally conditioned.* No circumspect attempt at liturgical reform, liturgical inculturation, or cultural critique can glibly assume that liturgy is not shaped by its cultural environment."
Barnard, Cilliers and Wepener would support this idea, noting that "culture forms the bed in which the streams of religion and faith flow."[142] Participants "are inculturated human beings whose lives are irrevocably shaped by the culture in which they live."[143] Their actions reflect political and religious context, and local culture.[144] The diversity of cutures provides "diversity in the Body of Christ, including diversity in forms of Christian worship.[145] The

---

141. Witvliet, *Worship Seeking Understanding*, 109–123.

142. Barnard, Cilliers, and Wepener, *Worship in the Network Culture. Liturgical Ritual Studies. Fields and Methods, Concepts and Metaphors*, 44.

143. Barnard, Cilliers, and Wepener, 107.

144. "There are no aspects of Christian liturgy that are not derived from the various cultures through which it has passed in its historical evolution (e.g. Jewish meals, Greek rhetoric, Roman models of leadership, Byzantine court ceremonial, Mediterranean solstice festivals, etc.)." (Senn, *Christian Liturgy Catholic and Evangelical*, 676.).

145. White, *Groundwork of Christian Worship*, 186.

matter is only in how it influences and to what degree the various components of worship have experienced the influence of the local or foreign culture.

As studies in worship formation and its contexts prove, the influence is revealed in patterns of communication,[146] or music, festivals, language, or architecture. This brings to mind once more the impact of the Orthodox environment and the context of persecution on these elements of Baptist worship in Belarus (see sections 4.2 and 4.3; and regarding architecture, section 5.4.1). A study of Baptist worship practice in different parts of Belarus (e.g. in the churches of south-west and north of Belarus) might reveal additional elements of local culture, which have contributed to the formation of the given form of services.[147] A comparative analysis of different evangelical subcultures (Charismatic, Pentecostal, and Baptist) is of special interest. It shows how local and Western influences manifest themselves in different communities (compare, for example, the "restrained" attitude to prayer among the Baptists and the loud praises of Pentecostal prayer, often shifting to shouting). Understanding the cultural conditioning of worship allows one to start a dialogue between worship and culture, which may turn out to be very productive.

2. "*The relationship between liturgy and culture is theologically framed by the biblical-theological categories of creation and incarnation.* Inculturation is both possible and necessary because of the twin claims that 'in the beginning God created the heavens and the earth' and 'the Word became flesh and lived among us.'"

The second thesis, which directs attention to the theology of creation and incarnation, is of special significance in the context of the Russian-speaking Baptist movement, which was shaped under persecution from the state. The total control of the communist regime over literature, theater, cinema, visual art, and other kinds of arts, as well as the antireligious orientation of art, contributed to the negative attitude among Baptists to mass culture in general (even though classical works of writers, artists, and composers of the pre-revolution period enjoyed acceptance among believers). The main texts defining this attitude were "the whole world lies in the power of the

---

146. Witvliet, *Worship Seeking Understanding*, 114.

147. See footnotes @@ and @@ about the influence of the Orthodox or Catholic context on Easter celebrations in churches in different regions of Belarus.

evil one" and "Do not love the world nor the things in the world. If anyone loves the world, the love of the Father is not in him."[148] Little attention is paid to the continuous action of common grace and the providential work of God in the world, which is expressed in the first chapters of Genesis and Psalms,[149] including people being created in His likeness and image who are able to create.

If we see culture as an enemy, then it will be impossible to either influence it, or adapt and change it to some new forms on the basis of *"the biblical-theological categories of creation and incarnation."*[150] Yet the development of the idea of creation opens doors to "full participation in and critique of culture,"[151] and wise stewardship of God's gifts that we receive through nature and people's abilities. One could take "Jubal's music"[152] and use it in worship (Jubal and Tubal-cain, the descendants of Cain, can be considered as representatives of secular society). "Hiram from Tyre" could build and decorate houses of prayer using "Tubal-cain's hammer."[153] It is possible that electronic musical instruments, popular musical styles, as well as Belarusian folk instruments like the duda, zhaleyka, and dulcimer, fine art, and drama,[154] will find their place in worship. In such manner the church would "return"

---

148. 1 John 5:19; 2:15.

149. Schmemann discusses the sacramental nature of the world, understanding it as "an epiphany of God, a means of His revelation, presence, and power" (Schmemann, "Worship in a Secular Age," 120). Unfortunately, he does not spend much time in supporting and clarifying his point.

150. Witvliet, *Worship Seeking Understanding*, 115.

151. Witvliet, 116.

152. Gen 4:21.

153. 1 Kings 7:13; Gen 4:22.

154. In 2013–2017 a group of enthusiasts, consisting of the members of evangelical churches, prepared some theater plays related to the history of Christianity in Belarus: 600th anniversary of the preaching of Jerome of Prague, a Czech reformer, in the Great Duchy of Lithuania (in Vil'no, Vitebsk, and Polotsk) in 2013; 500th anniversary of a prominent figure of Belarusian and western European Reformation Nikolai Radzivill Cherny in 2015; 500th anniversary of the publication of a Belarusian Bible by Francis Scorina in 2017. The plays took place in a number of theaters in Belarus and they or their parts were performed at various celebrations and church worship times. The audience appreciated/valued them as a mighty tool of Gospel presentation, which was suitable even inside the house of prayer.

what belongs to Him.¹⁵⁵ A secular culture would be redeemed, and that is a pressing task.¹⁵⁶

Doctrines of creation and incarnation provide the basis for using anything that has been created, and for the sanctification of any earthly vessel (including cultural life) that has been created by the Creator or by people created in His image and likeness. Attention to incarnation in its turn contributes to the idea of God entering into the everyday life of the world and His involvement in the activities of the world. Even our mundane daily routines can be transformed and offered to God. Grasping the incarnation in relation to worship enables crossing the boundaries between sacred and secular, filling the forms that are used in this world (whether those are verbal, musical, or other) and giving them a new meaning as they are used in the life of the church.

3. "*Liturgical inculturation requires theologically informed cultural criticism of one's own cultural context.*" People ought to study not only history and worship but the basic moments of cultural context,¹⁵⁷ cultures of conduct, and characteristic traits of people. Those who wish to reform worship need to consider the conservatism and traditionalism of Belarusians, their tendency to preserve their traditions and the existing order of things (which is reflected in their attitude to politics), and their patience and submissiveness to their fate, which is clearly revealed in poems, especially such significant ones as "Ya muzhyk-belarus . . ." ("I am a muzhik-Belarusian") and "Nash rodny kray" ("Our native land") by the famous Belarusian poets of the past, Yanka Kupala (1882–1942)¹⁵⁸ and Yakub Kolas (1882–1956).¹⁵⁹ Nevertheless, the desire to preserve the *status quo* and avoid changes could equally be a manifestation of the unhelpful qualities of laziness, cowardice, passiveness, and insecurity, which ought to be overcome.

In relation to Belarusian national culture, elements of folklore, rituals, and rites related to agriculture are often mentioned in society. However, such concepts do not play a significant role in people's lives today due to the prevalence

---

155. Matt 22:21. "Then render to Caesar the things that are Caesar's; and to God the things that are God's."

156. Davis, "Ghetto or Desert," 21.

157. Witvliet, *Worship Seeking Understanding*, 116–117.

158. True name is Ivan Dominikovich Lutsevich.

159. True name is Konstantin Mikhailovich Mitskevich.

of the Russian language, urbanization, and the "Americanization" of culture. The young generation is strongly influenced by IT, Western music, and the television industry. However, culture is pluralistic, and, in considering it, attention needs to be paid to the various groups of people to which the church is oriented as well as the region it is in. For example, the Transfiguration Feast (19th of August) could be very popular among villagers since the feast is related to harvest, planting, and the dedication of fruit in an agricultural society. In such instances it is not only important to engage people in worship and refer to local culture, "but rather to discern how particular cultural traits both enhance and obscure the nature and purpose of liturgy."[160] If certain cultural elements and traditions are able to make the Gospel clearer, then their inclusion in worship is going to contribute to a more profound worship in the local culture.[161] Generally speaking, the goal of Baptists in Belarus is to plant new churches, and their focus is on the spiritual maturity of Christians rather than having resources or being in a position to influence mass culture.[162] Nevertheless, transformation could at least occur in the lives of Christians and their relatives when worship is engaged in everyday life and it goes beyond the limits of the house of prayer. This occurs when a family practices Bible reading and singing, or when shared dinner turns into a small piece of worship. This makes the ties between worship and life stronger.

Basically, the relationship of worship and life is a two-way road. Way of life transforms worship and worship forms actions, traditions, lifestyle, and most certainly spiritual practices that extend beyond worship. Worship in the house of prayer is reflected in prayers in the home of a Christian when they incorporate church requests into their prayers, and pray for ministers, brothers and sisters in Christ, and other churches. The Sunday sermon encourages people to read and meditate over the Bible texts that have been read in worship during their devotions at home. The praxis of fasting is determined by

---

160. Witvliet, *Worship Seeking Understanding*, 118.

161. "Nairobi Statement on Worship and Culture," 3.1, in, ed., *Christian Worship Worldwide: Expanding Horizons, Deepening Practices*, ed. Charles E. Farhadian (Grand Rapids: William B. Eerdmans, 2007), 285–290.

162. The exception is the music concert put on by "City of Light" in Brest, which attracts thousands of young people. It has been running for several years in the summer on City Day in the main city square or sports grounds. ECB church "Salvation" is the organizer of the event, and in this way the church tries to share the light of love and kindness with the youth culture.

church life and the needs of the community. In this way worship considerably defines the spiritual discipline of worship participants.

4. *"The extremes of either complete identification with or rejection of a given culture are to be avoided at all costs."*

Considering inculturation one should avoid thoughtless imitation, or "cultural capitulation," on the one hand, and escapism and "cultural irrelevance" on the other.[163] The second extreme is more typical for traditional worship. In essence, worship as well as education, business, and politics does not appear to be a sphere of cultural engagement.[164] If politics is regarded as a secular business, unacceptable for a Christian (and that is why dialogue is impossible), then worship is too sacred to introduce the "world" into it. Representing traditional worship, one musician and choir conductor in Minsk explained, "I can listen to secular music at home but worldly music styles are unacceptable in church and only church music should be used. 'House clothes' are not suitable for coming to church." Splitting a Christian's life into their life in the house of prayer and their life beyond it leads to the profanation of life and the extreme sacralization of worship, which is not helpful in terms of their dialogue. This type of approach needs to be corrected. In the evangelical context, people should be reminded that Christianity is primarily a lifestyle and not a worship style, and in this manner the boundary between ethics and worship should be removed.[165]

> Wise is the church that seeks to be "in" but not "of" the world (John 15:19), resisting aspects of the culture that compromise the integrity of the gospel, and eagerly engaging its culture with the good news of the gospel of Jesus Christ who comes to each culture, but is not bound by any culture.[166]

---

163. Witvliet, *Worship Seeking Understanding*, 119.

164. Witvliet, 107.

165. Alexander Schmemann calls for the "'reconciliation' and mutual reintegration of liturgy, theology, and piety." (See Fisch, ed., *Liturgy and Tradition*, 42). However, in Schmemann's understanding this reconciliation is important not for changing worship but for the intensification of the influence of liturgy on life and theology.

166. World Communion of Reformed Churches, "Worshiping the Triune God: Receiving and Sharing Christian Wisdom Across Continents and Centuries," 1.4. This statement was adopted by the newly formed World Communion of Reformed Churches in 2010 (https://worship.calvin.edu/resources/articles/worshiping-triune-god-receiving-and-sharing-christian-wisdom-across-continents, last accessed 16 May 2019).

5. *"Liturgical action must reflect common elements in the Christian tradition through the unique expressions of a particular cultural context. There must be a judicious balance of particularization and universality."*

Witvliet's model calls for a *"balance of particularization and universality."*[167] Worship crosses over the boundaries of primitive repetition and the blind, mechanical transfer of customs and forms.[168] It reflects elements of local culture, but at the same time it does not exclude the opportunity for full participation by a representative of another culture, and it even reinforces the Gospel through the given characteristics of the given culture. In traditional worship such balance is revealed through the same basic elements (sermons, songs, and prayers) in different forms. These may appear especially different if compared to Baptist churches in the West. For example, Baptists kneeling down for prayer and saying extempore prayers from each person's place reflects their understanding of being in awe of God and freedom in the Spirit. It is interesting that Belarusian contemporary worship shows very little signs of such particularity. There is little difference from similar forms in the United Kingdom or the United States apart from the language. Contemporary worship is drawn more towards unification than differentiation, but John Witvliet believes that "the universal is expressed most clearly through the particular."[169] For example, in regard to music, wind instruments or folk instrument orchestras could provide an opportunity for the inculturation of worship in the local context. On the other hand, the traditional approach does not pay enough attention to the globalization of culture, insisting on last-century traditions, and the practice of modern worship could be analyzed as an illustration of an alternative attempt to balance *particularization and universality* in modern reality.[170]

---

167. Witvliet, *Worship Seeking Understanding*, 119.

168. "Four basic dualities that define judicious liturgical inculturation" by Anita Stauffer may be good tools for successful inculturation. In her opinion, liturgy should be "authentic and relevant," "Lutheran [that is, oriented to a particular tradition] and catholic," "local and global," "Christocentric and anthropocentric." (Stauffer, "Christian Worship: Towards Localization and Globalization," 9–10.) These opposites help to evaluate components of the worship, and bring to light local extremes and the mechanical transfer from other traditions.

169. Witvliet, *Worship Seeking Understanding*, 120.

170. Hislop writes concerning three laws of liturgical development. "The first may be called the principle of survival . . .", "The second principle appears the antithesis of the first. It is the law whereby the living faith is ever freeing itself from dead tradition and conventional expression. The wine of the Spirit is ever bursting the skins of tradition . . .", "The third principle

6. "*This balance of particularization and universality requires 'a mediating strategy' for liturgical inculturation.* Often such strategies are summarized in a single phrase: 'transforming culture,' 'dynamic equivalence,' 'creative assimilation.'"

The sixth thesis offers *"a mediating strategy"* for inculturation. Referring to Roman Catholic Anscar Chupungco, John Witvliet offers such methods as "dynamic equivalence," "creative assimilation," and "organic progression,"[171] which suggest the corresponding replacement of a ritual by its local equivalent, or the assimilation of certain forms of culture or the development of new forms in dialogue with the local culture. Implementation of these methods requires a creative approach and out-of-the-box-solutions, in the same way that the church has done from its very beginning by transforming Jewish or Pagan forms, filling them with new content, and often shaping the form of the element. "Proselyte baptism is transformed into Christian baptism, and pagan myths are transformed into Christian parables."[172] The Easter meal became the Lord's Supper, the Day of the Invincible Sun turned into Christmas. Rhetoric found its expression in sermons. In the years of persecution, the conditions forced Christians to look for dynamic equivalents: Christians in prisons and camps narrated that in order to do Communion without any wine or grape juice they used beet juice. Similar examples may become models for finding equivalents or ways of assimilation and introducing local traditions (if they are not associated with superstitions) into worship. Folk tunes or secular celebrations such as Victory Day (May 9) or Independence Day (July 3) may be appropriate places to start. (For other contemporary examples see section 8.3.3.)

---

harmonizes the two formers. We might call it the law of expansion. In its operation it preserves the old rite but attaches a new meaning to it. The Faith, ever seeking new forms of expression, adopts ceremonies, symbols, and rites which have sprung from alien sources." (Hislop, *Our Heritage in Public Worship*, 6–7.)

171. Chupungco, *Liturgical Inculturation: Sacramentals, Religiosity, and Catechesis*, 37, cited in Witvliet, *Worship Seeking Understanding*, 120–121.

172. Witvliet, *Worship Seeking Understanding*, 121.

7. *"The constituent liturgical actions of the Christian church – including proclamation of the Word, common prayer, baptism, and Eucharist – are among the 'universal' or common factors in the Christian tradition . . ."*

Referring to other authors, Witvliet suggests a kind of canon for worship – a set of nonnegotiable common aspects that include proclamation of the Word, common prayer, baptism, and Eucharist.[173] Belarusian Baptists would indeed accept this "canon," overlaying it with singing. Sermons, prayer, and singing are presented in various proportions in worship, but even with all the controversy around the number and length of sermons, various forms of prayer, and varying music styles, their existence as core elements has been never argued in regular worship. In contrast, baptism is regarded as a separate event rather than a part of regular worship, and in most churches it is only practiced once a year[174] while the Lord's Supper is practiced once a month. Yet any restriction in the frequency of a celebration is compensated by special attention to these elements and the solemnity of the occasions of baptism and the Lord's Supper. In any case, focus on key elements helps to preserve the crux of the service, and worship does not lose its identity even though it may transform in terms of culture.

In this way, as made clear in the theological model suggested by John Witvliet, conscious efforts towards inculturation, require the thorough study and analysis of: the theology of worship, the context of formation, worship in church history, and in other traditions and contexts such as local traditions and culture. Taking into consideration respect for the traditions of middle-aged and older Belarusians, especially religious ones, we understand that any changes cannot be undertaken without pastoral sensitivity, patience, and love. The pastor's credibility, good relationships, and patience become key factors in inculturation, as well as persistence and consistency in decisions.

---

173. Witvliet, 121–122. Gordon Lathrop, in his book *Holy Things* and again in his *Holy People*, has developed a shorthand way of describing this deep tradition of worship. He speaks of Book, Bath, and Meal. Book, of course, refers to the reading of Scripture, and not only its reading but its interpretation, and some kind of proclamation. Bath refers to baptism, whether preceded by teaching or followed by teaching. And Meal refers to the Lord's Supper, the Eucharist or Holy Communion. Lathrop would identify Book, Bath, and Meal as the essentials of Christian worship or what he prefers to describe as the "central things." See Byars, *The Future of Protestant Worship: Beyond the Worship Wars*, 40.

174. See discussion about baptisteries in this thesis, section 5.4.2.2. Interior spaces.

The call to evangelism and teaching the truths of faith do not leave the church any choice other than ongoing renewal of worship in dialogue with culture.

8.3.3. Inculturation: Building a Bridge in the Practice of Traditional Baptist Worship

For Belarusian Baptists, with their emphasis on the centrality of the Bible, inculturation may well begin with the Bible. Using the *koine,* the common language of the Greek-speaking empire, the New Testament provides a serious theological and historical argument for the use of modern translations in the common language of the people. Their use in worship (perhaps starting as a separate piece of reading) would gradually change the language of sermons, prayers, and singing, serving to demystify worship and bringing worship language closer to everyday usage.[175]

Traditionalists argue that there is no need to abandon the "inspired and infallible" Synodal translation, all the more so because it has proved to be effective, having transformed their lives and continuing to transform people. They would say that it is not difficult to learn and remember several hundred Slavonic terms. In fact, zealous Orthodox Christians in Belarus say similar things about the Church Slavonic translation, but in practice this good aspiration does not work, especially since this involves separate style as well as separate words.[176]

"Theologically informed cultural criticism" (see Witvliet's Thesis 3) requires avoiding extremes (Thesis 4), and considering church composition, various age groups, and attitudes towards religion in society. Martie McMane's caution should be taken seriously, that "Language that is too formal or stilted does not invite people in. Language that is too colloquial or folksy may not

---

175. New translations are already widely used in personal worship by many believers and Bible study groups. In September 2012, when the Minsk Theological Seminary received nine full-time students for a one-year program, the theology teacher immediately faced a new problem because all the students were using a new translation by the Russian Bible Society, published in 2011, whereas the theology course was based on the Synodal translation. Five of the students were originally from churches practicing contemporary worship styles, but it is possible to speak about this tendency in many places.

176. In my Homiletics class, when teaching Russian-speaking groups in Belarus, Russia, Ukraine, Kazakhstan, Kyrgyzstan, Estonia, and Moldova, I often ask about old words from the Synodal version, and even preachers cannot explain the meaning of some Slavonicisms without a dictionary.

convey enough *importance or* reverence."[177] Nevertheless, some steps in this direction could be taken. One of the options is publishing a revised Synodal version, where outdated words and phrases, or the ones which have acquired new meaning, could be replaced.[178]

The issue of the translation and interpretation of the Bible is directly related to the practice of preaching. One of the maladies of traditional preaching is homiletic heresy, which Clyde Fant calls "the leaven of the Pharisees."[179] The heresy finds its expression in homiletic Docetism, which is avoiding the human side of the sermon. Emphasis is put on the original meaning of the text and its historical and cultural analysis, and the exposition is done in church language and with an inflated style.[180] In regards to preaching in the churches in Belarus, one could hardly complain about the passion for exegesis. Nevertheless, the terms and topics reflect the world of the Bible. Bridging the gap means building a bridge to the modern world, to the world of the audience, which is done through application, addressing urgent topics, responding to the needs of people, and through using real-life illustrations, secular literature and arts, and comprehensive language. At the same time, Fant argues that this actualization should not lead to another extreme, "the heresy of Sadducees, ignoring the authority and power of the Bible and exaggerated attention to [the] human factor."[181]

An interesting attempt to make the sermon relevant was described in a report by the Deputy Commissioner for Religious Affairs in the Brest Region of 11 May 1986. While describing Easter worship in Baptist churches, he notes that "most of the sermons were traditional and repetitive, the same accounts of Christian doctrine were revealed over and over again."[182] The report continues, "The sermons, especially in Fortechnaya str. in Brest and

---

177. McMane, "That They May Have Life," 42. (Emphasis in original).

178. The publishers of a Russian-language version of *The MacArthur Study Bible* (Slavic Gospel Association) took this approach by substituting some of the borrowings from other languages and archaic words and expressions with their equivalents, which are clear to a modern reader. However, this publication is appreciated more as a commentary, and it is primarily used for sermon preparation and Bible study.

179. Fant, *Preaching for Today*, 30–41.

180. Fant.

181. Fant.

182. This is probably the evaluation of "the ministry of the word" by a stranger when he has the opportunity to listen to 3 or 4 sermons on the same topic of the resurrection of Jesus Christ.

other communities, were abounding in illustrations of so-called secular character: the poems by E. Eutushenko were quoted, as well as records by Mamin-Sibiriak and local poetry."[183] The Baptists turned to the authoritative sources under the pressure of an atheist regime in order to prove that their faith was legitimate. In the twenty-first century the conflict between atheism and faith lost its urgency and the apologetic element became less relevant. Yet quoting great scholars such as Newton and Pascal, or writers and poets such as Dostoevsky and Lermontov, or Belarusian writer Vasil' Bykau and Nobel Prize winner in Literature (2015) Svetlana Alexievich, could contribute to relevant, yet indigenous sermons.

Another element to consider is singing. Its relation in maintaining traditional attitudes toward change is not fundamentally different from the question of using Bible translations. Of course, there is more flexibility with respect to this element, especially in terms of individual and group singing, which allows a lot of room for creativity. Yet communal singing is not subject to any major changes, since *Song of Revival* is its main (and mostly only) source. Popular old songs offer important emotional and spiritual ties to the Christians of other generations and traditions. They should not be excluded from worship and, moreover, we should go further back than the nineteenth and twentieth centuries to include hymns from the Reformation and other periods. However, borrowed and new indigenous hymns will enrich worship and build better relationships with the present. In this area Prokhanov's example[184] can serve as a good precedent for the translation and writing of new songs that reflect the spiritual experiences of believers in the twenty-first century. We could connect this back to Witvliet's Thesis 2, affirming the constructive role of creativity in Christian calling and practice.

Historical studies provide some curious local examples of adaptation to the local culture and customs in the search for new effective methods. Several cases show how familiar forms, filled with new content, were used in evangelism during the first third of the twentieth century. For instance, regarding worship, evangelicals were accused of using the words of well-known songs

---

183. NARB, Stock 136, File 1, Case 88, 155.
Eugeny Eutushenko (born in 1932) is a Russian Soviet poet, writer, director, scriptwriter, and publicist. Dmitry Mamin-Sibiriak (1852–1912) was a Russian novelist and playwright.

184. See section 3.2.1.

to promote their ideas. The following example is a famous song in the Soviet Union called "Suliko," composed by Varinka Tseretely to words from Akaky Tseretely in 1895. The first lines in translation from the Russian by Naum Grebnev are as follows:

> I was looking for the grave of my beloved –
> And could find it nowhere!
> I was weeping bitterly and saying all the time:
> "My darling, where are you?"

Its edited "Christianized" version is:

> I was looking for peace to my soul,
> But it was hard to find.
> I prayed for a long time and suffered.
> I went a long way looking for it.[185]

A second example is actually a re-working of the lyrics to the music of the National Anthem of the Soviet Union (1944–1991).[186]

> United Forever in Friendship and Labour,
> Our mighty Republics will ever endure.
> The Great Soviet Union will Live through the Ages.
> The Dream of a People their fortress secure.
> Through Days dark and stormy where Great Lenin Lead us
> Our Eyes saw the Bright Sun of Freedom above
> and Stalin our Leader with Faith in the People,
> Inspired us to Build up the Land that we Love.[187]

Baptists put it this way:

> An unbreakable union of great freedom,
> The great love joined together forever to stand.
> We are faithful to our One Lord,
> And we have been washed in His blood.
> Through tempests and storms of the sea of life

---

185. Mitrokhin, *Baptizm: istoriya i sovremennost'*, 450.
186. Prokhorov, chief ed., *Sovetskiy entsiklopedicheskiy slovar'*, izd. 4 [The Soviet Encyclopedic Dictionary, ed. 4], 305.
187. Mikhalkov, *Anthem of the Soviet Union*, the first and second stanzas. English version by Paul Robeson.

> We'll go forward fearless of our mighty foes.
> Christ will help us, because we are strong in Him,
> And He is the Firstborn, He has paved the way![188]

Even though they are creative, these examples do not sit comfortably in worship, especially the Anthem. It was often performed many times just as music without lyrics, and the tune brings to mind the original meaning, associated with socialism, the Communist Party, and the names of Lenin and Stalin (in the first version of the Anthem). Even new words cannot completely remove the associations. The same is partly true for another interesting case, the rearrangement of "Hallelujah," the song of Canadian poet and singer Leonard Cohen.[189] It became popular in Belarus because of the animated film *Shrek*.[190] Considering that many older listeners are not necessarily familiar with *Shrek*, its performance does not awake so many associations with the characters and situation of the film. Below is the first stanza of the song as performed by a music group in "Bethlehem" church:

> I love You with all my soul.
> You have chosen me from the eternity.
> And now, my God, I sing praise to you
> You gave me grace from heaven.
> I would like to tell everybody about it.
> I sing Hallelujah from all my heart.[191]

Considering its existing biblical connotations, a better example of modern adaptation might be the song of the choir of Jewish slaves: "You Are Beautiful, oh, Our Motherland" from Giuseppe Verdi's opera "Nebuchadnezzar"[192] and rearranged in 2001 by the Music Department of Minsk Theological Seminary. The first stanza of the hymn is:

---

188. Mitrokhin, *Baptizm: istoriya i sovremennost'*, 451. Text put in poetry in English by Oksana Ostapovich.

189. Leonard Cohen, "Hallelujah," from *Various Positions* (Columbia Records, December 1984).

190. Directed by Andrew Adamson and Vicky Jenson (PDI/DreamWorks, 2001).

191. Text in Russian is written by Sergei Luk'yanov, Minsk Theological Seminary's dean and pastor (since 2016) of "New Covenant" Baptist Church in Minsk.

192. Giuseppe Verdi, "Nebuchadnezzar," 1841.

> Eternal God, You are the source of the creation,
> Your expanses are immense.
> Ears of grain in the field sing a praise hymn,
> And the fields are covered with flowers.
> The mighty rivers are full of water,
> They are clothed in luxurious green, the forests rustle;
> The song for You will never cease
> On earth, on water and in heaven.[193]

When talking about the inculturation of the music component of public worship, the notion of "translatability" can be of good service.[194] It is "more than just translation of words," "more than just translation."[195] Marcel Barnard and other authors, using case studies from Malawi and Zimbabwe as illustrations, oppose "the uncritical transportation (transfer) of melodies from one culture to the other," as well as "the creation of hymns that pursue and express certain forms of culture uncritically."[196] They call for the development of a hymnology that "meets the sounds of a particular culture," and at the same time "reaches out to find those sounds of life across all cultures that resonate with the gospel of Life."[197] This kind of work demands knowing languages as well as having a deep understanding of culture and the Gospel.

Opportunities for changing/adapting public worship do not end with using new Bible translations and learning new songs while maintaining the existing heritage. Testimonies about God's providence in life, experiences of living with the Lord, and healings (all of which reveal that the Lord is at work in the lives of Christians), may also connect worship with life. They can serve as a powerful tool to speak directly into lives through the experiences of others, and to break through the wall between worship and life. In this way, the link between public worship and the daily life of Christians gets stronger, and "daily living, family, society and workplace are seen as the

---

193. Patsuk, ed., *Poyte Gospodu, svyatyye Yego . . . Khorovoy sbornik dlya smeshannogo khora s soprovozhdeniyem*, tom 2 [Sing to the Lord, His Saints . . . Choral Compilation for a Mixed Choir with Accompaniment, vol. 2], 20–24.

194. Barnard, Cilliers, and Wepener, *Worship in the Network Culture. Liturgical Ritual Studies. Fields and Methods, Concepts and Metaphors*, 200–206.

195. Barnard, Cilliers, and Wepener, 205.

196. Barnard, Cilliers, and Wepener, 206.

197. Barnard, Cilliers, and Wepener.

arenas of faithfulness, and worship is seen as the place where we rehearse this faithfulness."[198] The same could be said about intercessory prayers. Lukas Vischer writes insightfully about prayers for government, and the victims of political or economic oppression.[199] The aforementioned book by Karl Barth could serve as a good example or pattern for these kinds of prayers.[200]

Another area to be carefully considered is how some holidays and memorial days could be "baptized" and used in Christian worship. The dedication of some events to Yahweh in the Jewish tradition that are related to time spans (the new year and month, weeks, agricultural cycles),[201] and the transformation of Jewish and pagan feasts in church history are good examples. The short history of the evangelical movement in the Soviet Union displays some evidence of this idea, as seen in the accusations leveled against the Christians by atheists set out below.

First, the sectarians oppose evangelical holidays to the revolutionary ones. They replace International Day of Working Women with a "Day of a Christian Woman." As a rule, during the day there are special meetings for women, and women generally preach on that day. "A Week of Evangelism" is dedicated to Lenin's Days and they also have some more "Weeks of Evangelism." Instead of May 1 being a Holiday of International Solidarity of the Working Class, they celebrate "Day of Evangelical International." In contrast to the Day of Harvest and Collectivization they have "Harvest Day" where they send groups of "teams" around villages (3–5 people each).[202]

Modern examples are attempts to Christianize Saint Valentine's Day and International Women's Day, although a fully-fledged integration of International Women's Day is hampered by socialist (Soviet) connotations.[203]

---

198. Ellis, "Gathering Struggles: Creative Tensions in Baptist Worship," 18.

199. Vischer, "Worship as Christian Witness to Society," 418.

200. Barth, *Molitva*.

201. Morrill, *Anamnesis as Dangerous Memory. Political and Liturgical Theology in Dialogue*, 99.

202. Yartsev, *Sekta evangel'skikh khristian* [The Sect of Evangelical Christians], 18.

203. Guiver offers the concept of defumigation for the integration of some cultural elements in the service. "Cultures often have to go through a period of 'defumigation' before the liturgy can take them on board. A country where tribal drum music is associated with devil-worship means drums will be unusable until they have known some decline, which may require the wait of a generation. An example of a defumigation process getting stuck is the early banning of musical instruments from worship . . . The principle of defumigation applies even today: churches wanting to introduce modern music tend to opt for styles at least a

Nowadays, Saint Valentine's Day is celebrated on February 14 in some churches in Minsk, receiving more importance than the feast of the Meeting of the Lord on the following day, February 15. Some churches do not celebrate the latter and have some special activities for youth on the day before.[204] The celebration is used as a good pretext for discussion about relationships between boys and girls, and eventually about God's love. In addition, some churches, such as "Salvation" in Kolodishchi, Minsk region, use the secular celebration on March 8 for a day of thanksgiving and prayer for mothers and wives.[205] Yet there is no single approach to celebrations. Some churches try to transform celebrations by rejecting their primary meaning, and others add new meanings to the secular ones.

Adhering to uniformity is perhaps not the key issue. As Kathleen Hughes suggests, there are various approaches to the adaptation of feasts: opposition, identification, purification [adding new meaning], paradox [using both primary and new meaning], and transformation [when celebration becomes a symbol of a deeper meaning].[206] For example, variety in methods could encourage creative assimilation[207] in celebrating Constitution Day (March 15), when people might be reminded about their civil duties and pray about their country; Labor Day (May 1), when people could dedicate their labor to God and be encouraged to work diligently;[208] Chernobyl Catastrophe Day (April 26), which could become the day of supplication for suffering people and the collection of finances for mercy and charity activities and/or also an occasion to talk about the environment and our responsibility to care for the

---

generation out of date. Power of association brings problems for inculturation that can leave Christians preferring to dress their worship in weak examples of cultural tradition rather than the most lively and vigorous." (Guiver, *Vision Upon Vision. Processes of Change and Renewal in Christian Worship*, 81.)

204. "Bethlehem," "New Earth," Minsk. (Dmitriy Mamoiko and Jacob Timofeev, Personal interview with author, Minsk, 21 November 2014 and 15 October 2015 [Personal notes, 80b].)

205. Nikolai Sinkovets, Personal interview with author, Minsk, 28 May 2013 (Personal notes, 80b).

International Women's Day is celebrated each year on 8 March in a number of countries as "Women's Day." Historically it started in the US as a day of solidarity of working women in the struggle for equal rights and emancipation.

206. Hughes, "Liturgical Year: Conflict and Challenge," 71.

207. "Nairobi Statement on Worship and Culture," 3.4.

208. Hughes, "Liturgical Year: Conflict and Challenge," 73.

world God created in love.[209] Christian connotation and meaning can also be given to the increasingly popular Family Day (15 May) and Mother's Day (14 October), with attention devoted to young people (on the last Sunday in June), to elderly people (1 October, the Day of the Elderly), and to the disabled (3 December).

Yet another matter to consider is the extent to which liturgical and secular calendars match the life routines of most people. Writing from an American perspective, Hughes points to the fact that for the majority of the population, a new life cycle starts with the beginning of the school year in September.[210] Since the academic year reflects the life of society, "our cycle of feasts and seasons needs to acknowledge this rhythm and to accommodate this experience of time, of new beginnings, of completion and joyous endings, and of certain shadow experiences inherent in both."[211] This is a fair observation that can be applied to the rhythm of life of Belarusians as well. In reality, many churches do lift up their prayers at the beginning of September for children and students, but this does not impact the direction of the whole process of worship, and they become only one of its numerous components.

Secular culture challenges Christianity by strong promotion of secular inculturation. As a result, there is evisceration of the religious meaning of Christmas and Easter, even though their social status has been lifted up and they are officially included into days of celebration. Christmas, both "Orthodox" (Eastern calendar) and "Catholic" (Western calendar) has been declared a public holiday, in stark contrast to the Soviet era when both Christmas and Easter time were enforced as working days. Evangelical churches strive to share the meaning of Christmas and Easter with the world by using this time for evangelistic events. Strong reiteration of their meaning is important, but intentionally assimilating some folk and state holidays into worship could enrich worship as well as deepen the role of faith in the everyday life of Christians and their family and friends.

Various life events could be included in worship along with celebrations. The birth of a child, marriage, or news about someone's death are quite often a part of worship. The list could be completed by including: entrance to college

---

209. Thanks to Lina Toth (Andronovienne) for reminding me about the environment.
210. Hughes, "Liturgical Year: Conflict and Challenge," 78.
211. Hughes, 82.

or university, graduation, a new job, and significant milestones such as silver or golden wedding anniversaries. Depending on the size of the church, current joys and sorrows of church members and visitors could be incorporated into an evening service or become an addition to the service and be celebrated during a shared tea-time for example.[212] This should not detract from worship staying Christocentric and focussed on the saving acts of God in Christ.

Inculturation is not an easy task, and one should take into consideration biblical content, Baptist identity, historical heritage, and appropriate forms for the given context and time. Charles Davis calls for prudence in such changes. Old forms "at least [have] an aura of venerable tradition," and reforms do not always meet expectations.[213] Passionate keepers of tradition have reason to be apprehensive about too rapid and drastic changes in public worship under new political circumstances. A Ukrainian Baptist minister, Volodimir Matviiv, notes that for a long time Christians were limited by the four walls of the house of prayer, "and often bound by restrictions: you could not do this and you could not do that. Now, having come out into the wide open and into the fresh air, we feel dizzy."[214] That is why Catholic authors of the *Constitution on the Sacred Liturgy* point out "that any new forms adopted should in some way grow organically from forms already existing."[215]

If the church is aware of its responsibility before the world, it undergoes a constant process of inculturation. *Ecclesia reformata et semper reformanda*

---

212. Martin Stringer goes even further regarding national customs and traditions in the process of inculturation. He highlights the example of India to prove the point; there the churches "went much further than simply adapting the music and language to local tastes. Attempts were made to incorporate Indian practices and organizations [even from Hinduism] into the church" (Stringer, *A Sociological History of Christian Worship*, 225–226.). George Guiver mentions "optional readings from Hindu scripture" as "the readings from the daily offices" (Guiver, *Vision upon Vision. Processes of Change and Renewal in Christian Worship*, 79). The elements of such an approach can be found in Belarus with the Orthodox and Catholic churches. For example, Catholic churches hold special worship services on November 2 devoted to All Souls' Day. Worship in memory of the dead stirs much interest, and overcrowded churches are evidence of that, but Baptists are apprehensive about such inculturation of rituals and superstitions.

213. Davis, "Ghetto or Desert," 10.

214. Matviiv, Svyashchenodii pastora, 287.

215. *Sacrosanctum Concilium*, ch. 1.3.23. It is possible that an example of such organic growth might be a presenter and congregation taking turns in order to read a new translation of Psalms at the beginning of the church service. For Baptist worship, such unconventional forms would combine antiquity and novelty, and "a tribute would be rendered" both to the Bible and modern age.

secundum verbum Dei,[216] for the boldest steps cannot release tensions between the sacral and secular once and for all. Firstly, this is due to the dual nature of worship itself, which belongs not only to the material world, but also to the spiritual one. Worship invades spiritual realms, and visible forms are used to build a bridge to the invisible world. The conflict that emerges at the intersection of worlds will only disappear in the heavenly liturgy.[217]

Secondly, a final decision about the translation of the language of the worship service into more contemporary language is not possible due to the relativity of cultural concepts, its fragmentation and the different perception of its elements by people of different ages, different preferences and tastes, and different understandings of culture. Continuous changes in culture doom the project, or at least make the adaptation process very complicated, especially considering the technological progress and the limited nature of church resources in comparison to the wider world. Yesterday's "ultramodern" becomes "modern" today, and "obsolete" tomorrow. Or, according to Hitchcock, "perhaps the greatest irony of the search for relevance is the fact that nothing so quickly becomes irrelevant as that which seemed intensely relevant only a short time before."[218] So, in every worldview context, in each geographical location, at any given moment of time, the church decides anew on the use of the language of the local culture and the time of the service for the community, to make it as clear and obvious as possible, so that, as 1 Corinthians 14:8 puts it, the trumpet would sound a clear call.[219] To describe the existing tensions, Davis uses the image of believers "wandering in a desert, without liturgy or public worship, until a return to the promised land becomes possible."[220] Duncan Forrester, Ian McDonald, and Gian Tellini sum up the situation as follows:

---

216. Latin for the "Church Reformed and always reforming according to the Word of God."

217. The notion of liminality, which is characterized by a state of uncertainty, ambivalence, and openness, could support this way of thinking. See Barnard, Cilliers, and Wepener, *Worship in the Network Culture. Liturgical Ritual Studies. Fields and Methods, Concepts and Metaphors*, 2–4, 65, 68–69.

218. Hitchcock, *The Recovery of the Sacred*, 29.

219. 1 Cor 14:8.

220. Forrester, McDonald, and Tellini, *Encounter with God*, 228.

> But although there are no appropriate forms of liturgy available, the believer cannot live without worship, so privately and in small groups believers will soldier on, sometimes using antiquated or despised forms inherited from the past, sometimes developing a variety of experimental forms of worship for themselves.[221]

This approach may not be perfect, but it still seems more preferable than the ghetto or state of permanent confrontation with secular culture.[222] In "a reciprocal dialogue between faith and culture"[223] worship is born, which transforms both culture and the participants of worship.

Bridging the cultural gap is a labor-intense and challenging task. However, by engaging in inculturation, the church continues to overcome the tension in worship between freedom and form, as well as the personal and social aspects of worship, by keeping in sight the structure and content of the worship service and its individual components, and by involving all the participants in the process. Stopping along the way is similar to death.[224] While the church walks in "the wilderness," the inculturation process will continue, and the congregation will be enriched in life-sustaining tensions between freedom and form, individual and communal aspects of worship, and the sacral and secular dimensions of worship.

---

221. Davis, "Ghetto or Desert," 19–23.
222. Forrester, McDonald, and Tellini, *Encounter with God*, 228.
223. Robert Taft, S.J., "The Missionary Efforts of the Eastern Churches as an Example of Inculturation," in Pecklers, *Worship*, 136–137.
224. Taft.

Conclusion

In this study I have analyzed traditional worship in Baptist churches in Belarus, seeking an answer to the following research question: How is the implicit theology, as it is embodied in traditional and present Baptist worship in Belarus, related to understandings of established Baptist worship? This led me to research the historical, political, religious, and theological contexts and their influence on traditional Baptist worship. Following that, I explored the relationship between implicit theology and present Baptist worship as expressed in structure, content, duration, shape, and physical spaces of worship as well the theological emphases of traditional public worship. Bringing all these aspects together, I studied their interaction and the inherent tensions that emerge between form and freedom, the communal and personal aspects in worship, and between the traditional form of worship and culture today. Finally, I have considered methods and approaches which might help to resolve the tensions, proposing that rather than seeing these tensions as limiting factors that need to be fully harmonized, holding a sense of creative tension allows the traditional and distinct forms of Baptist worship to maintain their character whilst making room for a contextually sensitive development of public worship and a broader understanding of worship itself.

I began this project by investigating the importance of worship in the reference to the system of life and belief for Belarusian Baptists, especially in the days of persecution when worship became a source of spiritual life in difficult times, a key mode for self-actualization, a refuge from the sinful world, a unique place of fellowship, and an expression of an alternative lifestyle. Thus, in Part One I made a thorough exploration of the context of the period when traditional worship was shaped. Studies on the origins of evangelical churches in Belarus highlight a variety of influences and connections.

Evangelical Christianity reached Belarus from different geographical sources: southern and northwestern Ukraine, Siberia, Germany, the United States, the Baltic region, Poland, and some others. In many cases the awakening was conditioned by relations within a Russian-speaking environment, whereas others were more determined by relations with German and English-speaking believers. The process of adjusting some Western forms to Eastern context resulted in conflict between local and foreign traditions. An example of such issues is varied perceptions concerning the rigid structure of worship services, or the preaching schedule within services. In other cases, Western and Eastern traditions merged and gave birth to an Eastern Slavic form of evangelical Christianity. An example of this is the heritage of hymns used in worship services, and particularly a collection of songs, Pesn' Vozrozhdeniya, which contains hymns translated from English and German languages, as well as indigenous hymns. In the conflict of traditions, Baptist identity did not remain fixed but continued to develop during the Soviet period, and the issue of contextualization became fresh again after the fall of the Iron Curtain, when Western forms and practices were reintroduced to Russian-speaking churches.

The study of the theological, religious, and political background drew attention to the theological basis of the movement, the influence of the Orthodox context, and persecution in the process of formation. Belarusian Baptists' lives and teaching reflect their desire to live and worship according to the Scriptures, and to return to the teachings and practices of the New Testament church. In regard to worship, this expresses itself in the denial of the division of believers into clergy and laity, and in the rejection of practices seen as 'non-biblical,' such as compulsory confession, making the sign of the cross, special rules for fasting, and infant baptism. The main focus is on the practices of preaching, teaching, prayer, and singing. However, limited information on early church worship services precludes full engagement with potential biblical models. Even so, practices and models arising out of readings of the Old and New Testaments offer some firmness and stability in the midst of what feels like frightening diversity.

It was noted that the Eastern Orthodox milieu left its mark on the formation of the spirit of public worship, characterized by reverence and awe, as well as on its content and form, including services dedicated to events of the life of Christ, such as the Lord's Baptism, the Meeting of the Lord, Annunciation

Day, and others. At the same time, a decisive split from Orthodox liturgy was expressed in the rejection of elaborate rites and icons and their use as objects of worship, along with the removal of candles, special garments, a clear-cut division between the priesthood and the laity as expressed in worship, and placing preaching at the center of the worship service. Thus, Baptists in Belarus build their theology on denial of the Orthodox form, but their worship continues to reflect the spirit and character of Orthodoxy.

Life during long-time persecution, opposition, and separation from the world explains motifs of struggle, suffering, and eschatological aspirations together with strong beliefs in retribution and hope reflected in sermons, songs, and poems. The recent decline in persecution has led to less emphasis being placed on the idea of struggle and a decrease in tension regarding eschatological expectations or motifs of suffering, but still the spirit of the worship service reflects the difficult history of the survival of evangelical Christians.

Part Two provided detailed analysis of the structure, time, content, and physical space, and the key theological values promoted by traditional Baptist worship, such as the centrality of Scripture, the principle of edification, the task of evangelism, and simplicity. As this part of the study was based on long-term and immersive participant observation, it presented an accurate and wide-ranging picture of the actual practices of most of the very wide spread of the traditional-style Baptist churches in Belarus, and of the views of pastors and church members as to the meaning, efficacy, and impact of that worship as they understood it.

The study of the structure and content of Baptist services in Belarus reflects the fact that it is composed of a combination of preaching, singing, and prayer (essential worship components), in different forms, numbers, proportions, and orders of service. Preachers and other participants usually speak on different topics that are based on "the inspiration of the Spirit." However, they have a common motif: namely, Christ, or a Christocentric message. The time factor of the worship is conceptualized in the part of the weekly cycle with its focus on the Sunday morning worship service. Other cycles include the monthly circle of services which revolves around the Lord's Supper, and the yearly circle which embraces all holidays related to the events of Christ's life and the life of the church. Although the focus on Christian holidays is weakening (except Christmas and Easter), they still serve as a kind of compass in church life and preaching. An examination of the design and the role of the houses of prayer in worship reveals inner contradictions between the practice and declared character of worship, which can be seen in the ambiguous status of the houses of prayer: house of prayer as "a building" and as "a temple." Worship halls are decorated with biblical texts as a reminder of the conflict with the Orthodoxy, reflected in this case in replacing icons with "talking" pictures. The changes also impacted the structure of the sanctuary. For example, there has been an observed shift from the pulpit to the stage; the barrier between the hall and the stage is diminishing, and the space of worship acquires and increasingly non-hierarchical arrangement.

Part Two also offers a more detailed and specific examination of the theological emphases of traditional worship services. Their review again turns attention to the decisive role of the context, in terms of theological, religious, and political impacts on the formation of these values. It also points to an inner conflict within local worship services in terms of their practical realization, such as the shift from the Bible to the sermon, the imbalance of worship in favor of (poor) edification or evangelism, or the simplification that comes in place of simplicity.

Part Three evaluates these findings, analyzing the nature of the internal conflicts between freedom and forms in worship, the individual and corporate aspects of the service, and the sacral and secular character of worship. Such analysis seeks ways of developing a dynamic theology of worship under the changing context. At the same time, it keeps its own theological emphases and its Baptist identity.

Examination of the structure and the individual worship components reveals that the pursuit of freedom and spontaneity is expressed in flexibility, encouragement, greater involvement of the congregation, and in openness to the Holy Spirit manifesting Himself through believers for the benefit of members. A rigid attitude toward forms can limit freedom in Christ and quench both the Spirit and the expression of gifts. At the same time this approach tends to lead to unsystematic teaching, low quality, or even disorder.

In worship practice, the "priesthood of all believers" is manifested in a variety of participants within the service, and allows individuals to express feelings and desires. It also brings dynamism and adds some color to it. Yet paying exaggerated attention to individual participants can underestimate the significance of the church as a body of believers. The edifying element suffers from an individual and a subjective dimension.

Traditional worship, that has naturally preferred the model of "Christ against culture," traditional style and topics, and which is marked by a special worldview, is sometimes difficult to reconcile with the needs and understanding of outsiders and young believers. The language of worship, which is based on Synodal translations, as well as music styles or dress styles, are part of the cultural gap between church and the "sinful world." Due to earlier hostility and persecution by the state and society, this separation led to the creation of a subculture and understanding of worship service as a shelter or refuge. Thus, some theological and practical steps are needed to address the tension between freedom and forms in worship, the individual and corporate aspects of the service, and the sacral and secular character of worship.

Thus, the final chapter proposed some theological grounds for, and practical ways of, reducing the tensions, enriching worship services, and utilizing all the potential of worship. These include a proper understanding of the opposites (such as structure and freedom) and their reciprocal concessions to each other, a clarification of the nature of the church and of the concept of priesthood, a clarification of the essence of corporate worship which leads to disciplined participation, and an inculturation that begins with the foundation of worship and the Bible and continues with sermons and music.

Summarizing the tension between freedom and form, it is important to note that it cannot be considered in isolation from the heritage formed by historical and interethnic relationships, and the context determined by the religious and political environment (such as by persecution and limited opportunities in the Soviet period). Understanding these factors and their expression in the practice of worship makes it possible to accept the relativity of forms, and focus on the purpose of gatherings, subordinating to it both the inspiration of the Spirit and forms in worship. Thus, balance between freedom and form can be achieved, and benefits drawn from their invisible rivalry.

In the churches of Belarus, it is necessary to clarify the nature of the church as a Body of Christ at the theological level, and to differentiate between public and private worship. The definition of the very concept of "participation in a worship service" must be clarified; the same can be said of the understanding of the priesthood of all believers in terms of worship. In practical terms, this requires careful planning and preparation for worship, as well as a more serious approach to corporate aspects of worship, including the selection of active participants in the worship service, and limiting the participation of some while encouraging the participation of others.

While critically approaching the local expression of secular culture, the church must also look for traces of God's providence in the history of Belarus and the work of non-believing contemporaries in order to find a place for them in worship. Worship leaders should avoid both complete identification with, and radical rejection of, the customs, habits, and values of Belarusians. An awareness of the country's history and other Christian traditions enables maintaining the key elements of worship in balance and expressing them in a way that bears in mind the specific context of the country, region, or even a particular church. However, in this work I stress that the tensions cannot be solved once and for all, as, to some extent, they are an integral part of worship and arise from the nature of worship and the church itself. Moreover, they are important for viability, vitality, openness, and durability, so that inculturation becomes an ongoing process.

The completed analysis of traditional public worship suggests some areas for future work. First of all, there is a need for wider historical research. There are a lot of documents of the Council for Religious Affairs in the National Archives of the Republic of Belarus. Many of these documents have not been studied in detail. They are primarily of interest in relation to state and church relationships, but at the same time they contain much information on worship. Visiting regional archives in Mogilev, Brest, and Grodno, as well as archives in Belostok and Warsaw (Poland), which I was not able to do due to constraints of the present project, would be a fruitful and rewarding task in terms of more deeply understanding the significant factors that influenced the shape and nature of Baptist church life and worship in Belarus. Also, more magazines published by evangelicals in the first third of the twentieth century are now available to view, and they could clarify some questions concerning the formation of the traditional patterns of worship.

> Secondly, it would be beneficial to give attention to a closer study and analysis of cultural context and public worship which would cover more churches geographically (specially the northern and eastern part of Belarus) and obtain more extensive feedback from worship participants, primarily regular congregation members. Data from a study like this could help in measuring

the effectiveness and relevance of worship in a given context at a given time. As I have analyzed the worship service as a whole, there is value in more research going deeper into particular components of worship, or into the content of sermons and songs. Thirdly, one could continue working on a theology of worship in a Russian-speaking context. The work of theologians representing other traditions and Baptists scholars from other countries, not just in the West, as well as research from the perspective of cultural studies, and possibly anthropology and psychology,[1] could be helpful in developing the theological tradition and understanding of the culture of worship in Belarus and other Russian-speaking countries. From a practical point of view such studies could be a good basis for building a culture of worship, developing resources to assist pastors and those who lead worship and music ministry with the goal of realizing the potential of gathering and the execution of the commands of Christ to worship "in spirit and truth."[2]

Here are some last words about the future of traditional worship. In its present state the structure and content of traditional worship satisfies many believers. This is confirmed by the viability of the practice of such worship not just in small towns and villages with only one church and no alternative, but also in regional centers and in the capital, where Christians have a choice of various forms, including contemporary worship. As Cherenkov states, "Evangelical churches have not yet resolved to make a risky step into the future, so the traditional evangelical Christianity is currently the dominant type."[3] The dynamics of change in Baptist Union churches in Belarus suggests that the traditional form will retain its position in the foreseeable future. However, it will no longer be seen as undisputed and the only acceptable form. Indeed, the understanding of traditional worship as such is gradually going

---

1. People may be either extroverts or introverts, depending on the direction of their activity; thinking, feeling, sensing, intuitive, according to their own information pathways; judging or perceiving, depending on the method in which they process received information. Jung, *Psychological Types*, 330–407. Different people prefer different types of worship. Some prefer order and organization, others like spontaneity and freedom.

2. John 4:24.

3. Cherenkov, *Litsom k litsu. Evangel'skaya vera v sovremennoi kul'ture*, 54.

to change along with the changing context, as a result of engagement with other traditions, the arrival of new people in the church, and the development of theological education (the observed decrease in the number of sermons during the last decades is a part of this process). The question is whether the churches are ready to manage the change, or whether the rapidly changing context will make its changes, regardless of their desires and strategies. In any case, the study of the history and the context of Baptist formation in Belarus, the analysis of the present situation within traditional style churches, and a better understanding of a theology of worship and other traditions of worship require a revision of the tradition.[4] This research sets a context in which the necessity of the revision of tradition can be seen more clearly, but in a way that seeks to honor the history of its formation and give a more theologically grounded voice to those aspects of the tradition that can enrich worship in the future.

---

4. Christopher Ellis thinks "it likely that amongst those local churches which continue to decline there will be a preponderance of traditional worship styles, namely the 'hymn sandwich' more properly called 'interspersed singing'" ("Understanding Worship: Trends and Criteria," 33.). It would take additional study to apply this conclusion to the Belarusian situation.

Bibliography

English

Abba, Raymond. *Principles of Christian Worship*. New York and London: Oxford University Press, 1966.

Abernethy, William Beaven. *A New Look for Sunday Morning*. Nashville: Abingdon Press, 1975.

Allmen, Jean-Jacques von. *Worship: Its Theology and Practice*. London: Lutterworth Press, 1965.

Anderson, Fred R. "Protestant Worship Today." *Theology Today*, vol. 43, no. 1 (1986): 63–74.

Andronoviene, Lina. "As Songs Turn into Life and Life into Songs: On the First-Order Theology of Baptist Hymnody." In *Currents in Baptist Theology of Worship Today*, edited by Keith G. Jones and Parush P. Parushev, 129–142. Praha: IBTS, 2007.

———. *Involuntarily Free or Voluntarily Bound: Singleness in the Baptistic Communities of Post-Communist Europe*. IBTS Occasional Publications Series. Vol. II. Prague, International Baptist Theological Seminary, 2003.

———. "Transforming the Struggles of Tamars: Singleness in Intentional Baptistic Communities." PhD diss., University of Wales, 2012.

Andronoviene, Lina and Parush R. Parushev, "Church, State, and Culture: On the Complexities of Post-Soviet Evangelical Social Involvement," *Bogoslovskie razmyshleniya* [Theological Reflections], no. 3 (2004): 161–213.

Andronoviene, Lina and Keith Jones, "Women in Baptist life." In *A Dictionary of the European Baptist Life and Thought*, edited by John Briggs, 529–531. Bletchley: Paternoster, 2009.

Aune, Michael B. "The Corporate and Confessional Character of Worship: The Common Service Debate." *Word & World*, vol. 8, no. 1 (1988): 32–42.

Baab, Lynne M. *Personality Type in Congregations: How to Work with Others More Effectively*. New York City: The Alban Institute, 1988.

Baldovin, John F. "Hippolytus and the Apostolic Tradition: Recent Research and Commentary." *Theological Studies*, vol. 64 no. 3 (Sep. 2003): 520–542.

Balley, Raymond. "The Changing Face of Baptist Worship in Review and Expositors." *The Changing Face of Baptists*, vol. 95, no. 1 (Winter 1998): 47–58.

Barnard, Marcel, Johan Cilliers, and Cas Wepener. *Worship in the Network Culture*. Liturgical Ritual Studies. Fields and Methods, Concepts and Metaphors. Leuven: Peeters, 2014.

Barth, K. *Church Dogmatics, IV/1*. Translated by G.W. Bromiley. Edinburgh: T. & T. Clark, 1956.

Basden, Paul. *The Worship Maze: Finding a Style to Fit Your Church*. Downers Grove: InterVarsity Press, 1999.

Bebbington, David W. "Evangelicals and Public Worship, 1965–2005." *Evangelical Quarterly*, vol. 79, no. 1 (2007): 3–22.

Bekus, Nelly. "'Hybrid Linguistic Identity of Post-Soviet Belarus." *Journal on Ethnopolitics and Minority Issues in Europe*, vol. 13, no. 4 (2014): 26–51.

Bolshakoff, Serge. *Russian Nonconformity*. Philadelphia: The Westminster Press, 1949.

Borchert, Gerald L. "The Lord of Form and Freedom: A New Testament Perspective on Worship." *Review and Expositors*, vol. 80, no. 1 (Winter 1983): 6–16.

Bosch, David J. *Transforming Mission. Paradigm Shifts in Theology of Mission*. Maryknoll: Orbis Books, 1992.

Bottroff, J. L. "Using Videotaped Recordings in Qualitative Research." In *Critical Issues in Qualitative Research Methods*, ed. by J. Morse, 244–261. Thousand Oaks: Sage, 1993.

Bourdeaux, Michael. *Religious Ferment in Russia*. London: Macmillan, 1968.

Brackney, William H., ed. *Baptist Life and Thought, A Source Book*. Rev. ed. Valley Forge: Judson Press, 1998.

Bradley, C. Randall. "Congregational Song as Shaper of Theology: A Contemporary Assessment." *Review and Expositors*, vol. 100, no. 3 (Summer 2003): 351–373.

Bria, Ion. *The Liturgy After the Liturgy: Mission and Witness from an Orthodox Perspective*. Geneva: The World Council of Churches, 1996.

Briggs, John H.Y., gen. ed. *A Dictionary of the European Baptist Life and Thought*. Bletchley: Paternoster, 2009.

Brown, David M. *Transformational Preaching. Theory and Practice*. College Station: Virtualbookworm.com Publishing, 2003.

Byars, Ronald P., *The Future of Protestant Worship: Beyond the Worship Wars*. Louisville: Westminster John Knox Press, 2002.

Carson, D.A. *Christ and Culture Revisited*. Grand Rapids: Wm. B. Eerdmans, 2008.

———. ed. *Worship by the Book*. Grand Rapids: Zondervan, 2002.

Chafin, Kenneth L. *1, 2 Corinthians. The Communicator's Commentary*. Waco: Word Book, 1985.

Chambers, P. Franklin. "The Renaissance of Worship." *The Baptist Quarterly*, vol. 2 (1924–1925): 10–14.

Chan, Simon. *Liturgical Theology*. Downers Grove: Inter-Varsity Press, 2006.

Cheprasov, Timofey, "Formative? Informative? Neither? Towards Understanding of the Practice of Proclamation, the Core Element of Russian Baptist Worship." PhD diss., University of Wales, 2015.

———. *Like Ripples on Water*. Eugene, Oregon: Wipf & Stock, 2018.

Cherry, Constance M. "Merging Tradition and Innovation in the Life of the Church." In E. Todd and E. Johnson, ed., *The Conviction of Things Not Seen: Worship and Ministry in the 21st Century*. Grand Rapids: Brazos Press, 2002.

Chupungco, Anscar J. "Liturgy and the Components of Culture." In S. Anita Stauffer, ed., *Worship and Culture in Dialogue*. Geneva: Lutheran World Federation, 1994.

Clifton-Soderstrom, Michelle A. David D. Bjorlin, *Incorporating Children in Worship: Mark of the Kingdom*. Eugene: Wipf & Stock, 2014.

Cohen, Leonard. "Hallelujah." In *Various Positions*. Columbia Records, December 1984.

Coleman, Heather J. "Baptist Beginning in Russia and Ukraine." *Baptist History and Heritage*, vol. 42, no. 1 (Winter 2007): 24–36.

———. *Russian Baptists & Spiritual Revolution 1905–1929*. Bloomington, Indianapolis: Indiana University Press, 2005.

Cornou, Maria Eugenia. "Worship as a Formative Practice: The Worship Practices of Methodists, Baptists, and Free Brethren in Emerging Protestantism in Argentina (1867–1930)." PhD diss., Vrije Universiteit Amsterdam, 2016.

Cottrell, Jack, *The Faith Once for All: Bible Doctrine for Today*. Joplin: College Press Publishing Company, 2002.

Cox, James W. *Preaching*. San Francisco: Harper & Row, 1985.

Creswell, John W. *Qualitative Inquiry & Research Design. Choosing Among Five Approaches*. 2nd. Ed. Thousand Oaks: Sage Publications, 2007.

Cross, Anthony R. and Philip E. Thompson. *Baptist Sacramentalism. Studies in Baptist History and Thoughts*. Vol. 5. Carlisle: Paternoster Press, 2003.

Davis, Charles. "Ghetto or Desert: Liturgy in a Cultural Dilemma." In Vos Wiebe, ed., *Worship and Secularization*. Bussum: Published by Paul Brand, 1970.

Davies, Horton. *The Worship of the English Puritans*. Glasgow: The University Press, 1948.

———. *Worship and Theology in England from Watts and Wesley to Maurice, 1650–1850*. Princeton: Princeton University Press, 1961.

Davies, J.G. ed., *A Dictionary of Liturgy & Worship*. London: SGM Press, 1972.

Denscombe, Martin. *The Good Research Guide for Small-Scale Social Research Projects*. 2nd. Ed. Philadelphia: Open University Press, 2003.

Dix, Dom Gregory. *The Shape of the Liturgy*. Westminster: Dacre Press, repr. 1954.

Dunn, James D.G. *Unity and Diversity in the New Testament. An Inquiry into the Character of Earliest Christianity*. 2nd. Ed. London: SCM Press; Valley Forge: Trinity Press International, 1990.

Dyck, Johannes. "Revival and Baptist Beginning in Russia." *Baptistic Theologies*, vol. 1, no. 1 (Spring 2009): 14–22.

Ellis, Christopher J. "Duty and Delight: Baptist Worship and Identity." *Review and Expositors,* vol. 100, no. 3 (Summer 2003): 329–349.

———. *Gathering. A Theology and Spirituality of Worship in Free Church Tradition*. London: SCM Press, 2004.

———. "Gathering Struggles: Creative Tensions in Baptist Worship." *The Baptist Quarterly*, vol. 42, no. 1 (2007): 4–21.

———. "Understanding Worship: Trends and Criteria." In *Currents in Baptistic Theology of Worship Today*, edited by Keith G. Jones, and Parush P. Parushev, 25–40. Praha: IBTS, 2007.

———. "Who is Worship For? Dispatches from the War Zone." *Perspectives in Religious Studies*, vol. 36, no. 2 (Summer 2009): 179–185.

Engle, Paul E., ser. ed., Paul A. Basden, gen. ed. *Exploring the Worship Spectrum*. Grand Rapids: Zondervan, 2004.

Erickson, Craig Douglas. *Participating in Worship. History, Theory, and Practice*. Lousville: Westminster/John Knox Press, 1989.

Fagerberg, David W. "A Theology of the Liturgy." *Liturgical Ministry,* vol. 14 (Fall 2005): 169–179.

Fairbairn, Donald. *Eastern Orthodoxy Through Western Eyes*. Louisville. London: Westminster John Knox Press, 2002.

"Faith and Inculturation." International Theological Commission. (1988). http://www.vatican.va/roman_curia/congregations/cfaith/cti_documents/rc_cti_1988_fede-inculturazione_en.html. Accessed 27 December 2016.

Fant, Clyde E. *Preaching for Today*. New York: Harper&Row, 1975.

Farhadian, Charles E., ed. *Christian Worship Worldwide: Expanding Horizons, Deepening Practices*. Grand Rapids: William B. Eerdmans Publishing Company, 2007.

Fetterman, David M. "Ethnography." In Michael S. Lewis-Beck, Alan Bryman, and Tim Futing Liao, eds. *The SAGE Encyclopedia of Social Science Research Methods*. Vol. 1. Thousand Oaks: SAGE Publications, 2004.

Fiddes, Paul S. "Theology and a Baptist Way of Community." in Paul S. Fiddes, Brian Haymes, Richard L. Kidd, Michael Quicke, Eds., *Doing Theology in a Baptists Way*. Oxford: Whitley Publications, 2000.

Fink, Peter E. "Public and Private Moments in Christian Prayer." *Worship*, 58 (1984): 482–499.

Florovsky, George. *Bible, Church, Tradition: An Eastern Orthodox View*. Belmont: Nordland, 1972.

Flower, Stanley K. *More Than a Symbol: The British Baptist Recovery of Baptismal Sacramentalism, Studies in Baptist History and Thoughts*, vol. 2. Carlisle: Paternoster, 2002.

Forrester, Duncan B. J., Ian H. McDonald, and Gian Tellini. *Encounter with God: An Introduction to Christian Worship and Practice*. Edinburgh: T&T Clark, 1996.

Frank, Rees, D. "The Worship of All Believers." *The Baptist Quarterly*, vol. 41, no. 3 (July 2005): 175–189.

Franklin, James H. "Troubles Created for Baptists in Russia by American-Trained Baptists," 1. American Baptist Historical Society. BIM, 65–13.

Freeman, Curtis W., James Wm. McClendon Jr. Velloso da Silva, and C. Rosalee, *Baptist Roots, A Reader in the Theology of a Christian People*. Valley Forge: Judson Press, 1999.

Gay, David H.J. *Baptist Sacramentalism. A Warning to Baptists*. Biggleswade: Brachus, 2011.

Gibson, Barbara E. "Videorecording." In Lisa M. Given, Ed., *The Sage Encyclopedia of Qualitative Research Methods*, vol. 2. Thousand Oaks: SAGE Publications, 2008.

Geertz, Clifford. "Thick Descriptions Toward an Interpretive Theory of Culture." In Glifford Geertz, *The Interpretation of Cultures: Selected Essays*. New York: Basic Books, 1973.

Glesne, Corrine. *Becoming Qualitative Researchers. An Introduction*. 2nd. ed. New York: Longman, 1999.

Grace Community Church, *Official Website*. Accessed 16 May 2019. https://www.gracechurch.org.

Green, Michael. *To Corinth with Love*. Waco: World Books, 1988.

Grenz, Stanley J. *Theology for Community of God*. Grand Rapids: William B. Eerdmans, 1994.

Guiver, George. *Vision Upon Vision. Processes of Change and Renewal in Christian Worship*. Norwich: Canterbury Press, 2009.

Harmon, Steven R. *Toward Baptist Catholicity, Essays on Tradition and Baptist Vision*. Bletchley: Paternoster Press, 2006.

Harris, Mark J. *Toward an Understanding of Russian Baptist Worship*. Portland: CMC International, 1997.

Hauerwas, Stanley and William H. Willimon. *Resident Aliens: Life in the Christian Colony*. Nashville: Abingdon Press, 1989.

Haymes, Brian. "Theology and Baptist Identity," in Paul S. Fiddes, Brian Haymes, Richard L. Kidd, Michael Quicke, eds., *Doing Theology in a Baptist Way*. Oxford: Whitley Publications, 2000.

Hebly, J.A. *Protestants in Russia*. Belfast: Christian Journals, 1976.

Hilborn, David. "An Evangelical Perspective on Orthodox Liturgy. The Place of Liturgy in Orthodoxy and Evangelism." In I. M. Randall, Ed., *Baptist and the Orthodox Church. On the Way to Understanding*. Praha: IBTS, 2003.

Hinson, E. Glenn. "Private Springs of Public Worship." *Review and Expositor*, vol. 80, no. 1 (Winter 1983): 110–118.

Hislop, D.H. *Our Heritage in Public Worship*. Edinburgh: T&T Clark, 1936.

Hitchcock, James. *The Recovery of the Sacred*. New York: The Seabury Press, 1974.

Hobsbawn, Eric and Terence Ranger. *The Invention of Tradition*. Cambridge University Press, 1983.

Hoon, Paul Waitman. *The Integrity of Worship*. Nashville: Abingdon Press, 1971.

Hughes, Kathleen. "Liturgical Year: Conflict and Challenge." In *The Church Gives Thanks and Remembers*, Ed. by Lawrence J. Johnson. Collegeville: The Liturgical Press, 1984.

Hughes, Kent. "Free Church Worship: The Challenge of Freedom." In D.A. Carson, Timothy Keller, Mark Ashton, and Kent Hughes, Eds., *Worship by the Book*. Grand Rapids: Zondervan, 2002.

Irvine, Christopher. "Space." In Juliette Day and Benjamin Gordon-Taylor, eds., *The Study of Liturgy and Worship*. Collegeville: A Pueblo Book, 2013.

Irwin, Kevin. "Lex Orandi, Lex Credendi – Origins and Meaning: State of the Question." *Liturgical Ministry*, 11 (Spring 2002): 57–69.

Johnson, Todd E., ed. *The Conviction of Things Not Seen: Worship and Ministry in the 21st Century*. Grand Rapids: Brazos Press, 2002.

Jones, Ilion T. *A Historical Approach to Evangelical Worship*. New York, Nashville: Abingdon Press, 1954.

Jones, Keith G. "On Abandoning Public Worship." In Keith G. Jones, and Parush P. Parushev, eds., *Currents in Baptistic Theology of Worship Today*. Praha: IBTS, 2007.

———. *A Shared Meal and a Common Table: Some Reflections on the Lord's Supper and Baptists*. Praha: IBTS, 2004.

———, "Towards a Model of Mission for Gathering, Intentional, Convictional Koinonia." *Journal of European Baptist Studies*, vol. 4, no. 2 (January 2004): 5–13.

Jones, Paul H. "We Are *How* We Worship: Corporate Worship as a Matrix for Christian Identity Formation." *Worship*, vol. 69 no 4 (July 1995): 346–360.

Joseph, Blosser. "Ritual Revival for Playful Protestant Preaching." *Encounter*, vol. 67, no. 3 (Summer 2006): 245–272.

Julien, Heidi. "Survey Research." In Lisa M. Given, ed., *The Sage Encyclopedia of Qualitative Research Methods*. Vol. 2. Thousand Oaks: SAGE Publications, 2008.

Jung, C.G. *Psychological Types*. Princeton: Princeton University Press, 1971.

Kainova, Maria. "Russian Protestant Conversions." *East-West Church & Ministry Report*, vol. 15, no. 1 (Spring 2007): 1–3.

Kauflin, Bob. *Worship Matters: Learning Others to Encounter the Greatness of God*. Wheaton: Crossway Book, 2008.

Kavanagh, Aidan. "Liturgical Needs for Today and Tomorrow." *Worship*, vol. 43, no. 8 (Jan. 1969): 2–12.

Kay, J. Alan. *The Nature of Christian Worship*. New York: Philosophical Library, 1954.

Keifert, Patrick. "Guess Who's Coming to Worship? Worship and Evangelism." *Word & World*, vol. 9, no. 1 (Winter 1989): 46–51.

Klomp, Mirella. *The Sound of Worship*. Leuven: Peeters, 2011.

Kolarz, Walter. *Religion in the Soviet Union*. London: MacMillan, 1961.

Lathrop, Gordon W. *Holy Things: A Liturgical Theology*. Minneapolis: Fortress Press, 1993.

———. *Holy People: A Liturgical Ecclesiology*. Minneapolis: Fortress Press, 2006.

Lewis, W.O. "Report on Baptists in Poland." American Baptist Historical Society. BIM, 65–1.

Liesch, Barry. *People in the Presence of God. Models and Directions for Worship*. Grand Rapids: Zondervan Publishing Company, 1988.

Longhurst, Christine, "Worship Music: Varied Styles, A Common Goal," *Direction*, vol. 22, no. 2 (Fall, 1993): 25–30.

Lukken, Gerard. *Ritual in Abundance. Critical Reflections on the Place, Form and Identity of Christian Ritual in our Culture*. Leuven: Peeters, 2005.

Lunkin, Roman, and Anton Prokof'yev. "Molokans and Dukhobors: Living Sources of Russian Protestantism." *Religion, State & Society*, vol. 28, no. 1 (March 2000): 85–90.

MacIntyre, Alasdair. *After Virtue: A Study in Moral Theory*. 3rd ed. Notre Dame: The University of Notre Dame Press, 2007.

Macquarrie, John. *Christian Theology*. Rev. ed. London: SCM Press Ltd, 1977.

Madil, Anna, "Ethnography." In Lisa M. Given, ed., *The Sage Encyclopedia of Qualitative Research Methods*. Vol. 1. Thousand Oaks: SAGE Publications, 2008.

May, Tim. *Social Researcher. Issues, Methods and Process*, sec. ed. Philadelphia: Open University Press, 1997.

McClendon, James Wm Jr. *Doctrine, Systematic Theology*. Vol. 2. Nashville: Abingdon Press, 1994.

———. *Ethics, Systematic Theology.* Vol. 1, reprinted edition with new introduction by Curtis W. Freeman. Waco: Baylor University Press, 2002.

McGowan, Andrew B. *Ancient Christian Worship. Early Church Practices in Social, Historical, and Theological Perspective.* Grand Rapids: Baker Academic, 2014.

McKibbens, Thomas R. Jr., "Our Baptist Heritage in Worship." *Review and Expositors,* vol. LXXX, no. 1 (Winter 1983): 53–70.

McMane, Martie Source. "That They May Have Life." *Liturgy,* vol. 20 no. 2 (2005): 39–46.

McSwain, Larry L. Ed., Wm. Loyd Allen, historical consultant. *Twentieth-Century Shapers of Baptist Social Ethics.* Macon: Mercer University Press, 2008.

Merton, Thomas. "Liturgy and Spiritual Personalism." *Worship,* vol. 34, no. 9 (Oct. 1960): 494–507.

Metford, J.C.J. *The Christian Year. An Indispensable Companion to the Holy Days, Festivals and Seasons of the Ecclesiastical Year.* New York: The Crossroad Publishing Company, 1991.

Moody, Dale. *The Word of Truth: A Summary of Christian Doctrine Based on Biblical Revelation.* Grand Rapids: Eerdmans, 1981.

Morgenthaler, Sally. "Worship Evangelism: Sally Morgenthaler Rethinks Her Own Paradigm." *Rev!* (May/June 2007): 49–50.

Morrill, Bruce T. *Anamnesis as Dangerous Memory. Political and Liturgical Theology in Dialogue.* Collegeville: The Liturgical Press, 2000.

———. Ed., *Bodies of Worship. Explorations in Theory and Practice.* Collegeville, Minnesota: The Liturgical Press, 1999.

Murphy, Nancey, Brad. J. Kallenberg and Mark Thiessen Nation. *Virtues & Practices in the Christian Tradition, Christian Ethics after MacIntyre.* Harrisburg: Trinity Press International, 1997.

"Nairobi Statement on Worship and Culture." In Charles E. Farhadian, Ed., *Christian Worship Worldwide: Expanding Horizons, Deepening Practices.* Grand Rapids: Eerdmans, 2007.

Negrov, Alexander. "Hermeneutics in Transition: Three Hermeneutical Horizons of Slavic Evangelicals in the Post-Soviet Period." *Theological Reflections,* no. 4 (2004): 33–55.

Nettleton, Nathan. "Making Meaning in Worship." *Currents in Baptistic Theology of Worship Today,* edited by Keith G. Jones and Parush P. Parushev, 85–93. Praha: IBTS, 2007.

Newman, Elizabeth. "The Priesthood of All Believers and the Necessity of the Church." In Philip E. Thompson, and Anthony R. Cross, eds., *Studies in Baptist History and Thought.* Vol. 11. *Recycling the Past or Researching History? Studies in Baptist Historiography and Myth.* Milton Keynes: Paternoster, 2005.

Nichols, Gregory L. The Development of Russian Evangelical Spirituality: A Study of Ivan V. Kargel (1849–1937). Eugene: Wipf & Stock, 2011.

———. "Evangelical Spirituality and Russian Baptists." In Parush R. Parushev, Ovidiu Creanga and Brian Brock, eds., *Ethical Thinking at the Crossroads of European Reasoning*. Praha: IBTS, 2007.

———. "Ivan Kargel and the Fulfillment of Revival: The Fullness of Salvation Which Leads to Sanctification." *Baptistic Theologies*, vol. 1, no. 1 (Spring 2009): 23–39.

Niebuhr, H. Richard. *Christ and Culture*. San Francisco: Harper & Row, 1951.

Nikol'skaya, Tatiana. "Russian Protestantism at the Stage of Legalization: 1905–1917." *Theological Reflections*, no. 4 (2004): 182–201.

Noyes, Morgan Phelps. *Preaching the Word of God*. New York: Charles Scribner's Sons, 1943.

Ohlmann, Eric H. "The Essence of Baptists: A Reexamination." *Perspectives in Religious Studies*, vol. 13 (Winter 1986): 83–104.

Ong, Walter. *Orality and Literacy: The Technologizing of the Word*. London: Methuen, 1982.

Oswald, Roy M. and Otto Kroeger. *Personality Type and Religious Leadership*. New York City: The Alban Institute, 1988.

Overbeck, T. Jerome. "The Worship Environment." In Robert E. Webber, ed., *The Complete Library of Christian Worship*, vol. 4, no. 2. Nashville: Star Song Publishing Group, 1994.

Parushev, Parush R. "Gathered, Gathering, Porous: Reflections on the Nature of Baptistic Community." *Baptistic Theologies*, vol. 5, no. 1 (Spring 2013): 35–52.

———. "Marxism and Christianity." In Martin Davie, Tim Grass, Steven R. Holmes and John McDowell, eds., *New Dictionary of Theology: Historical and Systematic*, 2nd rev. ed. Nottingham, Downers Grove: Inter-Varsity Press, 2016.

———. "Mission as Established Presence and Prophetic Witness in Culturally Orthodox Contexts." In Mihai Malancea and Vladimir Ubeivolc (eds.), *Evangelical Mission in the Eastern European Orthodox Contexts: Bulgaria, Romania, Moldova and Ukraine*. Chișinău, Moldova: Universitatea Divitia Gratiae, 2013.

———. "Walking in the Dawn of the Light: on the Salvation Ethics of the Ecclesial Communities in the Orthodox Tradition from a Radical Reformation Perspective." PhD diss., the School of Theology, Fuller Theological Seminary, 2006.

Parushev, Parush R. and Toivo Pilli. "Protestantism in Eastern Europe to the Present Day." In Alister E. McGrath and Darren C. Marks (eds.), *The Blackwell's Companion to Protestantism*. Oxford: Blackwell Publishing Ltd., 2004.

Patton, Michael Quinn. *Qualitative Research & Evaluation Methods*. 3rd ed. Thousand Oaks: Sage Publications, 2002.

Peck, David G. *Living Worship*. London: Eyre and Spottiswoode, 1944.
Pecklers, Keith F. *Worship*. London: Continuum, 2003.
Perry, Michael, ed. *The Dramatised Bible*. London: Marshall Pickering/Bible Society, 1989.
Phillips, Elizabeth. "Charting the 'Ethnographic Turn': Theologians and the Study of Christian Congregations." In Pete Ward, ed., *Perspectives on Ecclesiology and Ethnography*. Grand Rapids: William B. Eerdmans, 2012.
Pickstock, Catherine. "Liturgy and Modernity." *Telos*, vol. 113 (Fall 1998): 19–41.
Pilli, Toivo. "Baptists in Estonia 1884–1940." *The Baptist Quarterly*, vol. XXXIX, no. 1 (Jan. 2001): 27–28.
———. "Evangelical Christians-Baptists of Estonia: The Shaping of Identity, 1945–1991." PhD diss., University of Wales, 2007.
Popov, Alexander. "The Evangelical Christians-Baptists in the Soviet Union as a Hermeneutical Community: Examining the Identity of the All-Union Council of the ECB (AUCECB) Through the Way the Bible was Used in its Publications." PhD diss., University of Wales, 2010.
Prokhorov, Constantine. "Baptists and the Orthodox Church." In I.M. Randall, Ed., *Baptist and the Orthodox Church. On the Way to Understanding*. Praha: IBTS, 2003.
———. "Between the West and the East: Notes on the Origin of the Evangelical Movement in Russia," *Theological Reflections*, vol. 13 (2013): 79–105.
———. "Russian Baptist and Orthodoxy, 1960–1990: A Comparative Study of Theology, Liturgy, and Traditions." PhD diss., University of Wales, 2011.
———. "The State and the Baptist Churches in the USSR (1960–1980)." In K.G. Jones and I.M. Randall, eds., *Counter-Cultural Communities. Baptist Life in Twentieth-Century Europe*, 1–62. Milton Keynes: Paternoster, 2008.
Pyzh, Yaroslav. "The Confessional Community as the Ecclesiological Core of the Baptists in the Soviet Union, 1960–1990." PhD diss., the School of Theology, Southwestern Baptist Theological Seminary, Fort Worth, 2012.
Quill, Timothy C.J. "Liturgical Worship." In J. Matthew Pinson, ed., *Perspectives on Christian Worship, 5 Views*, 18–98. Nashville: Broadman & Holman Publishers, 2009.
Randall, Ian M. *Baptist and the Orthodox Church. On the Way to Understanding*. Praha: An Occasional Publication of the IBTS, 2003.
———. *Communities of Conviction. Baptist Beginnings in Europe*. Schwarzenfeld: Neufeld Verlag, 2009.
Randall, Ian M., Toivo Pilli and Anthony R. Cross. *Baptist Identities. Studies in Baptist History and Thoughts*, vol. 27. Carlisle: Paternoster Press, 2006.
Ratliff, F. William. "The Place of the Lord's Supper in Worship: Afterthought or Central Focus?" *Review and Expositors*, vol. 80, no. 1 (Winter 1983): 85–96.

Redman, Robert R., Jr. "Welcome to the Worship Awakening." *Theology Today*, vol. 58, no. 3 (Oct. 2001): 369–383.

Redman, Robb. "Worship Wars or Worship Awakening?" *Liturgy*, vol. 19, no. 4 (2004).

Remmel, Meego. "'Wake up, my Heart, and Glorify the Creator in Singing!' Sense of Virtue in the Primary Theology of Anabaptist and Estonian Baptistic Hymnody." PhD diss., University of Wales, 2011.

Resner, André, Jr. "To Worship or To Evangelize? Ecclesiology's Phantom Fork in the Road." *Restoration Quarterly*, vol. 36, no. 2 (1994): 65–80.

Robinson, W. "The Nature and Character of Christian Sacramental Theory and Practice." *The Baptist Quarterly*, vol. 10 (1940–1941): 411–420.

Ross, Melanie. "Lefts and Rites: One Evangelical's Perspective." *Liturgy*, vol. 23, no. 1 (Jan.-March 2008): 35–40.

Rowe, Arthur J. "1 Corinthians 12–14: the Use of a Text for Christian Worship." *The Evangelical Quarterly*, vol. 77, no. 2 (2005): 119–128.

Sacrosanctum Concilium. Constitution on the Sacred Liturgy. 4 December 1963. Accessed 7 December 2016. http://www.vatican.va/archive/hist_councils/ii_vatican_council/document s/vat-ii_const_19631204_sacrosanctum-concilium_en.html.

Samaritan's Purse. *Official Website*. Accessed 26 November 2016. https://www.samaritanspurse. org.

Sandelowski, Margarete. "Qualitative research." In Michael S. Lewis-Beck, Alan Bryman, and Tim Futing Liao, eds., *The SAGE Encyclopedia of Social Science Research Methods*. Vol. 1. Thousand Oaks: SAGE Publications, 2004.

Sawatsky, Walter. "Orthodox-Evangelical Protestant Dialogue on Mission-Challenges." *Acta Missiologiae. Journal for Reflection on Missiological Issues and Mission Practice in Central Europe*, vol. 1 (2008): 11–32.

Schaff, Philip. *History of the Christian Church. Vol. 1, Apostolic Christianity*. New York: Charles Scribner's Sons, 1888.

Schattauer, Thomas H. "Liturgical Studies: Discipline, Perspectives, Teaching." *International Journal of Practical Theology*, vol. 11, iss. 1 (Aug. 2007): 106–137.

Schmemann, Alexander. *For the Life of the World*. Crestwood: St. Vladimir's Seminary Press, 1963.

———. *Introduction to Liturgical Theology*. Crestwood: St. Vladimir's Seminary Press, 1996.

———. "Liturgical Theology: Remarks on Method." In T. Fisch, ed., *Liturgy and Tradition: Theological Reflections of Alexander Schmemann*. Crestwood: St. Vladimir's Seminary Press, 1990.

———. "Worship in A Secular Age." In Alexander Schmemann, Ed., *For the Life of the World*. Crestwood: St. Vladimir's Seminary Press, 1973.

Schwandt, Thomas A. *The SAGE Dictionary of Qualitative Inquiry.* 3rd ed. Thousand Oaks: SAGE Publications, 2007.

Searle, Mark. "The Church Gives Thanks and Remembers." In *The Church Gives Thanks and Remembers,* edited by Lawrence J. Johnson, 13–36. Collegeville: The Liturgical Press, 1984.

Segler, Franklin M. *Christian Worship, Its Theology and Practice.* Nashville: Broadman Press, 1967.

Senn, Frank C. *Christian Liturgy Catholic and Evangelical.* Minneapolis: Fortress Press, 1997.

———. *Introduction to Christian Liturgy.* Minneapolis: Fortress Press, 2012.

Sevastian, Dimitru. "'Christ's Way:' Biography as Theology in the Literature of F.M. Dostoevsky." PhD dissertation, University of Wales, 2012.

Sheeley, Steven M. "Baptists and the Bible Translation: Toward a Deeper Understanding." *Baptist History and Heritage,* no. 2, vol. XLII (Spring 2007): 8–18.

Shepherd, Massey H., Jr. *The Worship of the Church.* Greenwich: Seabury Press, 1952.

Shrek, Directed by Andrew Adamson and Vicky Jenson. PDI/DreamWorks, 2001

Silverman, David. *Doing Qualitative Research.* 4th ed. Thousand Oaks: SAGE Publication, 2013.

Stamoolis, James J., ed. *Three Views on Eastern Orthodoxy and Evangelism.* Grand Rapids: Zondervan, 2004.

Stauffer, S. Anita. "Christian Worship: Towards Localization and Globalization." In *Worship and Culture in Dialogue,* edited by S. Anita Stauffer, 9–10. Geneva: Lutheran World Federation, 1994.

Stewart, J.A. *A Man in a Hurry: The Story of the Life and Work of Pastor Basil A. Malof.* Asheville: The Russian Bible Society, 1968.

Stringer, Martin D. *A Sociological History of Christian Worship.* Cambridge University Press, 2005.

———. *On the Perception of Worship. The Ethnography of Worship in Four Christian Congregations in Manchester.* Birmingham: The University of Birmingham, 1999.

Taft, Robert S.J. "'Eastern Presuppositions' and Western Liturgical Renewal." Accessed 30 January 2011. https://www.archeparchy.ca/wcm-docs/docs/Taft_Eastern_Presuppositions.pdf.

Tedlock, Barbara. "Ethnography and Ethnographic Representation." In Norman K. Denzin, and Yvonna S. Lincoln, eds., *Handbook of Qualitative Research.* 2nd ed., 455–486. Thousand Oaks: SAGE Publications, 2000.

Thompson, Philip E. "Re-Envisioning Baptist Identity: Historical, Theological, and Liturgical Analysis." *Perspectives in Religious Studies,* vol. 27, no. 3 (Fall 2000): 287–303.

Underhill, Evelyn. *Worship*. New York: Harper&Row, 1936.
Verdi, Giuseppe. "Nebuchadnezzar." 1841.
Vischer, Lukas. "Worship as Christian Witness to Society." In *Christian Worship in Reformed Churches: Past and Present*, edited by Lukas Vischer, 415–442. Grand Rapids: Eerdmans, 2003.
Wainwright, Geoffrey. *Doxology: The Praise of God in Worship, Doctrine and Life*. London: Epworth Press, 1980.
———. "Renewing Worship: The Recovery of Classical Patterns." *Theology Today*, vol. 48, no. 1 (Apr. 1991): 45–55.
Ward, Pete, ed. *Perspectives on Ecclesiology and Ethnography*. Grand Rapids: William B. Eerdmans Publishing Company, 2012.
Wardin, Albert W. Jr, "How Indigenous Was the Baptist Movement in the Russian Empire," *Journal of European Baptist Studies*, vol. 9, no. 2 (Jan. 2009): 29–37.
Warren, Rick. *Purpose Driven Church: Growth Without Compromising Your Message and Mission*. Grand Rapids: Zondervan, 1995.
Watts, Isaac. "A Guide to Prayer; or a Free and Rational Account of the Grace and Spirit of Prayer with Plain Directions How Every Christian may Attain Them." In *The Works of the Reverend and Learned Isaac Watts, D.D.*, edited by J. Doddridge, 105–196. London: J. Barfield, 1715.
Webber, Robert E. *Ancient-Future Time: Forming Spirituality Through the Christian Year*. Grand Rapids: Baker Books, 2004.
———. "An Evangelical and Catholic Methodology." Ch. 8 in *The Use of the Bible in Theology: Evangelical Options*, edited by Robert K. Johnston. Atlanta: John Knox, 1985. Accessed 26 January 2011. https://www.religion-online.org/article/an-evangelical-and-catholic-methodology/.
———. *Worship Old & New: A Biblical, Historical, and Practical Introduction*. Rev. ed. Grand Rapids: Zondervan, 1994.
White, James F. "A Protestant Worship Manifesto." *The Christian Century*, vol. 27 (Jan. 1982): 82–86.
———. "Worship and Culture: Mirror or Beacon?" *Theological Studies*, vol. 35, no. 2 (Jan. 1974): 288–301.
———. *Protestant Worship: Traditions in Transition*. Lousville: Westminster/John Knox Press, 1989.
White, James F. and Susan J. White. *Church Architecture. Building and Renovating for Christian Worship*. Nashville: Abingdon Press, 1988.
White, Susan J. *Groundwork of Christian Worship*. Peterborough: Epworth Press, 2000.
Whitley, W.T., ed. *The Works of John Smyth*. Vol. 1. Cambridge: Cambridge University Press, 1915.
Wieczynski, Joseph L. "Religion and Culture in Early Russia and Ukraine." *The Catholic Historical Review*, vol. 85, no. 1 (Jan. 1999): 77–79.

Wierzchowski, Zbigniew. "Between the Wars: Golden Years for Polish Baptists." *Baptistic Theologies*, vol. 1, no. 1 (Spring 2009): 86–101.

Winward, S.F. *The Reformation of Our Worship*. London: The Carey Kingsgate Press, 1964.

Witvliet, John D. *Worship Seeking Understanding*. Grand Rapids: Baker Academic, 2003.

"Word of Grace" Church. Official Website. Accessed 1 January 2017. http://www.slovo.org.

World Communion of Reformed Churches. "Worshiping the Triune God: Receiving and Sharing Christian Wisdom Across Continents and Centuries." Accessed 7 August 2015. http://worsh ip.calvin.edu/resources/r esource-library/worshiping-the-triune-god-receiving-and-sharing-christian-wisdom-across-continents-and-centuries/.

Yates, Nigel. Liturgical Space. *Christian Worship and Church Buildings in Western Europe 1500–2000*. Hampshire: Ashgate Publishing, 2008

Zumr, Jozef. "Slavophilism." *Routledge Encyclopedia of Philosophy*. Vol. 8, edited by Edward Craig, 807–813. London: Routledge, 1998.

Russian, Belarusian, Ukrainian, and Polish

Adamovich, Georgiy. "Poteryanny Khristos" [Lost Christ]. *Krynitsa Zhyttsya* [The Source of Life], no. 1 (1995): 43–46.

A., I.K. "Evangel'skaya pesn'" [Evangelic Song]. *Utrennyaa Zvezda* [The Morning Star], no. 3–5 (1922): 15–16.

Akentiev, Vadim. *Operatsiya na serdtse ili kak yevangel'skiy Khristianin-baptist pereshel v Pravoslavnuyu Tserkov'* [Heart Surgery or How an Evangelical Christians-Baptist Converted to the Orthodox Church]. Kemerovo, 2004.

Akinchyts, Stanislav. ". . . Kab dlya nashaga naroda byla vydadzena Svyataya kniga" [. . . So that the Holy Book Would be Given to Our People]. *Krynitsa Zhyttsya*, no. 6 (2008): 14–16.

Alexandrenko, N.A. *Gomiletika* [Homiletics]. Odessa: Bogomyslie, 1997.

Alexeeva, L.M. *Istoriya inakomysliya v SSSR. Noveishy Period* [History of Heterodoxy in the USSR. The Newest Period]. Vilnius: "Vest'," 1992.

Archive. Church ECB in Lesovnia, Soligorsk district, Minsk region.

Arhiwum Akt Nowych w Warszawie. – Ministerstwo Wyznań Religijnych i Oświecenia Publicznego. Referat wyznań ewangielickich. – Sygn. 1455, l. 215. Archives of Modern Records in Warsaw. Ministry of Religious Affairs and Public Education. Department of Evangelical Churches.]– Sygn. 1455, l. 215.

Balikhin, F.P. "Moya poezdka zagranitsu" [My Trip Abroad]. *Baptist*, no. 1 (1907): 13–20.

Baltrushevich, Natallya. "Uzajemadačynienni dziaržavy i pratestanckich cerkvau u BSSR u 1965-1985 hh." [Mutual Relations of Protestant Churches in the Byelorussian SSR in 1965-1985]. In *Jevanhielskaya tsarkva Bielarusi: gistoryya i suchasnasc'. Vypusk II: (*da 500-hoddzia Mikalaja Radzivila Chornaha): zbornik materyjalaŭ II Mizhnarodnaj navukova-praktychnaj kanfierentsyi (Minsk, 5 sniezhnia 2015 h.*)* [Evangelical Church of Belarus: History and the Present. Issue II: (for the 500th anniversary of Nikolai Radziwill the Black): A Collection of Materials and the International Scientific-Practical Conference (Minsk, 5 December 2015), 220-237. Minsk: Pazityu-tsentr, 2016.

Baptist [Baptist], no. 3, 9 (1927), no. 17 (1909).

Baptist Ukrainy [Baptist of Ukraine], no. 11 (1928).

Barsov, N.I. *Istoriya pervobytnoy khristianskoy propovedi do IV veka* [The History of Primitive Christian Preaching to the IV Century]. Moskva: "Librokom," 2012.

Barth, Karl. *Molitva* [*Prayer*]. Moskva: Bibleysko-Bogoslovskiy Institut sv. Apostola Andreya, 2010.

Bednarczyk, Krzysztof. *Historiya Zborow Baptystow w Polsce do 1939 roku*. [History of Belarusian Churches in Poland Until 1939]. Warszawa: "Slowo Prawdy," 1997.

Belousov, A.S. "Gospod' sila moya i pesn'" [The Lord My Power and Song]. *Bratskiy Vestnik* [Fraternal Messenger], no. 2 (Moskva: VSEKhB, 1966): 74-78.

Belov, A.V. *Sekty, sektantstvo, sektanty* [Sects, Sectarianism, and Sectarians]. Moskva: "Nauka," 1978.

Belyakova, N.A. and M. Dobson. *Zhenshchiny v yevangel'skikh obshchinakh poslevoyennogo SSSR. 1940-1980-ye gg. Issledovaniye i istochniki* [Women in the Evangelical Communities of the Post-War USSR (1940s-1980s). Documents and Analysis] Moskva: "Indrik," 2015.

Berdyaev, N.A. *Sochineniya* [Essays]. Moskva: Raritet, 1994.

"Bethlehem" Church in Minsk. Official Website. Accessed 9 March 2017. http://iisus.by/otserkvi /история.

Bezbozhnik [Atheist], vols. 1-24 (1928).

Bibliya. Knigi Svyashchennogo Pisaniya Vetkhogo i Novogo Zaveta. Kanonicheskiye [The Bible. The Books of the Holy Scriptures of the Old and New Testament. Canonical]. Moskva: Rossiiskoye bibleyskoye obshchestvo, 2000.

Bokova, Olga A. "Bibleiskaia Ekzegetika i Germenevtika Sovremennikh Evangelskikh Khristian – Baptistov: Traditsii i Novatsii" [Biblical Exegetics and Hermeneutics of Contemporary Evangelical Christians-Baptists: Traditions and New Trends]. *Vestnik Leningradskogo Gosudarstvennogo Universiteta im. A. S. Pushkina* [Messenger of Leningrad State University], Issue 2, Vol. 2. St. Petersburg (2013): 216-226.

Bokun, A.I., ed. *Lukaš Dzekuts'-Maley i Bialaruskiya piaraklady Biblii* [Lukash Dzekuts-Maley and Belarusian Translations of the Bible]. Brest: "Al'ternatyva," 2011.

———. *Yevanhielskaya tsarkva Bielarusi: gistoryya i suchasnasc'* (da 600-hoddzia Yevanhielskai Tsarkvy ŭ Bielarusi): zbornik materyjalaŭ Mizhnarodnaj navukova-praktychnaj kanfierencyi (Minsk, 7 sniezhnia 2013 h.) [Evangelical Church of Belarus: History and the Present (the 600th Anniversary of the Evangelical Church in Belarus): The Collection of Materials of the International Scientific-Practical Conference (Minsk, 7 December 2013). Minsk: Pazityu-tsentr, 2014.

———. *Yevanhielskaya tsarkva Bielarusi: gistoryya i suchasnasc'. Vypusk II:* (da 500-hoddzia Mikalaja Radzivila Chornaha): zbornik materyjalaŭ II Mizhnarodnaj navukova-praktychnaj kanfierentsyi (Minsk, 5 sniezhnia 2015 h.) [Evangelical Church of Belarus: History and the Present. Issue II: (for the 500th anniversary of Nikolai Radziwill the Black): A Collection of Materials of the International Scientific-Practical Conference (Minsk, 5 December 2015). Minsk: Pazityu-tsentr, 2016.

———. Yevanhielskaya tsarkva Bielarusi: gistoryya i suchasnasc'. Vypusk III: (da 500-hoddzia Refarmatsyi i 500-hoddzia belaruskay Biblii): zbornik materyjalaŭ III Mizhnarodnaj navukova-praktychnaj kanfierentsyi (Minsk, 9 sniezhnia 2017 h.) [Evangelical Church of Belarus: History and the Present. Issue III: (for the 500th Anniversary of Reformation and the 500th Anniversary of Belarusian Bible): a Collection of Materials of the International Scientific-Practical Conference (Minsk, 9 December 2017). Minsk: Pazityu-tsentr, 2018.

———. "Gistoryya pierakladu Biblii na belaruskuyu movu" [The History of Bible Translation into the Belarusian Language], in *Lukaš Dziekuć-Maliej i bielaruskiya pieraklady Biblii. Zbornik materyjalau, artykulaý i dakumientau* [Lukash Dzekuts Malei and Belarusian Translations of the Bible. Collection of Materials, Articles and Documents]. Brest: "Al'ternatyva," 2011.

Bol'shaya sovetskaya entsyklipedia [Big Soviet Encyclopedia]. Vol. 3. Moskva: Sovetskaya entsyklopedia, 1970.

Bol'shaya entsyklopedia v 66 tomah [Big Encyclopedia in 66 vols]. Vol. 5. Moskva: "Terra," 2006.

Bonch-Bruevich, V.D. *Iz mira sektantov* [From the World of Sectarians]. Moskva: Gosudarstvennoe izdatel'stvo, 1922.

Bondarenko, I. *Tri prigovora* [Three Verdicts]. Odessa: "Khristianskoe prosveshchenie," 2006.

Borisov, Alexander. *Pobelevshie nivy. Razmyshleniya o Russkoi Pravoslavnoi Tserkvi* [Whitened Fields. Reflections on the Russian Orthodox Church]. Moskva: "Put'," 1994.

Bortkovskiy, N. "Shtundobaptizm" [Stundobaptists]. In *Russkiye sektanty, ih uchenie, kul't i sposoby propogandy* [Russian Sectarians: Their Teaching, Cult and Propaganda Techniques], edited by M. A. Kal'nev, 117–128. Odessa: Y. I. Fesenko's Printing Office, 1911.

Brother Andrew. *God's Smuggler*. London: Hodder & Stoughton, 2008.

Bulgakov, Sergei. *Pravoslavie* [Orthodoxy]. Moscow: ACT, 2003.

Cathedral of Intercession of the Most Holy Theotokos in Minsk. Official Website. http://pokrovhram.by/index.php?id=7. Accessed 7 March 2017.

Cherenkov, M.M. *Évropeys'ka reformatsiya ta ukrains'kyy évanhel's'kyy protestantyzm: Henetyko-typolohichna sporidnenist' i natsional'no-identyfikatsiyni vymiry suchasnosti* [European Reformation and Ukrainian Evangelical Protestantism: Genetic-Typological Affinity and Contemporary National Identification Dimensions]. Odessa: "Khrystiyanska Prosvita," 2008.

———. *Litsom k litsu. Yevangel'skaya vera v sovremennoy kul'ture sektantov* [Face to Face. Evangelical Faith in Contemporary Culture]. Odessa: "Khristianskoye prosveshcheniye," 2008.

———. "Yevangel'skaya vera v postateisticheskikh soobshchestvakh. Khristianskoye soobshchestvo Rossii: kriticheskiy samoanaliz na fone dukhovnoy situatsii vremeni" [Evangelical Belief in Post Atheistic Communities. The Christian Community in Russia: a Critical Self-Analysis with the Background of Spiritual Situation of the Time], in *Materialy kruglogo stola* [Roundtable Materials], 13–17. Moskva: Assotsiatsiya "Dukhovnoye vozrozhdeniye," 2007.

Chernov, A.S. "Fenomen Rossiyskoy kontrkul'tury na primere natsional'nogo samosoznaniya dukhovnykh khristian-molokan" [Phenomenon of Russian Counter-Culture of the Example of National Self-Consciousness of Spiritual Christians-Molokans]. *Vestnik TGU* [TGU Herald], no. 9 (89) (2010): 229–233.

———, "Inoskazaniye kak kharakternaya osobennost' ucheniya dukhovnykh khristian-molokan" [Circumlocution as Feature of Study of Spiritual Christians-Molokans]. *Vestnik TGU* [TGU Herald], no 6 (110) (2012): 282–288.

Chistovich, I.A. *Istoriya perevoda Biblii na russkiy yazyk* [History of Translating the Bible into the Russian Language]. Moskva: Rossiiskoye bibleyskoye obshchestvo, 1997.

Colligan, J. Hay. "White Russia – A Visitor's Impression." *The Times* (7 September, 1926). In Guy Picarda, *Nyabesnae polymya. Pratestantskaya tsarkva i belaruski natsyyanal'ny rukh na pachatku XX stagoddzya* [The Heavenly Fire. The Protestant Church and Belarusian National Movement in the Beginning of the 20th Century]. Minsk: Knigazbor, 2006: 12–44.

Corrado, Sharyl. *Filosofiya sluzheniya polkovnika Pashkova* [The Philosophy of Ministry of Colonel Vasiliy Pashkov]. Sanct-Peterburg: "Bibliya dlya vsekh," 2005. Originally published as "The Philosophy of Ministry of Colonel Vasiliy Pashkov." MA Thesis, Wheaton College, 2000.

Dal', V.I. *Tolkovyy slovar' zhivogo velikorusskogo yazyka v chetyrekh tomakh* [Explanatory Dictionary of the Russian Language in Four Volumes], edited by I.A. Boduen. Vol. 2. Moskva: Tsitadel', 1998.

Deklamatsiya – trud tozhe otvetstvennyy" [Recitation Is Also an Important Ministry]. *Vestnik Istiny* [Herald of Truth], *Spiritually-Edifying Journal of the CCECB*, no. 3 (2003): 48–50.

Dever, Mark and Paul Alexander. *Produmannoye sozidaniye tserkvi: sluzheniye, osnovannoye na Evangelii* [Thoughtful Building of the Church: A Ministry Based on the Gospel]. Minsk: "Printcorp"/Slavyanskoye evangel'skoye obshchestvo, 2009. Originally published as *The Deliberate Church: Building Your Ministry on the Gospel*. Wheaton: Crossway Books, 2005.

"Doklad P.V. Ivanova-Klyshnikova na 4-m Vsemirnom Kongresse Baptistov 25 iyunya 1928 g. Toronto, Canada" [P.V. Ivanov-Klyshnikov Report on the 4th World Baptist Congress, June, 25, 1928, Toronto, Canada]. In Leonid Kovalenko, *Oblako svidetelei Khristovyh* [A Cloud of Witnesses of Christ]. Kiev: Centr Khrisianskogo Sotrudnichestva, 1997: 297–300.

Dostoevsky, F.M. *Dnevnik Pisatelya, 1873* [Writer's Diary, 1873], collected works in 15 vols. Vol. 12. Sanct-Peterburg: "Nauka," 1992.

Dyck, Johannes. "Stanovleniye evangel'skogo baptistskogo bratstva v Rossii (1860–1887)" [Formation of Evangelical Baptist Brotherhood in Russia (1860–1887). In conference materials of *140 let rossijskomu baptismu. Proshloe, nastoyashchee, perspektivy* [140th Anniversary of Russia's Baptists. Past, Present and Prospects], 5. Moskva, October 19–20, 2007.

Ellis, Geoffry H. and L. Wesley Jones. *Drugaya revolyutsiya. Rossiyskoye yevangelicheskoye probuzhdeniye* [The Other Revolution. Russian Evangelical Revival]. Sanct-Peterburg: Vita International, 1999. Originally published as *The Other Revolution: Russian Evangelical Awakenings*. Abilene: ACU. Press, 1996.

Ermakov, P.E. "Biographiya brata L.D. Prymachenko" [Biography of brother L.D. Prymachenko]. *Baptist*, no. 3 (1927): 26–27.

Fedorenko, F. *Secty, ikh vera i dela* [Sects, Their Faith and Acts]. Moskva: Political Literature Publisher, 1965.

Firisiuk, Alexander. *Radost' seyaniya so slezami* [The Joy of Sowing with Tears]. Minsk: Union of Evangelical Christians of Baptists in the Republic of Belarus, 2017.

Florovskiy, Georgiy. *Puti russkogo bogosloviya* [Ways of Russian Theology]. Paris: YMCAPress, 1937.

Fountain, David. *Lord Radstok i dukhovnoye probuzhdeniye v Rossii* [Lord Radstock and a Spiritual Awakening in Russia]. Odessa: Alfom, 2001. Originally published as *Lord Radstock and the Russian Awakening*. Revival Literature, 1988.

Gardzienka, A. *Religiynaya apazitsyya na Belaruskim Pales'si u 1960–1980-ya gady*. Zagaroddze-3. Materyyaly navukova-krayaznauchay kanferentsyi "Palesse u XX stagoddzi" [Religious opposition in Belarusian Polesie in 1960–80-ies. Zagaroddze-3. Proceedings of Regional Research Conference "Polesie in the twentieth century"]. Minsk, 2001.

Garkavenko, F.I. *Khristianskoe sektantstvo v SSSR. Avtoreferat dissertatsii na soiskanie uchenoi stepeni kandidata philosophskikh nauk* [Christian Sectarianism in the USSR. Abstract of Dissertation for the Degree of Candidate of Philosophical Sciences]. Moskva: Institut narodnogo khozyaistva im. G.V. Plekhanova, 1964.

Geychenko, A. "Neobkhodimost' propovedi Yevangeliya s tochki zreniya sovremennogo evangel'skogo bogosloviya" [The Need for the Preaching of the Gospel in Terms of Contemporary Evangelical Theology]. In *Bogosloviye v evangelizme* [Theology in Evangelism]. Zaporozhie: Piligrim (2007): 79–96.

Gistoryia Bielarusi [History of Belarus]. Vol. 6. Minsk: Sovremennaya shkola, Ekoperspektiva, 2011.

Gladky, A.L. and A.I. Firisiuk. "80 let razluk i vstrech" [80 years of Partings and Meetings]. *Krynitsa Zhyttsya*, no. 2 (2007): 18–21.

Glan, Y. *Antireligioznaya literatura za 12 let (1917–1929)* [Anti-Religious Literature for 12 years (1917–1929)]. Moskva: "Bezbozhnik," 1930.

Gnida, I.S. "Poryadok provedeniya bogosluzhenii v tserkvakh evangel'skikh khristian-baptistov" [The Order of Worship in the Churches of Evangelical Christians-Baptists]. *Bratskiy Vestnik*, no. 4 (1988): 71–80.

Golodetsky, L. "Kakim byt' domu molitvy" [What Should the House of Prayer Be Like]. *Bogomyslie* [Contemplation of God], no.1 (1990): 263–266.

Golst, G.R. *Religiya i zakon* [Religion and Law]. Moskva: "Yuridicheskaya literatura," 1975.

Goncharenko, Y.S. "Izdanie sbornikov dukhovnykh pesen v kontekste razvitiya dukhovnoi muzyki evangel'skikh khristian-baptistov Rossii" [The Publication of Collections of Spiritual Songs in the Context of Development of Sprirtual Music of Evangelical Christians-Baptists of Russia]. In conference materials of *140 let rossiiskomu baptism. Proshloe, nastoyashchee, perspectivy* [140 anniversary of Russian Baptists. Past, Present and Prospects], Москва, October, 19–20, 2007.

———. *Muzyka i dukhovnoe vozrastanie tserkvi* [Music and the Spiritual Growth of the Church] (Moskva: Logos, 2002), p. 4.

Goricheva, Tatiana. "Freid i "homo liturgikas"" [Freud and the 'Homo Liturgikas']. *Foma* [Thomas], (Feb. 2010): 74–77.

Gorkiy, M. *O religii* [On Religion]. Moskva: Gosudarstvennyy anti-religioznyy izdatel'skiyt dom, 1941.

Greshnitsa [Sinner], directed by F. Philippov. Mosfilm, 1962.

Grygor'eva, V.V., V.M. Zavalniuk, U.I. Navitski and A.M. Filatava. *Kanfesii na Belarusi (kanets XVIII–XX st.)* [Confessions in Belarus (the end of XVIII–XX centuries)]. Minsk: VP "Ekaperspektyva," 1998.

Gutsul, Ivan. "Khristianskaya simvolika v sakral'noi arkhitekture protestantov Ukrainy – visual'noe vyrazheniye dukhovnosti veruyushchikh" [Christian Symbolism in Protestant Sacred Architecture in Ukraine – The Visual Expression of the Spirituality of Believers]. *Bogomyslie* [Contemplation of God], no. 17 (2016): 327–345.

———. "Molitvennyy dom – sakral'nyy khram ili mnogofunktsional'nyy kompleks?" [Is the House of Prayer a Sacral Temple or a Multifunctional Complex?]. *Bogomyslie* [Contemplation of God], no.19 (2016): 73–95.

Hunt, Dave. *V Rossiyu s lyubov'yu* [To Russia With Love]. Dukhovnoe vozrozhdenie, 2014

Hury, N. *Kościół Chrystusowy w RP. 90 lat w skrócie* [Church of Christ in RP. 90 years in short]. Warszawa: Chrześcijański Instytut Biblijny, 2012.

Hymn SSSR. Accessed 17 January 2015. https://ru.wikipedia.org/wiki/Гимн_СССР.

Ignatenko, L.M. *Osobennosti psikhologii baptistov*. Avtoreferat dissertatsii na soiskanie uchenoi stepeni kandidata philosophskikh nauk [Peculiarities of Baptist Psychology. Abstract of Dissertation for the Degree of Candidate of Philosophical Sciences]. Minsk: Akademiya nauk, 1968.

"Instruktivnoe pis'mo Soveta po delam religioznyh kul'tov" [Letter of Instruction of the Council for the Affairs of Religious Cults]. The Website of the Russian Association of Researchers of Religion. Accessed 31 March 2011. http://www.rusoir.ru/president/works/214/.

"Instruktivnoe pis'mo starshim presviteram VSEKhB" [Letter of Instruction to AUCECB Senior Pastors]. Accessed 2 December 2016. http://baptistru.info/index.php?title=Инструктивное_пись мо_и_Положение_ВСЕХБ.

International Union of Churches of ECB. Accessed 16 July 2014. http://dic.academic.ru/dic.nsf/r uwiki/1133416.

Istoriya evangel'skikh khristjan-baptistov v SSSR [History of Evangelical Christians-Baptists in the USSR]. Moskva: Izdanije Vsesoyuznogo soveta evangel'skikh khristian-baptistov, 1989.

Istoriya Evangel'skogo dvizheniya v Evrazii [History of the Evangelical Movement in Eurasia], Primary sources, CD-ROM, 1.1. Euro-Asian Accrediting Assosiation, 2001.

---. CD-ROM, 2.0. EAAA, 2002.

---. CD-ROM, 3.0 EAAA, 2003.

---. CD-ROM, 4.0 EAAA, 2005.

Ivanov, M.V. *Dukhovnost' evangel'skikh Khristian-baptistov* [Spirituality of Evangelical Baptist Christians]. Moscow: *Dukhovnost' evangel'skikh Khristian baptistov* [Spirituality of Evangelical Christians-Baptists]. Moskva: Rossiisky soyuz evangel'skikh khristian-baptistov, 2010.

Ivanov, V. "Obshchiny i presvitery" [Communities and Pastors]. *Baptist*, no. 21–24 (1914).

K., B. "O muzyke i penii" [On Music and Singing]. *Bratskiy Vestnik*, no. 1 (1977): 69.

Kahle, Wilhelm. *Evangel'skie khristiane v Rossii i Sovetskom Soyuze* [Evangelical Christians in Russia and the Soviet Union]. Wuppertal: Oncken-Verlag, 1978.

Kalinicheva, Z.V. *Social'naya sushchnost' baptisma* [Social Essence of Baptists]. Leningrad: "Nauka," 1972.

Kanatush, Pavel. "Svidetelstvo o pape" [Testimony about My Dad]. *Krynitsa Zhyttsya*, no. 6 (2010): 24–26.

Kanatush, V.Y. "Istoriya evangel'skogo dvizheniya v Belarusi" [The History of Evangelical Movement in Belarus]. *Krynitsa Zhyttsya*, no. 2 (1998): 24–32.

---. "Istoriya evangel'skogo dvizheniya v Belarusi" [The History of Evangelical Movement in Belarus]. *Krynitsa Zhyttsya*, no. 4 (1998): 16–20.

---. *Taina Apokalipsisa* [The Mystery of the Apocalypse]. Minsk: "Probuzhdenie," 1993."

Kantor, Vladimir. "Impersky kontekst russkogo pravoslaviya" [The Imperial Context of Russian Orthodoxy], *Vtoraya navigatsiya* [Second Navigation]. Zaporozh'e: Dikoe pole (2006): 35–56.

Karetnikova, M.S. "Ivan Veniaminovich Kargel'" [Ivan Veniaminovich Kargel]. In I.V. Kargel', *Sobraniye sochineniy* [Collection of Works]. Sanct-Peterburg: "Bibliya dlya vsekh" (2000): 684–688.

Karev, A.V. "Russkoe evangel'sko-baptistskoe dvizhenie" [Russian Evangelical Baptist Movement]. In *Al'manakh po istorii russkogo baptizma* [Almanac on the History of Russian Baptists], edited by M.S. Karetnikova, 85–186. Sanct-Peterburg: "Bibliya dlya vsekh," 1997.

---. "Slovo Bozhie" [The Word of God]. *Bratskiy Vestnik*, no. 2 (1964): 6–16.

---. "Svyashchennodeistviya tserkvi" [Sacred Rites of the Church]. *Bratskiy Vestnik*, no. 1 (1963): 36–48.

---. "Zloupotrebleniya otlucheniyami" [Abuse of Excommunications]. *Bratskiy Vestnik*, no. 1 (1971): 66–69.

Kargel', I.V. *Sobraniye sochineniy* [Collected Works]. Sanct-Peterburg: "Bibliya dlya vsekh," 2000.

Kasataya, T.U. "Evangel'skiya khrystsiyane-baptysty u BSSR u 1944 – pachatku 1950-kh gg." [Evangelical Christian Baptists in USSR in 1944- The Beginning of 1950s]. *Arche*, no. 1–2 (2012): 138–150.

———. "Samvydat evangel'skikh khrysstiyan-baptystau u BSSR" [Samizdat of Evangelical Christian Baptists in the Byelorussian SSR]. *Arche*, no. 3 (2017): 190–212.

———. "Sud nad baptystami': savetskiya kinastuzhki yak metad barats'by suprats' yevangel'skikh khrystsiyan baptystau u BSSR" [The Baptists' Trial: Soviet Movies as a Method of Fighting Against Evangelical Christian Baptists in BSSR]. In Bokun, ed., *Yevanhielskaya tsarkva Bielarusi: gistoryya i suchasnasc'. Vypusk II*, pp. 240–251.

Kharlov, L.I. "Iz istorii muzikal'no-pevcheskogo sluzheniya nashego bratstva" [From the History of Music and Singing Ministry of Our Brotherhood]. *Bratskiy Vestnik*, no. 6 (1981): 46–52.

Khaytun, D. and P. Kapayevich. *Suchasnaye sektantstva na Belarusi* [Modern Sectarianism in Belarus]. Minsk: Belaruskaye dzyarzhaunaye vydavetstva, 1929.

Kholm, Vardo. "Poyte Gospodu" [Sing to the Lord]. *Bratskiy Vestnik*, no. 1 (1957): 28–32.

Khrapov, N. *Dom Bozhii i sluzhenie v nem. Prakticheskoe posobie dlya sluzhiteley tserkvi. Pererabotannoe izdanie* [The House of God and the Ministry There. Practical guide for Ministers. Revised Edition]. Souz tserkvei evangel'skikh khristian-baptistov, 2003. Accessed 2 December 2016. http://www.blagovestnik.org/books/00280.htm#40.

Klimenko, A.E. "Materialy Plenuma AUCECB, Iyun' 1981 Goda" [Materials of a Plenum of the AUCECB, June 1981]. *Bratskiy Vestnik*, no. 5 (1981): 52–66.

Klopot, Vladimir. "Bozh'e voditelstvo" [God's Guidance]. *Gost'* [Guest], no 5–6 (2014): 14–16.

Kolesnichenko, Leonid. "Gomel'skoi tserkvi 100 let" [100 Anniversary of the Gomel Chucrh]. *Krynitsa Zhittsya*, no. 3 (2007): 8.

Kolesnikov, N.A. *Khristianin! Znaesh li ty kak dolzhno postupat' v dome Bozhiem?* [Christian! Do You Know How to Act in the House of God?]. Moskva: "Druzhba i blagaya vest'," 1998.

Komisarenko, V.I. "Osobennosti blagovestiya v russkoy kul'ture" [Special Characteristics of Evangelism in Russian Culture]. *Bogomyslie* [Contemplation of God], no. 10 (2004): 60–87.

Konzevenko, Ol'ga. *Istoriya EKhB v Mogileve* [ECB History in Mogilev]. Minsk: Minsk Theological Seminary, 2002, Unpublished.

Koryakov, U.B. "Yazykovaya situatsiya v Belorussii i tipologiya yazykovykh situatsiy. Dissertatsiya na soiskaniye uchenoy stepeni kandidata philosophskikh nauk" [Language Situation in Belarus and the Typology of

Language Situations. Thesis for the Degree of Candidate of Philosophical Sciences]. Moskva: Moskovskiy Gosudarstvennyy Universitet im. M.V. Lomonosova, 2002. Unpublished.

Kovalenko, Leonid. *Oblako svidetelei Khristovykh* [A Cloud of Witnesses of Christ]. Kiev: Centr Khrisianskogo Sotrudnichestva, 1997.

Krapivin, M.Y. *Nepridumannaya tserkovnaya istoriya: vlast' i tserkov' v Sovetskoy Rossii (oktyabr' 1917-go – konets 1930-kh godov)* [True Church History: Power and the Church in Soviet Russia (October 1917–Late 1930s)]. Volgograd: Peremena, 1997.

Krasovitskaya, M.S. *Liturgica* [Liturgics]. Moskva: Pravoslavnyy Svyato-Tikhonovskiy Bogoslovskiy Institut, 1999.

Kreshchuk, Oleksandr. "Faktory natkhnennya tserkovnoyi muzyky. Dopovid na 4-y Pastorskiy konferentsiyi, 2009 r., Kyyev" [Factors of Inspiration in Church Music. Report on the 4th Pastoral Conference, 2009, Kiev]. Accessed 20 June 2011. http://ecbua.info/index.php?option=co m_content&task=view&id=118 2&Itemid=62.

Kreyman, V. "Nekotorye voprosy dukhovnogo muzykal'nogo tvorchestva" [Some Issues in Sacred Musical Creativity]. *Bratskiy Vestnik*, no. 4 (1980): 57–61.

Kruedener, Yulia and Anna Lion. *Evangelist. Zhizn' i sluzhenie Ivana Onishchenko* [An Evangelist: The Life and Ministry of Ivan Onishchenko]. Accessed 15 August 2014. http://www. blagovestnik.org/books/00092.htm.

Kuraev, Andrei. *Protestantam o pravoslavii. Nasledie Khrista* [To Protestants on Orthodoxy. Legacy of Christ]. Klin: "Khristianskaya zhizn," 2006.

Latyshonak, A. and Y. Miranovich. *Gistoryya Belarusi ad syaredziny XVIII st. da pachatku XXI st* [History of Belarus from the Middle of the 17th Century to the Beginning of the 21st Century]. Smalensk: "Inbelkult," 2013.

The Law of the Byelorussian SSR from 14.11.1939. Accessed 26 January 2017. https://ru.wikiso urce.org/wiki/Закон_БССР_от_14.11.1939_Западная_Белоруссия.

Leahu, Victor. "K voprosu o vzaimodeistvii teologii bogosluzheniya i teologii kul'tury v liturgicheskom opyte neoprotestantisma" [On the Interaction of Theology of Liturgy and Theology of Culture in the Liturgical Experience of Neoprotestantism], in *Bogoslovie i bogoslovskoe obrazovanie v sovremennom obshchestve. Material konferencii Bogoslovskogo obshchestva Evrazii* [Theology and Theological Education in Modern Society. Conference Material of the Theological Society of Eurasia]. Odessa: Euro-Asian Accrediting Assosiation, 2002: 44–69.

Lensu, M.Y. and E.S. Prokshina, eds. *Baptizm i baptisty* (Sotsiologicheskiy ocherk) [Baptism and Baptists (Sociological Essay)]. Minsk: "Nauka i tekhnika," 1969.

Leshchuk, I. *Labirinty dukhovnosti* [Labyrinths of Spirituality]. Cherkassy: "Smirna," 2008.

Leskov, N.S. *Zerkalo zhizni* [The Mirror of Life]. Sanct-Peterburg: "Bibliya dlya vsekh," 1999.

Levindanto, Nikolai. "Blagochinie pomestnyh tserkvey ili tserkovnaya distsiplina" [Godliness of Local Churches or Church Discipline]. *Bratskiy Vestnik*, no. 3–4 (1955): 10–24.

Lewis, C.S. "Khristianstvo i kul'tura" [Christianity and Culture], in *Sobraniye sochineniy v 8 tomakh* [Collection of Works in 8 Volumes], edited by C.S. Lewis, vol. 2, 249–257. Moskva: Vinograd, 1998.

"Light of Gospel" Church in Minsk. Official Website. Accessed 9 March 2017. http://www.glchu rch.by.

Linkevich, V.N. *Mezhkonfessional'nye Otnoshenia v Belarusi (1861 – 1914gg.)* [Interdenominational Relationships in Belarus *(1861 – 1914)*. Grodno: Grodnenskiy gosudarstvennyy universitet im. Y. Kupaly, 2008.

———. "Novyye techeniya protestantizma v Belorussii vo II pol. XIX – nach. XX vv." [New Movements of Protestantism in Belarus in the Second Half of the 19th – Beginning of the 20th Centuries], *Novaya ekonomika* [New Economy], no. 1 (67) (2016): 198–205.

Lisovskaya, T.V. "Deyatel'nost' protestantskih obshchin i organizatsiy v Zapadnoy Belarusi v 1921–1939 gg. [The Activities of Protestant Churches in Western Belarus from 1921–1939]. *Ves'nik Grodzenskaga dziarzhaunaga universiteta imia Yanki Kupaly* [Grodno State University of Y. Kupala Messenger], no. 1, 2 (67) (2008): 77–82.

———. "Neoprotestantizm v Zapadnoi Belarusi v 1921–1939 gg." Dissertatsiya na soiskaniye uchenoy stepeni kandidata istoricheskikh nauk [Neoprotestantism in Western Belarus in 1921–1939. Thesis for the Degree of Candidate of Historical Sciences]. Minsk: Belorusskiy gosudarstvennyy universitet, 2008.

———. "Novye protestantskie denominatsii na zapadnobelorusskih zemliah v kontse XIX – 20 gg. XX veka: Faktory i putsi poyavleniya" [New Protestant Denominations in West Belarusian Territory Between the Late Nineteenth Century and the 1920s: Factors and Ways of Emergence]. *Ves'nik Brestskaga universiteta* [Brest University Messenger], no. 2 (30) (2007): 41–49.

———. "Problema ispol'zovaniya belorusskogo yazyka v deyatel'nosti baptistskikh i pyatidesyatnicheskikh obshchin Zapadnoi Belarusi v 1921–1939 gg." [The Problem of Use of Belarusian Language in the Activities of Baptist and Pentecostal Communities in Western Belarus in 1921–1939]. In *Slavyanskie yazyki: sistemno-opisatel'ny i sociokul'turny aspekty issledovaniya. Material IV Mezhdunarodnoi nauchno-metodicheskoi konferentsii, ch. 2* [Slavic Languages: Systemic-Descriptive and Socio-Cultural Aspects of the Study. The Material of the IV International Scientific Conference, Part 2]. Brest: Brestskiy gosudarstvennyy universitet im. A.S. Pushkina (2010): 74–79.

———. "Struktura yevangel'sko-baptistskogo dvizheniya Zapadnoy Belarusi v 1921–1939 gg." [The Structure of the Evangelical-Baptist Movement of Western Belarus in 1921–1939]. *Vestnik Brestskogo universiteta* [Brest University Messenger], no. 6 (84), (2013): 22–24.

Liven, S.P., *Dukhovnoe probuzhdenie v Rossii. Vospominaniya knyazhny S.P. Liven* [Spiritual Revival in Russia. Memories of Princess S.P. Lieven]. Chicago: Slavic Gospel Press, 1989.

Makarevich, Pavel. *Prorochestva Biblii* [Prophecy of the Bible]. Minsk, 1993.

Margaritov, S. *Istoria russkih misticheskih i racionalisticheskih sekt* [History of Russian Mystic and Rationalistic Sects]. 4th ed., Corrected and Supplemented. Simpheropol': Tavrich. gub. tip., 1914.

Martsinkovskiy, V.F. *Zapiski veruyushchego* [A Believer's Notes]. Novosibirsk: "Posokh," 2006.

Matviiv, V. *Svyashchennodii pastora* [Pastor's Sacred Rites]. Kiev: Vseukraïns'kyi Soyuz ob'ednan' evangel's'kykh khrystyian-baptystiv, 2004.

Matyash, Tamara. "Pravoslavie kak kul'turny phenomen" [Orthodoxy as a Cultural Phenomenon], in *Russkaya pravoslavnaya tserkov' v prostranstve Evrasii. Materialy IV Vsemirnogo Russkogo Narodnogo Sobora* [Russian Orthodox Church in Eurasia. Materials of the VI World Russian People's Council]. Moskva: Eurasia (2002): 107–115.

Mel'gunov, S.P. *Iz istorii religiozno-obshchestvennykh dvizhenii v Rossii XIX v.* [From the History of Religious and Social Movements in Russia in the XIX Century]. Moskva: Zadruga, 1919.

———. *Tserkov' i gosudarstvo v Rossii* [Church and State in Russia]. Moskva, Zadruga, 1907.

Men', Aleksandr. *Pravoslavnoye bogosluzheniye. Tainstvo, Slovo i obraz* [Orthodox Worship. Sacrament, Word, and Image]. Moskva: SP Slovo, 1991.

Mitskevich, A.I., *Istoriya Evangel'skikh khristian-baptistov* [The History of Evangelical Christians-Baptists]. Moskva: Rossiisky soyuz evangel'skikh khristian-baptistov, 2007.

———. "Vseobshcheye svyashchenstvo I sluzhiteli tserkvi" [Pristhood of All Believers and Church Ministers]. *Bratskiy Vestnik*, no. 3 (1965): 29–36.

Mikhalkov, Sergei. Anthem of the Soviet Union. Moscow: Gosudarstvennoye musykal'noye izdatel'stvo, 1944.

Mikhovich, Leonid. "Pokloneniye i bogosluzheniye" [Worship and Public Worship] In *Slavyanskiy bibleyskiy kommentariy: sovremennaya yevangel'skaya perspektiva* [Slavic Biblical Commentary: Modern Evangelical Perspective], edited by S.V. Sannikov, 177–178. Kiev, EAAA, 2016.

Milovidov, A.I. *Sovremennoye shtundo-baptistskoye dvizheniye v Severo-Zapadnom kraye* [Modern Stundist-Baptist Movement in the Northwestern Region]. Vilna: Russky Pochin, 1910.

Minsk Theological Seminary. Official Website. Accessed 9 March 2017. http://www.mbseminary.org/index.php.

Minutes of the Church Council Meeting, no. 017, 22 March 2016 Church in Borovliany, Minsk region.

Minutes of the Council of the ECB Union in Belarus, no. 59, 30 October 2002); 60, 18–19 December 2002; and 141, 21 May 2019 Minsk, Belarus.

Minutes of the Membership Meetings, no. 04 (2 April 2014); and no. 06 (14 February 2016). Church in Borovliany, Minsk region.

Mironova, Ekaterina. "Predstavleniya o brake i brachnyye praktiki yevangel'skikh veruyushchikh v Sovetskom Soyuze v 1940–1980-ye gg. Po materialam obshchin yevangel'skikh khristian-baptistov tsentral'no-chernozemnogo regiona" [Marriage Ideas and Practices Among Evangelical Believers in the Soviet Union in 1940–1980s. The Case of Central Black Earth Region]. Gosudarstvo, religiia, tserkov' v Rossii i za rubezhom [State, Religion and Church in Russia and Abroad], no. 36 (2) (2018): 131–162.

Misiruk, S.N. "Tserkov' Khrista – eto maloe stado . . ." [The Church of Christ is a Little Folk . . .]. *Vestnik Istiny*, no. 2 (1996): 2–3.

Mitrokhin, L.N., *Baptizm: istoriya i sovremennost'* [Baptists: History and Modernity]. Sanct-Peterburg: Russkiy khristianskiy gosudarstvennyy institut, 1997.

———. ed., *Khristianstvo. Slovar'* [Christianity. Dictionary]. Moskva: "Respublika," 1994.

———. and E.Y. Lyagushina. "Nekotoryye cherty sovremennogo baptizma" [Some Features of the Modern Baptists]. *Voprosy filosofii* [Questions of Philosophy], no. 2 (1964): 62–73.

Mogilevskie eparhial'nye vedomosti [Mogilev Diocese Gazette], no. 8 (1906), 21 (1910), 20 (1912).

Moody, D.L. *Pol'za i naslazhdeniye ot izucheniya Biblii* [Pleasure and Profit in Bible study]. Korntal': Svet na Vostoke, 1990.

The Moscow Central Church of ECB. Accessed 15 May 2019. http://mbchurch.ru/publications/b rotherly_pdf/.

Motorin, I. "O bogosluzhenii v dni apostolov i v nashi dni" [On Worship in the Days of the Apostles and Today]. *Bratskiy Vestnik*, no. 1 (1957): 7–10.

M., P. "Istoki evangel'skogo dvizheniya v Rossii" [Backgrounds of Evangelical Movement in Russia]. *Vestnik Istiny*, no. 6 (2007): 33–40.

Nastol'naya kniga presvitera [The Pastor's Handbook], sec. ed. Moskva: Vsesoyuznyy sovet evangel'skikh khristian-baptistov, 1987.

Nastol'naya kniga presvitera, tom 1 [The Pastor's Handbook, vol. 1]. Moskva: Izdanie Rossiiskogo soyuza evangel'skikh khristian-baptistov, 2010.

Navitski, U.I., et. al, *Jevanhielskija chryscijanie u Bielarusi: piat́ stahoddziau historyi (1517-2017 hh.)* [Evangelical Christians in Belarus: Five Centuries of History (1517-2017)]. Minsk. Pasityu-centr, 2019.

Nesteruk, Vladimir. *Khristianstvo i estetika.* Diplomnaya rabota [Christianity and Aesthetics. Diploma Thesis]. Minsk: Minskaya bogoslovskaya seminariya, 2003, Unpublished.

Nikol'skaya, T, "Kto takiye 'otdelennyye'?" [Who Are the 'Separated'?]. *Mirt* [Myrtle], no. 5 (30) (2001): 1-2. Accessed 16 June 2014. http://dic.academic.ru/dic.nsf/ruwiki/1133416.

———. *Russkiy Protestantism i gosudarstvennaya vlast' v 1905-1991 godakh* [Russian Protestantism and the Government in 1905-1991]. Sanct-Peterburg: Evropeisky universitet v Sankt-Peterburge, 2009.

———. "Russkiy protestantizm na etape utverzhdeniya legalizatsii (1905-1917 gg.)" [Russian Protestantism at the Stage of Legalization: 1905-1917]. *Theological Reflections*, no. 4 (2004): 161-181.

———. "Uroki istorii dlya EKhB" [History Lessons for ECB]/ *Mirt* [Myrtle], no. 2 (57) (2007): 10.

Notny sbornik dukhovnykh pesen, tom 3, chast 1 [Music Collection of Spiritual Songs, vol. 3, part 1]. Moskva: Vsesoyuznyy sovet evangel'skikh khristian-baptistov, 1988.

Novoe vremya, no. 802 [The New Time, no. 802] (May 23, 1878). In *Vestnik Istiny,* no. 6 (2007): 33-40.

"Novyy khristianskiy kul'turnyy tsentr" [The New Christian Cultural Center]. *Krynitsa Zhytstsya* [The Source of Life], no. 4 (2004): 7.

Nursultanov, Marat. A Poll Among the Members of the Baptist Church in Orsha, Vitebsk Region. March 2008.

"Obnovliat'sia i byt' samobytnym" [Be Replendished and Be Original]. *Logos: The Bible. Education. Music,* no. 1(13) (2005). Moskva: Khristianskiy tsentr [Logos].

Odintsov, M. I. "Sovet po delam religioznyh kul'tov pri SM SSSR i evangel'skoe dvizhenie v Sovetskom Soyuze v 1956-1965 gg." [Council for the Affairs of Religious Cults of the USSR Council of Ministers and the Evangelical Movement in the USSR in 1956-1965]. Accessed 31 March 2011. http://www.rusoir.ru/president/works/214/.

Odintsov, N.V. ed. *Ispovedanie very khristian-baptistov, 1928* [Christian Baptist Confession, 1928]. https://slavicbaptists.com/2012/02/10/verouchenie1928/, last accessed 16 May 2019.

"O kharizmatii" [On Charismatics]. Open Letter of the Union Council of Baptist Churches in Russia to Baptist Churches. Accessed 1 April 2012. http://ehbtambov.ru/archives/2142.

Orlov, M.A. "The Report by M.A. Orlov on His Trip to Belarus." *Bratskiy Vestnik*, no. 3 (1948): 46–48.

Orthodox encyclopedia under the editorship of Cyrill, Patriarch of Moscow and all Russia. Vol. 9. On-line version. http://www.pravenc.ru/text/155522.html. Accessed 6 March 2017.

Pashkovtsy's evangelical confession. http://slavicbaptists.com/2012/06/01/pashkavconfession/. Accessed 26 November 2016.

Panych, Olena. "Children and Childhood Among Evangelical Christians-Baptists During the Late Soviet Period (1960s-1980s)." *Bogoslovskie razmyshleniya* [Theological Reflections], no. 13 (2012): 155–179.

Patsuk, D.Y., ed. *Poyte Gospodu, svyatyye Yego . . . Khorovoy sbornik dlya smeshannogo khora s soprovozhdeniyem*, tom 2 [Sing to the Lord, His Saints . . . Choral Compilation for a Mixed Choir with Accompaniment, vol. 2]. Minsk: Muzykal'nyy otdel Minskoy bogoslovskoy seminarii Soyuza YEKHB v Belarusi, 2004–2006.

Pavlov, F.P. ed., *Ispovedanie very khristian-baptistov. Razdel X. O tserkvi Gospodnei* [Confession of Faith of Christian Baptists. Section X. On the Church of God]. 1906.

Pavlov, P.V. "Doklad na 3-m Vsemirnom kongresse baptistov v Stockgolme, Shvetsiya, 26.07.1923" [Report on the 3rd World Congress of Baptists in Stockholm, Sweden, 26.07.1923]. In Leonid Kovalenko, ed., *Oblako svidetelei Khristovykh* [A Cloud of Witnesses of Christ]. Kiev: Centr Khrisianskogo Sotrudnichestva (1997): 218–220.

Pavlov, V.G. "Pravda o baptistakh. Ocherk istorii, tserkovnogo ustroystva i printsipov baptistskikh obshchin" [The Truth about Baptists. Essay on History, Church Organization and Principles of Baptist Communities]. In M.S. Karetnikova, ed., *Al'manakh po istorii russkogo baptizma* [Almanac on the History of Russian Baptists]. Sanct-Peterburg: "Bibliya dlya vsekh" (1997): 220–272.

Pekun, S. "Krestnyy put' Brestskoy tserkvi YEKHB" [The Way of the Cross of Brest ECB Church]. *Krynitsa Zhyttsya*, no. 2 (1997): 23–26.

———. "Krestnyy put' Brestskoy tserkvi YEKHB" [The Way of the Cross of Brest ECB Church]. *Krynitsa Zhyttsya*, no. 3 (1997): 14–19.

———. "Luka Nikolaevich Dzekuts'-Maley: zhizn' i sluzhenie" [Luka Nikolaevich Dzekuts-Maley: Life and Ministry]. *Krynitsa Zhyttsya*, no. 2 (2000): 6–9.

Pesn' Voskhozhdeniya. Sbornik tserkovnykh gimnov i pesnopeniy [Song of Ascents. Collection of Hymns and Chants]. Bryansk: Muzykal'no-khorovoy otdel Bezhitskoy tserkvi EKhB, 2009.

Pesn' Vozrozhdeniya – 2500. Sbornik dukhovnykh gimnov i pesen evangel'skih tserkvey [Song of Revival – 2500. The Collection of Spiritual Hymns and

Songs of Evangelical Churches]. Moskva: Mezhkonfessional'nyy khristianskiy tsentr, 2001.

Pesn' Vozrozhdeniya. Sbornik dukhovnykh gimnov i pesen evangel'skih tserkvey [Song of Revival], Collection of Hymns and Songs of Evangelical Churches. Minsk, Church of Christian of Evangelical Faith, 1996.

Pesn' Vozrozhdeniya. Sbornik dukhovnyh gimnov i pesen evangel'skih tserkvey s notami, tom 1 [Song of Revival. Collection of Spiritual Hymns and Songs of Evangelical Churches with Music, vol. 1], Samohvalovichi: ODO "Dubki," 2006.

Podberezskiy, I.V. *Byt' protestantom v Rossii* [To Be a Protestant in Russia]. Moskva: Blagovestnik, 1996.

———. *Vera po Yevangeliyu v Rossii* [Faith According to the Gospel in Russia]. Moskva: Khristianskoye slovo, 2000.

"Polnoe sobranie zakonov rossiiskoy imperii." Sobranie 3. T. 3. Sanct-Peterburg, 1886. [Complete Collection of Laws of the Russian Empire. Collection 3, vol. 3. Sanct-Peterburg, 1886]. Accessed 10 November 2012. http://nauka-i-religia.narod.ru/religioved/garadga/docum.ht ml. 2012.

Polnyy pravoslavnyy bogoslovskiy entsiklopedicheskiy slovar', t. 1 [Unabridged Orthodox Theological Encyclopedic Dictionary, v. 1]. Moscow: Vozroszdenie, 1992.

"Polozheniye sektantstva v predelakh Mogilevskoy yeparkhii i mery dlya bor'by s nim. Iz raporta Yeparkhial'n. missionera na imya Yego Preosvyashchenstva" [Position of Sectarianism within the Mogilev Diocese and Measures to Fight It. From the Report of the Diocesan Missionary to His Eminence]. *Mogilevskiye yeparkhial'nyye vedomosti* [Mogilev Diocesan Gazette], no. 8 (1906): 296.

Popov, V.A. "Otechestvennaya shkola propovedi v tserkvakh evangel'skikh khristian baptistov" [National School of Preaching in Evangelical Christian Baptist Churches]. In *Traditsiya podgotovki sluzhiteley v bratstve evangel'skikh khristian-baptistov. Istoriya i perspektivy: Sbornik statey* [Tradition of Training Ministers in the Brotherhood of Evangelical Christian Baptist Churches. History and Perspective: Collection of Articles], 36–47. Moskva: Rossiisky soyuz evangel'skikh khristian-baptistov, 2013.

———. *I.S. Prokhanov. Stranitsy zhizni* [Prokhanov. Pages of Life]. Sanct-Peterburg: "Bibliya dlya vsekh," 1996.

———. *Stopy Blagovestnika* [The Feet of an Evangelist]. Moskva: "Blagovestnik," 1996.

Pospelovsky, D.V. *Russkaya pravoslavnaya tserkov' v XX veke* [Russian Orthodox Church in the 20th Century]. Moskva: Izdatel'stvo "Respublika," 1995.

———. "Stalin i tserkov': "konkordat" 1943 i zhizn' tserkvi" [Stalin and the Church: The "Concordat" of 1943, and the Life of the Church], *Continent*, no. 103 (2000): 220–239.

Predko, T.I. *Dinamika sinkreticheskoy religioznosti zhiteley belorusskogo Poles'ya*. Avtoreferat dissertatsii na soiskaniye uchenoy stepeni kandidata filosofskikh nauk [Dynamics of Syncretic Religion in Belarusian Polesye. Abstract of Dissertation for the Degree of Candidate of Philosophical Sciences]. Minsk, Belorusskiy gosudarstvennyy universitet, 2009.

Prokhanov, I.S. *V kotle Rossii* [In the Cauldron of Russia]. Chicago: World Fellowship of Slavic Evangelical Christians, 1992.

Prokhanov, I.S. and Y.I. Zhidkov, eds. *Pesni pervykh khristian* [The Songs of the First Christians]. Leningrad: Vsesoyuznyy sovet evangel'skikh khristian-baptistov, 1927.

Prokhorov, Konstantin. *Mezhdu Zapadom i Vostokom: Zametki o nachale evangel'skogo dvizheniya v Rossii* [Between East and West: Notes on Early Evangelical Movement in Russia]. *Bogoslovskie razmyshleniya* [Theological Reflections], no. 13 (2012): 53–78.

Puzynin, Andrei. *Tradiciya evangel'skikh khristian. Izuchenie samoidentifikacii i bogosloviya ot momenta ee zarozhdeniya do nashih dnei* [The Tradition of Evangelical Christians. The Study of Identity and Theology from Its Inception to the Present Day]. Moskva: Bibleisko-bogoslovskiy institut sv. Apostola Andreya, 2010.

R., A. "Khristianin v bytu" [A Christian in Everyday Life]. *Bratskiy Vestnik*, no. 5 (1977): 65–67.

Rekuts, I.F. *Protestantism i khudozhestvennaya kul'tura Belarusi* [Protestantism and Artistic Culture of Belarus]. Minsk: Belorusskiy gosudarstvennyy universitet, 1995. Accessed 14 March 2016. https://religia.by/.

Rizhskiy, M.I. *Istoriya perevodov Biblii v Rossii* [History of Bible Translations in Russia]. Novosibirsk: "Nauka," 1978.

Rogozin, Pavel. *Otkuda vse eto poyavilos'?* [Where Did It All Come from?]. Gummersbach: Missiya Vestnik Mira, 1996.

The Roman Catholic Church in Belarus. Official Website. Accessed 6 June 2015. http://www.catholic.by/2/belarus/dioceses.html.

Rozhdestvensky, A. *Yuzhnorussky Shtundism* [Southrussian Shtundism]. Sanct-Peterburg: Tipographiya Departamenta Udelov, 1889.

Rudenko, Anatoliy. "Kul't propovedi i sluzheniye slova" [The Cult of Sermon and Ministry of the Word]. http://gazeta.mirt.ru/?2-37-1364. Accessed 14 August 2014.

Rudnichenko, T.S. "Pesnopeniya v religioznykh ritualakh dukhoborov i molokan Rostovskoy oblasti: sovremennoye sostoyaniye" [Chants in Religious Rituals

of the Doukhobors and Molokans in the Rostov Region: Current State]. *Vestnik TGU* [TGU Herald], no. 4 (168) (2015): 173–179.
Russian Bible Society. Official Website. Accessed 2 June 2014. http://www.biblia.ru/reading/new_translations/sinodal.htm.
Ryabushkin, N.V. *Kto takiye sektanty* [Who Are the Sectarians]. Ivanovo: Ivanovo Publishing House, 1961.
Ryaguzov, Vl.S. 'O tserkovnoy arkhitekture' [On Church Architecture]. *Bogomyslie* [Contemplation of God], no. 1 (1990): 250–261.
Ryaguzov, Viktor, *Zhizn' vopreki* [Life in Spite of]. Samara: Izdatel'ski dom "Dobrusich, 2011.
Rydz'koýski, A. "Vedats' tavaryshcha pa audytoryi" [Know Your Comrade in the Auditorium], *Chyrvonaya zmena*, no. 206 (Oct. 20, 1959), p. 3.
S.,V. "Voprosy dukhovnoy zhizni" [Issues of Spiritual Life]. *Bratskiy Vestnik*, no. 2 (1964): 17–23.
Satsevich, H. and N. Hury, *Slowo i zycie* [Word and Life], no. 4–6 (1995).
Savik, M. "Radost' vsyakoy dushe" [The Joy of Every Soul]. *Khristianskiy Soyuz*, no. 9–10 (September-October, 1928): 164.
Savinskiy, S.N. *Istoriya evangel'skikh khristian-baptistov Ukrainy, Rossii, Belorussii. Chast' II (1917–1967)* [History of Evangelical Christians-Baptists in Ukraine, Russia and Belarus. Part II (1917–1967)]. Sanct-Peterburg: "Bibliya dlya vsekh," 2001.
———. "Istoriya russko-ukrainskogo baptizma. Uchebnoye posobiye" [History of Russian-Ukrainian Baptists. Study Manual]. Odessa: Odesskaya bogoslovskaya seminaria, Bogomyslie, 1995.
Sawatsky, Walter. *Evangelicheskoye dvizheniye v SSSR posle Vtoroy mirovoy voyny* [Evangelical Movement after World War II]. Moskva: Filial Tsentral'nogo komiteta mennonitov v Rossii, 1995. Originally published as *Soviet Evangelicals Since World War II*. Kitchener, Ontario: Herald Press, 1981.
Schmemann, Aleksandr. "Missionerskiy imperativ" [The Missionary Imperative]. In Iakov Stamulis, ed., *Pravoslavnoye bogosloviye missii segodnya* [Orthodox Theology of Mission Today]. Moskva: Pravoslavnyy Svyato-Tikhonovskiy Bogoslovskiy Institut (2002): 385–396.
"Seven Baptist Principles." Official Website of the Union of ECB in Belarus. Accessed 29 November 2016. http://baptist.by/faith/principles.
Sevyarynets, Paval. *Lyublyu Belarus': 200 fenomenau natsyyanal'nay idei* [I love Belarus: 200 Phenomenon of National Idea]. Vil'nya: Institut belarusistyki, 2008.
Shchavelin, N. "O blagogovenii v dome molitvy" [On Reverence in the House of Prayer]. *Bratskiy Vestnik*, no. 5 (1955): 41–43.
Shenderovsky, Ludvig. *Ivan Prokhanov*. Toronto: "Evangel'skaya Vera," 1986.

Shipkov, Georgy. "Molitva Gospodnya" [The Lord's Prayer]. *Baptist*, no. 17 (Sep. 1909): 4–9.

"Simvol yevangel'skoy very pashkovtsev" [Pashkovtsy's Evangelical Creed]. Accessed 8 August 2014. http://slavicbaptists.com/2012/06/01/pashkavconfession/.

Sinichkin, A.V. "Vlast' i sluzhiteli tserkvi na etape formirovaniya VSEKHB (s 1944-go po 1949 g.)" [Authorities and Church Officials at the Stage of AUCECB Formation (from 1944 to 1949)]. In *Traditsiya podgotovki sluzhiteley v bratstve evangel'skikh khristian-baptistov. Istoriya i perspektivy: Sbornik statey* [The Tradition of Training of Ministers in the Brotherhood of Evangelical Christians-Baptists. History and Prospects: Collected Papers], 148–162. Moskva: Rossiiskiy soyuz evangel'skikh khristian-baptistov, 2013.

Slowo Pojednania [Word of Reconciliation], vol. 4, no. 1 (Jan.–Feb. 1939).

Sokolov, E. "V.V. Ivanov." *Bratskiy Vestnik*, no. 1 (1982): 47–52.

Sokolov, Ivan. *Otnoshenie protestantizma k Rossii v XVI i XVII vekakh* [The Relation of Protestantism to Russia in the 16–17th centuries]. Moscow: Tipographia E. Lissner and Y. Roman, 1880.

Somov, K. V. "O propovedi I propovednikakh" [About Preaching and Preachers]. *Bratskiy Vestnik*, no. 2 (1964): 33–43.

———, "Pesnya v zhizni khristianina" [A Song in the Life of a Christian]. *Bratskiy Vestnik*, no. 4 (1964): 29–34.

———, "Tserkov' Khrista i ejo svyashchenstvo" [The Church of Christ and Its Priesthood]. *Bratskiy Vestnik*, no. 4 (1963): 53–65.

Stamulis, Iakov. *Pravoslavnoye bogosloviye missii segodnya* [Orthodox Theology of Mission today]. Moscow: Pravoslavnyy Svyato-Tikhonovskiy Bogoslovskiy institut, 2003.

State Acts Governing the Life of Evangelical Believers in the Russian Empire. Accessed on 30 July 2014. http://anabaptist.ru/obmen/hystory/ist1/files/books/book_002/0060_t.html.

Stikhotvoreniya, declamatsii, istorii [Poems, Recitations, Stories]. Lipniki, 1960s., Unpublished.

Sulackov, A. *Na iskhode nochi* [At the End of Night]. Alma-Ata: "Kazakhstan," 1966.

Svod zakonov Rossiiskoi imperii [Code of Laws of the Russian Empire], vol. 14, part 1. St. Petersburg, 1982.

Tervits, Y.E. "Muzyka i dukhovnoye vozrastaniye veruyushchikh" [Music and Spiritual Growth of Believers]. *Bratskiy Vestnik*, no. 3 (1981): 58–63.

Teteryatnikov, Konstantin. "Blagovestiye: vchera i segodnya." [Evangelism: Yesterday and Today] Accessed 7 November 2019. https://www.christianmegapolis.com//благовестие-вчера-и-сегодня/.

Timoshenko, Mikhail. "Baptisty i ikh protivniki" [Baptists and Their Adversaries], *Baptist*, no. 9 (1911).

Torbet, Robert G., Albert W. Wardin, and Sergei Savinsky. *Istoriya baptizma* [A History of the Baptists]. Odessa: Bogomyslie, 1996.

Trans World Radio in Belarus. Official Website. Accessed 3 February 2017. http://twr.fm.

Trubchik, V.P., *Vera i traditsiya* [Faith and Tradition]. Minsk: Soyuz YEKHB, 2009.

"Tserkov' dolzhna ostavat'sya tserkov'yu. Neobratimyye desyatiletiya: 1917–1937 gody v istorii evangel'skogo i baptistskogo dvizheniy. Dokumental'nyy material ob istorii tserkvi EKhB v Rossii" [The Church Should Remain a Church. Irreversible Decade: 1917–1937 in the History of the Gospel and of the Baptist Movement. Documentary Material About the History of Baptist Church in Russia]. Mezhdunarodnyy sovet tserkvei evangel'skikh khristian-baptistov, Istoriko-analiticheskiy otdel, 2007.

"Tserkov' v derevne Rubel'" [Church in the Village of Rubel]. *Krynitsa Zhyttsya*, no. 3 (2009): 22–25.

Tuchi nad Borskom [Clouds over Borsk], directed by V. Ordynsky. Mosfilm, 1961.

Ubeivolc, Vladimir. "Rethinking *Missio Dei* Among Evangelical Churches in an Eastern European Orthodox Context." PhD diss., University of Wales, 2011.

"Ukaz ob ukreplenii nachal veroterpimosti 1905" [Decree on Making Toleration Foundation Stronger 1905]. Accessed 11 June 2012. https://ru.wikisource.org/wiki/Указ_Об_укреплении_н ачал_веротерпимости_(1905).

Union of Evangelical Christians-Baptists of Russia. Official Website. Accessed 5 November 2019. http://baptist.org.ru/read/article/96272.

The Union of Militant Atheists of the Russian Federation. Official Website. Accessed 24 June 2014. http://svb.net.ru/.

Unuchak, Andrus'. "Centr Abjadnańnia Cerkvau Chrystovych u Kobrynie (1929–1930 hh.)" [Union Center of the Churches of Christ in Kobryn]. In Bokun, ed., *Yevanhielskaya tsarkva Bielarusi: gistoryya i suchasnasc'*, pp. 178–185.

———. "S'vyatar, patryyot, perakladchyk" [Priest, a Patriot Translator], in *Lukash Dzekuts'-Maley i belaruskiya pieraklady Biblii. Zbornik materyyalau, artykulaý i dakumentau* [Lukas Dzekuts Maley and Belarusian Translations of the Bible. Collection of Papers, Articles and Documents], 8–16. Brest: Al'ternatyva, 2011.

———. "Tserkvy Khrystovyya na Kobrynshchyne u 1920-ya gg.: da pytannya denaminatsyynay toyesnas'tsi i arganizatsyynaga stanaulennya" [The Churches of Christ in Kobrin Area in the 1920s: The Issues of Confessional Identity and Organizational Development], in Bokun, ed., *Yevanhielskaya tsarkva Bielarusi: historyjya i suchasnasc'. Vypusk II*, pp. 203–213.

Vabishchevich, A. "Zachodniaja Bielarus pad uladaj Pol'shchy. Dukhounaje zhytsia va umovakh palanizatsyi" [Belarus under the Rule of Poland. Spiritual Life in Polanization]. In *Historyia Bielarusi* [History of Belarus] Vol. 5, 483–441. Minsk: Ekaperspektyva, 2006.

Vdovichenko, P.I. *Kritika ideologii sovremennogo baptizma (po materialam Belorusskoy SSR).* Avtoreferat dissertatsii na soiskaniye uchenoy stepeni kandidata filosofskikh nauk [The Critique of Modern Baptist Ideology (According to the Records of Belarussian SSR). Abstract of Dissertation for the Degree of Candidate of Philosophical Sciences]. Minsk: Belorusskiy gosudarstvennyy universitet, 1966.

Vereshchagin, Victor. "O samobytnosti russkoi kul'tury v kontekste globalizatsii" [On the Uniqueness of Russian Culture in the Context of Globalization]. In *Russkaya pravoslavnaya tserkov' v prostranstve Evrasii. Materialy IV semirnogo Russkogo Narodnogo Sobora* [Russian Orthodox Church in Eurasia. Materials of the VI World Russian People's Council], 116–125. Moskva: Eurasia, 2002.

Verhovih, E.Y. "Kanon v Arkhitekture pravoslavnoy tserkvi" [Canon in Architecture of the Orthodox Church]. *Akademicheskiy vestnik Uralniiproyekt RAASN* [Academic Bulletin of Uralniiproekt RAASH], no. 4 (2010): 26–33.

Verouchenie evangel'skikh khristian-baptistov v Belarusi, prinyatoe na 43-m s'ezde evangel'skikh khristian-baptistov (1985 g.). [Doctrine of Faith of Evangelical Christian Baptists in Belarus, adopted on the 43rd Congress of Evangelical Christian Baptists, 1985. Unpublished material.

Verouchenie evangel'skikh khristian-baptistov v Belarusi, prinyatoe na s'ezde EKhB v Belarusi 15.03.2003 goda. [Doctrine of Faith of Evangelical Christian Baptists in Belarus, adopted at the Congress of ECB in Belarus 15.03.2003]. Unpublished material.

Verouchenie Ob'edinionnoi tserkvi khristian very evangel'skoi v Respublice Belarus', izd. 2 [Doctrine of Faith of the United Church of Christians of Evangelical Faith in Republic of Belarus, 2nd ed.]. Minsk: Positive-center, 2012.

Vestnik Istiny, no. 3 (2001).

Vestnik Istiny, no 4 (2001).

Vestnik Istiny, no. 4–5 (2009).

Vezikova, Galina. "Khochetsya li v nebo" [Do You Want to be Taken to Heaven?]. http://www.blagovestnik.org/books/00430/db/v838593.html. Accessed 31 July 2014.

———, "V poiskakh puti" [In Search of the Way]. Accessed 16 May 2019. http://www.blagovestni k.org/books/00430/db/v4599835.html.

Vil'chinskiy, Vladimir. *Nedarom prolityye slezy* [Tears Shed not in Vain]. Brest, 2011.

Viske, Gyunter and Genrick Leven ml., *Oni sledovali za Iisusom* [They Followed Jesus]. Cherkassy: "Smirna," 2001.

The "Voice of the Ands." Accessed 3 February 2017. History. http://www.hcjb.ru/history.htm.

Volchanskiy, V. "O sluzhenii orkestrov" [About Orchesta Ministry]. *Bratskiy Vestnik*, no. 3 (1982): 54–56.
Voskoboynikov, V.M. *Illyustrirovannaya pravoslavnaya entsiklopediya. Tolkovaniye simvolov i obryadov. Opisaniye glavneyshikh pravoslavnykh svyatyn'* [Illustrated Orthodox Encyclopedia. Interpretation of Symbols and Rituals. Description of the Main Orthodox Holy Places]. Moskva: EKSMO, 2008.
"Vsesoyuznoye soveshchaniye yevangel'skikh khristian i baptistov v Moskve s 26 po 29 oktyabrya 1944 g. (Zapisi zasedaniy)" [All-Union Conference of Evangelical Christians and Baptists in Moscow from October 26 to October 29, 1944 (Recordings of Meetings)], *Bratskiy Vestnik*, no. 1 (1945): 11–38.
Vukashinovich, Vladimir. *Liturgicheskoye vozrozhdeniye v XX veke* [Liturgical Revival in the XX Century]. Moskva: Khristianskaya Rossiya, 2005.
Vvedenskiy, A. "P'yanstvo i sektantstvo (k nashey polemike s sektantami)" [Drunkenness and Sectarianism (About Our Polemic with Sectarians)]. *Mogilevskiye yeparkhial'nyye vedomosti* [Mogilev Eparchy News], no. 20 (1912).
Vysotskiy, N.I. "Znacheniye i sila dukhovnoy muzyki" [Power and Strength of Christian Music]. *Bratskiy Vestnik*, no. 5 (1978): 57–66.
Yanouskaya, V.V. *Hrystsiyanskaya tsarkva u Belarusi 1863–1914 gg.* [Christian Church in Belarus in 1863–1914]. Minsk: Belaruski dziarzhauny universitet, 2002.
Yartsev, A. *Sekta evangel'skikh khristian* [The Sect of Evangelical Christians]. Moskva: "Bezbozhnik," 1930.
Yasevich-Borodayevskaya, V.I. *Bor'ba za veru* [Fighting for Faith]. Sanct-Peterburg, 1912.
Yemelyakh, L.I. *Proiskhozhdenie Khristianskogo kul'ta* [Origins of the Christian Cult]. Leningrad: Lenizdat, 1972.
Yevseyev, I.E. *Sobor i Bibliya* [The Council and the Bible]. Sanct-Peterburg: Sinodal'naya Tipographiya, 1917.
Yevtukhovich, Georgy. *Zhit' – znachit verit'. Iz istorii evangelicheskoi tserkvi v Belarusi* [To Live Means to Believe. From the History of an Evangelical Church in Belarus]. Minsk: Publisher A.N. Varaksin, 2006.
Yuny Bezbozhnik, (1931).
Zayavleniye very evangel'skikh khristian-baptistov v Belarusi, Mart 2002 [Statement of Faith of Evangelical-Christians-Baptists, March 2002]. Unpublished.
Zhidkov, Y.I. "Nashi prazdniki" [Our Celebrations]. *Bratskiy Vestnik*, no. 2 (1946): 13–20.

Photographs of the Houses of Prayer and Sanctuaries

Fig.3. Photograph of Fortechnaya 61/1 church building, Brest.

Fig.4. Photograph of Jackshitsy house of prayer, Minsk region.

Fig.5. Photograph of Voropaevo house of prayer, Vitebsk region.

Fig.6. Photograph of the "Arc," house of prayer, Volkovysk, Grodno region.

Fig.7. Photograph of Central Baptist church, Kobrin, Brest region.

Fig.8. Photograph of "Light of Gospel" church building, Minsk.

Fig.9. Photograph of "Bethany" church building, Kobrin, Brest region.

Fig.10. Photograph of "Bethlehem" church building, Minsk.

**Fig.11. Photograph of textual decoration in
Malech house of prayer, Brest region.**

Texts from left to right: "We preach Christ crucified, resurrected and coming again." "And behold, I come quickly" (Rev 3:11a). "The kingdom of God is at hand; repent and believe in the gospel" (Mark 1:15).

Fig.12. Photograph of textual decoration in Sadovyi house of prayer, Brest region.

Texts from left to right: "Ascribe to the LORD glory and strength" (Psalm 29:1b). "The earth is satisfied with the fruit of His works" (Psalm 104:13b). "The LORD is my light and my salvation" (Psalm 27:1a).

Fig.13. Photograph of textual decoration in Pruzhany house of prayer, Brest region.

Texts from left to right: "We preach Christ crucified" (1 Cor 1:23a). God is love. "For it is time to seek the LORD" (Hosea 10:12b).

Fig. 14. Photograph of textual decoration in Zavelev'e house of prayer, Brest region.

Texts on the left, in the center (top to bottom) and on the right: "Bless the LORD, O my soul, and forget none of His benefits" (Psalm 103:2). "We preach Christ crucified." "In everything give thanks" (1 Thess. 5:18). "You shall remember all the way which the LORD your God has led you" (Deut 8:2a). "Because He has fixed a day in which He will judge the world" (Acts 17:31a).

Fig.15. Photograph of worship hall Man'kovichi church/house of prayer, Brest region.

Fig.16. Photograph of worship hall "Golgotha" church, Minsk.

Photographs of the Houses of Prayer and Sanctuaries 361

**Fig.17. Photograph of worship space Liuban'
house of prayer/church, Minsk region.**

**Fig.18. Photograph of worship hall Shatsk house
of prayer/church, Minsk region.**

Fig.19. Photograph of the worship hall Central Baptist church, Gomel (2002).

Fig.20. Photograph of the worship hall/space after renovation Central Baptist church, Gomel (2007).

Fig.21. Photograph of elevated platform Central Baptist church, Kobrin (2008).

Fig.22. Photograph of elevated platform after renovation, Central Baptist church, Kobrin (2017).

Langham Literature, with its publishing work, is a ministry of Langham Partnership.

Langham Partnership is a global fellowship working in pursuit of the vision God entrusted to its founder John Stott –

> *to facilitate the growth of the church in maturity and Christ-likeness through raising the standards of biblical preaching and teaching.*

Our vision is to see churches in the Majority World equipped for mission and growing to maturity in Christ through the ministry of pastors and leaders who believe, teach and live by the word of God.

Our mission is to strengthen the ministry of the word of God through:
- nurturing national movements for biblical preaching
- fostering the creation and distribution of evangelical literature
- enhancing evangelical theological education

especially in countries where churches are under-resourced.

Our ministry

Langham Preaching partners with national leaders to nurture indigenous biblical preaching movements for pastors and lay preachers all around the world. With the support of a team of trainers from many countries, a multi-level programme of seminars provides practical training, and is followed by a programme for training local facilitators. Local preachers' groups and national and regional networks ensure continuity and ongoing development, seeking to build vigorous movements committed to Bible exposition.

Langham Literature provides Majority World preachers, scholars and seminary libraries with evangelical books and electronic resources through publishing and distribution, grants and discounts. The programme also fosters the creation of indigenous evangelical books in many languages, through writer's grants, strengthening local evangelical publishing houses, and investment in major regional literature projects, such as one volume Bible commentaries like the Africa Bible Commentary and the South Asia Bible Commentary.

Langham Scholars provides financial support for evangelical doctoral students from the Majority World so that, when they return home, they may train pastors and other Christian leaders with sound, biblical and theological teaching. This programme equips those who equip others. Langham Scholars also works in partnership with Majority World seminaries in strengthening evangelical theological education. A growing number of Langham Scholars study in high quality doctoral programmes in the Majority World itself. As well as teaching the next generation of pastors, graduated Langham Scholars exercise significant influence through their writing and leadership.

To learn more about Langham Partnership and the work we do visit langham.org

www.ingramcontent.com/pod-product-compliance
Lightning Source LLC
Chambersburg PA
CBHW052010290426
44112CB00014B/2193